AMERICAN LAW

MADE SIMPLE

Le **droit américain** facile

Jean-Éric Branaa

Maître de Conférences Université Panthéon-Assas (Paris 2)
Chercheur au Centre de Droit Public Comparé (CDPC)

Illustrations de **Dimitri Champain**

ellipses

Du même auteur chez le même éditeur

American Government Made simple. Le gouvernement americain facile,
2014, 336 p.
(Illustrations : Antonio Meza).

English Law Made Simple, *le droit anglais facile*, 2013, 304 p.
(Illustrations : Antonio Meza).

La Constitution américaine et les institutions, coll. « Les essentiels de civilisation
anglo-saxonne »,1999, rééd. 2008, 176 p.

ISBN 9782340-000667
©Ellipses Édition Marketing S.A., 2014
32, rue Bargue 75740 Paris cedex 15

DANGER
LE
PHOTOCOPILLAGE
TUE LE LIVRE

www.editions-ellipses.fr

THAT'S THE LAW

(First steps into the American Law)

Imagine that you are shopping in a grocery store in Virginia when a little old woman in line at the checkout starts screaming that she's been pick-pocketed. The police arrive on the scene and the woman identifies you as someone who suspiciously brushed against her. The police arrest you and throw you in jail. Later, they seek to interrogate you without informing you of your right to have a lawyer present.

Legal Issues:

Some possible legal issues raised by these facts include:

☐ *Is pick pocketing a crime in Virginia? If so, under what law?*

☐ *Did the police have probable cause to arrest you based on the identification of the old woman?*

☐ *How reliable was the old lady's identification?*

☐ *How long can the police hold you?*

☐ *Were any of your Constitutional rights violated during the police's arrest and interrogation of you?*

☐ *If you are found guilty, can the little old lady also sue you in civil court for infliction of emotional distress or another tort?*

Step 1: After you have brainstormed all the possible legal issues the facts raise, determine whether the legal issues are governed by Federal or State law.

Step 2: Which Court Are You In?
Determining which court you are in is a two-part inquiry. First, ask yourself whether you are in Federal or State Court. Dual sovereignty means that each sovereign has its own court system: the States each have courts and the United States has courts, which are called Federal courts. Federal Courts are located throughout the United States – not just in Washington, D.C.
Second, ask yourself whether you are in a Trial Court, a mid-level appeals court, or a supreme court. Most American court systems – whether they a re Federal or State – have a similar structure, consisting of Trial Courts, mid-level appeals courts, and supreme courts. In the Federal court system, the Trial Courts are called United States District Courts. The Federal Courts of appeals each cover a geographical area called a circuit and are, accordingly, called Circuit Courts. States vary in the names they give to their courts, but regardless of the nomenclature, the structure is the same.

Look at the documents on the next page: a table of the organization of the courts, the State court system the sequence of event in the criminal justice system - Answers are to be found on page 304.

Federal and State Courts

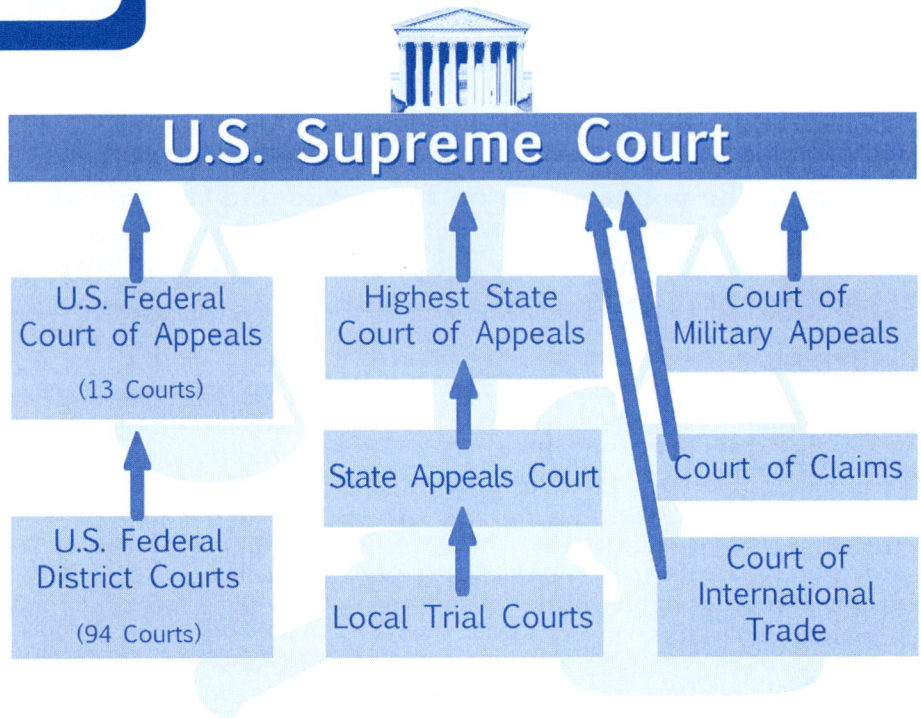

U.S. Supreme Court

U.S. Federal Court of Appeals (13 Courts)	Highest State Court of Appeals	Court of Military Appeals
	State Appeals Court	Court of Claims
U.S. Federal District Courts (94 Courts)	Local Trial Courts	Court of International Trade

The State Court system

State Supreme Court	→	hears appeals from lower courts
Superior Court	→	hears serious cases most trials held here
Special Courts: Juvenile, Divorce, Family, Housing	→	specific cases heard
County, Municipal, Traffic, Magistrate, etc.	→	minor cases, arraignments

The sequence of events in the criminal justice system

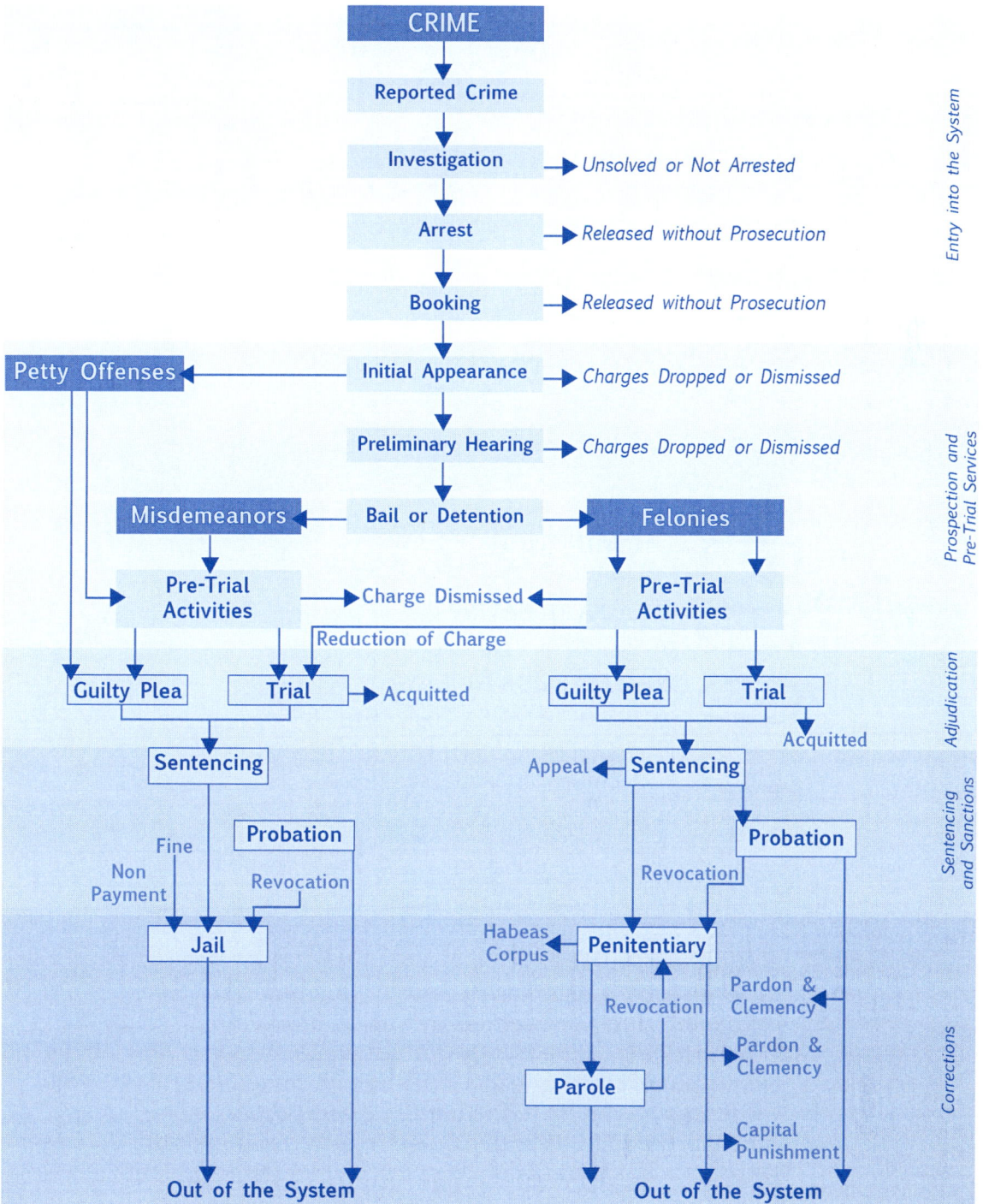

```
                        CRIME
                          │
                          ▼
                    Reported Crime                              Entry into the System
                          │
                          ▼
                    Investigation  ──▶ Unsolved or Not Arrested
                          │
                          ▼
                       Arrest  ──▶ Released without Prosecution
                          │
                          ▼
                      Booking  ──▶ Released without Prosecution
                          │
                          ▼
  Petty Offenses ◀── Initial Appearance ──▶ Charges Dropped or Dismissed
                          │
                          ▼                                     Prosecution and
                  Preliminary Hearing ──▶ Charges Dropped or Dismissed    Pre-Trial Services
                          │
                          ▼
  Misdemeanors ◀── Bail or Detention ──▶ Felonies
        │                                     │
        ▼                                     ▼
    Pre-Trial  ──▶ Charge Dismissed ◀──   Pre-Trial
    Activities       Reduction of Charge   Activities
        │                                     │
        ▼                                     ▼                 Adjudication
 Guilty Plea   Trial ──▶ Acquitted    Guilty Plea   Trial
                  │                      │            │
                  ▼                      ▼            ▼ Acquitted
             Sentencing          Appeal ◀── Sentencing          Sentencing
                  │                           │                 and Sanctions
        Fine      │    Probation              ▼
        Non       │       │  Revocation    Probation
       Payment    ▼       ▼                   │ Revocation
                Jail                          ▼                 Corrections
                                 Habeas ◀── Penitentiary ◀── Pardon & Clemency
                                 Corpus       │                  │
                                     Revocation│                 ▼ Pardon & Clemency
                                              ▼
                                           Parole ──▶           Capital Punishment
        │                                     │
        ▼                                     ▼
  Out of the System                   Out of the System
```

Err... Law?

Introduction

The discovery of America took a long time. The people who explored, and then settled this land, brought with them their knowledge and ideas of what Law was. Nevertheless, when living far from the large cities, they sometimes took some "concessions" with what would be acceptable as Law... especially in the Wild West. We may see in this an important debate that arises: should Law be created from top to bottom?

PART 1 – THE FUNCTION OF LAW

We know that Law occupies an important place in our society. We cannot avoid it if we want to live in a peaceful world without problems. However, it is not so obvious when we think about the early days of the United States. Thinking about the "outlaws" of the Wild West like Jesse James, we may wonder if laws were part of the daily lives of the pioneers. Could these people live a peaceful life and live together in harmony? Of course, everybody knows that there were sheriffs to enforce the laws in the new territories, but were they really powerful? And did they obey the same exact system of laws? In other words, was there a clear and shared definiton of the idea of Law at that time? And what kind of organization was established to make sure everybody would obey the laws?

Law is a human creation. It is up to each person to decide if he or she will respect the laws created by the majority, or not. Those who decide not to respect the laws do not place themselves in mortal danger; so there is no correlation between the laws of Nature and those of Man. Laws were simply created to bring a bit of justice and equality to our society. The Courts and the governments are responsible for enforcing them and making sure that everyone is answerable to these laws on equal terms within their sphere of influence.

Law provides protection for victims and defines punishment of those who break the law. Law does not only consist of options among which one may just pick and choose the best solution:

> **When a society has no legal system that allows each person to live in harmony with others, living well together is not possible.**

those who don't obey it should be aware that they will have to face the consequences. When a society has no legal system that allows each person to live in harmony with others, living well together is not possible. In such a society, one might imagine that people would decide everything based only on their own desires, and that they might also commit any and all crimes freely if such was their wish: to steal, kill, injure, destroy, pollute, rape, assault, or terrorize would thus be possible, and no one would be able to stop it.

So, one might say that it would be a disaster if each of us could act upon his or her own desires without any limits. If laws did not exist, nothing would stop people who would be free to take revenge or behave badly, knowing that there would be no consequences, whether we do good or bad. Society is actually brimming with crime, murder and unlawful actions.

Each country needs a legal system to allow people to live freely and in peace. A judicial system is a set of rules for a group of people, which thus corresponds to a specific culture or society. The goals and objectives of laws and rules is to protect the rights of each one.

In the United States, the legal system is a bit complicated, because many legal systems are actually super-imposed: at the Federal, State and local levels. Each level creates its own laws, which citizens must obey. Each also has its own judicial organization. Far removed from what their ancestors were doing in the time of the Wild West,

American people now easily use, and sometimes overuse, the potential of their legal system to settle their disputes. They have certainly become the world champions for this very particular sport: going to court.

How are laws made?

As concerns the laws passed by Congress, everything begins with a Bill, introduced into Congress by one of the two houses (the House of Representatives or the Senate); neither takes precedence over the other. Then, each law is debated in committee before being discussed by members in the respective houses. When adopted by one house, it is then sent to the other house where the process is repeated. Finally, after being passed by both houses, the Bill is then sent to the President, who must either sign it into Law with his signature, or veto it.

ACTIVITY

A. What do you imagine life was like in the Old West?

....

....

....

....

B. Is it possible to live in a world without laws?

....

....

....

....

C. Why does the American legal system seem to be so complicated today?

....

....

....

....

FRONTIER JUSTICE

Enforcing the law

The three great threats to the lives of the settlers on the frontier were nature and the elements, Native Americans, and lawbreakers. Men like Bat Masterson and Wyatt Earp became famous for enforcing the law. But it was not easy because everyone was armed and a single lawman was often the only law for 200 or 300 miles around. Judges, like the famous Roy Bean, administered law on a circuit and conducted hearings in local saloons with a law book in one hand and a pistol in the other. Desperados were not always the colorful or spectacular kind. Most crimes had to do with swindlings and thefts, the work of claim jumpers, confidence men, card sharks, and rustlers. If caught, these men often faced rough justice, if not at the hands of an individual, then at the hands of vigilantes or a lynch mob. But the Old West had a deep ambivalence about the Law. It admired tough and independent characters, gamblers who took chances and won, people who knew how to fight for, and keep, what was theirs. It admired a tough lawman but was suspicious of government. That ambivalence is apparent in the reputations enjoyed by men like the Dalton boys, Billy the Kid, Sam Bass, and Frank and Jesse James: notorious outlaws who were feared but, in a sense, also admired.

The O.K. Corral case

In 1876, Wyatt Earp moved to Wichita, Kansas, where his brother Virgil had opened a new saloon. There, he also began working with a part-time police officer on rounding up criminals. The adventure and the little bit
5 of press Earp received from the job appealed to him, and eventually he was made City Marshal in Dodge City, Kansas. He then reinvented himself as a lawman. In December 1879, Earp joined his brothers Virgil and Morgan in Tombstone, Arizona, a booming frontier town
10 that had only recently been erected when a speculator discovered the land there contained vast amounts of silver. His good friend Doc Holliday, whom he had met in Kansas, joined him
But the silver riches the Earp brothers hoped to find
15 never came, forcing Earp to return to law work. In a town and a region desperate to tame the lawlessness of the cowboy culture that pervaded the frontier, Earp was a welcome sight.
In March 1881, Earp set out to find cowboys that had
20 robbed a Tombstone stagecoach and its driver. In an effort to close in on the outlaws, he struck a deal with a rancher named Ike Clanton, who regularly dealt with the cowboys working around Tombstone. In return for his help, Earp promised Clanton he could collect a
25 $6,000 reward.

But the partnership quickly dissolved. Clanton, paranoid that Earp would leak the details of their bargain, turned against Earp. By October, Clanton was out of his mind, drunk and parading around Tombstone's saloons,
30 bragging that he was going to kill one of the Earp men. Everything came to a head on October 26, 1881, when the Earps, along with Doc Holliday, met Clanton, his brother Billy, and two others, Frank McLaury and his brother, Tom, on a small lot on the edge of town near
35 an enclosure called the O.K. Corral. There, the greatest gunfight in the West's history took place. Over the course of just 30 seconds, a barrage of shots was fired, ultimately killing Billy Clanton and both of the McLaury brothers. Virgil and Morgan Earp, as well as Holliday,
40 were all injured. The only one remaining unharmed was Wyatt. The battle drove tensions between the cowboy community and those who were looking for a more settled West to emerge. Ike Clanton planned the shooting of Virgil Earp and the assassination of Morgan Earp.
45 As a result of Morgan's death, Wyatt Earp set off in search of vengeance. With Holliday and a group of men, he killed so many people that they made headlines around the nation, earning the group both praise and condemnation for taking on the West's wild cowboy
50 culture.

Judge Roy Bean

DOCUMENT 3

Although many colorful characters have become legends of the Old West, "Hanging Judge Roy Bean," who held court sessions in his saloon along the Rio Grande River in a desolate stretch of the Chihuahuan Desert of West Texas, remains one of the most fascinating. Calling himself the "Law West of the Pecos," he is reputed to have kept a pet bear in his courtroom and sentenced dozens to the gallows, saying "Hang'em first, try'em later."

Roy Bean was born in Mason County, Kentucky around 1825. At age 15 he left home to follow two older brothers out West seeking adventure. After killing a local hombre in New Mexico, Roy fled to California, to stay with his brother Joshua, who would soon become the first mayor of San Diego. In 1852, Roy was arrested after wounding a man in a duel. He escaped and headed back to New Mexico, where brother Sam Bean had become a sheriff. Roy tended bar in Sam's saloon for several years while smuggling guns from Mexico through the Union blockade during the Civil War. He married a Mexican teenager.

In 1882, the Galveston, Harrisburg and San Antonio Railroad hired crews in Texas to link San Antonio with El Paso, across 530 miles of scorching Chihuahuan Desert, infested with rattlesnakes and scorpions. Fleeing his marriage and illegal businesses in San Antonio, Roy headed to Vinegaroon to become a saloonkeeper, serving railroad workers whiskey from a tent. As his own best customer, he was often drunk and disorderly.

The nearest courtroom was a week's ride away and County Commissioners were eager to establish some sort of local law enforcement. They appointed Roy Bean Justice of the Peace for Precinct No. 6, Pecos County, Texas. Roy built a small saloon, and above the door, posted signs proclaiming "ICE COLD BEER" and "LAW WEST OF THE PECOS." From here Roy Bean began dispensing liquor, justice and various tall tales. Roy Bean's justice was not complicated by legalities; it was characterized by greed, prejudice, a little common sense and lots of colorful language. "It is the judgment of this court that you are hereby tried and convicted of illegally and unlawfully committing certain grave offenses against the peace and dignity of the State of Texas, particularly in my bailiwick," was a typical Bean ruling. "I fine you two dollars; then get the hell out of here and never show yourself in this court again. That's my rulin'."

One of Bean's most outrageous rulings occurred when an Irishman was accused of killing a Chinese worker. Friends of the accused threatened to destroy Roy's bar if he was found guilty. Court in session, Bean browsed through his law book, turning page after page, searching for another legal precedent. Finally, rapping his pistol on the bar, he proclaimed, "Gentlemen, I find the law very explicit on murdering your fellow man, but there's nothing here about killing a Chinaman. Case dismissed."

As a legend, Judge Roy Bean is a merciless dispenser of justice, often called "The Hangin' Judge." But that title goes to Isaac Parker of Fort Smith, Arkansas, who sentenced 172 men to hang and actually strung up 88 of them. In his book *Judge Roy Bean Country*, Jack Skiles says that although Bean threatened to hang hundreds, "there's no evidence to suggest that Judge Roy Bean ever hung anybody." One or two were sentenced and taken to the gallows, but allowed to escape.

ACTIVITY

A. Read the three documents. Why was it so difficult to enforce the law on the frontier? How would you describe the kind of justice that was administered then?

B. What legal education did the judges practicing in the West receive? What was the equivalent for an English judge at that time (the 1850s and after)?

PART 2 – WHAT ARE LAWS?

NATIONAL LAW

STATE LAW

So what is a law? Imagine your family sitting down to play a board game. You need to know the rules in order to play, right? The same thing goes for your day-to-day life – you need to know the rules or laws. Every country has their own set of laws and each is unique to that country. For example, in the United States, the law says that people must drive on the right-hand side of the road. In England, on the other hand, their Law states they drive on the left. You could really do some damage if you didn't know that law and started driving on the wrong side of the road!

In the U.S.A., the situation is complex because there are several levels: the Federal, the States and the local levels. Laws can be made by the national government or by individual State governments. National laws are those laws that everyone in the country must follow. Laws made by individual States are only valid in that State. It is also important to distinguish between different types of laws and actions, or lawsuits, brought before the courts and of the redress the law provides in each type of case.

Civil and Criminal

PLAINTIFF

DEFENDANT

LITIGATION

BEYOND A REASONABLE DOUBT

PREPONDERANCE OF EVIDENCE

Courts hear two kinds of disputes: civil and criminal. A civil suit involves two or more private parties, at least one of which alleges a violation of a statute or some provision of common law. The party initiating the lawsuit is the plaintiff; the opponent, the defendant. A defendant can bring a counterclaim against a plaintiff or a cross-claim against a co-defendant, so long as they are related to the plaintiff's original complaint. Courts prefer to hear all the claims arising from one dispute in a single lawsuit. Business litigations, breaches of contract, or tort cases, in which a party alleges he has been injured by another's negligence or willful misconduct, are civil cases.

While most civil litigations are between private parties, the Federal government or a State government is always a party to a criminal suit. In the name of the People, it prosecutes defendants charged with violating laws that prohibits certain conduct as injurious to the public welfare. Two businesses might litigate a civil action for breach of contract, but only the government can charge someone with murder.

The standards of proof and potential penalties also differ. A criminal defendant can be convicted only upon the determination of guilt "beyond a reasonable doubt." In a civil case, the plaintiff needs only show a "preponderance of evidence," a weaker formulation that essentially

Courts of Equity

In 13th century England, "courts of law" were authorized to decree monetary remedies only. These damages were sufficient in many instances, but not in others, such as a contract for the sale of a rare artwork or a specific parcel of land. During the 13th and 14th centuries, "Courts of Equity" were formed. These tribunals created equitable remedies like specific performance. By the 19th century, most American jurisdictions had eliminated the distinction between law and equity. Today, with rare exception, U.S. courts can award either legal or equitable remedies as the situation requires.

means "more likely than not." A convicted criminal can be imprisoned, but the losing party in a civil case is liable only for legal or equitable remedies.

Legal and equitable remedies

The U.S. legal system offers a wide, but not limited, range of remedies. The criminal statutes typically list the range of fines or prison time a Court may impose for a given offense. Other parts of the criminal code may allow stiffer penalties for repeat offenders in some jurisdictions. Punishment for the most serious offenses, or felonies, is more severe than for misdemeanors. In civil actions, most American courts are authorized to choose among legal and equitable remedies. The distinction means less today than in the past, but is still worth knowing.

ACTIVITY

A. Why is it important to know the particular laws of a country?

....

....

....

B. What different categories of Law can you define?

....

....

....

C. What is an equitable remedy?

....

....

....

Civil

OOPS!

Criminal

BEING LEGAL

DOCUMENT 4

Great Wedding! But was it legal?

George Clooney to marry Angelina... in the role of a priest.

The actor, 52, recently went online to get a licence allowing him to officiate weddings. And his friends said the nuptials of Brad Pitt and Angelina Jolie would be his first outing as "Reverend George". The couple are expected to tie the knot later this year in a series of summer ceremonies. Brad, 50, has asked his long-time pal to conduct the service. "Now he's started calling him Reverend George Clooney. He is taking it all very seriously and has already had discussions about what kind of service they'd like."

In an era when couples obsess about the band playlist and hand towels for the restrooms, one question may be forgotten: Is the person performing the wedding legally able to do so?

10 Daniel Morales and Gwendolyn Baxter thought they knew. Their outdoor ceremony two summers ago in Farmington, Conn., was performed by a friend who had been ordained online by the Universal Life Church. Having heard of other couples who were 15 married that way, they assumed it was legal.

But Connecticut is one of a half-dozen places that do not recognize marriages performed by someone who became a minister for the sole purpose of marrying people. Such a minister "doesn't meet the require-20 ments of the State statutes," said William Gerrish, a spokesman for the Connecticut Department of Public Health. The penalty in Connecticut for an unauthorized performance of a marriage is a fine of up to $500 and a year in jail for the officiant, though Richard 25 Blumenthal, the Connecticut Attorney General, said prosecution is unlikely. As for the marriage, the statute is clear, Mr. Blumenthal said. Nonetheless, he encouraged couples not to panic; unless the issue is forced through divorce or death, the judicial system 30 tends to grant couples the benefit of the doubt. "If the marriage is performed by someone unauthorized, but the two people having the marriage still believe it to be valid, it may continue to be valid until someone challenges it," he said. But, he said, "They are at risk." 35 With so many people turning to friends and relatives to perform their marriage ceremonies, more are bound to discover that they may not be legally married. But finding out what is allowed can be daunting. Marriage laws are often vague and vary from State to State and 40 county by county. And misimpressions are rampant.

The Universal Life Church alone has ordained more than 18 million ministers since it was founded in 1959 in Modesto, Calif. The 45 organization ordains 10,000 people a month, twice as many as in 2000, according to Andre Hensley, the church's President. Eighty percent join the fold solely to perform weddings, he said. The Church of Spiritual Humanism, the Rose Ministries and the Temple of 50 Earth, which describes itself as a "religion-free religion," also have online ministry sites.

Somehow forgotten is that marriage is a legal contract. And three States besides Connecticut – Alabama, Virginia and Tennessee – as well as other jurisdictions, 55 prohibit weddings performed by ministers who do not have active ministries. Even in Las Vegas, that city's no-holds-barred image notwithstanding, it is illegal for individuals to perform a marriage if they do not have a congregation. Yes, Elvis may be in the house, 60 but he may face up to six months doing the *Jailhouse Rock* unless an authorized minister is there to sign the license. In many other States, including New York, the rules about ministers ordained online are less clear. Often, even city, county and State officials 65 are uncertain of the parameters.

As a clerk at the Marriage License Bureau in Philadelphia, who did not want to be named because she is not allowed to speak to reporters, said, "People call us and ask if it's legal or not, and we don't know 70 if it's legal." The laws regarding officiants are there to ensure that only people of sufficient standing perform a ceremony that is a keystone of society. Elnora Douglas, the office coordinator of the St. Louis County marriage license department, finds it odd that 75 couples would want to circumvent them. "It's like you want your favorite cousin to perform a surgery, so they go online to get a medical degree," she said. Still, she said, "Everyone saw that episode of 'Friends' where Joey got ordained, and we've been bombarded." 80

DOCUMENT 5

What's wrong?

Five years later

ACTIVITY

A. What may be problematic in Brad Pitt and Angelina Jolie's choice of George Clooney as minister for their wedding ceremony?

B. *Document 5*. What do you imagine the final image might be?

C. Consider *Document 4* and *Document 5*. Explain if they are Civil or Criminal cases, and why.

PART 3 – WHO MAKES THE LAWS?

National laws are made in Congress, which is part of the Legislative Branch, and is made up of the House of Representatives and the Senate. Usually, Congress can make laws on all kinds of matters, such as setting speed limits on highways or regulating how much radon may be found in drinking water.

Sources of ideas for legislation are unlimited. Proposed drafts of bills come from many different sectors. Primary among these is the idea and draft conceived of by a Member or Delegate. This may emanate from the election campaign during which the Member had promised, if elected, to introduce legislation on a particular subject. In addition, the Member's constituents, either as individuals or through citizen groups or associations, may use their right to petition and transmit their proposals to the Member.

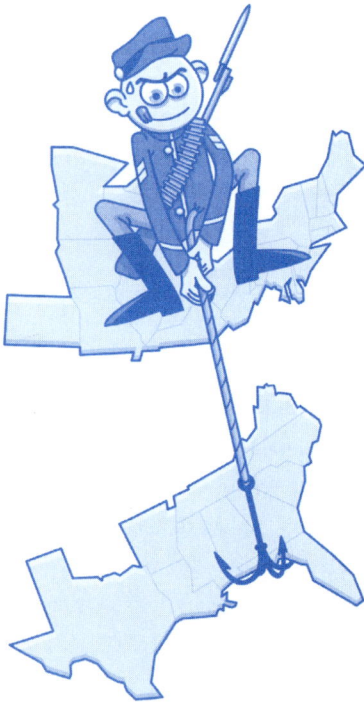

The role of State Law in the Federal system

The Constitution specifically forbids the States from adopting certain kinds of laws (like entering into treaties with foreign nations or coining money). Also, the Article VI *Supremacy Clause* prohibits State laws that contradict either the Constitution or Federal law. Even so, large parts of the legal system remain under State control. The Constitution has carefully specified the areas where Congress might enact legislation, thus specifically forbidding the Federal government from adopting other certain kinds of laws. The Tenth Amendment to the Constitution (1791) makes explicit that State Law would take precedent elsewhere: "*The powers not delegated to the United States by the Constitution, nor prohibited by it are reserved to the States, respectively, or to the people.*"

There nonetheless remained considerable tension between the Federal government and the States – over slavery, and ultimately over the right of a State to leave the Federal union. The civil conflict of 1861-65 resolved both disputes. It also produced new restrictions on the State role within the legal system: under the Fourteenth Amendment (1868), "*No State shall... deprive any person of life, liberty or property, without due process of law; nor deny to any person within its jurisdiction the equal protection of the laws.*" This amendment greatly expanded the Federal Courts' ability to invalidate State laws. *Brown v. Board of Education* (1954), which forbade racial segregation in the Arkansas State school system, relied upon this "equal protection clause."

Procedural due process
It is one of the fundamental characteristics of the U.S. legal system. It implies the guarantee of a fair hearing, procedure or proceeding will be afforded to the individul before the Federal or State government can deprive him of life, liberty or property.

Substantive due process
It is derived from the due process clauses of the Fifth and Sixth Amendments and provides the individual with the substantive right to challenge arbitrary governmental action taken through legislation.

Beginning in the mid-20th century, a number of the trends outlined above – the rise of the administrative State, a more forceful and expansive judicial interpretation of due process and equal protection, and a similar expansion of Congress's power to regulate commerce – combined to enhance the Federal role within the legal system. Even so, much of that system remains within the State domain. While no State may deny a citizen any right guaranteed by the Federal Constitution, many interpret their own constitutions as bestowing even more generous rights and privileges. State Courts applying State Law continue to decide most contractual disputes. The same is true of most criminal cases, and of civil tort actions. Family Law, including such matters as marriage and divorce, is almost exclusively a State matter. For most Americans, most of the time, the legal system means the Police of their own State, or of the various municipalities and other political subdivisions within that State.

ACTIVITY

A. What is the Legislative Branch of government?

....

....

....

B. Why is Article VI so important for the States when making legislation?

....

....

....

C. What is the importance of the Tenth Amendment?

....

....

....

POWER OF STATE COURTS

Defense of the power of State Courts

DOCUMENT 6

Had the health of Chief Justice Oliver Ellsworth allowed him to serve six months longer than he did, Jefferson rather than Adams would have appointed his successor; and Jefferson would not have appointed John Marshall but (as he later said) Judge Spencer Roane of Virginia Supreme Court to lead the United States Supreme Court. If this had happened, the subsequent history of the United States might have been very different, for Roane's position was directly opposed to that of Marshall: Roane was a strict constructionist of the Constitution, an advocate of limited government powers, and a firm believer in States' rights. The following abbreviated version of two articles, written by him under the pseudonym "Hampden", originally appeared in the _Richmond Enquirer_ on June 11 and 15, 1819. The articles were inspired by and directed against Marshall's decision in _McCulloch v. Maryland_.

I beg leave to address my fellow citizens... on a momentous subject... Although some of them will, doubles, lend a more willing ear than others to the important truths I shall endeavor to articulate, none
5 can hear them with indifference. None of them can be prepared to give a carte blanche to our Federal rulers, and to obliterate the State governments, forever, from our political system.

It has been the happiness of the American people to
10 be connected together in a confederate republic; to be united by a system which extends the sphere of popular government and reconciles the advantages of monarchy with those of a republic; a system which combines all the internal advantages of the latter with
15 all the force of the former. It has been our happiness to believe that, in the partition of powers between the general and State governments, the former possessed only such as were expressly granted, or passed therewith as necessary incidents, while all
20 the residuary powers were reserved by the latter. It was deemed by the enlightened founders of the Constitution as essential to the internal happiness and welfare of their constituents to reserve some powers to the State governments; as to their external
25 safety, to grant others to the government of the Union. This, it is believed was done by the Constitution, in its original shape; but such were the natural fears and jealousies of our citizens, in relation to this all-important subject, that it was deemed necessary to
30 quiet those fears by the Tenth Amendment to the Constitution. It is not easy to devise stronger terms to effect that object than those used in that amendment. Such, however, is the proneness of all men to extend and abuse their power – to "feel power and forget
35 right" – that even this article has afforded us no security. That legislative power, which is everywhere extending the sphere of its activity and drawing all power into its impetuous vortex, has blinked even the strong words of this amendment. That judicial
40 power, which, according to Montesquieu is "in some

measure, next to nothing"; and whose province this great writer limits to "punishing criminals and determining the disputes which arise between individuals"; that judiciary which in Rome, according
45 to the same author, was not entrusted to decide questions which concerned "the interests of the State, in the relation which it bears to its citizens"; and, which, in England, has only invaded the Constitution in the worst of times, and then, always, on the side
50 of arbitrary power, has also deemed its interference necessary in our country. It will readily be perceived that I allude to the decision of the Supreme Court of the United States, in the case of _McCulloch against the State of Maryland_.

55 The warface carried on by the legislature of the Union against the rights of "the States" and of "the people" has been with various success and always by detachment. They have not dared to break down the barriers of the Constitution by a general act
60 declaratory of their power. That measure was too bold for these ephemeral duties of the people. The people hold them in check by a short rein, and would consign them to merited infamy, at the next election...

They have adopted a safer course. Crescit eundo
65 is their maxim; and they have succeeded in seeing the Constitution expounded, not by what it actually contains but by the abuses committed under it.

A new mode of amending the Constitution has been added to the ample ones provided in that instrument, and the strongest checks established in it have been
70 made to yield to the force of precedents! The time will soon arrive if it is not already at hand, when the Constitution may be expounded without ever looking into it – by merely reading the acts of a renegade Congress, or adopting the outrageous doctrines of
75 Pickering, Lloyd, or Sheffey!

The warfare waged by the judicial body has been of a bolder tone and character. It was not enough for them to sanction, in former times, the detestable doctrines of Pickering & Co., as aforesaid; it was not enough

80 for them to annihilate the freedom of the press by incarcerating all those who dare, with a manly freedom, to canvass the conduct of their public agents; it was not enough for the predecessors of the present judges to preach of justice and bolster 85 up the most unconstitutional measures of the most abandoned of our rulers; it did not suffice to do the business in detail, and ratify, one by one, the legislative infractions of the Constitution. That process would have been too slow, and perhaps too 90 troublesome...

They resolved, therefore, to put down all discussions of the kind, in future, by a judicial coup de main; to give a general letter of attorney to the future legislators of the Union; and to treat under foot all those parts and articles of the Constitution 95 which had been, heretofore, deemed to set limits to the power of the Federal legislature. That man must be a deplorable idiot who does not see that there is no earthly difference between an unlimited grant of power and a grant limited in its terms, but accompanied with unlimited means of carrying it 100 into execution.

The Supreme Court of the United States have not only granted this general power of attorney to Congress, but they have gone out of the record to do it, in the case in question. It was only necessary, 105 in that case, to decide whether or not the bank law was 'necessary and proper', within the meaning of the Constitution, for carrying into effect some of the granted powers; but the Court have, in effect, expunged those words, from the Constitution... The power of the Supreme Court is indeed great, but it 110 does not extend to everything; it is not great enough to change the Constitution...

ACTIVITY

A. What shows you that Hampden (Judge Roane) was suspicious about the power of the national goverment?

B. From what you understand in the text, what is _McCulloch v. Maryland_ about?

PART 4 – LITIGANTS AND INTEREST GROUPS

In this vast and complex organizations of justice, the American people find their own paths to take their grievances to Court. In some cases, the litigants are individuals, whereas in other cases the litigants may be a government agency, a corporation, a union, an interest group, or a university, for example.

What motivates them to take their case to Court? In criminal cases, the answer to this question is quite simple. A State or Federal criminal statute has allegedly been violated, and the government prosecutes the party charged with violating the statute. In civil cases, the answer is not quite so easy. Although some people readily take their grievances to court, many others avoid this route because of the time and expense involved.

Judges are called upon to resolve two kinds of disputes: private law cases and public law controversies. Private law disputes are those in which one private citizen or organization sues another. In public law controversies, a citizen or organization contends that a government agency or official has violated a right established by a constitution or a statute.

A classic example of private, or ordinary, compensation-oriented litigation is when a person injured in an automobile accident sues the driver of the other car in an effort to win monetary damages as compensation for medical expenses incurred. This type of litigation is personal and is not aimed at changing governmental or business policies. Some private law cases, however, are policy-oriented or political in nature. Personal injury suits and product liability suits may appear on the surface to be simply compensatory in nature but may also be used to change the manufacturing or business practices of the private firms being sued. Most political or policy-oriented lawsuits, however, are public law controversies. That is, they are suits brought against the government primarily to stop allegedly illegal policies or practices. They may also seek damages or some other specific form of relief. Political or policy-oriented litigation is more prevalent in the Appellate Courts than in the Trial Courts and is most common in the U.S. Supreme Court. Ordinary compensatory litigation is often terminated early in the judicial process because the litigants find it more profitable to settle their dispute or accept the verdict of a Trial Court. However, litigants in political cases generally do little to advance their policy goals by gaining victories at the lower levels of the judiciary. Instead, they prefer the

Private Law

Public Law

Interest groups at court

Throughout the 1960s, interest groups with liberal policy goals fared especially well in the Federal Courts. Public interest law firms pursue cases that serve the public interest in general – including cases in the area of consumer rights, employment discrimination, occupational safety, civil liberties, and environmental concerns.

In the 1970s and 1980s, conservative interest groups turned to the Federal Courts more frequently than they had before. This was in part a reaction to the successes of the liberal interest groups. It was also due to the increasingly favorable forum that the Federal Courts provided for conservative viewpoints.

more widespread publicity that is attached to a decision by an appellate tribunal. Pursuing cases in the Appellate Courts is expensive. Therefore, many lawsuits that reach this level are supported in one way or another by interest groups.

Although interest groups are probably better known for their attempts to influence legislative and executive branch decisions, they also pursue their policy goals in the courts. Some groups have found the Judicial Branch to be more receptive to their efforts than either of the other two branches of government. Interest groups that do not have the economic resources to mount an intensive lobbying effort in Congress or a State legislature may find it much easier to hire a lawyer and find some constitutional or statutory provision upon which to base a court case. Involvement of interest groups in the judicial process may take several different forms, depending upon the goals of the particular group. However, two principle tactics stand out: involvement in test cases and presentation of information before the courts through *Amicus Curiae* (Latin, meaning "friend of the court") Briefs.

ACTIVITY

A. What are some of the different reasons that may result in taking a case to Court?

....
....
....

B. Give an example of a private case.

....
....
....

C. Give an example of a public law case.

....
....
....

GOING TO COURT

Test cases

DOCUMENT 7

Because the judiciary engages in policy making only by rendering decisions in specific cases, one tactic of interest groups is to make sure that a case appropriate for obtaining its policy goals is brought
5 before the court. In some instances this means that the interest group will initiate and sponsor the case by providing all the necessary resources. The best-known example of this type of sponsorship is *Brown v. Board of Education of Topeka* (1954). In that case,
10 although the suit against the Board of Education of Topeka, Kansas, was filed by the parents of Linda Brown, The National Association for the Advancement of Colored People (NAACP) supplied the legal help and money necessary to pursue the case all the way
15 to the Supreme Court. Thurgwood Marshall, who later became a U.S. Supreme Court Justice, argued the suit on behalf of the plaintiff and the NAACP. As a result, the NAACP gained a victory through the Supreme Court's decision that segregation in public
20 schools violates the equal protection clause of the Fourteenth Amendment.

Interest groups may also provide assistance in a case initiated by someone else, but which nonetheless raises issues of importance to the group. A good
25 example of this situation may be found in a freedom of religion case, *Wisconsin v. Yoder*. That case was initiated by the State of Wisconsin when it filed criminal complaints charging Jonas Yoder and others with failure to send their children to school
30 until the age of 16 as required by State law. Yoder and the others, members of the Amish faith, believed that education beyond the eighth grade led to the breakdown of the values they cherished and to "worldly influences on their children."
35 An organization known as the National Committee for Amish Religious Freedom (NCARF) came to the defense of Yoder and the others. Following a decision against the Amish in the Trial Court, the NCARF appealed to a Wisconsin Circuit Court, which upheld the trial's court decision. An appeal was made to the 40 Wisconsin Supreme Court, which ruled in favor of the Amish, saying that the compulsory school attendance law violated the free exercise of religion clause of the First Amendment. Wisconsin then appealed to the U.S. Supreme Court, which on May 15, 1972, 45 sustained the religious objection that the NCARF had raised to the compulsory school attendance laws.

As these examples illustrate, interest group involvement in litigation has focused on cases concerning major constitutional issues that have 50 reached the Supreme Court. Because only a small percentage of cases ever reaches the nation's highest court, however, most of the work of interest group lawyers deals with more routine work at the lower levels of the judiciary. Instead of fashioning major test 55 cases for the Appellate Courts, these attorneys may simply be required to deal with the legal problems of their groups' clientele.

During the civil rights movement in the 1950s and 1960s, for example, public interest lawyers not 60 only litigated major civil rights questions; they also defended African Americans and civil rights workers who ran into difficulties with the local authorities. These interest group attorneys, then, performed many of the functions of a specialized legal aid society, they 65 provided legal representation to those involved in an important movement for social change. Furthermore, they performed the important function of drawing attention to the plight of African Americans by keeping cases before the courts. 70

Lucas v. South Carolina Coastal Council

A case decided by the U.S. Supreme Court, *Lucas v. South Carolina Coastal Council*, provides a good example. South Carolina's Beachfront Management Act forbade David H. Lucas from building single-family houses on two beachfront lots he owned. A South Carolina Trial Court ruled that Lucas was entitled to be compensated for his loss. The South Carolina Supreme Court reversed the Trial Court decision, however, and Lucas appealed to the U.S. Supreme Court. The High Court ruled in Lucas's favor, saying that if a property owner is denied all economically viable use of his or her property, a taking has occurred and the Constitution requires that he or she gets compensation.

Amicus Curiae briefs

DOCUMENT 8

Submission of *Amicus Curiae* briefs is the easiest method by which interest groups can become involved in cases. This method allows a group to get its message before the court even though it does not control the case. Provided it has the permission of the parties to the case or the permission of the court, an interest group may submit an *Amicus* brief to supplement the argument of the parties. The filing of *Amicus* briefs is a tactic used in appellate rather than Trial Courts, at both the Federal and the State levels.

Sometimes these briefs are aimed at strengthening the position of one of the parties in the case. When the *Wisconsin v. Yoder* case was argued before the U.S. Supreme Court, the cause of the Amish was supported by *Amicus Curiae* briefs filed by the General Conference of Seventh Day Adventists, the National Council of Churches of Christ in the United States, the Synagogue Council of America, the American Jewish Congress, the National Jewish Commission on Law and Public Affairs, and the Mennonite Central Committee.

Sometimes friend-of-the-court briefs are used not to strengthen the arguments of one of the parties, but to suggest to the court the group's own view of how the case should be resolved. *Amicus Curiae* briefs are often filed in an attempt to persuade an Appellate Court to either grant or deny review of a lower-court decision. A study of the US Supreme Court found that the presence of *Amicus* briefs significantly increased the chances that the Court would give full treatment to a case.

Unlike private interest groups, all levels of the government can admit *Amicus* briefs without obtaining permission. The Solicitor General of the United States is especially important in this regard, and in some instances the Supreme Court may invite the Solicitor General to present an *Amicus* brief.

Lakey v. Sta-Rite Industries (1997)

A case litigated in North Carolina provides a good example. The case began in 1993 after a five-year-old girl, Valerie Lakey, got stuck in the drain of a wading pool after another child had removed the drain cover. Such a powerful suction was created that, before she could be rescued, the drain had sucked out most of her large and small intestines. As a result, the girl will have to spend about 11 hours per day attached to intravenous feeding tubes for the rest of her life. In 1997, a jury awarded the girl's family $25 million in compensatory damages and, before the jury was to have considered punitive damages, the drain manufacturer and two other defendants settled the case for $30.9 million. The plaintiff's attorney said that the lawsuit revealed similar incidents in other areas of the country and presented a stark example of something industry insiders knew, but others did not. Not only did the family win its lawsuit, but the North Carolina legislature also passed a law requiring multiple drains to prevent such injuries in the future.

ACTIVITY

A. Why is a case called a test case?

B. What is an *Amicus Curiae* brief?

Important Words

Due process
Plaintiff
Defendant
Interest group
litigant
Amicus Curiae

The function of law

Law did not always exist everywhere in the United States: what about the American West at the time of the conquest? Law is a human invention, and necessary so that we can all live together. Those that do not respect it are punished. This is what makes us feel safe. The Courts are there to enforce the laws. Without them, and without laws, everyone could do what they want, even kill, rape and steal, if they so wished. It would no longer be possible to live together in society. That is why each country has established a legal system allowing each person to live freely and in peace. In the United States, there are however many systems piled on top of one another: at the Federal level, the State level and the local level. Each level has created its own legal system that citizens must obey. Laws are passed by Congress: a bill is introduced and examined in committee, then debated in each chamber, before being sent to the President, who may veto it.

What are laws?

Law is complicated. It is even more complicated in the United States because it may be created by the Federal government (national law), or by the 50 different States (State law). It may be civil, or criminal, according to the case, between two disputing parties; or brought by the State, seeking to protect society from an individual. This is true for business litigation, breaches of contract, or tort cases. The person who brings a case against another person is the Plaintiff, if it is a civil case. To win against another person, the Defendant, they need to show a "preponderance of evidence". In criminal cases, we speak of the Accused, and the determination of guilt is made "beyond reasonable doubt". Here, a person may be imprisoned, while in civil cases a person must pay damages. The sentences that may be imposed on criminals are numerous, and are listed in the Penal Code. The most extreme punishments, such as the death penalty, are reserved for the most serious crimes, called felonies. Less serious crimes are called misdemeanors.

Who makes the laws?

Congress passes laws. It is composed of two chambers: a House of Representatives and the Senate. There is no limit to the types of laws the Senate may adopt. Members of Congress are elected by the people and are their representatives. On the other hand, the Constitution formally forbids States to adopt certain kinds of laws, such as those allowing to enter into treaties with foreign nations, or to coin money. Article VI, which is called the Supremacy Clause, forbids all laws that contradict those passed by the Federal government. But the 10th Amendment declares that all powers not explicitly granted to Federal power in the Constitution return to the States, which are the only ones to be able to make decisions and pass the laws that they want. This, however, is not without problems, as can be seen in the subject of slavery or segregation. The 14th Amendment introduced the question of due process of law, and granted new powers to the Federal Courts to take care of these problems between the Federal government and the States. Nevertheless, the States still have strong prerogatives on certain issues, such as Family Law or contractual disputes.

Litigants and interests groups

In some cases the litigants are individuals, whereas in other cases the litigants may be a government agency, a corporation, a union, or an interest group, for example. In criminal cases, the reason for going to Court is obvious. In civil cases, it is not always so clear. Many people avoid resolving their problems in Court, because it is very costly. There are two major types of civil cases: private law cases and public law controversies. A private law case consists in requesting damages to pay hospital bills after an accident, for example. Public law controversies are concerned with complaints against the government. They are primarily handled by the Courts of Appeal, or the U. S. Supreme Court. Bringing a case before these Courts is extremely expensive; this is why they are most often led by interest groups, finding there a more efficient method in making their cause known, than lobbying Congress.

A. Are the following statements true or false? Check the correct box.

	True	False
All the laws are the same in all the 50 States in the U.S.A.		
Litigation is the action of going to court.		
Equity is a system of law tried in a separate court called "Court of Chancery."		
A bill is a proposal for a new law.		

B. What are the different levels of jurisdiction in the U.S.A.?

....

....

C. How are laws made?

....

....

D. What is the difference between civil and criminal cases?

....

....

E. What is the punishment in a Criminal case?

....

....

F. What is the punishment in a Civil case?

....

....

REFERENCES :

Page 7. "Chuckwagon in Texas", Wikimedia. http://commons.wikimedia.org/wiki/File:Chuckwagon_Texas_1900.jpg
Page 8. "Frontier justice", by Dimitri Champain
Page 10. "Enforcing the law", adapted from "Western Frontier life", Jrank encyclopedia, http://www.jrank.org/encyclopedia/pages/cm7l11kf68/Western-frontier-life.html
"The O.K. Coral case", adapted from Prelinger H. The Kansas historical quarterly, Kansas State Historical Society, Topeka, Kansas, 1960. Vol 1.
"Gold Prospector", by Tony Oliver Wikimedia. http://commons.wikimedia.org/wiki/File:Gold_prospector.jpg?uselang=fr
Page 11. "Judge Roy Bean", adapted from "Law West of the Pecos: The Hanging Judge", in Desert USA, http://www.desertusa.com/desert-people/judge-roy-bean.html
"West of the Pecos" .Wikimedia. http://commons.wikimedia.org/wiki/File:%22Judge_Roy_Bean,_the_%60Law_West_of_the_Pecos,%27_holding_court_at_the_old_town_of_Langtry,_Texas_in_1900,_trying_a_horse_th_-_NARA_-_530985.tif?uselang=fr
Page 13. "Civil v. criminal", by Dimitri Champain
Page 14. "Great Wedding! But is it legal?" adapted from "George Clooney to marry Brad Pitt...in the role of a vicar", by Devan Sipher, New York Times, August 5, 2007
"George Clooney", by Georges Biard Wikimedia. http://commons wikimedia.org/wiki/File:George_Clooney_2000.jpg?uselang=fr
"Wedding". by Anna Maj Michelson, Wikimedia. http://commons.wikimedia.org/wiki/File:AMJ-wedding-4656.jpg?uselang=fr
Page 15. "What's wrong", by Dimitri Champain, adapted from law for kids: http://badwebcomicswiki.shoutwiki.com/wiki/Law_for_Kids
Page 16. "A federation", by Dimitri Champain
Page 18. "Defense of the power of State Courts" from Spencer Roanes, The Annals of America, The John P. Branch Historical Papers of Randolph-Macon College, June 1905, Volume 4, page 539.
Page 19. "State powers", by Dimitri Champain
Page 20. "Private law v. public law", by Dimitri Champain
Page 23. "Amish Man", by Ernest Mettendorf, Wikimedia. http://commons.wikimedia.org/wiki/File:Amish_man.jpg
Page 24. "Summary", by Dimitri Champain
Page 25. "Review", by Dimitri Champain
pp. 9, 11, 13, 15, 17, 19, 21, 23   "Activity", by Dimitri Champain

Early American Law

Introduction

The Constitution of the United States establishes the form of government that Americans have today. It was created in Philadelphia during the summer of 1787 by a group of 55 delegates from the new States that had recently gained their freedom from British rule. These men brought with them a considerable knowledge of government. They had gained this knowledge by studying the writings of political philosophers and historians who had written about government over the past 2,000 years. It was this knowledge and experience that they referred to when they wrote the Constitution.

"GIVE ME LIBERTY, OR GIVE ME DEATH !"

PART 1 – THE HISTORICAL CONTEXT

The first Colonists to cross the Atlantic Ocean in the 17th century to live in the New World brought their knowledge with them, notably on a judicial level. The English Colonists brought with them their Common Law, their socie-tal rights, and their legal institutions. It is to them that we especially owe the introduction of the Justice of the Peace and the hierarchy of the Courts; colonization was organized by and placed under the control of the Crown: businesses had to obtain a Charter issued by the Crown, before taking any further steps. With this document in hand, the immigrants thought they were covered by all the rights and privileges claimed by all other English sub-jects. But this Charter granted them even a bit more, by authorizing a certain form of self-governing. During the first year of settlement, the English allowed the Colonies to moderately develop this idea of self-government, leaving

DID YOU KNOW?
The 'Charter of 1606', also known as the First Charter of Virginia, is a document from King James Ist of England to the Virginia Company, assigning land rights to colonists for the stated purpose of propagating the Christian religion.

them to create their own local political and legal systems, based on the necessity of adaptation and experience.

The first Americans were passionate, but also pragmatic. Speaking of Law, they had to modify it often, because the highly complex English institutions had no place in those new territories. In the first place, they had to adapt Law to their daily lives, which were very different than in Europe: laws were modified, and new rules and regulations created. Law developed differently in the different Colonies. In Virginia, for example, society was dominated by plantation owners who were dynamic and had an extremely developed business sense, and whose primary interest was to make money. They endeavored

> # The law developed differently from colony to colony.

The Colonial judicial systems varied
This variety was born from the numerous origins of the Colonies and in the legal interests that did not always correspond with each other. Towards the end of the 17th century, the Courts began to take on a new role, acting as a glue holding society together: because, through the cases that they had to resolve, the American Courts enabled everyone, rich and poor, to identify themselves as belonging to the same group. These Courts had already gotten rid of the sophisticated procedures present in the English Courts; on the contrary, they were open and attuned to the reality of the actual lives of the Colonists.

to establish regulations, within the House of Burgesses, related to their activity, and to create "labor rights", which mainly consisted of laws authorizing indentured servants and slavery. In the meantime, England was brandishing its *Habeas Corpus*... In Massachusetts, society did not resonate with the same mercantile rhythm: there, it was important to construct a society that respected the precepts taught in the Bible. The laws promoted by the Colony Assemblies and Town Councils in the regions of the Northeast were primarily aimed at dictating people's behavior. It must be remembered that their rights, liberties and property were protected under the Code of Laws: *The Law and Liberties* (1648).

The American judges and magistrates, who only rarely possessed the same education in Law as their English peers, delivered justice that was rapid, even simple, and often filled with generosity. This was not beneficial to the development of the legal practice, since lawyers were not frequently well liked and in whom little trust was given. Thus, the Colonies created and developed a unique judicial culture based on usefulness. Their judicial seclusion came to an end with the Glorious Revolution in their Mother Country (1688-89). William III had set up an administration whose bureaucratic rigor finally got the better of this atypical justice, in taking control of, and in moving closer to, the principles typically honored in England.

Yet, other influences were affected the birth of American Law: the Native Americans' interplay with the Spanish,

DID YOU KNOW?
In 1671, in its attempt to ensure a fair legal system, the English Common Law Courts introduced Habeas Corpus, a Latin phrase meaning "may you have the body", giving the judge the possibility to determine if a person was detained legally or not.

The Glorious Revolution

The Glorious Revolution established the victory of Parliament over the King of England. Various contested issues of power were resolved in favor of Parliament. Parliament had to be convened regularly. All new taxes had to be approved by Parliament. The King and his family had to belong to the Anglican religion. New political arrangements were made with Scotland.

the French and the English. Each learned from the other, even when it came to Law. The Europeans learned, notably, the importance of bartering (exchanging ideas) with the Native Americans. The Spanish instilled a law based on religious precepts, while attempting to subjugate these peoples whom they judged inferior. But the Native Americans resisted Christianization, and fittingly relied on moral law to defend their cause. They also resisted attempts to introduce Civil Law into their societies and then taught their principles and the importance they ascribed to ancestral customs to the French. The English, arriving later, made use of the knowledge already garnered, and tried not to impose their Law on the Native Americans, but preferred trading with them, exchanging gifts and negotiating treaties.

ACTIVITY

A. Why did the Colonists create laws that were so different from one Colony to another?

....

....

....

....

....

....

B. What was the infuence of the Indians in the development of the law?

....

....

....

....

....

CODIFYING THE LAW

The Laws and Liberties of Massachusetts

DOCUMENT 1

The Laws and Liberties of Massachusetts, enacted in 1648, served as the basis for civil and criminal law in the colony until the eighteenth century. This code was a revision of a 1641 code known as *The Body of Liberties*, which was written by Nathaniel Ward, a Puritan minister and teacher. *The Laws and Liberties* reflect the Puritans' concern that members of the community should live a Christian life true to the principles of the sect. Laws were meant to guide the righteous and punish the wicked, but they were also to be administered fairly. Religious heresy was severely punished as were fornication, adultery, and other behavior that violated the moral teachings of the colonists. Nevertheless, the code mandated that individuals could not be punished without *Due Process of Law*.

To Our Beloved Brethren and Neighbours the Inhabitants of the Massachusetts, the Governour, Assistants and Deputies assembled in the General Court of that Jurisdiction with grace and peace in our Lord Jesus Christ;

5 So soon as God had set up Political Government among his people Israel he gave them a body of laws for judgment both in civil and criminal causes. These were brief and fundamental principles, yet withall so full and comprehensive as out of them 10 clear deductions were to be drawn to all particular cases in future times. For a Commonwealth without lawes is like a Ship without rigging and steeradge. Nor is it sufficient to have principles or fundamentalls, but these are to be drawn out 15 into so many of their deductions as the time and conditions of that people may have use of. And it is very unsafe & injurious to the body of the people to put them to learn their duty and libertie from generall rules, nor is it enough to have lawes 20 except they be also just. Therefore among other priviledges which the Lord bestowed upon his peculiar people, these he calls them specially to consider of, that God was neerer to them and their lawes were more righteous then other nations. God was 25 sayd to be amongst them or neer to them because of his Ordinances established by himselfe, and their lawes righteous because himselfe was their Lawgiver: yet in the comparison are implyed two things, first that other nations had something of 30 Gods presence amongst them. Secondly that there was also somewhat of equitie in their lawes, for it pleased the Father (upon the Covenant of Redemption with his Son) to restore so much of his Image to lost man as whereby all nations are disposed 35 to worship God, and to advance righteousnes: ...

They did by nature the things contained in the law of God. But the nations corrupting his Ordinances (both of Religion, and Justice) God withdrew his presence from them proportionably whereby they were given up to abominable lusts. ... Wheras if 40 they had walked according to that light & law of nature they might have been preserved from such moral evils and might have injoyed common blessing in all their natural and civil Ordinances: now, if it might have been so with the nations who 45 were so much strangers to the Covenant of Grace, what advantage have they who have interests in this Covenant, and may injoye the special presence of God in the puritie and native simplicitie of all his Ordinances by which he is so neer to his owne 50 people. This hath been no small priviledge, and advantage to us New-England that our Churches, and civil State have been planted and growne up (like two vines) together like that of Israel in the wilderness by which we were put in minde (and 55 had opportunity put into our hands) not only to gather our Churches, and set up the Ordinances of Christ Jesus in them according to the Apostolick patterne by such lights as the Lord graciously afforded us: but also withall to frame our civil Politie, 60 and lawes according to the rules of his most holy word whereby each do help and strengthen other (the Churches the civil Authoritie, and the Civil Authoritie the Churches) and so both prosper the better without such emulation, and contention for 65 priviledges or priority as have proved the misery (if not ruine) of both in other places.

Harvard College

One of the most remarkable facts of the early history of New England is that the Colonists of Massachusetts, only six years after the founding of Boston [in 1630], should have set about
5 establishing a college. These people had come into the wilderness for the sole purpose of enjoying and perpetuating their peculiar religion, one of the most essential features of which was a learned ministry. But as the English Universities were
10 under the control of the Episcopal Church, and the Nonconformists in England were persecuted and discouraged in every way, there was no reason to expect that England would long continue to supply the growing colonies with competent clergymen.
15 The Colonists, therefore, were compelled to provide for this difficulty, or give up the object of their founding the Colony. A nursery for the education of clergymen was one of the necessities of the situation, and the first college was founded for that purpose.
20 Almost as soon as the Colony was planted, in 1630, the people began to think of rearing clergymen, and a few young men were lodged in the families of ministers, from whom they received instruction in the languages and theology.
25 There was then living at Charlestown, on the other side of Charles River, an invalid clergyman named John Harvard, who had brought with him from England some property and a considerable number of books. He had been educated at Cambridge, in England, and had emigrated to Massachusetts in 30 1637, the very year of the Pequot War, and the year after the four hundred pounds had been voted for a college. An opinion was current at the time that the voyage across the Atlantic and a residence in New England were good for consumptives; and there is 35 some reason to believe that John Harvard, sharing this opinion, had removed to Massachusetts for the restoration of his health.

He does not appear to have preached in America, nor, as far as we know, to have contemplated prea- 40 ching. But after struggling with disease for about a year, he died of consumption. When his Will was opened, it was found that he had left his whole library of two hundred and sixty volumes, and one half of his estate, to the proposed college, – his 45 estate being worth nearly sixteen hundred pounds sterling. Provided thus with a fund of nearly twelve hundred pounds, the trustees went forward, erected a building, established the college, and conferred upon it the name of its first benefactor. 50

ACTIVITY

A. Who made *The Laws of Massachusetts*? Justify your answer.

B. What is defined by *Due Process of Law*?

C. Was Harvard College founded to supply for educated judges and lawyers?

PART 2 – LIFE IN THE COLONIES

Beginning in 1700, the simple and rapid justice that prevailed in the Colonies started to decline. It was in this same period that the number of cases increased drastically, the Colonists turning more and more easily toward the Courts to resolve their disagreements. The reasons that explain this outcome were rather ordinary: problems with indebtedness or contracts, which were typical consequences of the growing commerce that was thriving more and more, as well as the decrease in the influence of local institutions as the Colonists gradually increased in number. Most people went to Court for wrongs committed against them or damage done to their property. The rich and influential knew very well how to manipulate the Courts in order to persecute or punish their enemies. This explosion of cases encouraged the emergence of a legal profession, which did not stop expanding and becoming increasingly important. This also provided work for provincial legislatures to whom it was required to request the drafting of laws in response to particular situations that could appear within their circle of influence. These laws were progressively more numerous, as well as more precise and detailed. Lawyers rapidly became elected to legislatures, helping to further complicate the writing of laws, their precision and their technical nature. The legislatures dealt especially with the question of private property.

Laws became so complicated and exhaustive that the judges could no longer settle for simple and pragmatic solutions to disputes; they turned to English case law (precedents) and the "Anglicization" of American Law began. American Law became structured, more strict and conventional: men practicing Law were increasingly men educated in Law Schools and Universities, and the majority were quite simply educated in England, in Oxford, Cambridge or London. Law books, dictionaries, and manuals became more and more commonplace, slowly giving rise to a modern legal culture.

Colonial Law adopted English Law, but notable exceptions still existed in many sectors: real estate, inheritance, marriage and divorce, relations between the Church and the State, Criminal Law, trial procedure, questions pertaining to the jury, to the presence of a lawyer. But the

Colonial Law v. English Law.
Certain aspects of Colonial Law, in absolute opposition to English Law, are quite surprising: for example, in using "the deed and record system", Americans simplified the transfer of property, rendering it more egalitarian. Thus, they moved away from Birthright Citizenship and Child Law, to replace this system with a more general Family Law (one was thus able to deed property or land to any relative).

The Black Codes
During the presidency of Andrew Johnson, the Southern governments passed laws imposing severe restrictions on newly freed slaves such as prohibiting their right to vote, forbidding them to sit on juries, limiting their right to testify against white men, carrying weapons in public places, and working in certain occupations.

most obvious difference was the existence of the right to own slaves, which brought about the voting of *The Black Codes*, totally unheard of in England.

Using the Law became a very efficient social and political weapon, which became widely employed by various groups. This would bring about tensions that had not existed previously.

Americans began reacting emphatically when English Parliament imposed new taxes and new Customs duties, starting in 1760. It was a serious crisis. The Colonists were persuaded that Parliament in London was usurping the power of the Colonial Legislative Assemblies, which had progressively become miniature parliaments, capable of governing a society that had started to become well organized. These Assemblies focused on three Federal powers: legislative, administrative and judicial.

ACTIVITY

A. What may explain the important rise in the use of "justice" in the Colonies?

....

....

....

....

....

B. What were the *"Black Codes"* and why were they an American specificity?

....

....

....

....

....

A DIFFICULT START

DOCUMENT 3

Salem Witch Trial

In 1692, 24 people died during the hysteria of the Salem witch trials. Although we have detailed accounts of the events, historians are still trying to determine the reasons for this tragedy. It may be difficult for us to understand how people in a community turned on their neighbors. There may be a tendency to see the people of Salem as ignorant or cruel. But in many ways, these people were like us – with their own beliefs, fears, challenges, petty disagreements, even jealousies. Search the Internet and get a closer look at what life was like in Salem in 1692 and comment on the following paintings.

DOCUMENT 4

The Scarlet Letter

In *The Scarlet Letter* by Nathaniel Hawthorne, adulteress Hester Prynne must wear a scarlet «A» to mark her shame. Her lover, Arthur Dimmesdale, remains unidentified and is wracked with guilt, while her husband, Roger Chillingworth, seeks revenge.

Nathaniel Hawthorne, describing "a tale of human frailty and sorrow", insisted that *The Scarlet Letter* was "a Romance", not a novel. This distinction, in his mind, was important. Where a novel, as he put it, "aims at a very minute fidelity, not merely to the possible, but to the probable and ordinary course of man's experience", a romance expressed "the truth of the human heart". Here, in short, is the prototype of the psychological novel, a brilliant and groundbreaking example of a new genre within 19th-century fiction. Hawthorne's tale has a stark simplicity. In the 17th-century town of Boston, a young woman, Hester Prynne, is publicly disgraced for committing adultery and giving birth to an illegitimate child, a girl named Pearl. Forced to wear a scarlet "A", Hester slowly redeems herself in the eyes of Puritan society. Over many years, she challenges the two men in her life – her husband and her lover – with the dark truth of their emotional responsibilities and failures, while at the same time wrestling with her own sinful nature. After seven long years of painful rehabilitation, she emerges as a strong, inspiring woman, while the pastor, Arthur Dimmesdale, who seduced her, dies of shame. Hester, too, eventually dies, and is buried near Dimmesdale under a tombstone marked with a simple "A".

Such a bare summary does few favors to an extraordinary work of the imagination that burns from page to page with the fierce simplicity of scripture and an almost cinematic clarity of vision. *The Scarlet Letter* is an astounding book full of intense symbolism, as strange and haunting as anything by Edgar Allan Poe, a writer whom we know Hawthorne much admired.

The process of Hester Prynne's acquisition of self-knowledge, the recognition of her sin and her ultimate restoration in a sequence of enthralling scenes, punctuated by moments of confrontation with Dimmesdale, is utterly compelling and, at times, deeply moving. Nathaniel Hawthorne's understanding of the emotional transactions of the sexes is profound and modern, too. And very interesting about the price paid for the loss of love. Hester's reflections on her relationship with Dimmesdale ("How deeply had they known each other then! And was this the man? She hardly knew him now") could be found in many modern novels.

The most memorable and original aspect of *The Scarlet Letter* lies in Hawthorne's portrait of Hester Prynne, who has been described as "the first true heroine of American fiction", a woman whose experience evokes the biblical fate of Eve. Hawthorne's achievement is to make her passion noble, her defiance heartbreaking and her frailty inspiring. She becomes the archetype of the free-thinking American woman grappling with herself and her sexuality in a cold, patriarchal society. Hester Prynne is more than just a mother with a baby, she is an outcast woman who will ultimately be welcomed back into American life, purged and cleansed of her sin. Readers of *The Scarlet Letter* during, for instance, the Monica Lewinsky scandal of the 1990s, could not fail to miss the resonance of Hawthorne's "romance" with that bizarre political drama.

ACTIVITY

A. What does *The Scarlet Letter* tell you about the life in the Colonies in the late 18th century? Was it a fair law?

B. How would you defend Chillingworth if there were a trial in the novel *The Scarlet Letter*? (Read the novel...)

PART 3 – A REVOLUTION

A growing centralizing resistance to imperial administration was led by a group of lawmen, half-politicians, half-lawyers, well-educated, and confident in the future. They justified their unhappiness, first, in the name of Common Law, then, in the name of Fundamental Laws. Their protests were brought before Courts of Justice where they exercised their talents in famous trials and cases, such as the Parson's Cause, the writs of assistance case, the Alexander McDougall case, and the Boston Massacre trials.

These men also made their opinions heard in numerous pamphlets, written as legal memoirs, and debated on the Mother Country's violations of their rights. In this way, they were using Law to try to resolve a political controversy.

In 1776, the Americans renounced their allegiance to their sovereign, because the King and his administration had not respected Common Law, or the contract binding them to the Colonies.

In taking their oaths, the Americans made a distinction between Common Law and Fundamental Laws. Fundamental Laws and freedoms were the true sovereign of the People. The people, who thus became the source of power and Law that had served as a justification for the Revolution, would become the People's protector, and not the King, who could not any longer fulfill this role.

The royal government was replaced by governments that were created in each of the States. But power was carefully defined and limited: republican constitutions were drafted, in every State as well, to give everyone a voice in the exercise of power. The Constitutional Assemblies were highly concerned with inscribing the principle of equal powers and a system of checks and balances in these constitutions. And, more importantly, they established one of the Revolutionary principles that Locke and Montesquieu had imagined: a separation of the powers. Translating these concepts into Law was the single greatest rupture with colonial England.

When the Colonists won the War, they invented a political system that was very different from the one they had experienced when they were English. Their first obligation was to establish a more egalitarian society, and thus more democratic. The immigrants found authentic opportunities in this Land that had not existed in England, especially that of having land of their own, or participating in community life, or even being elected to a city assembly.

DID YOU KNOW?

In his Second Treatise of Government (1689), John Locke had argued that the idea of a social contract could exist between members of society and a government, on the condition, however, that the government be the protector of the life, liberty and property of said members of society. This idea led to the development of the idea of inalienable rights.

The theory of Natural Law
Natural Law theory is a philosophical and legal belief that all humans are governed by basic innate laws, or laws of nature, which are separate and distinct from laws which are legislated. The origins of Natural Law theory lie in Ancient Greece.

The Colonists, and notably the Founding Fathers, had adopted ideas based on the Theory of Natural Law, in vogue in the 17th and 18th centuries.

Under the spell of these Revolutionary ideas, the Americans threw themselves into creating their government, with a real fear of centralized power: their first move was to limit themselves to a confederation, each State jealously safeguarding its sovereignty. The Federal government had such limited power, that it was not actually able to do anything. The approval of 9 of the 13 States was needed. Neither executive nor judicial power had been planned. The typical Colonial Assembly was used as a model.

ACTIVITY

A. Who was King of England at the time of the Revolution, and what do you know about him?

....

....

....

....

....

....

B. Why did the States write their own Constitutions?

....

....

....

....

....

....

REVOLUTION AT THE COURT?

DOCUMENT 5

The Parson's Cause

The "Parson's Cause" was an important legal and political dispute in the Colony of Virginia often viewed as an important event leading up to the American Revolution. Colonel John Henry, father of Patrick Henry, was the judge who presided over the court case and jury that decided the issue. The relatively unknown Patrick Henry advocated in favor of colonial rights in the case.

In 1758, the Virginia colonial legislature passed the Two Penny Act. According to legislation passed in 1748, Virginia's Anglican clergy were to be paid 16,000 pounds of tobacco per year, one of the Colony's
5 major commodity crops. Following a poor harvest in 1758, the price of tobacco rose from two to six pennies per pound, effectively inflating clerical salaries. The House of Burgesses responded by passing legislation allowing debts in tobacco to be paid in currency at
10 a rate of two pennies per pound. King George III of Great Britain vetoed the law, causing an uproar in the Colony. Many Virginia legislators saw the King's veto as a breach of their legislative authority.

The Reverend James Maury, a clergyman who had
15 sued in Hanover County Court (April 1st, 1762) for back wages on behalf of all the ministers involved, effectively becoming a representative of the British cause. The court ruled (Nov. 5th, 1763) that Maury's claim was valid, but that the amount of damages had to be determined by a jury, which was called 20 for in December 1763. Patrick Henry, then relatively unknown, rose to prominence by defending Hanover County against Maury's claims. Henry argued in favor of the Two Penny Act. As reported by the plaintiff Maury in a letter (Dec. 12th, 1763) to fellow Anglican 25 minister John Camm shortly after the trial, Henry argued in substance "that a King, by disallowing Acts of this salutary nature, from being the father of his people, degenerated into a Tyrant and forfeits all right to his subjects' obedience." 30

The jury awarded Maury one penny in damages. The award effectively nullified the Crown veto, and no other clergy sued.

DOCUMENT 6

George Cooke's 1834 depiction of Patrick Henry arguing the "Parson's Cause" case at the Hanover County Courthouse.

The Parson's opinion

DOCUMENT 7

The Parson's opinion of the "Parson's Cause",
by Reverend James Maury (1763)

To the Reverend John Camm,

DEAR SIR: — Now that I am somewhat more at leisure, than when I wrote to you by Major Winston, from Hanover County, Virginia, some few days ago, I have sat down to give you the best account I
5 can of the most material passages in the trial of my cause against the Collectors in that Court, both to satisfy your own curiosity, and to enable the lawyer, by whom it is to be managed in the General Court, to form some judgment of its merits. I believe, sir,
10 you were advised from Nov'r Court, that the Bench had adjudged the Two-Penny Act to be no law; and that, at the next, a jury, on a writ of inquiry, were to examine whether the Plaintiff had sustained any damages, and what. Accordingly, at December Court,
15 a select jury was ordered to be summoned; but, how far they who gave the order, wished or intended it to be regarded, you may judge from the sequel. The Sheriff went into a public room, full of gentlemen, and told his errand. One excused himself (Peter Robinson
20 of King William County) as having already given his opinion in a similar case. On this, as a person then present told me, he immediately left the room, without summoning any one person there. He afterwards met another gentleman (Richard Sq. Taylor) on the green,
25 and, on his saying he was not fit to serve, being a church warden, he took upon himself to excuse him, too, and, as far as I can learn, made no further attempts to summon gentlemen.

These, you'll say, were but feeble endeavors to comply
30 with the directions of the Court in that particular. Hence, he went among the vulgar herd. After he had selected and set down upon his list about eight or ten of these, I met him with it in his hand, and on looking over it, observed to him that they were not such jurors as the Court had directed him to
35 get, being people of whom I had never heard before, except one, whom, I told him, he knew to be a party in the cause, as one of the Collector's Securities, and, therefore, not fit for a juror on that occasion. Yet this man's name was not erased. He was even called
40 in Court, and, had he not excused himself, would probably have been admitted. For, I cannot recollect, that the Court expressed either surprise or dislike that a more proper jury had not been summoned. Nay, though I objected against them, yet, as Patrick
45 Henry (one of the Defendant's lawyers) insisted they were honest men, and, therefore, unexceptionable, they were immediately called to the book and sworn. Three of them, as I was afterwards told, nay, some said four, were Dissenters of that denomination called
50 New Lights, which the Sheriff, as they were all his acquaintance, must have known. Messrs. Gist and McDowall, the two most considerable purchasers in that county, were now called in to prove the price of tobacco, and sworn. The testimony of the former
55 imported, that, during the months of May and June, 1759, tobacco had currently sold at 50s. per hundred, and that himself, at or about the latter end of the last of those months, had sold some hundreds of hogsheds at that price, and, amongst the rest,
60 one hundred to be delivered in the month of August, which, however, were not delivered till September. That of the latter only proved, "That 50s. was the current price of tobacco that season." This was the sum of the evidence for the Plaintiff.

ACTIVITY

A. Briefly explain what the Parson's Cause was and its importance at the time.

B. Read the description made by Reverend James Maury, what are the elements of English justice that you may find?

PART 4 – MAKING A NEW NATION

George Washington
Washington had won the respect of his countrymen as Commander of the Continental Army. His fellow delegates elected him President of the Constitutional Convention because they held him in high esteem. His job was to keep the meetings orderly and effective.

DID YOU KNOW?
There were 55 Delegates to the Constitutional Convention, 34 of which were lawyers.

Alexander Hamilton
(1755-1804). He was a Founding Father of the United States, Chief of Staff of George Washington, one of the most influential interpreter and promoter of the Constitution, the founder of the nation's financial system, and the founder of the first American political party (the Federalists).

Bills of Attainder
Legislative acts declaring an individual or group of individuals guilty of some crime and which punishes them without the benefits of either due process or a judicial trial.

The first organization that had been imagined, under the *Articles of Confederation*, did not work well. A Constitutional Convention was thus organized in Philadelphia in May 1787, presided by George Washington. Everybody, or almost, agreed on the idea that a strong national government was necessary. But worries were voiced, especially from States having little territory or small populations, and who feared being dominated by larger, more populated States. It was decided to create an assembly with two chambers: the House of Representatives and the Senate. The former would represent the populace, giving dominance to heavily populated States. The latter, would represent the States; all would have an equal number of seats, no matter how big it was or the number of people living in the State.

The government was also divided into 3 branches:

- Congress would be in charge of passing laws, though not in an unlimited fashion, because a list of specific powers would be established. By this, we mean powers "listed" in the Constitution. The Constitution, the laws passed by Congress and the treaties all together would thus become "the Supreme Law of the Nation." The States, on their side, would keep all powers not expressly delegated to the Federal government.
- A President would be elected for a period of four years and would have the right to veto bills passed by Congress.
- There would also be a Supreme Court, which would be independent.

A Constitution was drafted. It had to be approved by nine States. Each knew that if one of the large States did not approve it, it would have little chance of being ratified. The State of New York was particularly in doubt. Alexander Hamilton, an influential Federalist, decided to throw himself into a vigorous campaign in favor of adopting the Constitution. Assisted by John Jay and James Madison, he published a series of fundamental articles (85 in total) in defense of this idea. Starting October 27th, 1787, they were printed in newspapers throughout New York State, all signed with the pen name "*Publius*", to convince the population of the merits of this Constitution. Today, we refer to these articles as the *Federalist Papers* and they represent a key element in understanding the American political system.

One point not in their favor, however, was that a Consti-

Ex-post facto laws
Ex-post facto *means "after the fact". In simplest terminology, you cannot be held criminally responsible for an action that was not a crime at the time it took place. For example, a person gambles on a riverboat on Monday when it is legal. But on Tuesday, a law is passed saying anyone who gambled on Monday has committed a crime.*

tution undoubtedly did not contain much about the protection of individual freedoms, apart from the mention of a right to *Habeas Corpus*, the ban of *ex-post facto laws,* and bills of attainders. For the Federalists, the fact of having limited the Federal government's power by establishing a precise list should have sufficed. But many were not convinced by this argument. The Constitution was finally ratified after a last-minute commitment was made for the adoption of a Bill of Rights.

The promised Bill of Rights was finally adopted in 1791. It forbade the Federal government from limiting the rights enumerated in the first 10 Amendments, by Law. So, no person or body, not even Congress, may limit the rights endowed by the Constitution. This limitation was later extended to the States through the Doctrine of Selective Incorporation (14th Amendment).

ACTIVITY

A. What were the achievements of the Constitutional Convention held in 1787?

....

....

....

....

....

....

B. What do you know about Publius?

....

....

....

....

....

....

UNDERSTANDING THE CONSTITUTION

DOCUMENT 8

The Federalist Papers
No. 78
The Power of the Judiciary

WE PROCEED now to an examination of the judiciary department of the proposed government.... According to the plan of the convention, all judges who may be appointed by the United States
5 are to hold their offices during good behavior... In a monarchy it is an excellent barrier to the despotism of the prince; in a republic it is a no less excellent barrier to the encroachments and oppressions of the representative body. And it is the best expedient
10 which can be devised in any government, to secure a steady, upright, and impartial administration of the laws. Whoever attentively considers the different departments of power must perceive, that, in a government in which they are separated from each
15 other, the judiciary, from the nature of its functions, will always be the least dangerous to the political rights of the Constitution; because it will be least in a capacity to annoy or injure them. The Executive not only dispenses the honors, but holds the sword of the
20 community. The legislature not only commands the purse, but prescribes the rules by which the duties and rights of every citizen are to be regulated. The judiciary... may truly be said to have neither FORCE nor WILL, but merely judgment; and must ultimately
25 depend upon the aid of the executive arm even for the efficacy of its judgments. This simple view of the matter suggests several important consequences. It proves incontestably, that the judiciary is beyond comparison the weakest of the three departments of
30 power; that it can never attack with success either of the other two ... that ... the general liberty of the people can never be endangered from that quarter; I mean so long as the judiciary remains truly distinct from both the legislature and the Executive. For I
35 agree, that "there is no liberty, if the power of judging be not separated from the legislative and executive powers." And it proves, in the last place, that as liberty can have nothing to fear from the judiciary alone, but would have every thing to fear from its union
40 with either of the other departments... and that as nothing can contribute so much to its firmness and independence as permanency in office, this quality may therefore be justly regarded as an indispensable ingredient in its constitution, and, in a great
45 measure, as the citadel of the public justice and the public security. The complete independence of the courts of justice is peculiarly essential in a limited Constitution. By a limited Constitution, I understand one which contains certain specified exceptions to
50 the legislative authority; such, for instance, as that it shall pass no bills of attainder, no *ex-post facto* laws,

and the like. Limitations of this kind can be preserved in practice no other way than through the medium of courts of justice, whose duty it must be to declare all acts contrary to the manifest tenor of the Constitution 55 void. Without this, all the reservations of particular rights or privileges would amount to nothing.... If it be said that the legislative body are themselves the constitutional judges of their own powers, ... it may be answered, that this cannot be the natural presump- 60 tion, where it is not to be collected from any particular provisions in the Constitution. It is not otherwise to be supposed, that the Constitution could intend to enable the representatives of the people to substitute their will to that of their constituents. It is far more 65 rational to suppose, that the courts were designed to be an intermediate body between the people and the legislature, in order, among other things, to keep the latter within the limits assigned to their authority. The interpretation of the laws is the proper and peculiar 70 province of the courts. A constitution is, in fact, and must be regarded by the judges, as a fundamental law. It therefore belongs to them to ascertain its meaning, as well as the meaning of any particular act proceeding from the legislative body. If there should 75 happen to be an irreconcilable variance between the two, that which has the superior obligation and validity ought, of course, to be preferred; or, in other words, the Constitution ought to be preferred to the statute, the intention of the people to the intention of 80 their agents. Nor does this conclusion by any means suppose a superiority of the judicial to the legislative power. It only supposes that the power of the people is superior to both ... If, then, the courts of justice are to be considered as the bulwarks of a limited 85 Constitution against legislative encroachments, this consideration will afford a strong argument for the permanent tenure of judicial offices, since nothing will contribute so much as this to that independent spirit in the judges which must be essential to the 90 faithful performance of so arduous a duty....Upon the whole, there can be no room to doubt that the convention acted wisely in copying from the models of those constitutions which have established good behavior as the tenure of their judicial offices, in point 95 of duration; and that so far from being blamable on this account, their plan would have been inexcusably defective, if it had wanted this important feature of good government. The experience of Great Britain affords an illustrious comment on the excellence of 100 the institution.
PUBLIUS

DOCUMENT 9

The Anti-Federalist Papers
No. 78-79
The Power of the Judiciary

...The Supreme Court under this constitution would be exalted above all other power in the government, and subject to no control. ...

The judges in England, it is true, hold their offices during their good behavior, but then their determinations are subject to correction by the House of Lords; and their power is by no means so extensive as that of the proposed Supreme Court of the Union. ...

The judges in England are under the control of the legislature, for they are bound to determine according to the laws passed under them. But the judges under this constitution will control the legislature, for the Supreme Court are authorised in the last resort, to determine what is the extent of the powers of the Congress. They are to give the constitution an explanation, and there is no power above them to set aside their judgment. ... There is no power above them, to control any of their decisions. There is no authority that can remove them, and they cannot be controlled by the laws of the legislature. ... this court will be authorised to decide upon the meaning of the constitution; and that, not only according to the natural and obvious meaning of the words, but also according to the spirit and intention of it. In the exercise of this power they will not be subordinate to, but above the legislature. .... The Supreme Court then have a right, independent of the legislature, to give a construction to the constitution and every part of it, and there is no power provided in this system to correct their construction or do it away. If, therefore, the legislature pass any laws, inconsistent with the sense the judges put upon the constitution, they will declare it void; and therefore in this respect their power is superior to that of the legislature. In England the judges are ... subject to have their decisions set aside by the House of Lords, for error, ...But no such power is in the legislature. The judges are supreme and no law, explanatory of the constitution, will be binding on them.

When great and extraordinary powers are vested in any man, or body of men, which in their exercise, may operate to the oppression of the people, it is of high importance that powerful checks should be formed to prevent the abuse of it. ...I suppose the supreme judicial ought to be liable to be called to account for any misconduct, by some body of men, who depend upon the people for their places; and so also should all other great officers in the State, who are not made amenable to some superior officers....

BRUTUS

Thomas Jefferson
(1743-1826) He was an American Founding Father, the principal author of the Declaration of Independence and the 3rd President of the United States.

ACTIVITY

A. *Document 9*: **According to the document, how does the Supreme Court of the United States differ from the highest court in Great Britain?**

B. **What is the author's attitude towards the proposed Supreme Court of the United States?**

C. **How would the United States be different today if the proposals outlined in the *Anti-Federalist Papers* had been accepted?**

D. **Compare Document 9 with *Federalist Number 78*. What are the major points on which the authors disagree? On which points do they agree?**

Important Words

Common Law
Fundamental Laws
Confederation
Constitution
Ex-post facto laws
Bill of attainder

The historical context

The English Colonists brought their knowledge and their Law with them; we especially owe them their Justice of the Peace and the hierarchy of the Courts. However, the English allowed the Colonists to develop a form of local government from the beginning, and even the legal system in response to new living conditions. Laws were modified according to local situations and major differences appeared between the different Colonies, the laws having been geared more towards issues of commerce in the South, for example, while they became more rigid in regards to behavior and morals in the North. Judges were less educated than the judges in England and they applied practical justice, based on efficiency. Many other influences came into play: the influence of Spanish and French law, and even Native American traditions, from which the English borrowed their standards of trade.

Life in the Colonies

An important change took place starting in 1700: society became more complex, and justice along with it. This complexity was the result of a higher number of Colonists, and thus, more and more cases to hear in Court, especially because of the commerce that was becoming progressively significant. A profession of legal experts developed and law became more complicated. Then, they got themselves elected to Assemblies, which contributed to making laws even more specific, convoluted and structured. It was at that moment when American Law became Anglicized. Some exceptions were to note, however, in Property Law, marriage, inheritance, Church/State relations, and certain issues related to Criminal Law. The Colonists wanted the laws passed by the Assemblies to be recognized, especially rejecting the taxes imposed on them without their say by the central power in London.

A Revolution

Resistance began to develop around some men, half-politicians and half-legal experts, who based their demands on Common Law: they first defied the English King's and Parliament's power in the halls of justice. But they also pursued the battle on a more political level, by publishing pamphlets and organizing debates aimed at alerting the Colonists to the fact that the pact between the King and his subjects, thus Common Law, was not being respected. They made a distinction between Common Law and Fundamental Laws, which encouraged them to say that the People were the true sovereigns. From there, they created a republican power, inspired by Locke's and Montesquieu's notion of the separation of the powers. These concepts were transformed into Law and resulted in the rupture with England. Their greatest fear was to recreate a centralized power, so they preferred to create a confederation, with the Colonial Assembly as a model.

Making a new nation

A Constitutional Convention was organized in 1787 in Philadelphia. If the political system was to be changed, it was important to respect the balance of powers between small and large States or of those more populated and those that were not. A Congress with two chambers was created, one to represent the People, and the other, the States. A Constitution was drafted, but some were concerned by the absence of a protection of individual rights in the text. To convince people to accept this Constitution, men such as John Jay and James Madison led a victorious campaign by writing pamphlets for newspapers. The articles came to be known as the *Federalist Papers*. It was finally decided to adopt a Bill of Rights, which was done in 1791: 10 Amendments that protected individual rights were added to the U.S. Constitution.

A. Fill in the text:

The U.S. .... was written in 1787. The Constitutional Convention was held in........................... ... . This document is a plan for .... It explains the government's responsibilities. There are three branches of government: the .... Branch, the .... Branch and the .... Branch. Some powers are given to the national government and some powers are given to the .... The beginning of the Constitution is called the .... Article V of the Constitution States how changes can be made to the Constitution. These changes are called ....

B. Why was family life in New England so different from life in the South?
....
....

C. Who was George Washington?
....
....

D. What was the Constitutional Convention?
....
....

E. What were the powers kept by the States after the Revolution?
....
....

F. What are *The Federalist Papers*?
....
....

REFERENCES :

Page 27. "Patrick Henry", Wikimedia. http://commons.wikimedia.org/wiki/File:Patrick_Henry_speaking_before_the_Virginia_Assembly.tiff

Page 29. "Indian law", by Dimitri Champain

Page 30. "The Laws and Liberties of Massachusetts", from The Laws and Liberties of Massachusetts: Reprinted from the Unique Copy of the 1648 Edition in the Henry E. Huntington Library, Huntington Library Pres, 1998

page 31. "Harvard College", from 'Harvard University Founded in Celebrate Boston. http://www.celebrateboston.com/cambridge/harvard-college-founded.htm
"Harvard Paul Revere", Wikimedia. http://commons.wikimedia.org/wiki/File:HarvardPaulRevere.jpg?uselang=fr

Page 32. "Lawyers in the colonies", by Dimitri Champain

Page 34. "The Witch", Wikimedia. http://commons.wikimedia.org/wiki/File:TheWitch-no3.jpg?uselang=fr
"Salem Witch trial", Wikimedia. http://commons.wikimedia.org/wiki/File:Salem_witch.jpg
"Matteson-jacobs", Wikimedia. http://commons.wikimedia.org/wiki/File:Matteson-jacobs.jpg?uselang=fr

Page 35. "The Scarlet Letter", adapted from "The 10 best novels: N°16 – The Scarlet Letter by Nathaniel Hawthorne (1850)", by Robert McCrum, The Observer, January 5, 2014.

"The Scarlet Letter", Wikimedia. http://commons.wikimedia.org/wiki/File:The_Scarlet_Letter_%281917%29_1jpg?uselang=fr

Page 36. "A revolution", by Dimitri Champain

Page 38. "Parson's Cause by Cooke", Wikimedia. http://commons.wikimedia.org/wiki/File:Parson%27s_Cause_by_Cooke.jpg?uselang=fr

Page 39. "The Parson's opinion ", from The Parson's opinion of the "Parson's cause", by Reverend James Maury (1763), in The World's best orations, Vol.1, Gutemberg Project, http://www.gutenberg.org/files/14182/14182.txt

Page 40. George Washington. Wikimedia. http://commons.wikimedia.org/wiki/File:Portrait_of_George_Washington.jpeg
Alexander Hamilton, Wikimedia. http://commons.wikimedia.org/wiki/File:Hamilton_small.jpg

Page 43. "Official portrait of Thomas Jefferson". Wikimedia. http://commons.wikimedia.org/wiki/File:Official_Presidential_portrait_of_Thomas_Jefferson_%28by_Rembrandt_Peale,_1800%29.jpg

Page 44. "Summary", by Dimitri Champain

Page 45. "Review", by Dimitri Champain

pp. 29, 31, 33, 35, 37, 39, 41, 43. "Activity", by Dimitri Champain

The U.S. Legal System

Introduction

U.S. Law is more than statutes passed by Congress. In some areas, Congress authorizes administrative agencies to adopt rules that add detail to statutory requirements. And the entire system rests upon the traditional legal principles found in English Common Law. Although both the Constitution and statutory laws supersede common law, courts continue to apply unwritten Common Law principles to fill in the gaps where the Constitution is silent and Congress has not yet legislated.

3

PART 1 – SUPREMACY OF FEDERAL LAW

After obtaining their independence, between 1781 and 1788, the Colonies agreed upon a text defining the type of government that they wished to have. The *Articles of the Confederation* became, in some ways, the first constitution adopted by the United States. This text established a very limited government, with a weak Congress, holding few powers. It granted actual authority to the different States that had just come into being, each one within the frontiers of the ex-Colonies. The *Articles* made no mention of judicial power, apart from a Maritime Court that was retained.

The drafting of the Constitution reflected a general consensus about the need to strengthen Federal power. The legal system received particular attention and this resulted in the creation of the Supreme Court. The addition of a Supremacy Clause in Article IV also reinforced the new powers of the Judicial Branch. For this paragraph established the primary principle of American Law: that which is written in the Constitution may not be contradicted by any State. It is neither, however, very clearly stated if this principle applies to the Federal State itself, nor what the role of each State's legal systems is in all of the areas that were not "enumerated" in the Constitution as being conferred to Federal power.

The Constitution gave Congress the power to create Law.

A busy Congress
Over the two-year duration of each Congress, Senators and Representatives introduce about 10,000 bills. During that time, about 650 bills are passed by Congress, and then signed into law by the President.

The Constitution gave Congress the power to create Law. A major restriction was added though, giving the President the power to veto, even if the veto could be overturned by a ¾ vote of the two Houses. Federal Laws are called statutes. The United States Code is the compilation and codification of Federal Statutory Law. The Code is not Law in and of itself, but it presents the statutes in a logical and easily understandable order. For example, Title 8 contains all of the texts related to Agriculture; Title 10, those related to the Army; and Title 20, those related to Education. This code may be consulted and downloaded freely at uscode.house.gov. Thus, all citizens have access to it.

Congress' legislative power is nevertheless limited by the Constitution itself, which clearly states jurisdictions of the national legislators. These areas are defined in Article I, section 8. They are very broad, such as the right to regulate commerce between States and foreign countries, or highly specific, such as the one that establishes Postal Service, but they are logical because they respond to emergencies and needs of the situation at that time. Article I, section 9 also forbids Congress' passing *ex-post facto* laws, which means it cannot pass a law which would be applied retroactively (after the fact).

The power for interpreting the text of the laws, especially the Constitution, was not as clearly planned, though it would seem primordial! The Judicial Branch does it today, since it assumed that responsibility from the beginnings of the young republic.

Powers granted to the Federal Judicial Branch are also limited by what was originally intended in the Constitution. Although, the need for a Judicial Branch was not as defined in the mind of the Framers of the Constitution and they only truthfully imagined the situations that were presented to them at that precise moment: in the end, they are highly limited but clearly listed in Article III. Among them, one can see: "all cases in Law and equity…", diversity cases, or disputes between residents of two different States. What seems to have been vital was avoiding an advantage for a plaintiff in holding the trial in his own State.

But another power appeared later. In a case that is now famous, *Marbury v. Madison* (1803), and that we may consider as the "founder" of judicial power, the Supreme Court itself thus considered that it held another more important power: that of determining if a law violated the Constitution, therefore actually interpreting it. In this way, the Supreme Court would be able to declare that a law is valid. The Court thus interpreted it to mean that it is unconstitutional when violating the rights granted to the People, because Article I does not authorize Congress to pass such laws.

ACTIVITY

A. How does the Constitution limit the powers on Congress?

....

....

....

....

....

B. What is the importance of *Marbury v. Madison* (1803)?

....

....

....

....

....

CONGRESS MAKES THE LAW

DOCUMENT 1

How a bill becomes a law

Introduction of a bill

A new piece of legislation or bill is introduced by a member of Congress. It can be introduced in either the House of Representa-
5 tives or the Senate, or both. One exception is that all appropriations or funding bills start in the House of Representatives. A bill number is assigned (S. 1, for instance, for
10 the first Senate bill introduced; or H.R. 50 for the 50th bill introduced in the House).

Committee consideration

Based on the issue addressed or for consideration, the bill then goes to the appropriate committee,
15 which will either kill the bill or refer it to a specific subcommittee. At this stage, a hearing is often held and the parties interested can testify for and against the bill. After the hearing, a mark-up occurs where amendments are debated and voted on to revise the
20 original bill. The bill is then voted out of the sub-committee to the full committee. More hearings and another mark-up may take place at this point. The committee votes to decide if the bill will be "reported out" of the committee for consideration by the entire
25 legislative body, or to stop the process here.

Floor action

The process differs somewhat in the House (House of Representatives) and the Senate, once the bill is reported out of the committee. In the Senate, the bill moves from committee passage to floor debate,
30 whereas in the House, the bill goes to the Rules Committee. This is where rules are given to the legislation that regulates time limits for debate and determines whether all members of the House can offer amendments.

Debate

35 Two members hold great power because of their responsibility for scheduling floor debate. These are the Speaker of the House and the Senate majority leader. A commonly used tactic for "killing" a bill is to delay scheduling of the bill so that it may not be voted on.

Once the bill is scheduled, floor debate takes place 40 and amendments can be suggested, if permitted by the rules of the House. The bill is then voted on for final passage. The same process occurs in the other chamber if it passes.

Conference

As a result of the amendments offered in the com- 45 mittees and on the floor, the legislation passed individually by the House and Senate usually differs. In order to work out the differences, each chamber's version must go to a conference committee made up of members from both chambers. A conference report 50 is issued which contains the bill with all compromises that have been agreed upon. Both the full House and the Senate must then vote on the conference report. If this passes, the bill becomes law, or is vetoed.

The bill becomes law or is vetoed

At this stage, the bill is sent to the President so that 55 it can be signed and become a law. The bill can be vetoed and returned to Congress if the President does not agree with the bill. Unless the required 2/3 majority in both the House and Senate overrides the veto, the bill dies. 60

ACTIVITY

A. Fill out the diagram, after reading *Document 1*.

INTRODUCTION

1

COMMITTEE ACTION

2

3A → OR → 3B

4

4A → OR → 4B

FLOOR ACTION

5

5A → OR → 5B

6   SAME PROCESS IN THE OTHER HOUSE

7

8A → OR → 8B

ENACTMENT

9A → OR → 9B

10A → OR → 10B

PART 2 – COMMON LAW

When no law (statute) or no constitutional principle exists, the Courts, whether Federal or State, turn toward Common Law. Common Law is a system that has prevailed in England for centuries. It includes a collection of legal rulings, jurisprudence, customs and principles that thus form a Law based on experience (Case Law).

Common Law is a legal system that appeared in England starting in 1066 with William the Conqueror; it developed gradually in numerous countries during the English conquests and the expansion of its Empire. A large number of countries use it today: Australia, India, Canada (except Quebec), New Zealand, and Malaysia. One major difference between Common Law countries and countries that apply Roman Law (like France), is that among the former, a judge explains the verdict rendered by the Court, which is not the case in the latter.

The United States is a Common Law country. Every State uses Common Law, with the exception of Louisiana, which applies Roman Law. When a case comes before a Court, jurisprudence must first be verified, unless other-wise specified in a law adopted by Congress (State or Federal). Common Law applies in civil cases, because a person cannot be convicted of a criminal offense, unless they break a law, which defines the procedure and the consequences of the violation. Once the legislative body has passed a law and the text is made public, it is said the law is "on the books".

In many of the States, Common Law is still vitally important in certain areas, such as Contract Law, Property Law, or civil liability, because Common Law covers more possibilities than the laws passed by the Assemblies of these States. For the States handle these areas of law, and they are not always legislated on issues that are presented to the Courts. But even for issues that are covered by specific laws at a State level from that point on, Common Law is there to fill in the gaps.

Common Law changes with the times, contrary to what happens at a Federal level, where Justice at a State level depends substantially on this evolution; we can see very different solutions from one State to the next. On a Fede-

Hierarchy
A judge's rank is determined on the basis of the court they were sitting in when they made a decision. The general idea of the system is that lower judges must follow the decisions of higher judges, i.e. that there exists a clear hierarchical relationship among the different courts.

ral level, the Courts have a more limited range of issues to deal with, which are most often addressed by laws passed by the U.S. Congress.

Common Law is a more flexible system that also leads to more complexity. Thus, a lawyer who must defend a case in Court will have to not only find the appropriate laws that contain the desired response, but also search within a tangled web of verdicts delivered that are related to a similar problem. Lawyers receive a highly advanced education that teaches them how to develop a meticulous legal sense and to be interested in the smallest detail, which might make a difference. The lack of uniformity between the States is so complicated that only legal experts can find the correct response, often at an exorbitant hourly rate!

ACTIVITY

A. How many States use Common Law in the United States? Why do they use it, or not?

....

....

....

....

....

B. What is the main problem in the use of Common Law for a lawyer?

....

....

....

....

....

IN THE NAME OF MY STATE

The Common Law right to change one's name

DOCUMENT 2

Historically, Anglo-American naming practices were far less formal and less regulated than they are today. Surnames did not become necessary until the 14th century, when
5 they started to be picked and applied at random – a man's physical, mental or moral characteristics, his occupation or his place of residence, even his real or fancied resemblance to an animal, supplied a myriad of surnames which still exist. These were
10 at first merely temporary, not always lasting as long as the lives of the persons so named, and were not transferred to descendants.

By the reign of Elizabeth I, beginning in 1558, surnames had become static and hereditary in
15 England. However, naming practices remained flexible. Historical flexibility in naming practices is reflected in the establishment early on of a common law right to change names without petition to the State. In theory, at common law even today, a per-
20 son may change names without State assistance. After sufficient time and consistent use by the named person and others, the new name becomes the person's legal name. In the United States, this right continues to be recognized by many courts
25 today, although nearly all States have also enacted statutory processes for changing names.

When enacted, such statutes were offered as an additional aid to changing one's name, rather than as a restriction on the common law tradition, and
30 were intended to help the government better keep records of citizen's names. Only a few States have explicitly abrogated the common law right. The precise contours of the common law right to change one's name may be, however, subject to some
35 debate. It seems unclear, unless one considers the common law right to allow change with legal effect, what the States that abrogated the common law right intended to abrogate. In contrast, the Maine Supreme Court noted the freedom to use addi-
40 tional names informally in an opinion in which it also declared the common law right "superseded." The court Stated: We recognize that a person may informally adopt a stage name, a *nom de plume*, or a business name or one for social purposes
40 which is not his true name and, while using such a name, may obligate himself legally and, under

certain conditions, enter into agreements which are binding upon other parties. On the other hand, there are situations in which the public interest entitles the State to demand that a person identify 45 himself by his true, legal name in connection with his performance of certain activities.

Thus it appears that the common law right to change one's name is as it sounds: it protects the right to make a legally recognized change. 50 Regardless of the contours of the right, however, changing one's name with any real effect today requires the assistance of the State. For example, although passport regulations permit issuance of a passport under a person's name changed by 55 common use, the regulations also require three public documents bearing the new name. One document must be a form of government-issued photo identification.

In new procedures instituted after September 11, 60 2001, the New York Department of Motor Vehicles (DMV) requires four to six points (each form of identification is awarded a value of 1–2 points) of identification information, such as other identification cards, credit cards, social security cards, 65 and so on, in order to receive State identification. The New York State DMV requires that the name on all of these documents match exactly.

It seems unlikely with these standards that a person could acquire identification with a name 70 other than that on already issued government documents.

Obtaining an identification card in California under a name different from that on one's birth certificate or legal presence document requires 75 verification with one of the following State-issued documents: adoption documents, name-change document, marriage certificate, domestic partnership certificate, divorce document, or medical information authorization form in conjunction with 80 a gender change. According to their case law, both New York and California retain the common law name-change right.

Yet, it seems unlikely that either State would issue identification materials with a name changed at 80 common law, given their application requirements.

DOCUMENT 3

Hello. What's your name?

In 2004, the New Mexico Court of Appeal permitted Snaphappy Fishsuit Mokiligon to change his name to Variable. A few years later, Variable petitioned to have his name changed to Fuck Censorship!

The Trial Court denied his petition, explaining that the desired name was "obscene, offensive and would not comport with common decency." The Appellate Court affirmed. The California Court of Appeal reached a similar decision in 1992, when it denied a petitioner's request to change his name to Misteri (pronounced Mister) Nigger. Although both petitioners argued that denying their requests violated their First Amendment rights, the courts concluded that the problems risked by permitting names that contain offensive content – or example those that might incite violence or be considered fighting words – warranted denial.

This particular concern does not really apply to other desired names, for example those with nonalphabetical characters or otherwise unusual characteristics, though State Courts have denied these petitions as well: The California Court of Appeal found no abuse of discretion after the lower court denied Thomas Boyd Ritchie III's request to change his name to III *(pronounce Three)*.

The Supreme Courts in Minnesota and North Dakota refused to change Michael Herbert Dengler's name to 1069.

In 1976, a New York court refused to allow a feminist to change her last name from "Cooperman" to "Cooperperson."

In contrast, other State Courts have granted petitions for unusual name changes. The journalist Jennifer Lee successfully changed her name to Jennifer 8. Lee.

In 2006, the California Court of Appeal found that a lower court did abuse its discretion in refusing to allow Darren Lloyd Bean to change his name to Darren QX Bean!

At times, courts have reached conflicting conclusions in cases in which petitioners have sought to change their names to single words, even though the courts were in the same State.

How do I implement my name change in the USA?

Whether you have changed your name by usage or by court order, the most important part of accomplishing your name change is to let others know you've taken a new name.

The practical steps of implementing a name change are:

• Advise the various government and business agencies with which you deal and have your name changed on their records. It is generally recommended that you first acquire a driver's license, then a Social Security card in your new name. Once you have those pieces of identification, it is usually fairly simple to acquire others or have records changed to reflect your new name.

• Tell your friends and family that you have changed your name and you now want them to use only your new one.

• Use only your new name. If you are employed or in school, go by your new name there. Introduce yourself to new acquaintances and business contacts with your new name.

ACTIVITY

A. What is the right to privacy in the United States and how is it protected?

B. May States place a restriction on name-changes or do the opinions of courts in these cases rely on custom?

PART 3 – JUDICIAL PRECEDENT

DID YOU KNOW?
Six Presidents of the United States – John Adams, John Quincy Adams, Theodore and Franklin Delano Roosevelt, Rutherford B. Hayes, and John Fitzgerald Kennedy – were graduates of Harvard.

I plead the Fifth!

The Courts deliver responses to accusations of violations of the law and in relation to the problem of understanding these same laws. This most often requires judges to interpret the laws. When engaging in such interpretations, judges believe that they are connected to what was previously decided by superior Courts, or ones on the same level. This is what we call *stare decisis*, or more simply put, legal precedence. This principle helps judges to establish a comprehensible system, which is substantial and allows justice to be predictable. The people on trial who go to Court with a case whose precedents are basically unfavorable will try to show that the facts of their case contain elements that differentiate them from the case at hand, and they must arrive at different conclusions with different reasoning.

Sometimes, the courts interpret laws quite differently, even those that are found in the Constitution: the 5th Amendment, for example, contains the clause, "that no person... shall be compelled in any criminal case to be a witness against himself."

We should realize that even such a clear amendment is in fact... not so clear! It does happen that some individuals refuse to respect a court order, or to testify, on the basis that their testimony may expose them to legal proceedings, because they might have broken the law, not in the United States, but in a foreign country. That is a complicated situation! Does the self-incrimination clause apply in this case? The Second Circuit Court of Appeals thought so, but the Fourth and Fifth Circuit Courts of Appeals thought not. This means that the Law is not the same in the U.S. from one Court to the next!

The Superior Courts regularly try to iron out these differences and to standardize them nationally. So the U.S. Supreme Court, which is able to choose the cases it hears, almost always chooses to hear cases in which the judgment will allow them to resolve a conflict within the Circuit Courts. In the example given in the former paragraph, the Supreme Court rendered arbitration in 1998, finding that the fear of legal proceedings in a foreign county did not fall within the context of the

self-incrimination clause of the 5th Amendment of the U.S. Constitution. This verdict is applied throughout the country now. That means that in all the States, even in the Second Circuit, all Courts are bound by the decision of the highest Court in the land.

In the same manner, an Appeals Court verdict (Circuit Court) binds all of the inferior District Courts. The rule of what is also applied in all States; in this way, the precedents grow in volume and the Law slowly becomes standardized.

ACTIVITY

A. What does *Stare Decisis* mean?

....

....

....

....

....

....

....

B. How can the system of law be standardized nationally?

....

....

....

....

....

....

....

BEHIND CLOSED DOORS

DOCUMENT 4

Precedents affect judges' decisions

You may have assumed that a trial judge simply hears the facts of a case and makes a decision based on those facts. After all, is that not the way it happens on television? Few people outside the legal community understand how many factors enter into a trial judge's decisions, and, in particular, how precedents govern those decisions.

Q: What is a precedent?

A: A precedent is a prior judicial decision involving the same legal issue that is currently being decided. For example, before 1996, when a police officer stopped a criminal defendant for a minor traffic violation, and found incriminating evidence (drugs, for example), the defendant would argue, sometimes successfully, that the traffic violation was just a "pretext," or an excuse, and that the real reason for the stop was the police officer's hunch that the defendant was involved in serious criminal activity. The defendant would argue that, because the police officer had no reason to believe that a serious crime was being committed, the evidence of that crime should not be used in evidence at trial. In 1996, both the United States Supreme Court and the Supreme Court of Ohio decided that, even when a minor traffic violation is not the real reason for stopping a motorist, the stop is legitimate if the driver has, in fact, committed a minor traffic violation. As a result of those decisions, Ohio trial judges may no longer throw out evidence just because it is obtained as the result of a "pretextual" stop.

Q: Must trial judges follow these precedents?

A: Yes. Our judicial systems, both Federal and State, are organized as hierarchies, so that when one court decides a legal issue, all courts below it in the hierarchy must follow its decision. All Ohio courts must follow decisions of the Supreme Court of Ohio; Ohio Trial Courts within an appellate district must follow decisions of that district's Court of Appeals.

Q: Why must trial judges follow decisions of higher courts?

A: We value uniformity in the law, which requires at least one court with the authority to decide, for the entire judicial system, what the law is. Also, a trial judge would not have the time to decide every legal issue that comes up from scratch. When a novel issue arises, the three judges of an appellate panel can bring their collective wisdom to bear on the issue, and the most important issues will be decided with the collective wisdom of seven justices of the Supreme Court of Ohio (or the nine justices of the United States Supreme Court).

Q: Suppose the judge disagrees with a higher court's precedent?

A: Because our judicial system is hierarchical, the judge must follow legal precedents decided by a higher court. A judge who feels strongly enough may express disagreement in his or her decision, while still following the higher court's decision.

For example, in a 2001 decision by the Ohio 2nd District Court of Appeals, the issue was whether a natural father's having sent his daughter just one Christmas card, in the year before the proposed adoption of the daughter by her stepfather, was enough contact with the child to require the father's consent to the adoption. The Supreme Court of Ohio had held that any communication, however slight, between a parent and a child within the year preceding a proposed adoption was enough to require the parent's consent. The Court of Appeals followed this decision, as required, but noted its disagreement with the decision in its opinion. Occasionally, the Supreme Court of Ohio may change its mind after having reviewed such an opinion.

Q: So does this mean higher courts sometimes overturn their old decisions?

A: Yes. Occasionally, a court will overrule itself not long (within a few years) after handing down a decision. The court might, for example, be made aware of legal authority it did not know about when it made the earlier decision. More common is the overruling of an older precedent. This can reflect changing social conditions, or changes in other areas of the law, or, it can reflect the recognition that, in the light of experience, the old decision just is not working out well.

DOCUMENT 5

Go ask your mother!

Gay marriage, medical marijuana, recreational marijuana, immigration... the list goes on and on of laws that are supposed to be decided State by State. Yes, you may say, "Well, they are." Truth is, no they aren't.

There are two basic levels in the U.S legal system: Federal law and State law. A Federal law applies to the nation as a whole and to all 50 States whereas State laws are only in effect within that particular
5 State. If a State law gives people more rights than a Federal law, the State law is legally supposed to prevail. This means State law will always supersede Federal law when the person in question stands to gain more from the State law, right?
10 Wrong. The law that applies to situations where State and Federal laws disagree is called the Supremacy Clause, which is part of article VI of the Constitution. The Supremacy Clause contains what is known as the doctrine of pre-emption, which
15 says that the Federal government wins in the case of conflicting legislation. Basically, if a Federal and State law contradict, then when you are in the State you can follow the State law, but the feds can decide to stop you. When there is a conflict between a State
20 law and Federal law, it is the Federal law that prevails. For example, if a Federal regulation prohibits the use of medical marijuana, but a State regulation allows it, the Federal law prevails.
Confused as to what really happens when State and
25 Federal laws clash? Let us take gay marriage for instance. The Supreme Court recently announced that it would be hearing two cases involving same sex marriage, both of which have implications for States' rights to recognize same sex marriage. The
30 decisions will almost certainly affect what role States can play in recognizing same sex marriage. Even President Obama has said that States, and States, alone should decide whether same sex marriage is legal within their borders. As of now, there
35 are 17 States that recognize same-sex marriage and 33 States that have a ban against it.
So, does Federal law recognize same-sex marriage? Yes. The Federal government must now recognize valid same-sex marriages according to the U.S.
40 Supreme Court's June 26, 2013 decision in *U.S. v. Windsor*. This decision cleared the way for same-sex married couples to receive Federal benefits. Yet not all facets of the Federal government adhere to that. The IRS recognizes same-sex marriage as married under all Federal tax provisions where marriage is a factor. The Social Security Administration however, 45 only recognizes marriages that are valid in the State where the couple lives for the purposes of granting Federal benefits. This means if you are in a same-sex marriage but live in a non-recognition State, you are not eligible for Social Security benefits on your 50 spouse's work record.
Let us move onto my favorite subject, pot. At the Federal level there is the Controlled Substances Act, which classifies marijuana as a Schedule I substance. This act considers pot to have a high poten- 55 tial for dependency and no accepted medical use, making distribution of marijuana a Federal offense. In October of 2009, the Obama Administration sent a memo to Federal Prosecutors encouraging them not to prosecute people who distribute marijuana 60 for medical purposes in accordance with State law. So what happens when you get caught with the green bud in a State that allows it (for now, let us say medicinally)? We can look at the case of Gerald Duval, Jr. Duval claims he is on the frontlines of 65 the war over medical marijuana. Michigan, Duval's home, allows the farming and use of medical marijuana. Duval, Jr. thought his Michigan pot farm was protected under State law – then the Feds came. Now, he will soon serve a 10-year prison sentence 70 for breaking the U.S. government's marijuana regulations. How can this even be fair?
Well, this my friends is how I see it... it's the "go ask your mother" law. Regress back into your childhood and think of your father as the State law and your 75 mother as the Federal law. You want to go to a party and stay out a little later past your curfew. Your father (State) says yes but your mother (Federal) says no. Who ultimately has the final say?
"Go ask your Mother." 80

ACTIVITY

A. Which Courts bind which other(s) in the United States?

B. Is it legal to smoke weed in America?

PART 4 – EQUITY

Maxims of Equity
The maxims of equity are basic rules upon which the rules of equity have been established. They reflect and represent fundamental moral ideas or themes that lie at the heart of equitable jurisdiction.

As for the differences we can observe in the various States, we must factor in the right to a fair trial. In civil proceedings, the Courts may decide between two solutions: they can choose a legal or equitable remedy. Equity was adopted during the Anglicization of American Law. Generally, it was applied when no solutions were available from Common Law, or yet Common Law only offered monetary solutions. For example, if a breach of contract cost a plaintiff $500, he could appeal in Court to win back this sum, and thus "obtain justice." This "accounting" aspect of justice, however, would rapidly become inadequate, and incapable of assessing the actual situation. A piece of land, for example, may be valued at $500/acre, but this would no longer be the case with farmland or a construction plot. And in the latter case, should land located on the coast be evaluated at the same price as land 15 miles inland? And how much do you value the land where you, and maybe your parents, or your ancestors, were born? This is how subjectivity came into play, assigning a value to a work of art or to a family heirloom. And the plaintiffs were no longer content with requesting damages, but claimed "real justice". Equity Courts developed in the 13th and 14th centuries, offering highly creative solutions based on common morals. These Courts were led by and were established under the authority of a Lord Chancellor, a powerful figure, Advisor to the King, who was also often a man of the cloth. Equity Courts notably invented and furthered "specific performances", which forced the person who lost his case to perform a specific task or to fulfill an obligation that he had promised to do. For example, deliver a product to a sub-contractor, which would allow him to create a derivative product from the delivered product.

Equity Courts, per their highly moral nature, were codified by customs and maxims, like "one who does not have clean hands may not enter into equity." These customs and maxims were conserved in the United States.

In the Federal system, there is no specific Court for equity. Therefore, the same judges use Common Law or equity at their own discretion. None of that brings clarity to justice. It may often seem quite difficult to say with certainty if the verdict is rendered under Common Law, or equity. But, like in England, Equity is the procedure used to obtain a more just decision. The Plaintiff would most often have pleaded that without this equity, irreparable or serious damages would follow. There is, howe-

Judicial Decree
It is a judicial decision, especially in an Equity or Probate Court. The main difference with a verdict is that it contains an order having force of law (for example, of doing a particular act).

ver, a notable difference in the two procedures, because there is no jury for an equity trial and the judge renders a decision on the Law, but also on the facts. Finally, his decision is not rendered in the form of a verdict, but as a judicial decree.

ACTIVITY

A. Have you heard of maxims of equity before? Could you give an example of them? (or search the Internet)

....

....

....

....

....

....

....

B. Describe the cartoon on page 60.
- **List the objects or people you see in the cartoon. Which of the objects are symbols? What do you think each symbol means? Which ones are missing?**
- **Is it a classical representation of Justice? Is it a good representation of Justice?**

....

....

....

....

....

....

....

MONEY, MONEY, MONEY?

Frivolous Lawsuits

DOCUMENT 6

Some people may think that it is possible to make big money by going to Court. Frivolous lawsuits in the American legal system make rousing news stories and attention-grabbing headlines. They are usually health-related cases in which the Plaintiff accuses the Defendant of significant mental and physical damages. However, many are not aware that these provocative news pieces are at the heart of one of the most heated debates of the modern American legal system—the issue of tort reform.

The 1994 product liability lawsuit, *Liebeck v. McDonald's,* is frequently cited as the first major frivolous lawsuit in America. The incident involved 79-year-old Stella Liebeck, who had purchased a McDonald's cup of coffee, spilled it in her lap, and experienced third-degree burns over six percent of her skin. During the trial, Liebeck claimed that McDonald's coffee was served too hot – between 180-189 degrees Fahrenheit – and therefore her burns were a result of McDonald's negligence. The twelve person jury decided that Liebeck should receive $200,000 in compensatory damages (later reduced to $160,000 since Liebeck was partially at fault for her burns) and $2.7 million in punitive damages (the equivalent of two days worth of McDonald's coffee sales). A judge subsequently reduced the latter award to $480,000.

Judith Haimes filed a medical malpractice suit against Temple University Hospital following an allergic reaction to a dye used in a CAT scan. In *Haimes v. Temple University Hospital and Hart,* Haimes claimed that she warned the doctor of her allergy, but that the doctor proceeded with the injections, which allegedly triggered an extreme allergic reaction that left her with migraines for several days. Haimes, a professional psychic prior to the incident, claimed that the hospital's carelessness ended her career as a psychic because she experienced severe headaches when attempting deep mental concentration. Haimes was originally awarded $986,000 in damages, but the judge ordered a retrial. The second suit was dismissed due to the lack of credibility of Haimes' medical expert. The second decision, affirmed in 1991 by a Pennsylvania Superior Court, resulted in no compensatory damages whatsoever for Haimes.

The media's messages to the public about frivolous lawsuits are commonplace, but such representations on seemingly frivolous lawsuits are often not factually accurate. First, the notion that frivolous lawsuits threaten the American justice system is derived mostly from the fact that much of the public does not actually understand the details surrounding the trials.

For example, numerous headlines trumpeted the fact that Stella Liebeck received $3 million from her suit and Judith Haimes received $1 million from her suit, when in fact Liebeck received $640,000 and Haimes received nothing.

Second, many could assume that the magnitude and intensity of media coverage of frivolous lawsuits is directly proportional to the quantity of lawsuits, and therefore that the extensive media coverage would indicate a large quantity of frivolous lawsuits. The fact that these articles and headlines often reference the growing number of frivolous lawsuits also contributes to this perception. To the contrary, however, the number of new tort cases filed in 2014 was 433,000, down from 547,000 in 2000, suggesting that the number of frivolous lawsuits per annum is actually decreasing. One key problem of media coverage of tort litigation is the fact that news outlets frequently publish these articles, not necessarily to support the tort reform movement, but rather because their "shock factor" generates interest and increases sales.

There is little argument over the claim that frivolous lawsuits are a problem that drains the resources of courts, businesses and the American public. There is similarly little room for argument over the claim that unscrupulous lawyers and opportunistic Plaintiffs have taken advantage of a legal system that affords them great latitude in pressing their claims. What is less clear is whether or not the basic right to a remedy for a perceived legal wrong is being reshaped and abridged by the public's lack of knowledge about the true scope and nature of supposedly frivolous lawsuits and the actual monetary damages awarded.

That's (also) America at court

Civil lawsuits cost the U.S. economy over 200 billion dollars per year! According to the U.S. Federal News, every taxpayer in the U.S. is now paying a "lawsuit tax" of around $700 – $800 per year. It is no surprise that personal injury lawyers are thriving in the States and that the law schools are packed to overflowing with potential new lawyers. Here are some of the bizarre lawsuits that these lawyers have had to handle. This list deals with recent lawsuits only.

Richard Overton v. Anheuser-Busch, 1991

For a while in the 1990s, Anheuser-Busch, the producers of Budweiser, ran a series of ads in which two beautiful women came to life in front of two truck drivers. A Michigan man bought a case of the beer, drank it, and failed to see two women materialize. Cue the lawsuit. He sued the company for false advertising, asking for a sum in excess of $10,000. Thankfully, the court dismissed the suit and the man remained penniless and dateless.

Medera City v. Tasers, 2002

Marcy Noriega, a California Police Officer decided to tase a suspect in the back of the Police car when he became uncontrollable and started kicking at the windows. Noriega drew her taser from her belt and fired it at the man. Unfortunately for the crook, the officer had accidentally drawn her gun instead, and she shot him in the chest – killing him. The city is now suing the taser company, arguing that any reasonable officer could mistakenly draw and shoot their gun instead of their taser. They are suing for the full costs of the wrongful death lawsuit, which the man's family has filed against the city.

Dukes Family v. Killer Whale, 1999

Daniel Dukes, a 27-year-old moron from Florida, hatched a clever plot so that he could have his life-long dream of swimming with a whale fulfilled. He hid from the security guards at Sea World and managed to stay in the park after closing. Shortly after, he dived into the tank containing a killer whale – fulfilling his dream. Daniel was killed by the whale. His parents proceeded to sue Sea World because they did not display public warnings that the whale (Tillikum) could kill people. They also claim that the whale is wrongly portrayed as friendly because of the stuffed toys sold there.

Allen Heckard v. Michael Jordan, 2006

Allen Heckard sued Michael Jordan and Nike founder Phil Knight for $832 million because Heckard claimed that he was tired of people thinking he looks like Jordan. He claimed to suffer defamation, permanent injury, and emotional pain and suffering because people often mistook him for the basketball star. Heckard dropped the lawsuit later that year.

Pearson v. Chung, 2007

Roy L. Pearson Jr., a 57-year-old Administrative Law Judge from Washington, D.C., claimed that a dry cleaner lost a pair of his pants, so he sued the dry cleaning shop for $65,462,500. Representing himself, Judge Pearson cried in court over the loss of his pants, whining that there certainly is not a more compelling case in the District archives. But the Superior Court judge was not moved: he called the case "vexatious litigation", scolded Judge Pearson for his "bad faith", and awarded damages to the dry cleaners. But Pearson didn't take no for an answer: he appealed the decision. The Court of Appeal rejected his case.

ACTIVITY

A. How much pain and suffering is enough to sue?

B. Which of the above cases is the most surprising for you, and why?

Important Words

Common Law
Equity
Case Law
stare decisis
self-incrimination
Rule of Law

Supremacy of Federal law

The first text that served as the U.S. Constitution was not suitable: the *Articles of Confederation* did not allow for decisions to be made that could be applied across the board and permit things to be standardized. So the U.S. Constitution was drafted within a broad consensus. Article IV granted a major power to the Federal government. The Constitution gave Congress the power to pass Federal laws, called *statutes*. They are compiled in the United States Code. The power to interpret these laws fell to the judges, but that had not been specified in the beginning. This power derives from one of the groundbreaking Supreme Court rulings in the *Marbury v. Madison* case, in 1803.

Common Law

When there is not a law that specifically applies to an issue raised, the judges turn to Common Law and look at the precedents. William the Conqueror introduced the Common Law system in England in 1066. It is still in effect today in most of the Anglophone countries, including the United States, except for Louisiana. Common Law is very widely used in certain sectors of law, such as Property Law, Contract Law, or civil liability. It has changed over time and adapted to the evolution of society, contrary to the laws passed by the Assemblies, which take much longer to change. The system, though, is also more complex, which requires a high level of expertise.

Judicial precedent

Judges offer solutions based on their interpretation of the Law. This interpretation falls into the broader context of verdicts rendered by other Courts in similar cases. They are bound by these other judgments, and this is referred to as *stare decisis*, or the rule of the precedent. Some Courts may interpret laws differently from what might have been done elsewhere. In this case, the Supreme Court is the final judge and its role very often consists in arbitrating. Little by little, it reduces these differences in interpretation between the Courts.

Equity

Everybody hopes that his or her case will be fair. For this to happen, the American Courts have the option of choosing between two systems: Common Law and Equity. Common Law is limited in the sense that it only permits presenting monetary solutions, a compensation for the damage that was caused. Equity is a system that allows a judge to impose, for example, and obligation to do something, such as resorting to a sub-contractor, otherwise nothing else can be done. In such cases, receiving money in payment for damages serves no purpose for the entrepreneur, who would prefer a long-term solution that would allow him to function normally. There is no specialized Court for Equity. All judges may choose one or the other.

A. In this lesson, the question of the the different law available was discussed. To revise this connect the proposed item to the appropriate law.

Law	Right implied
Common law	- it is fair justice.
Equity	- it can be vetoed by the President.
Statute law	- It is forbidden to drink alcohol under 18.
Federal law	- Courts decisions are binding lower Courts.
State law	- ex-post facto law are forbidden.

B. What is a committee in Congress?

....

....

C. What could be a Court's justification for denying you the right to be called Barack Obama, Hillary Clinton or Santa Claus?

....

....

D. What is known as a Court of Equity?

....

....

E. Do you know of any frivolous lawsuits, other than the ones presented? Which ones?

....

....

REFERENCES:

Page 47. "American law disgests", by Alan Shin, Wikimedia. http://commons. wikimedia.org/wiki/File:American_law_digests.jpg?uselang=fr
Page 48. "Supremacy of Federal law", by Dimitri Champain
Page 50. "How a bill becomes a law", Wikimedia. http://commons. wikimedia.org/wiki/File:State_of_the_Union.jpg
Page 52. "Case law", by Dimitri Champain
Page 54. "The Common Law Right to Change One's Name", adapted from "The right to control one's name", by Julia Shear Kushner, 57 UCLA Law Review 313 (2009) p.324
Page 55. "No Name, Colorado", by Dimi Talen,Wikimedia. http://commons. wikimedia.org/wiki/File:No_Name,_Colorado.jpg?uselang=fr
Page 56. "Pete Williams at SCOTUS", by Angela N., Wikimedia. http://commons.wikimedia.org/wiki/File:Pete_Williams_at_ SCOTUS.jpg?uselang=fr
Page 57. "Supreme Court rulings", by Dimitri Champain
Page 58. "Precedents affect judges' decisions", adapted from Judge

Mike Fain of the 2nd District Court of Appeals in Dayton, Ohio, February 20, 2013 on Ohiobar.org.
Page 59. "Go ask your mother!", adapted from Lesley Daunt, Hunffington Post, January 28, 2014.
Page 60. "Common law and Equity", by Dimitri Champain
Page 62. "Mc donald's chicken bacon onion brasil 2", Wikimedia. http:// commons.wikimedia.org/wiki/File:Mc_donalds_chicken_bacon _onion_brasil_2.jpg
Page 63. "Dry cleaner and other shops, St Marychurch Precinct", by Jean Vaughton, Wikimedia. http://commons.wikimedia.org /wiki/File:Dry_cleaners_and_other_shops,_St_Marychurch_ Precinct_-_geograph.org.uk_-_1207189.jpg
Page 64. "Summary", by Dimitri Champain
Page 65. "Review", by Dimitri Champain
pp. 49, 51, 53, 55, 57, 59, 61, 63. "Activity", by Dimitri Champain

UNIT 4 The Federal judicial system

Introduction

Article III of the Constitution anticipates that "judicial power of the United States shall be vested in one Supreme Court, and in such inferior Courts as the Congress may from time to time ordain and establish." It was decided that a Supreme Court should thus be created, but the U.S. Congress was granted the power to create Lower Courts if it wished and how it wished. Likewise, Congress has the power to abolish and create a new system if it wishes. However, this option has limits, because the Supreme Court is actually supreme and has learned to extract from the protection granted it by the Constitution all of the power to become a formidable opposing force to the two other branches of government.

PART 1 – ORGANIZATION OF THE FEDERAL SYSTEM

Original jurisdiction and appeals
The Supreme Court hears most cases on appeal. Litigants wishing to appeal their cases from a State Supreme Court or from a Federal Court of Appeals must file for a "writ of certiorari". If four of the nine Justices agree to issue a writ, the Court will hear the case. The Court also has limited "original jurisdiction" in some cases.

Generally, the Federal Courts handle civil and criminal issues related to Federal Law. The competences may sometimes be mixed, and some cases that should be in the domain of the Federal Courts might nevertheless be heard by a State Court.

Federal judges are usually nominated for life, which means until they retire, die or quit. The Constitution envisages their good behavior and they may be dismissed if they do not respect this clause, most frequently being if they are linked to a criminal case. The code of conduct for Federal judges is very strict. In each Court, personnel are there to assist with its functioning, particularly the Court Clerks.

In Section 2 of Article III, the U.S. Constitution defines the jurisdiction of the Federal Court: *"The judicial Power shall extend to all Cases, in Law and Equity, arising under this Constitution, the Laws of the United States, and Treaties made, or which shall be made, under their Authority; to all Cases affecting Ambassadors, other public Ministers* and Consuls; to all Cases of admiralty and maritime Jurisdiction; to Controversies to which the United States shall be a Party; to Controversies between two or more States; between a State and Citizens of another State; between Citizens of different States; between Citizens of the same State claiming Lands under Grants of different States, and between a State, or the Citizens thereof, and foreign States, Citizens or Subjects."

> **The judicial power shall extend to all cases, in law and equity, arising under the Constitution, the laws of the United States and treaties.**

Federal Court jurisdiction became even more restricted with the 11th Amendment, which forbids it from hearing cases "commenced or prosecuted against [a State] by Citizens of another State, or by Citizens or Subjects of any Foreign State." The Federal Courts may hear a case if:

1. The parties are citizens of two different States (including foreign countries) and the amount of damages reaches $75,000.

2. If the case addresses a Federal issue, that is to say, for example, a problem with interpreting the Constitution, a Law passed by Congress, or in a treaty with a foreign country.

3. If the Federal government is a stakeholder in the case. The Constitution plans for the Supreme Court having exclusive jurisdiction (original jurisdiction) "in cases affecting ambassadors and other diplomats, and in cases in which a State is a party."

In all other cases, the Supreme Court is an Appellate Court, which is almost always the case, except if it is a problem between two States.

The Supreme Court's power to hear appeals originates in the State Courts, created by the Judiciary Act of 1789. This power rapidly imposed itself as being a powerful prerogative of the Supreme Court, especially in cases like Martin v. Hunter's Lessee (1816) and Cohens v. Virginia (1821).

Function of the Supreme Court

The Constitution limits the Court to dealing with "cases" and "controversies". John Jay, the first Chief Justice, clarified this restraint early in the Court's history by declining to advise President George Washington on the constitutional implications of a proposed foreign policy decision. The Court does not give advisory opinions; rather its function is limited only to deciding specific cases.

Since Article III of the United States Constitution stipulates that Federal Courts may only entertain "cases" or "controversies", the Supreme Court avoids deciding cases that are moot and does not render advisory opinions, as the Supreme Courts of some States may do. For example, in *DeFunis v. Odegaard*, 416 U.S. 312 (1974), the Court dismissed a lawsuit challenging the constitutionality of a law school affirmative action policy because the Plaintiff student had graduated since he began the lawsuit, and a decision from the Court on his claim would not be able to redress any injury he had suffered. The mootness exception is not absolute. If an issue is "capable of repetition yet evading review", the Court will address it even though the party before the Court would not himself be made whole by a favorable result. In *Roe v. Wade*, 410 U.S. 113 (1973), and other abortion cases, the Court addresses the merits of claims brought by pregnant women seeking abortions even if they are no longer pregnant, because it takes longer than the typical human gestation period to appeal a case through the lower courts to the Supreme Court.

ACTIVITY

A. When may a Federal Court hear a case?

....

....

....

....

B. Does the Supreme Court act as a Trial Court, an Appellate Court or both?

....

....

....

....

....

CONSTITUTIONAL CONCERNS

The Justices of the Supreme Court

DOCUMENT 1

Appointment and tenure

Supreme Court justices are appointed by the President with the advice and consent of the Senate. Once confirmed, a Supreme Court Justice – like any other Federal judge – serves during "good behavior." Only one Justice, Samuel Chase, has ever been impeached by the House of Representatives, and the Senate failed to convict him. Usually, appointment to the Court represents the culmination of a career, and Justices tend to remain on bench until death or retirement. Justice Wendell Holmes, for example, did not retire until he was older than 90. The average tenure for Justices appointed during the 20th or beginning of the 21st centuries is more than 14 years.

Choosing Justices

On average, vacancies on the Court occur roughly every two years, so a president serving two full terms can expect to have a considerable impact on the composition of the Court, but there is no absolute rule on that matter: President Ronald Reagan named four Justices to the Court during his two terms; after him, Presidents Clinton, Bush and Obama named two each, even if also serving two terms. In making these appointments, presidents typically select persons with distinguished career in public life. Very often appointed Justices have previously served in Congress or held Cabinet posts. Although prior judicial experience is not a requirement, all Justices appointed since 1975 have served as appellate judges. Presidents also seek appointees who share their political affiliation (roughly 90 percent of appointees have been members of the President's party) and their constitutional views. Thus President Bush sought proponents of "judicial restraint," whereas President Obama pledged to appoint justices sympathetic to the "right to privacy." Finally, Presidents also consider demographic factors in their appointees. President Lyndon Johnson chose Thurgwood Marshall as the first African American on the Supreme Court, and when Marshall retired, President George Bush replaced him with another African American, Clarence Thomas. President Ronald Reagan selected Sandra Day O'Connor as the first woman on the High Court, and Barack Obama chose Sonia Sotomayor as the first Hispanic to the position.

The impact of appointments

Through their power to appoint Supreme Court Justices, Presidents frequently can influence the orientation of the Supreme Court. For example, appointments by Presidents Reagan and Bush (father and son) produced a substantially more conservative Court than existed before. Nevertheless, these presidential efforts do not always succeed. The Senate may refuse to confirm a president's nominee. 29 nominations have been unsuccessful on at least the first try, and 12 were fully considered and formally rejected by the Senate. Even when the Senate does confirm nominees, the process has sometimes been arduous; for example, Justice Clarence Thomas received Senate approval by a close 52-48 vote after accusations of sexual harassment were leveled against him during confirmation hearing. Moreover, once on the Court, Justices may not behave as the President expected. The President may have misjudged the prospective Justice's views, those views may change after the justice is appointed, or new issue may arise that the President did not anticipate in choosing a Justice. When a Justice fails to meet the President's expectation, there is nothing the President can do about it.

The Three-part structure of the Federal Courts

DOCUMENT 2

Supreme Court
– Highest court in the federal system
– Nine Justices, meeting in Washington, D.C.
– Appeals jurisdiction through certiorari process
– Limited original jurisdiction over some cases

Courts of Appeal
– Intermediate level in the federal system
– 12 regional "circuit" courts, including D.C. Circuit
– No original jurisdiction; strictly appellate

District Courts
– Lowest level in the federal system
– 94 judicial districts in 50 states & territories
– No appellate jurisdiction
– Original jurisdiction over most cases

ACTIVITY

A. What does "during good behavior" mean relative to a U.S. Supreme Court Justice?

B. Look at the flow chart on *Document 2* and describe how an individual civil case moves between the different levels of the court system.

C. Decide whether the following situations would be dealt with at State or Federal level. (They can be both)

Federal   State

1. Jack Silver, a young Bostonian, is accused of theft.
2. Natalie Anderwood, from Philadelphia, is accused of murder.
3. Santiago Herrera, a Latin American, accuses his boss of discrimination.
4. The Russian Ambassador is accused of espionnage.
5. Two men want to get married in Austin, Texas.
6. Edward Snowden makes NSA information classified as Top Secret public.
7. A woman files for divorce in New York City.
8. John Rupert aggresses Bill Crosby, his neighbor, over a private lane, which he says belongs to him.
9. Walmart accuses Visa of having colluded with banks to charge it fees it should not have had to pay.
10. Lacoste sues a company that is selling copies of its polo shirts in Dallas, TX.
11. Arthur MacCory is fired from his company in Florida.
12. A plastic surgeon in Las Vegas is accused of negligence.
13. In Arizona, Wells Fargo Bank is accused by Keith Ulahoop for having lied about the risks of buying stocks on the Stock Market.
14. An author of a crime novel in California sues another author in North Carolina for plagiary.
15. Julie Potter, from Seattle, refuses to pay her Federal income tax, under the pretext that she doesn't want to keep her American citizenship.
16. Wyoming and Montana have a dispute over a piece of land.
17. An Afghanistan war veteran living in Tennessee contests a denial to pay him disability benefits for being wounded in battle.
18. A North Korean warship opens fire on an American submarine.

PART 2 – DISTRICT COURTS

The 94 United States District Courts (also called Federal District Courts) are Federal Trial Courts of general jurisdiction. So all cases concerning the U.S. legal system are heard here. However, contrary to the Supreme Court that is created by the Constitution, these Courts are a work of Congress. This is at least what the Constitution foresees, in Article III (*"The judicial Power of the United States, shall be vested in one supreme Court, and in such inferior Courts as the Congress may from time to time ordain and establish."*). The first were created by the Judiciary Act of 1789, during the first session of the United States' first Congress. These Courts decide civil or criminal cases according to the rules of Anglo-Saxon Law systems, that is to say the rules of Common Law, Statute Law, Equity and Admiralty Law. They have jurisdiction in all civil and criminal cases as soon as they become Federal ones. When a person is arrested, a District Court Commissioner, a judicial officer, will review the charging documents and set pre-trial release. Clerks provide support for the Courts both within and outside the courtroom. They are responsible for a wide variety of activities, including scheduling cases, maintaining case files, distributing forms, and responding to requests for information.

There is at least one district per State (up to 4 in California, Texas, or New York) and one in the District of Columbia. For the unincorporated Territories, there is one for each following island or archipelago: Puerto Rico, the United States Virgin Islands, Guam, and the Northern Mariana Islands, but they are not technically District Courts in the eyes of Article III of the Constitution. Neither do the judges also do enjoy the same protection. Furthermore, they only serve for 10 years. Because the District Judges are nominated by the President of the United States, with a confirmation by the Senate, and take advantage of the rights described in Article III of the Constitution: they are nominated for life. The President most often applies the rule of senatorial courtesy, and places the State Senator into the nominees of new judges, or accepts that the Senator exercises a sort of veto right. Congress establishes the number of District Court judges in the United States Code. The number varies according to the importance of the Court. There are about 700 District Judges nation-

Congratulations, it's a district court!

Advisory opinions
The doctrines of mootness, ripeness, and standing prohibit District Courts from issuing advisory opinions. Other doctrines, such as the abstention doctrine and the Rooker-Feldman doctrine limit the power of lower Federal Courts to disturb rulings made by State Courts.

Abstention and Rooker-Feldman
The abstention doctrine and the Rooker-Feldman doctrine limit the power of lower Federal Courts to disturb rulings made by State Courts.

wide. Other judges, called Magistrate Judges, are recruited locally and help beginners with their jobs, though they are not nominated for life. They are typically recruited for 8-year terms, renewable. Usually only one judge presides over the trial at this level of jurisdiction, but in half of the cases, the Court uses a jury. For very important trials, there may be three judges on the bench (*in this case, the bench has two District Judges and one Circuit Judge*). A District Court often includes the jurisdictions of numerous counties (or their equivalent).

The official name of a District Court is "*the United States District Court for*" followed by the name of the district, for example: United States District Court for the Southern District of New York.

Each of the United States District Courts is answerable to the 11 Circuits of the United States Courts of Appeals that hear appeals from verdicts rendered in the lower courts. An appeal for a verdict from the District Court must be brought before the Appeals Court in the same Circuit. In very rare cases, the appeal may go directly before the U.S. Supreme Court.

ACTIVITY

A. Who does what in a District Court?

....
....
....
....
....

B. What does a district judge do?

....
....
....
....
....

DISTRICT JUSTICE

DOCUMENT 3

Vacant Texas Federal judgeships languish

Ten Federal judgeships have sat vacant in Texas for an average of nearly two years, creating a backlog of more than 12,000 cases, according to a report by two progressive advocacy groups that blame the problem on the State's U.S. Senators.

The report, given to *The Associated Press* ahead of its release Wednesday, says Republican Sens. John Cornyn and Ted Cruz have deliberately delayed potential nominees by President Barack Obama. Both Senators, however, say Obama hasn't moved fast enough with his nominees.

The report notes that only six judges have been appointed to U.S. District Court vacancies in Texas under Obama – and none since Cruz took office in January 2013. By contrast, 17 such vacancies had been filled by this point in Republican President George W. Bush's second term, when Cornyn and Cruz's predecessor, Sen. Kay Bailey Hutchinson, was in office.

"Senators Cornyn and Cruz have allowed politics to cloud important needs to have judges to fill our Federal Courts," said Phillip Martin, Deputy Director of Austin-based Progress Texas, which compiled the report with the Center for American Progress in Washington.

The lifelong Federal Court appointments are made by the White House but confirmed by the U.S. Senate. The report details three vacancies on the 5th U.S. Circuit Court of Appeals and seven in the Northern, Southern, Eastern and Western Districts of Texas. The 5th Circuit is based in New Orleans but three of its vacancies are designated Texas seats, and at least one is close to being filled.

Plus, upcoming retirements mean that 13 Texas-based Federal judgeships could be vacant by March 2015.

That potential problem is particularly worrisome for Federal Courts near the U.S.-Mexico border, like those in the Western and Southern Districts of Texas, which have some of the nation's heaviest caseloads. The longest vacancy is in Texas' Western District, where Judge W. Royal Furgeson, Jr. entered semi-retirement in November 2008. His slot remains open five years and four months later. That has required Senior U.S. District Judge David Alan Ezra to travel from Honolulu to San Antonio – on the government's dime – to hear cases.

A Southern District Court based in Corpus Christi has had a vacancy for nearly three years. The shortest-lived opening on the report's list is about nine months in the Northern District.

Cornyn and Cruz counter that Obama hasn't quickly nominated candidates to fill the vacancies. However, the White House doesn't push nominees without the support of the home-State Senators and waits for them to make suggestions, as mandated by Senate tradition.

Since creating the Federal Judicial Evaluation Committee to vet potential Texas nominees last April, Cornyn's office says it and Cruz have suggested at least three nominees to the White House for the seven district-court vacancies. More names are expected soon.

"Through the bipartisan FJEC, Sen. Cornyn has submitted several well qualified nominees to the White House for consideration," Cornyn spokeswoman Kate Martin said.

Catherine Frazier, a spokeswoman for Cruz, said her boss has been working closely with Cornyn and that "both of our offices have been in regular contact and working in good faith with the White House."

One of the 5th Circuit openings noted in the report as being vacant for more than two years is close to being filled. The Senate Judiciary Committee, which includes Cornyn and Cruz, last week approved Obama's nomination of Gregg Costa, currently a Southern District judge based in Galveston.

His nomination now only needs full Senate approval – though a vote hasn't been scheduled by the chamber's Democratic leadership. And the other nine openings on Texas' Federal benches don't even have nominees. There are 86 Federal judicial vacancies nationwide and 39 lack nominees – meaning Texas' account for nearly a quarter of all vacancies without nominees, according to data from the Administrative Office of the U.S. Courts.

And if approved, Costa's move to the 5th Circuit would create a new vacancy on Texas' Southern District's bench – and become one of the 13 possible future openings Wednesday's report warns may be a reality by next year.

"Sens. Cornyn and Cruz must put their constituents above political gamesmanship," the report says, "and end their unwavering obstruction of the Federal judicial nomination process."

DOCUMENT 4

How the case moved through the court system.
Regents of the University of California v. Bakke (1978)

Regents of the University of California v. Bakke: this precedent-setting case for Affirmative Action was the first case tried before the Supreme Court to qualify and define how Affirmative Action could be implemented in universities.

The Case: The case was tried before the Supreme Court in 1977 and a ruling was given in 1978. The plaintiff, Allan Bakke, had applied to the UC Davis Medical School twice (the first time in 1973, and the second in 1974) and was rejected both times. At the time, there were two programs for admissions to the UC Davis Medical School: the general admissions program and the special admissions program for those students who felt that they were either at an economic or an educational disadvantage in comparison with the other students. The students who were accepted through the second admissions program did not have to meet the same admissions requirements as the students who were accepted through the general admissions program. In addition, all the students who were accepted through this special program in the two years in which Bakke applied were minority students (even though there were white applicants to this program) with admissions scores significantly lower than Bakke's. Bakke then proceeded to sue UC Davis for admission, claiming that he was being unfairly discriminated against because of his race. The Trial Court and the California Supreme Court both ruled in favor of Bakke, finding that the UC Davis special admissions program was a quota system that was an unlawful violation of, among other things, Title VI of the Civil Rights Act of 1964, and that UC Davis had not accepted Bakke solely on account of his race.

The Verdict: The Supreme Court, although split 5-4, also ruled in favor of Bakke with Judge Powell as the deciding vote. It was decided that quota systems such as the one employed by UC Davis were violations of Title VI of the Civil Rights Act of 1964. However, race could still be used as a positive factor in the admissions process.

Supreme Court of the United States
Writing for a divided Court, Justice Powell holds that the quota system by the University of California at Davis medical school is unconstitutional, but that race could be used as a "plus" in the application process.
Regents of the University of California v. Bakke (1978)

Supreme Court of California
The California Supreme Court agrees with the Superior Court and declares the special permissions program unconstitutional. In addition, the Court orders that Bakke be admitted to the medical school at the University of California at Davis.
Bakke v. Regents of the University of California (1976)

Superior Court of Yolo County, Cali.
After his second rejection, Bakke files his case in trial court. The Superior Court declares that the special admissions policy "operated as a racial quota" and violates Federal and State Constitutions and Title VI. It also says that race cannot be used as a factor for admissions. However, the Court does not order Bakke's admission because he did not prove that he would have been admitted if the special admissions policy did not exist.
Bakke v. Regents of the University of California (1974)

ACTIVITY

A. Read **Document 3**. What do you understand about the nomination of District Judges?

B. Describe how a case moves from the bottom to the top, using the Bakke case (What was the complaint about? Where was the case first introduced? What happened next?, etc.).

PART 3 – COURTS OF APPEALS

The Courts of Appeal were created by Congress in 1891. They are called the Federal Courts of Appeal since 1948, although everyone says Circuit Courts. Yet, this name can be confusing because the Circuit Courts, which were created by the Judiciary Act of 1789, were intermediary Courts between the Trial Courts and the Supreme Court. These Circuit Courts were abolished with the adoption of the Judicial Code of 1911.

The United States is divided into 13 judiciary circuits. Originally, all of the judges were itinerant, traveling from town to town inside a sector assigned to them; they were already called circuits. They are either "numbered circuits" or "unnumbered circuits", and all have at least one Court of Appeal. Numbered circuits are 1 to 11, plus two unnumbered circuits: one for D.C. and one for the Federal Circuit, which was created in 1982, specialized in patents and trademarks and with a national responsibility – it's the only circuit that has no geographic limit. All appeals are heard by a panel of three judges. There may be more judges, according to the severity of the issue, with the number varying from one circuit to the next. The Court sits *en banc*.

The appeals are sometimes sent directly to the U.S. Supreme Court; this is especially the case if an appeal is directed against a verdict of the highest State Court. However, the Supreme Court hears no more than 100 cases per year. Thus, the Courts of Appeal have a strong influence on the evolution of Law in the country.

Since the creation of these Courts, all verdicts are published by a private company, West Publishing, in the *Federal Reporter*. West Publishing has published the *Law Reports* since 1880 and have become inescapable, to the point that some attorneys cite *Reports* in their references. West has contributed to organizing the indexation of American Law, first based on notes attached to verdicts, then by the establishment of a numbering system whose goal was to make looking for a verdict or a point of Law simpler. They are very influential in the sector of digitizing court records with *Westlaw* and *West American Digest System*, which are used by all American legal experts.

The Federal Court of Appeals have 179 judges that are nominated by the President of the United States and must be confirmed by the Senate, as Stated in Article III of the U.S. Constitution. The number of judges per circuit varies

Senior judges

Senior status is a form of semi-retirement for United States Federal judges, and judges in some State Court systems. After Federal judges have reached a certain combination of age and years of service on the Federal Courts (=active judges), they are allowed to assume senior status. A judge must be at least 65 and have served for 15 years to qualify, with one fewer year of service required for each additional year of age. When that happens, they receive the full salary of a judge but work only part-time.

greatly, between 5 (1st Circuit) and 29 (9th Circuit). These judges are nominated for life and are very well paid (almost $200,000 per year). These two conditions are essential for them to be able to resist outside influence and judge with a peace of mind.

The Courts of Appeal only deal with appeals, that is to say there are no cases as such, but only a re-examination of pieces of evidence entered into trial. The attorneys draft a brief, which can be a few pages or several hundred. Sometimes they must plead in person before the Court, but only them: the two parties are not allowed to say anything. Court procedure for the Courts of Appeal is defined by the Federal Rules of Appellate Procedure.

It is possible to appeal a verdict rendered by this Court. Since the adoption of the Judiciary Act of 1925, this appeal is not automatic and must be accepted by the Supreme Court. Such a request is called "petitioning for a writ of *certiorari*".

The Courts of Appeal verdicts establish a binding precedent, which means that Federal Courts of the same Circuit are bound in their future verdicts by those rendered in Courts of Appeal, even if the judges don't agree with them.

ACTIVITY

A. What is the difference between a Circuit Court and a District Court?

....

....

....

....

....

B. How do you file a petition for a writ of *certiorari*?

....

....

....

....

....

ON CIRCUIT

DOCUMENT 5

United States Courts of Appeals
11 numbered circuits

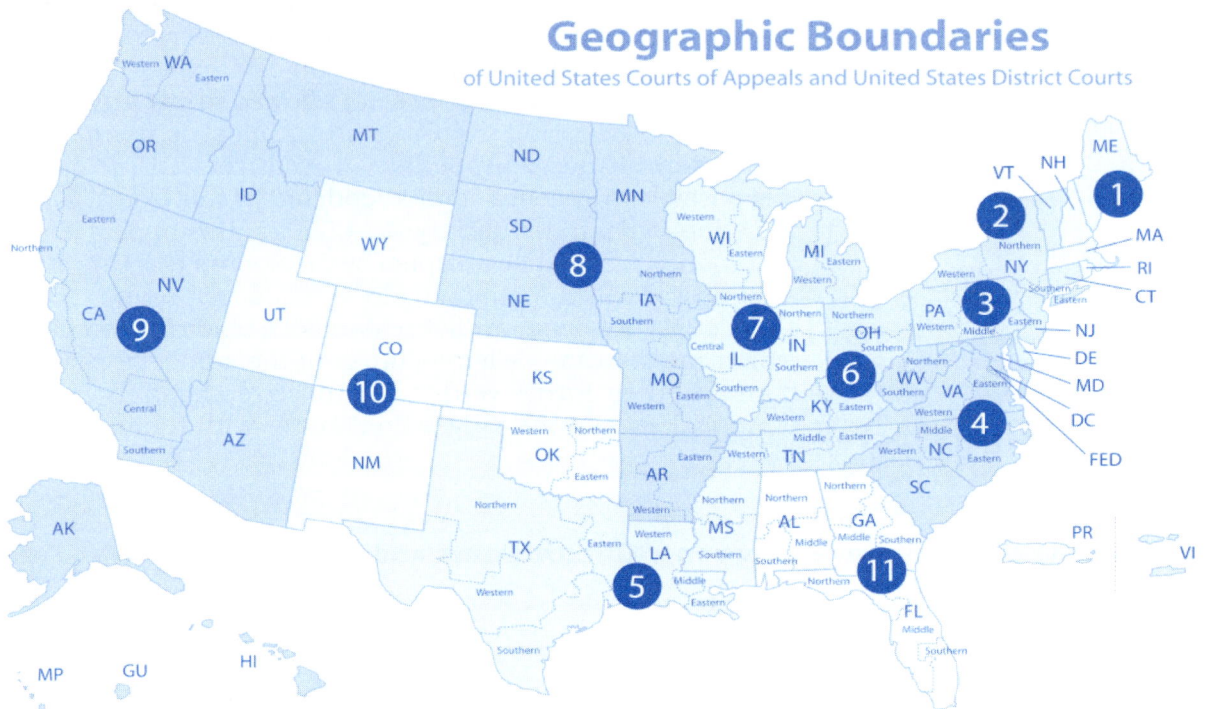

Geographic Boundaries of United States Courts of Appeals and United States District Courts

- First Circuit (Boston): Maine, Massachusetts, New Hampshire, Puerto Rico, Rhode Island
- Second Circuit (New York City): Connecticut, New York, Vermont.
- Third Circuit (Philadelphia): Delaware, New Jersey, Pennsylvania, Virgin Islands.
- Fourth Circuit (Richmond): Maryland, North Carolina, South Carolina, Virgina, West Virginia.
- Fifth Circuit (New Orleans): Louisiana, Mississippi, Texas.
- Sixth Circuit (Cincinatti): Kentucky, Michigan, Ohio, Tennessee.
- Seventh Circuit (Chicago): Illinois, Indiana, Wisconsin.
- Eighth Circuit (St. Louis): Arkansas, Iowa, Minnesota, Missouri, Nebraska, North Dakota, South Dakota.
- Ninth Circuit (San Francisco): Alaska, Arizona, California, Guam, Hawaii, Idaho, Montana, Nevada, Northern Mariana, Oregon, Washington.
- Tenth Circuit (Denver): Colorado, Kansas, New Mexico, Oklahoma, Utah, Wyoming.
- Eleventh Circuit (Atlanta): Alabama, Florida, Georgia.

  + Federal Circuit (Washington, D.C.)
  + District of Columbia (Washington, D.C.)

DOCUMENT 6

Example of a Circuit Court
United States Court of Appeals for the First Circuit

COMPOSITION OF THE COURT
as of September 2014:

Chief Justice:
- Sandra Lynch (nominated by Bill Clinton in 1995).

Circuit Judges:
- Juan R. Torruella (Reagan – 1982)
- Jeffrey R. Howard (G.W. Bush – 2002)
- Ojetta Rogeriee Thompon (Obama – 2010)
- William J. Kayatta, Jr. (Obama – 2013)

Senior Judges:
- Levin H. Campbell (Nixon – 1972)
- Bruce M. Selya (Reagan – 1986)
- Conrad K. Cyr (G.H. Bush – 1989)
- Michael Boudin (G.H. Bush – 1990)
- Norman H. Stahl (G.H. Bush – 1992)
  Kermit Lipez (Clinton – 1997)

Former Chief Justices:
- Levin H. Campbell (from 1983 to 1990)
- Juan R. Torruella (from 1994 to 2001)
- Michael Boudin (from 2001 to 2008)

Inactive Judges:
- Levin H. Campbell
- Conrad K. Cyr

The United States Court of Appeals for the First Circuit (in case citations, **1st Cir**.) is a Federal Court with appellate jurisdiction over the District Courts in the following districts:
- District of Maine
- District of Massachusetts
- District of New Hampshire
- District of Puerto Rico
- District of Rhode Island

The court is based at the John Joseph Moakley Federal Courthouse in Boston, Massachusetts (*see photo*). Most sittings are held in Boston, where the Court usually sits for one week most months of the year; in one of July or August, it takes a summer break and does not sit. The First Circuit also sits for one week each March and November at the *Jose V. Toledo Federal Building and United States Courthouse in Old San Juan, Puerto Rico,* and occasionally sits at other locations within the circuit.

With five active and four senior judges, the First Circuit is the smallest of the 13 United States Courts of Appeals. Since retiring as an active Justice of the United States Supreme Court, Associate Justice David Souter has sat on the First Circuit by designation in several cases.

ACTIVITY

A. Comment the divisions in Circuits. What does it suggest to you?

B. Why may be the justification of a *Federal Circuit*?

C. Comment the box «composition of the Court» in *Document 6*.

PART 4 – THE SUPREME COURT (SCOTUS)

Olympus?

Even better: SCOTUS!

The Supreme Court of the United States, sometimes shortened to United States Supreme Court or abbreviated as SCOTUS, was created by the U.S. Constitution (Article III), and first met in 1789. It is the highest level of judicial power in the United States, and the court of last resort. In accordance with Article III, the Supreme Court may hear any case related to the Constitution or the laws of the United States, and treaties it may have concluded.

It passes judgment in first instance (original jurisdiction) in some rare cases: cases involving one of the States of the Union, a foreign country, or a foreign diplomat. It has no power in all other cases. Its verdicts are without appeal, in all cases. It is usually limited to more important cases, and notably, in deciding if Federal or State laws conform to the Constitution, of which it is the definitive interpreter.

In 1908, Charles Evans Hughes, then-Governor of New York, is cited as saying, during an official speech before the Elmira Chamber of Commerce: "*The Constitution is what the Supreme Court says it is.*" In that respect, it's the Supreme Court that also defines the citizens' fundamental rights in the end, sometimes broadly, sometimes narrowly, and protects them effectively.

The power of judicial review, which is essential to the Supreme Court's power, is not Stated in the Constitution; the Court attributed it to itself in 1803 in the judgment *Marbury v. Madison*. Whether we consider it initially as legitimate or usurped, this power, after being in effect over 200 years, is no longer contested in its principle.

Judicial review in the United States, either concrete or diffuse, is completed *a posteriori*, meaning that it occurs after the law has been made known. It is concrete when the constitutionality of a law is only examined in the context of a particular case. So it is possible that a law be judged entirely or partially unconstitutional, for external legal reasons (it was adopted by a body that did not have the right, for example Congress passing legislation in a sector reserved for the States), or internal legal reasons (its contents contravene the provisions of the Constitution, for example, Fundamental Rights). A Supreme Court verdict applies *to inter partes*. It is not meant to repeal laws. However, it constitutes a precedent that other courts

The right order
As it is customary in American Courts, the nine Justices are seated by seniority on the Bench. The Chief Justice occupies the center chair; the senior Associate Justice sits to his right, the second senior to his left, and so on, alternating right and left by seniority.

Recessing but still working
During the recess period, the Justices study the argued and forthcoming cases and work on their opinions. Each week the Justices must also evaluate more than 110 petitions seeking review of judgments of State and Federal Courts to determine which cases are to be granted full review with oral arguments by attorneys.

must apply, rendering *ipso facto* inapplicable. Finally, constitutional control is diffuse when all Courts, whether Federal or State, and not only the Supreme Court, may examine the constitutionality of a legal standard.

The motto of the Supreme Court is *"Equal Justice under Law"*. It sits in Washington, D.C. in the Supreme Court building, not far from the Capitol. The Court is comprised of 9 Justices: a Chief Justice and 8 Associate Justices. They are nominated by the President of the United States and must be confirmed by the Senate. They are irremovable and serve for life. To dismiss a Justice, an impeachment process must be launched; it has happened only once at this level, and it was not successful. The Justices earn a bit more than $200,000 per year, and Congress cannot decrease their salaries as long as they are in office. Almost 10,000 cases are presented each year to be heard by the Supreme Court, but the Justices only accept around 100 to 150 cases per year. The cases they choose are up to them and they are not required to give a motive for their refusal to hear a case. The Court begins its term on the first Monday in October of each year.

ACTIVITY

A. How can a State be forced to follow a Supreme Court decision with which it disagrees?

....

....

....

....

B. How does the Supreme Court decide which cases to hear?

....

....

....

....

AT WORK

DOCUMENT 7

Jury verdict research using the Internet (*Reports for free*)

The plaintiff claims obstetrical malpractice led to her child's cerebral palsy. The question: If she is successful in convincing the jury, what is her likely recovery?
In Sacramento, CA, a jury awarded $18.5 million on similar facts. And in Bronx County, N.Y., a similar claim resulted in a $9.45 million award April 14.

These verdicts were found using services that report verdicts and settlements in tort cases. Such reporters are nothing new – personal-injury lawyers have turned to them for decades for guidance in valuing their cases.

What is different is that these were found on the Internet, through services that cost nothing. While verdict reports traditionally come in print or are stored in proprietary databases, a handful now make the Internet their home.

What follows is a survey of verdict and settlement reporting services on the Internet. The best of these are sites that publish full case reports online and offer them at no cost to the user.

Probably the most comprehensive, free source of trial reports on the Internet is the Verdicts and Settlements Database of Law Journal *EXTRA!*, *http://www.ljextra.com/cgi-bin/vds*. It contains all reports published since 1994 on the verdicts and settlements page of the *National Law Journal*, and is fully searchable using key words. The database is national in scope and, according to *LJX* Editor Al Robbins, should contain reports from throughout the U.S.

Plans are underway for the *New York Law Journal*, sister to the *NLJ*, to offer a similar database of New York verdicts and settlements on its Web site, *http://www.nylj.com*. The *NYLJ* recently began publishing these reports in its print edition, collected independently from those in the *NLJ*. Ed Adams, *NYLJ* online editor, confirms that plans are underway to publish these reports on the Web, although he is undecided as to when and whether to restrict access to subscribers.

After Law Journal *EXTRA!*, MoreLaw, *http://www.morelaw.com*, is the only Web service with free, nationwide verdict and settlement reports.

It covers all States and the District of Columbia, and has verdicts since December 1996. For any given State, the number of reports ranges from only a handful for the entire period to several a month.

Unique to MoreLaw is that trial reports are linked to the e-mail addresses or Web sites of the participating attorneys. Publisher Kent Morlan, a lawyer in Tulsa, OK., obtains the reports in various ways, canvassing local courts, receiving submissions from lawyers, and culling verdicts from newspaper reports and other sources.

The site's most serious flaw is the lack of a search engine – a significant omission on a site of this nature. Cases are listed by State and then, within each State, by date.

Other sites with free trial reports are more limited, mostly offering only a few reports and tending to focus on a particular jurisdiction or topic.

For example, the Philadelphia Trial Lawyers Association, *http://philatla.org*, publishes its monthly newsletter, The Verdict, online. Each month's issue includes 2-3 reports of notable verdicts or settlements. Each report includes a description of the facts and injuries, and provides the court, the judge, the outcome, the lawyers, and the experts. Issues since February 1996 are available.

The Cobb County (Georgia) Bar Association began offering verdicts and settlements involving local lawyers on its Web site in May 1995, *http://www.kuesterlaw.com/cobb*. As with PTLA, the reports were part of its monthly newsletter. But only a couple of issues of the newsletter contained case reports, and no new issues have appeared online for some time. Jeff Kuester, a lawyer who helped set up the site, told legal.online that upkeep fell behind due to reliance on volunteers, but that it would be resuming soon.

The Doctor's Reference Library of the New Jersey Optometric Association, *http://www.eyecare.org/legal/leglmain.html*, includes a feature, "Eye On Medicine," devoted to chronicling ophthalmologic malpractice in New Jersey. Among other things, it lists and describes

DOCUMENT 8

Being a woman or a judge?

adapted from "*Debate on whether female judges decide differently arises anew*", by Neil A. Lewis, in The New York Times, June 3rd, 2009.

Sandra Day O'Connor, the first woman to serve on the Supreme Court, is often quoted as saying that a wise female judge will come to the same conclusion as a wise male judge. But the opposing argument was bolstered force-fully in April by Justice Ruth Bader Ginsburg, currently the Court's only woman, in a case involving Savana Redding, a 13-year-old girl who had been strip-searched at school by the authorities on suspicion of hiding some ibupro-fen pills that may be bought over-the-counter.

"They have never been a 13-year-old girl," Justice Ginsburg said of her eight male collea-gues, several of whom had suggested during oral argument that they were not troubled by the search. "It's a very sensitive age for a girl," Justice Ginsburg went on to say in an inter-view with *USA Today*. "I didn't think that my colleagues, some of them, quite understood." Now that President Obama has nominated

Judge Sonia Sotomayor to become the third woman in the court's history, the question of how female judges may see and decide some cases differently is again being weighed.

Judge Sotomayor herself raised the issue of personal experience in judging and engendered mixed reviews recently for a speech she gave in 2001 in which she said, "I would hope that a wise Latina woman with the richness of her experiences would more often than not reach a better conclusion than a white male who hasn't lived that life."

But the idea that women may inherently view the law differently on occasion is something that troubles even several female judges who believe it may be so.

Judge Judith S. Kaye, who was the chief judge of New York State for 16 years until her recent retirement, said she had long avoided engaging others on the question. "I struggled with it for the 25 years I served as a judge," Judge Kaye said. But she said she had ultimately come to terms with defending the idea that women judges will, at times, see things differently. "To defend the idea that women come out different on some cases, I just feel it," Judge Kaye said. "I feel it to the depths of my soul," she added, because a woman's experiences are "just dif-ferent." Lawrence Robbins, a veteran litigator in Washington, disagreed, saying, "Any person in the real world should be highly reluctant to make these broad generalizations."

ACTIVITY

A. Does *Document 7* tell you how to find a case held in the Supreme Court?

B. In your opinion, does it make any difference in being a man or a woman when judging?

SUMMARY

Important Words

District Courts
Circuit
Justices
en banc
SCOTUS

Organization of the Federal system

The Federal Courts may hear cases on Federal, civil or criminal issues, though it is not uncommon for the State Courts to handle them. Federal judges are nominated for life. Their rights are defined in Article III of the Constitution, which describes the Judicial Branch. This article specifies that the authority of the Federal Courts extends to all issues in which the parties are from different States, to problems interpreting a Federal law, or to a treaty with a foreign country, or when the Federal government is one of the parties involved. In all other cases, the U.S. Supreme Court is an Appeals Court. It only deals with subjects that have yet to be ruled on, refusing to render advisory opinions, which is a prerogative of the higher U.S. Courts, or to render judgment in cases that have already been heard and have become moot cases. But this rule is not absolute, since, as what happened in *Roe v. Wade* (1973), the Court considered it was a situation prone to be repeated often.

District Courts

The 94 Federal District Courts are basic first-instance courts for Federal issues. They are not provided for in the Constitution and were created by Congress based on the *Judiciary Act* of 1789. There is at least one Court per State, or in the American territories, authorized to hear civil and criminal cases. The President appoints these Judges for life then the Senate confirms the nomination. The President usually applies the rule of Senatorial Courtesy to make his choice, which means involving the State Senators in the final choice. There are about 70 District Judges. Other judges, called District Magistrates, are found in the District Courts, and are hired for eight-year, renewable contracts. Typically, one judge presides over the case at this level, except for extremely important cases where there is a bench with three judges. All District Courts depend on a Circuit Court, which is the Appeals Court.

Courts of Appeals

Congress created the Appeals Courts in 1948. They are often called Circuit Courts, often confused with those created by the *Judiciary Act* of 1789, but today they have disappeared. The United States is divided into 13 Circuits, of which 11 are called numbered Circuits. The unnumbered Circuits are the one in Washington, D.C. and a Circuit that incorporates the entire USA. These Courts hear most of the cases appealed, because the Supreme Court only accepts about 100 per year. The opinions are published in the *Law Reports*. There are 179 judges at this level, all nominated by the U.S. President, with approval by the Senate. These Courts do not only deal with appeals cases. An appeal of their decision is nevertheless possible, in Supreme Court, but the latter must first accept it.

The Supreme Court (SCOTUS)

The U.S. Constitution created the U.S. Supreme Court, also called SCOTUS, in Article III. It deals with original cases or on appeal and limits itself to the most important cases. Its decisions are final: no other appeal is possible. The Supreme Court has the power of judicial review, which is not specified in the Constitution: it attributed it to itself in 1803, in the *Marbury v. Madison* verdict. Supreme Court decisions bind all other U.S. Courts. Its motto is "Equal Justice under the Law". It sits in Washington, D.C. It is composed of nine judges, called Justices: a Chief Justice and eight Associate Justices. They are all appointed for life by the President of the United States, but must be approved by a Senate confirmation.

A. Say if the following statements are true or false:

	True	False
1. – Federal judges are nominated for ten years.		
2. – If there is a dispute between two States, the case may be brought directly to the Supreme Court.		
3. – The United States are divide into 13 circuits.		
4. – The Constitution created the Federal District Court.		

B. What is the Ninth Circuit Court of Appeals?

....
....

C. What is *per incuriam*?

....
....

D. Can the U.S. Supreme Court review and overrule a State Supreme Court decision?

....
....

REFERENCES :

Page 67. "Contempention of Justice", by Matt Wade Photograph. Wikimedia. http://commons.wikimedia.org/wiki/File:ContemplationOfJustice.jpg

Page 68. "US Supreme Court interior". Wikimedia. http://commons.wikimedia.org/wiki/File:Ussupremecourtinterior.JPG?uselang=fr

Page 70. "Seal of the United States Supreme Court", Wikimedia. http://commons.wikimedia.org/wiki/File:Seal_of_United_States_Supreme_Court.svg

Page 71. "Three-part structure": "supreme Court": Wikimedia, http://commons.wikimedia.org/wiki/File:Supreme_Court_Front_Dusk.jpg; "Courts of Appeal": http://www.cafc.uscourts.gov/cache/thumbs/09e0f8cf71df4d29d7d3a9abb5b8fdd9.jpg; "District Courts": Wikimedia, http://commons.wikimedia.org/wiki/File:Spottswood_W._Robinson_III_and_Robert_R._Merhige,_Jr.,_Federal_Courthouse.jpg

Page 72. "It's a district court", by Dimitri Champain

Page 74. "Vacant Texas federal judgeships languish", adapted from Will Weissert, Associate Press, April 3, 2014, http://lubbockonline.com/texas/2014-04-03/vacant-texas-Federal-judgeships-languish#.Uz0WqseNAUE

Page 75 "How the case moved through the court system". adapted from Streetlaw: http://www.streetlaw.org/en/Page/633/How_the_Case_Moved_through_the_Court_System
"US Supreme Court". by Kjetil Ree, Wikimedia. http://commons.wikimedia.org/wiki/File:US_Supreme_Court.JPG?uselang=fr
"Supreme Court of California main courthouse", by Cool Caesar, Wikimedia. http://commons.wikimedia.org/wiki/File:Supremecourtofcaliforniamaincourthouse.jpg?uselang=fr;"Decatur Indiana superior court".Wikimedia. http://commons.wikimedia.org/wiki/File:Decatur-indiana-superior-court.jpg?uselang=fr

Page 76. "Circuit", by Dimitri Champain

Page 77. "Levita espalda". by Incal, Wikimedia. http://commons.wikimedia.org/wiki/File:Levita_espalda.jpg?uselang=fr

Page 78. "Court of Appeals and District Court map", by Tintazul, Wikimedia. http://commons.wikimedia.org/wiki/File:US_Court_of_Appeals_and_District_Court_map.svg?uselang=fr

Page 79. "Jose v. Toledo Federal Building and United States Courthouse – San Juan, Puerto Rico". Wikimedia. http://commons.wikimedia.org/wiki/File:Jose_V._Toledo_Federal_Building_and_United_States_Courthouse.JPG

Page 80. "SCOTUS", by Dimitri Champain

Page 81 : "Supreme Court State of the Union", by Chuck Kennedy, retouchée par KimChee, Wikimedia, http://commons.wikimedia.org/wiki/File:Supreme_Court_State_of_the_Union_2011.jpg?uselang=fr

Page 83. "Being a woman or a judge? ", adapted from «Debate on whether female judges decide differently arises anew», by Neil A. Lewis, in The New York Times, June 3, 2009.
"Ruth Bader Ginsberg, Wikimedia. http://commons.wikimedia.org/wiki/File:RuthBaderGinsburg.jpg

Page 84. "Summary", by Dimitri Champain

Page 85. "Review", by Dimitri Champain

pp. 69, 71, 73, 75, 77, 79, 81, 83 "Activity", by Dimitri Champain

UNIT 5 State Courts

Introduction

The United States is unable to see itself as a one entity: there are 50 States to take into consideration. Well before 1787, the new States that had grown out of the previous Colonies, had all written their own Constitution's, and so had already thought out their model of society. The present judicial system is, for the most part, based on this reality; there are no two States that have the same structure in the United States. Each State developed its own vision of the legal system and was free to create the Courts as they wished.

PART 1 – EVERY MAN FOR HIMSELF?

Far from being a well-organized system as seen at the Federal level, this is a disparate system that you must cope with when you want to study the organization of the judicial system at the State level. Even the names are not the same; as you can see, at the Federal level, a Trial Court is called a District Court and appeals courts are called Circuit Courts. And yet, in about 15 States, the Circuit Courts are Appellate Courts. The Trial Courts are often called Superior Courts, with the most extreme case being in New York State, because the Supreme Court is the name used to designate the Trial Court.

The Judicial System in Colonial Times

During the Colonial period, powers were concentrated in the hands of a governor who was appointed by the King of England. Executive, legislative and judicial powers were combined into his office, rendering the need for an elaborate court system useless.

The lowest judicial level was made up of local judges,

called Justices of the Peace, who were nominated by the Governor. At the next level were found the County Courts, like in England. It was possible to appeal a verdict rendered by a Justice of the Peace or the County court before the Governor and his council.

Juries (Grand and Petit) were also introduced during this period; they started to become popular in England from 1215, with the end of the Ordeals.

' In colonial times, the need for an elaborate court system was rendered useless. '

Grand and Petit Juries

A normal Petit Jury hears hears evidence of a case after the arrest and the arraignment of the accused. A Grand Jury hears evidence before the case is filed and may issue indictments based on the evidence presented by the Prosecutor alone. Additionally, a Petit Jury merely listen to testimony presented, as well as instructions of the judge. It then renders decisions based on the evidence and judge's instructions. Besides criminal cases, it also hears civil cases. A Grand Jury gets to ask witnesses questions and can actually start their own investigations into matters not even presented by the Prosecutor. (Prosecutors usually attempt to take charge of the jury, but it is actually the jury who is in charge. After hearing the evidence, it either bills (indicts), no bills (does not indict), or passes (takes no action), not by a unanimous vote as in criminal cases, but by 9 out of 12, as in civil cases.

Starting at the beginning of the 18th century, a large number of lawyers who had been educated at the Inns of Court in London settled in the Colonies, integrating into society, participating in Assemblies, and affecting the passing of Laws, which became more and more complicated and technical.

The New States

After the Revolution, a wind of defiance blew through the Colonies, taking with it the Governors' power, and also that of the attorneys and even that of English Common Law. Many Governors were stripped of their functions and many specialized Courts were angrily abolished.

The Supreme Court of the United States, a Federal Court, imposed its supremacy by declaring a large number of the Laws passed by the States as unconstitutional. This encouraged the State's distrust of the legal system. Judges and legislators had many disputes, the latter passing laws contrary to the spirit of the judges' rulings. The balance between States and Federal powers still had to be found.

The Situation Today

Starting with the Civil War, the State Courts were overflowing with new requests, brought on by world modernization, industrialization, and the rapid expansion of cities. Cases became more and more numerous and complex. The States' legal systems, which for the most part had been created in response to the needs of an agricultural society, had to be rethought. The States all responded differently to this problem: for some, new Courts needed to be created, while others insisted upon dividing authority into geographic areas; and even others responded that specialized Courts were needed. At the beginning of the 20th century, the States had systems very different from one another. Americans thus began searching for a way to bring together these varied systems, initiating a program known as the Court Unification Movement, which was advocated by men the likes of Roscoe Pound, Dean at Harvard Law School.

This unification movement was fraught with difficulty and encountered opposition from a large number of lawyers around the country. It was, however, a success in some States.

ACTIVITY

A. Who held authority over the judiciary in the Colonies in Colonial times?

....

....

....

....

....

....

....

B. How did the historical situation influence the modern judicial situation in the States?

....

....

....

....

....

....

A WORLD OF DIFFERENCE

Different places, different laws

DOCUMENT 1

Conflict of laws, that part of the law in each State, country, or other jurisdiction that determines whether, in dealing with a particular legal situation, its law or the law of some other jurisdiction, will be applied. An alternative term, widely used in Europe, is "private international law." An example of a situation that might involve the different laws of two places is that of a contract signed in one State and mailed to another. Complications may arise if one of the States provides that a contract so delivered is effective once mailed, while the other State provides that it is not effective until received. The conflict of laws rules that a court applies in these disputed situations are commonly designed to decide the case by the law of the territory having the closest connection with the transaction. An often expressed ideal is that of making the decision the same regardless of where the case is decided.

In the United States the existence of many States with legal rules often changing makes the subject of conflict of laws especially urgent. The Supreme Court ruled in 1938 that each Federal Court must apply the conflict of laws rules of the State in which it sits. Certain provisions of the U.S. Constitution deprive the States of complete freedom to determine how they will decide cases in this field. Most important is Article 4, Section 1, which provides, in part, "Full Faith and Credit shall be given in each State to the Public Acts, Records, and judicial Proceedings of every other State." The U.S. Supreme Court has interpreted this provision as requiring each State to treat as valid any judgment rendered by another State that had jurisdiction over the matter and to lend its powers of enforcement to the judgment; the sole exception is that the courts of one State do not enforce claims arising under the penal law of another. Jurisdiction in this context is defined as the capacity of the State to impose its authority on a transaction because of its intimate connection with the litigants and/or the subject of litigation.

There are especially difficult jurisdictional problems in the field of divorce. The chief problem occurs when only one of the parties appears and the other is merely notified of the action. In such cases the Supreme Court has ruled that the State had jurisdiction to divorce if the party appearing was domiciled there. The Court has defined 'domicile' as the place where a person is living, with the ultimate intention of making it his or her home. A person who obtains a divorce under these circumstances may seek alimony, or payment thereof, in any State and is immune from the charge of bigamy if he or she remarries.

Roscoe Pound

DOCUMENT 2

(born October 27th, 1870 – died July 1st, 1964)

U.S. legal educator and botanist. After studying botany at the University of Nebraska and law at Harvard University, he was admitted to the Nebraska Bar, and he practiced law while also teaching at the State university).
At the University of Nebraska he directed the State botanical survey and discovered a rare fungus (Roscopoundia). He later taught at several law schools, most notably Harvard, where he also served as Dean, instituting many reforms. He was perhaps the chief U.S. advocate of sociological jurisprudence, which holds that statutes and court decisions are affected by social conditions; his ideas apparently influenced President Franklin D. Roosevelt's Bew Deal Programs. After World War II, he helped reorganize the judicial system of Taiwan.

Dissatisfaction with the Administration of Justice

DOCUMENT 3

Passing to the third head, causes lying in our judicial organization and procedure, we come upon the most efficient causes of dissatisfaction with the present administration of justice in America. For I venture to say that our system of courts is archaic and our procedure behind the times.

Uncertainty, delay and expense, and above all the injustice of deciding cases upon points of practice, which are the mere etiquette of justice, direct results of the organization of our courts and the backwardness of our procedure, have created a deep-seated desire to keep out of court, right or wrong, on the part of every sensible business man in the community.

Our system of courts is archaic in three respects: (1) In its multiplicity of courts, (2) in preserving concurrent jurisdictions, (3) in the waste of judicial power which it involves. The judicial organizations of the several States exhibit many differences of detail. But they agree in these three respects. Multiplicity of courts is characteristic of archaic law. In Anglo-Saxon law, one might apply to the Hundred, the Shire, the Witan, or the king in person. Until Edward I broke up private jurisdictions, there were the king's superior courts of law, the itinerant justices, the county courts, the local or communal courts, and the private courts of lordships; besides which one might always apply to the king or to the Great Council for extraordinary relief. When later the royal courts had superseded all others, there were the concurrent jurisdictions of King's Bench, Common Pleas, and Exchequer, all doing the same work, while appellate jurisdiction was divided by King's Bench, Exchequer Chamber, and Parliament. In the Fourth Institute, Coke enumerates seventy-four courts. Of these, seventeen did the work that is now done by three, the County Courts, the Supreme Court of Judicature,

and the House of Lords. At the time of the reorganization by the Judicature Act of 1873, five Appellate Courts and eight courts of first instance were consolidated into the one Supreme Court of Judicature. It was the intention of those who devised the plan of the Judicature Act to extend the principle of unity of jurisdiction by cutting off the appellate jurisdiction of the House of Lords and by incorporating the County Courts in the newly formed Supreme Court as branches thereof. The recommendation as to the County Courts was not adopted, and the appellate jurisdiction of the House of Lords was restored in 1875. In this way the unity and simplicity of the original design were impaired. But the plan, although adopted in part only, deserves the careful study of American lawyers as a model modern judicial organization. Its chief features were (1) to set up a single court, complete in itself, embracing all superior courts and jurisdictions; (2) to include in this one court, as a branch thereof, a single court of final appeal. In the one branch, the court of first instance, all original jurisdiction at law, in equity, in admiralty, in bankruptcy, in probate, and in divorce was to be consolidated; in the other branch, the court of appeal, the whole reviewing jurisdiction was to be established. This idea of unification, although not carried out completely, has proved most effective. Indeed, its advantages are self-evident. Where the appellate tribunal and the court of first instance are branches of one court, all expense of transfer of record, of transcripts, bills of exceptions, writs of error, and citations is wiped out. The records are the records of the court, of which each tribunal is but a branch. The court and each branch thereof knows its own records, and no duplication and certification is required.

ACTIVITY

A. What are the various drawbacks of the American system according to Roscoe Pound (*Document 3*)?

B. Give an example of a conflict of laws that may arise in the United States.

C. What are some examples of Federal and State laws conflicting?

PART 2 – STATE COURTS ORGANIZATION

TRIAL COURTS OF LIMITED JURISDICTION

Types of crimes
In criminal matters, for example, the States can hear three types of crimes: minor offenses (the least serious), misdemeanors (more serious), and felonies (the most serious). These Courts are limited to only two categories. The maximum sentences they may impose may not exceed one year in prison and a fine of $1,000, generally. As for civil matters, the examine cases in which the amount does not exceed a very limited sum, most often $500.

TRIAL COURT OF GENERAL JURISDICTION

SPECIALIZED TRIBUNALS

Though certain States chose to join the unification movement, the systemic structure of each State Court varies from State to State. Each one exhibits different characteristics, but it is still possible generalize about some aspects. Most States have a Trial Court of limited jurisdiction that is presided over by only one judge who hears minor civil and criminal cases.

These Courts are the best known by Americans because they hear almost 90% of court cases. They can be called many things: Justice of the Peace Courts, Magistrates' Courts, Municipal Courts, Juvenile Courts, Domestic Relations Courts, Metropolitan Courts. Judges presiding over these Courts are not required to have completed Law School. They have a limited jurisdiction for the least important cases. In criminal matters, for example, the States can hear three types of crimes: **minor offenses** (the least serious), **misdemeanors** (more serious), and **felonies** (the most serious). Moreover, they are often concerned with highly specific questions, such as traffic violations, or domestic relations, for example. The sentences imposed by the Courts do not remain on your criminal record. An eventual appeal is brought before a Trial Court of General Jurisdiction for a case that is called *de novo* (new trial). Finally, in certain States, these Courts, just like English Magistrates' Court, are also responsible for the first stage of a felony criminal proceeding: hold arraignment, set bail, appoint attorneys for indigents and conduct preliminary examinations.

The States have a Trial Court of General Jurisdiction at their disposal as well, presided over by one judge. These Courts are typically called Circuit Courts, Superior Courts, or District Courts, and hear serious civil and criminal cases. They are also generally divided into legal districts or circuits. Most often, the States choose political borders (those of the counties) to define judicial districts, though this is not always the case. In urban areas, judges may be required to specialize in something. All judges at this level are required to have a Law degree. Some States have specialized Courts that only hear certain types of cases, such as those related to traffic circulation or family rights. All of the States have a higher court, usually called the State Supreme Court or the Court of Last Resort, which serves as an appeals court. In New York, this Court is called the Court of Appeals, just as in Maryland. In Maine and Massachusetts, it's called the Judicial Supreme Court, while in West Virginia, it's the Supreme Court of Appeals. The States of Oklahoma and Texas have two

SUPREME COURT

COURT OF APPEALS

higher Courts, one criminal and civil. The size differs from one State to the next, having between 3 and 9 Judges, sitting *en banc*. These Judges are the ultimate decision-makers for all questions judged within the State, depending on the State law. Most of these Courts follow a procedure that greatly resembles the one adopted by the U.S. Supreme Court: when a case is admitted, the opposing party has to fill out a brief and present its arguments orally. Then, the Judges deliver their verdicts in writing, with their reasons.

Many States also have an intermediary Court of Appeals and hear appeals of court judgments. If only 13 such Courts existed at the beginning of the 20th century, these Courts, which are generally recently created, are Federal Courts. Their primary function is to alleviate the higher Court's caseload. Here, the name or the size may differ from State to State as well; in Alaska, for example, this Court only has 3 Judges, while there are 80 appeals judges in Texas. The functioning is different as well: while in some States they sit *en banc*, others may also have a panel, permanent or rotating organization.

NEW YORK — Court Of Appeals

TEXAS — Higher Courts

WEST VIRGINIA — Supreme Court Of Appeals

MASSACHUSETTS — Judicial Supreme Court

ACTIVITY

A. Describe the general structure of courts in the States.

....

....

B. In which way are the States' Supreme Court and the Federal one alike?

....

....

WHAT'S GOING ON IN TEXAS?

The Court Structure of Texas

DOCUMENT 4

1.   State Highest Appellate Courts

Supreme Court	Court of Criminal Appeals
Civil Jurisdiction Only (9 Justices)	*Criminal Jurisdiction Only* (9 Judges)

↑ **civil appeals**   ↑ **criminal appeals**

2.   State Intermediate Appellate Courts

Court of Appeals

Intermediate Appellate Jurisdiction
(14 Courts)

3.   State Trial Courts of General & Special Jurisdiction

District Courts

Trial Courts of General Civil and Criminal Jurisdiction
(some courts specialize by subject matter)

4.   County Trial Courts of Limited Jurisdiction

Constitutional County Courts	County Courts at Law	Statutory Probate Courts
Limited Civil and Criminal Jurisdiction (1 in each county)	*Limited Civil and/or Criminal Jurisdiction*	*Limited to Probate Matters*

5.   Local Trial Courts of Limited Jurisdiction

Municipal Courts	Justice of the Peace Courts
Limited Criminal Jurisdiction	(Small Claims Courts) *Limited Civil and Criminal Jurisdiction*

Texas, court by court

DOCUMENT 5

• **Municipal Courts**
These are the City Courts of Texas. Terms, salaries, and qualifications for municipal judges vary across the State. Municipal Courts have criminal jurisdiction to hear violations of city ordinances. Most of them are not courts of record, requiring that appeals from them require a trial *de novo*. 84% of the cases are Class C misdemeanors dealing with traffic violations with fines up to $500.

• **Justice of the Peace Courts**
Each Texas county is required to have at least one and no more than 8 Justice of the Peace (J.P.) courts. The county commissioners draw these up and the voters in each precinct elect justices to a 4-year term. The only qualification for holding office is to be a registered voter! J.P. courts have criminal jurisdiction in Class C misdemeanors with fines up to $500 and civil jurisdiction in cases involving less than $5,000. J.P.s also function as Magistrate, Notary Public, and Coroner in counties with no medical examiner. They can also perform marriages and preside over small claims courts. Most criminal cases in J.P. courts involve traffic violations. There were 835 J.P. courts in Texas as of 2001.

• **County Courts**
Every county has a "constitutional county court", presided over by a county judge who is elected to a 4-year term. The only qualification is to be "well informed in the law"! County courts hear civil cases involving $200-$5,000 probate cases, and Class A and B misdemeanor criminal cases. The constitutional county judge has other administrative duties, the most important of which is presiding over the county's commissioners' court. To relieve this workload, the legislature created 187 County Courts-at-Law and Probate Courts. These courts have specialized jurisdiction and their judges are generally more qualified than a constitutional County Judge. County Courts at law have civil jurisdiction in cases under $100,000. There are 254 County Courts, 195 County Courts-at-Law, and 16 Probate Courts in Texas.

• **District Courts**
There are 418 District Courts in Texas. These are the major Trial Courts in the State and have both criminal and civil jurisdiction (3/4 of their cases are civil cases.) All felony cases begin at the District Court. They also hear civil cases involving $200 or more. District judges are elected to 4-year terms and must be at least 25 years old with four years' experience as a lawyer or judge. District Courts in urban counties usually specialize as either criminal or civil courts. Each county in Texas must have at least one court designated as a juvenile court and in most counties the District Court carries out this function.

• **Courts of Appeals**
Texas has 14 intermediate Appellate Courts, which hear cases originating in the courts within their "supreme judicial district." They have both criminal and civil jurisdiction. These courts are multi-judge panels whose members are elected to staggered 6-year terms. Qualifications are the same as for the Supreme Court level.

• **Court of Criminal Appeals**
This is the highest appeals court for criminal cases. The nine judges on the Court are elected to staggered 6-year terms. Qualifications are the same as for the Supreme Court. The Court of Criminal Appeals is the highest court for criminal cases in Texas. All death penalty appeals go directly the Court of Criminal Appeals (thus bypassing the Courts of Appeals.)

• **Texas Supreme Court**
The Texas Supreme Court is the highest court for civil cases only and has only limited original jurisdiction. In addition to hearing appeals, the court issues rules of civil procedure and licenses lawyers to practice in Texas. This Court is composed of nine justices who are elected to staggered 6-year terms. A justice must be 35 years old, a U.S. and Texas citizen, and have been a lawyer and/or court-of-record judge for 10 years.

ACTIVITY

A. What is the major difference betwwen the court structure in Texas, compared to what can be found in a traditional State structure?

B. Explain the terms and qualifications of the judges in each court. Specify if they are elected or appointed.

PART 3 - ADMINISTRATIVE AND STAFF SUPPORT

Just like at the Federal level, a great number of people work in the various State Courts.

Magistrates

The State Magistrates, who are sometimes called commissioners or referees, are often those who start civil, as well as criminal, cases. In some States, they may even have to render verdicts in very limited cases. A primary function of the Magistrate is to provide an independent, unbiased review of complaints of criminal conduct brought to the office by law enforcement or the general public. Magistrate duties include issuing various types of processes such as arrest warrants, summonses, bonds, search warrants, subpoenas, and certain civil warrants. Magistrates also conduct bail hearings in situations where an individual is arrested on a warrant charging him or her with a criminal offense. Magistrates provide services on an around-the-clock basis, conducting hearings in person or through the use of videoconferencing systems. They are the first level of contact with the public.

Law Clerks

Law Clerks are lawyers who work with a judge, notably in contributing their knowledge of the State's legal system. There are practically none in the Appellate Courts. It's not necessarily a life-long career. However, those who hang up their robes in Court are often called Staff Attorneys. Law Clerks are most usually junior lawyers, at the beginning of their career. For them, it is a good opportunity to get to know the judges and the lawyers in the area in which they might wish to settle. It also allows them to observe how a large number of lawyers work.

Some of them work permanently for the Court and for all of the judges in Court: they are called Court Clerks. Their work consists in logging cases, coordinating schedules, preparing meetings or hearings, following up on cases, and even drafting court judgments under the Judges' supervision, and collecting fines or case-related fees. In most States, these Clerks are elected and may be designated with another title, such as Administrator.

Administrative Office of the Court (AOC)

Each State now has an Administrative Office of the

Clerkship

Upon completing a judicial clerkship, a law clerk often becomes very marketable to elite law firms. However, some law clerks decide they enjoy the position so much they continue to serve the judge as a law clerk in a permanent capacity.

There's nothing we can do?

Nope, the judge is on vacation for a week.

BANK

Very influential

Law clerks can have a great deal of influence on the judges with whom they work. Some judges seek to hire law clerks who have not only excelled academically, but also share the judge's ideological orientation, especially at some State Supreme Courts levels.

Court, or an agency that performs its duties; its role is to oversee the smooth functioning of the State's entire legal administration, or of the County's, when created by the County as in certain States. Among these duties is preparing the budget, training and human resources. Certain legal tasks, such as probation or ADR (Alternative Dispute Resolution) [*see Unit 12 – p. 244*] may also be asked of them, according to the whims of the State Legislators.

The Administrative Director of the Courts is accountable to the State government (or the Council) and the Chief Justice for the performance of the Administrative Office of the Courts. The Administrative Director's responsibility is to accomplish the council's goals and priorities.

ACTIVITY

A. What qualifications do you think are important for State judges?

....

....

....

....

....

B. What is a law clerk?

....

....

....

....

....

AT THE COURT

Five methods of judge selection

DOCUMENT 6

A APPOINTMENT BY THE EXECUTIVE

1. Seven of the original 13 States provide for some judges to be appointed by the Governor and serve for life.

2. When judicial selection is by gubernatorial appointment, there is greater potential for the selection of judges who are competent.

3. However, it may not always ensure competence because governors may use judicial appointments to reward friends and repay political debts.

4. Also, most Governors, as do U.S. presidents, have used their appointive powers to select judges who share their political philosophy, which has sometimes raised questions of judicial competence.

5. Senatorial courtesy, which allows U.S. senators to limit the President's choices for appointment to Federal District Courts, can also influence gubernatorial appointments to the State judiciary.

6. While governors are unlikely to select unqualified people for judicial appointments, it does not necessarily lead to the appointment of the most competent persons.

7. Another criticism is that once appointed by the Governor, the judges are not responsive to voters and can exercise great independence in their decisions.

B. APPOINTMENT BY THE LEGISLATURE

1. Four States of the original 13 States allow the legislature to select the judges.

2. Appointment by the legislature is a system left over from colonial America.

3. This system tends to lead to the selection of former legislators as judges.

4. The party that controls the State Legislature tends to select judges that belong to their party, making political party loyalty somewhat more important than competence.

C. PARTISAN ELECTIONS

1. 13 States use partisan elections to select some or all of their State judges.

2. Judicial candidates must first run in a party primary and then, if they win the primary, must run in the general election.

3. Partisan elections do have the advantage of leading to greater responsiveness of judges to the public.

4. However, critics charge and, the data seems to indicate, that partisan elections can often lead to poorly qualified judges being elected because voters vote a straight-party ticket, or for the most familiar name on the ballot, regardless of merit.

5. Another criticism is that judges are less independent and

impartial in this method of selection, because of the influence of large campaign contributions, often given by law firms and interests who will have cases pending before the Court.

D. NON-PARTISAN ELECTIONS

1. 21 States use nonpartisan elections to choose some, or all, of their State judges.

2. In nonpartisan elections the judicial candidates run without any party affiliation indicated on the ballot.

3. Non-partisan elections often reduce the cost of campaigns because candidates do not have to run and win a primary election to be on the ballot in the general election.

4. Non-partisan elections also have the advantage of eliminating the problem of straight-ticket voting.

5. Non-partisan elections force the voters to base their decision on something other than a party label.

6. While this method of judge selection would not necessarily result in the selection of more competent judges, it would probably prevent the kind of large-scale changes that occurred in Harris County in 1994, due to straight-ticket voting.

E. THE MERIT OR MISSOURI SYSTEM

1. 21 States use some version of the "merit" or "Missouri system" to elect some judges.

2. The merit or Missouri system allows the Governor to appoint judges from a list submitted by a screening committee of legal officials.

3. After appointment, the judge serves for a set term and then must run in a retention election.

4. The retention election allows the voters to simply vote "yes" or "no" as to whether the judge remains in office – a majority of yes votes means the judges serves another term and a majority of no votes means the selection process begins anew.

5. In these retention elections, judges run unopposed.

6. Advocates of this method of judge selection argue that it leads to more competent judges being selected and keeps the judges responsive to the public because they must face voters in the retention election.

7. Critics allege that there is little evidence that it results in the selection of more competent judges (although it probably screens out the incompetent or poorly qualified).

8. Critics also charge that there is no evidence it leads to judge responsiveness to public opinion because the judge has no opponent in the retention election and it is difficult to defeat someone with no one; most judges are retained, with less then 1 percent ever removed.

Key terms in Court

DOCUMENT 7

Advisory opinion: a legal opinion issued by the Texas Attorney General, at the request of a legislator, on the constitutionality of a bill under consideration. While technically having no legal standing, if the opinion is that the bill is unconstitutional, that usually kills any chances that the bill will pass the Texas Legislature.

Appellate Courts: courts that possess only appellate jurisdiction, the power to hear cases on appeal from lower courts and decide points of law, not points of fact; in Texas, these include the 14 Courts of Appeals with 80 judges.

Appellate jurisdiction: the power to review the decisions of a lower court. (Such appeals do not involve a new trial, but simply a review of the law as it was applied in the original trial.)

Civil cases: cases involving a dispute between two parties and involve the idea of responsibility, not guilt.

Constitutional County Courts: established in each of the 254 counties in Texas by the State Constitution, which determines their jurisdiction.

County Courts-at-Law: courts created in larger urban counties by an act of the legislature; they replace the Constitutional County Court in the counties they operate in.

Criminal cases: cases brought against individuals for violations of law--crimes against society.

District Courts: the major Trial Courts in the State, hearing major criminal (felony) and civil cases.

Dual court system: Texas judicial system of having two high courts – the Texas Supreme Cour (the highest court for civil cases) and the Court of Criminal Appeals (the highest court for criminal cases).

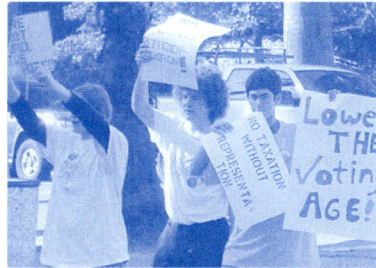

Grand Jury: a jury that decides whether to indict or formally charge and bring to trial a suspect; used as a screening mechanism to prevent arbitrary actions by Prosecutors.

Magistrate/Minor Courts: courts which hear cases involving misdemeanors and minor civil matters; in Texas these are Justice of the Peace and Municipal Courts.

Merit system/Missouri system: a method of judge selection that involves the Governor appointing judges from a list submitted by a screening committee of legal officials; after appointment, the judge serves a set term and is then subjected to a retention election (where the judge has no opponent and voters simply vote yes or no to retain or remove the judge).

Original jurisdiction: the power to try a case being heard for the first time

Petit Jury: the trial jury that determines guilt or innocence of the defendant and may decide the punishment.

Plea bargaining: the Defendant pleading guilty to a lesser charge in exchange for a lesser sentence agreed to by the accused and the Prosecuting Attorney

Standing: a rule of the courts that for an individual to file a lawsuit, the case must involve an actual controversy between two parties, and someone must have suffered real damage.

Stare Decisis: a Latin term that literally means "to stand that which has been decided before;" a common-law doctrine that once a case has been decided, subsequent cases with similar facts should receive similar decisions by following the earlier precedent.

Supreme Courts: courts of last resort; in Texas there are two – the Texas Supreme Court for civil cases and the Court of Criminal Appeals for criminal cases.

Trial de Novo Courts: courts that keep no record of the proceedings (all Justice of the Peace and most Municipal courts in Texas).

ACTIVITY

A. Explain briefly what the Missouri system is.

B. Who is more likely to be elected according to the different methods of judge selection used?

PART 4 – STATE COURT WORKLOAD

If the Federal Courts are overloaded with hundreds of thousands of cases to hear, what can be said about the State Courts, which have to sift through 93 million cases each year? In other words, 97% of all lawsuits filed in the USA are heard in State Courts, and not in Federal Courts; does that not mean that the State Courts have a more active and determining role in creating Law? Maybe not. But, in order to understand the importance of the American legal system in Americans lives more clearly, let's take a closer look at that statistic of 93 million: for each of these cases, we must take into account the involvement of at least two parties, a judge, at least two lawyers, a Law Clerk, some witnesses, journalists, and the jurists who were requisitioned for the hearing. Justice is first and foremost in the lives of Americans, not because of its Federal aspect and its important constitutional principles, but because of the State Courts. Every American is concerned, because they are part of a court case, by being involved in an accident, paying a fine for speeding, or being called for jury duty. The work of the Courts at a State level either affects their lives, their jobs, or their public affairs.

The ways in which Judges resolve cases that are brought before them may be complicated or banal. The case may be of minor or major importance, for a petty or a colossal sum of money. State Judges, and especially, Justices of the Peace, through the millions of verdicts rendered each year, mold a part of the American society. There is no limit to their power, since, for example, they may be led to pronounce judgment on life sentences, to rule in cases concerning human embryos, or on issues of cloning, or euthanasia. Thus, in 2005, the Florida Courts had to address a difficult issue in the case of Terry Schiavo. Following a stroke, this 41 year-old-woman was in a vegetative coma for 15 years, kept alive by a feeding tube in a Florida hospital. After having tried to help her recover from her condition, her husband Michael had finally come to the realization, in 1997, that she would never again lead a normal life. Her doctors' diagnosis was that she was in "a permanent vegetative State" and that there was no chance for her to get better.

Affirming that his spouse had previously confided in him her desire to not be kept alive

George Bush
Born on July 6, 1946, in New Haven, Connecticut, George W. Bush was the 43rd president of the United States. He narrowly won the Electoral College vote in 2000, in one of the closest and most controversial elections in American history. Bush led the United States' response to the 9/11 terrorist attacks and initiated the Iraq War. Before his presidency, Bush was a businessman and served as Governor of Texas.

artificially, Michael had decided to put an end to her suffering, against the wishes of her parents. He feeding tube was removed, and reinserted twice, in 2001 and 2003, in answer to court rulings. Congress and President George W. Bush seized upon this story as an opportunity to make her a symbol of the debate on when life ends and to defend religious convictions.

Contradicting the constitutional rights of patients to refuse to be kept alive in an artificial State, a specific law was urgently passed to allow the case to no longer be in the sole domain of Floridian Courts, but also in that of the Federal Courts. It was a pointless move: the Federal Courts refused to voice their opinion, just as the Supreme Court, 6 times in a row. A judge ordered that the feeding tube be removed for a third, and final time, on March 18th, 2005.

Notwithstanding cases this extreme, the State Courts must resolve numerous conflicts in everyday life, and this is done every day: divorce, custody battles, problems with inheritance, contracts not being respected, breaches of contract, problems between neighbors, or the 56 million fines to collect.

ACTIVITY

A. Why should State Courts be considered as important as Federal Courts?

....

....

....

....

B. Is a State judgeship less important than a Federal one?

....

....

....

....

CRIME AND PUNISHMENT

A case in Texas

DOCUMENT 8

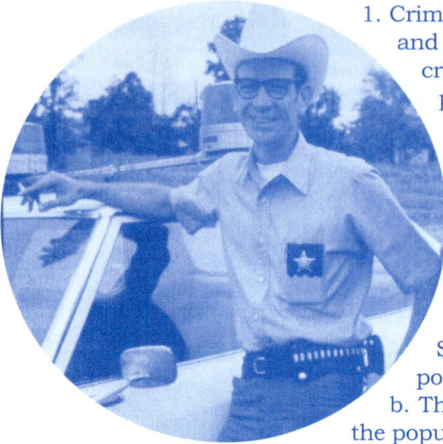

A. NATIONAL AND STATE CRIME STATISTICS

1. Crime rates and violent crime rates rose dramatically during the 1960s and have increased steadily in recent years (an average of 115,000 violent crimes per year in the past ten years compared to an average of 16,000 per year in the 1960s).

2. Although crime has increased, the increase is not as great as the news media or campaign rhetoric leads the public to believe.

3. Violent crime has increased in Texas more than in the nation as a whole.

4. Texas ranks 5th among the 50 States in total crimes committed per 100,000 people.

5. Many factors contribute to the crime rate.

   a. More crimes are committed in larger cities, in comparing the 50 States, there is a strong correlation between the percentage of the population living in urban (metropolitan) areas and crime rates.

   b. This partly explains the Texas crime rate, since about 80 percent of the population in Texas lives in metropolitan areas.

   c. There is also a strong correlation between age, sex, and crime.

   d. Almost 46 percent of crimes are committed by people below 25 years of age.

   e. Almost 82 percent of all crimes are committed by males.

   f. Race is also a factor in crime.

   g. African Americans constitute about 12 percent of the U.S. population, but constitute almost 30 percent of people arrested for crime (some argue that the key factor is not race, but socio-economic status – more blacks people are in lower socioeconomic status.

B. THE POLICY OF INCARCERATION

1. Texas has the highest rate of incarceration of any State or Western industrialized nation – the Texas philosophy is, if "**you do the crime, you do the time**".

   a. Texas incarcerates 636 prisoners per 100,000 people.

   b. Michigan is next with 428 per 100,000.

   c. The U.S. incarceration average is 387 per 100,000.

   d. For comparison purposes, here are some incarceration statistics for other Western industrialized nations:

      (1) Canada at 116 per 100,000.

      (2) Mexico at 97 per 100,000.

      (3) England at 93 per 100,000.

      (4) Spain at 90 per 100,000.

      (5) France at 84 per 100,000.

      (6) Italy and Germany at 80 per 100,000.

2. The Texas philosophy is that being tougher on criminals – more incarceration – will lead to a reduction in crime rates.

3. The fact that Texas leads the nation with the highest incarceration rate and ranks 5th among the 50 States in terms of total crimes committed per 100,000 people raises questions as to the validity of that philosophy.

C. CAPITAL PUNISHMENT

1. The death penalty has been used in the United States since Colonial times.
2. In recent years, many critics have attacked the death penalty as ineffective, unevenly applied, and unconstitutional.
3. In 1972, in *Furman v. Georgia*, the U.S. Supreme Court outlawed the death penalty for two reasons:
   - a. It was unevenly applied to many crimes.
   - b. There were a lack of safeguards in place in many States.
4. From 1965 until 1977, there were no executions in the United States.
5. Many States then rewrote their death penalty statutes to meet the procedural objections made by the U.S. Supreme Court in *Furman v. Georgia*.
6. Thus, in 1976, in *Gregg v. Georgia*, the U.S. Supreme Court ruled that if proper guidelines and procedures were followed, the death penalty did not violate the 8th Amendment ban against cruel and unusual punishment
7. Supreme Court guidelines include the following:
   - a. No mandatory death penalty laws are permissible.
   - b. A capital crime must involve the taking of a human life.
   - c. Consideration must be given to the Defendant's character and record.
   - d. Consideration must be given to relevant mitigating circumstances.
   - e. Jurors opposed to the death penalty cannot automatically be excluded from the jury in a capital felony case.
8. Since the *Gregg* decision, all but 16 States have reinstated the death penalty (34 in all).
9. Texas is the leading State in both sentencing people to death, and in the number of prisoners executed
   - a. Since the death penalty was reinstated in Texas in 1982, Texas has executed 510 of the 1,369 prisoners executed nationwide (since *Furman*, from 1976 to July of 2014).
   - b. Thus, Texas, with 7% of the U.S. population, has performed more than one-third of the executions.
   - c. As of 2014, there were 292 prisoners on death row awaiting execution in Texas (only Florida and California have more, with respectively 412 and 733).
   - d. At the rate of one execution a week, it would take 7 years to execute all of those prisoners.
   - e. In Texas, a few counties account for most of the death sentences: 25 of the 254 counties in the State have supplied all 510 prisoners executed in Texas since 1982, most of them in East Texas.
   - f. The Texas public heavily favors the death penalty, by a three-to-one margin.
   - g. Endless delays and appeals and the long span between the sentence and the execution reduce the effectiveness of the death penalty – the average time from sentence to execution in Texas is 9.1 years.
   - h. Also, the cost to taxpayers for executing felons is quite high.
10. Most executions (83%) have been in southern States, a reflection of the dominant traditionalistic culture of the South.
11. In Texas and most other southern States, juries can determine the sentence for all crimes, and juries seem more likely than judges to use the death penalty.
12. Some States sentence many prisoners to death but carry out few executions (California, Pennsylvania, and Illinois are three such States).

ACTIVITY

A. What could explain the high crime rate in Texas?

B. Do you think that Texas philosophy, "you do the crime you do the time" provides for a good solution to the problem of criminality?

C. Explain the evolution of the legislation for the death penalty in the United States.

SUMMARY

Important Words

Grand Jury
Petit Jury
felony
misdeameanor
Magistrate
clerk

Every man for himself

The legal system of each State is quite diverse. The differences are even obvious in their names, each State naming its Courts at their own discretions, sometimes with originality. For example, in New York, the Trial Court is called Supreme Court. We have to go back in time to the Colonies to understand these differences, when all powers rested in the Governor's hands, leaving little possibility for a judicial branch to develop, apart from some borrowings from England, such as the jury and the Justice of the Peace. After the Revolution, the new States defended their right to keeping these differences, meticulously avoiding any standardization. Law changed profoundly because of modernization and industrialization, though these changes, once again, took place without necessarily institutionalizing the structures and the Courts. Roscoe Pound launched a unification movement in the 20th century, but it was a difficult task.

State Courts organization

Some States chose to join the unification movement. Today, major differences are still visible, but we can distinguish a common structure. For minor offenses, there is a Trial Court. It is the one most Americans are the most familiar with, because 90% of cases are heard there. These Courts have a limited jurisdiction. That is the reason why the States created Courts of general jurisdiction, where the most important cases are tried. The judicial landscape is usually divided into districts, or circuits, which are often pre-existing administrative divisions. All cases may be appealed before an Appeals Court. In some special cases, the States have Higher or Supreme Courts, which also have different names from one State to the next.

Administrative and staff support

Court organization at a State level is fairly similar to what we find at a Federal level. The Magistrate may have various names: its role is to issue warrants and ensure that everything happens according to regulation. A judge's Law Clerks offer assistance, especially on legal issues. This job is usually reserved for lawyers just starting out, which allows them to get to know thoroughly how the legal system works, as well as the judges. This may be quite useful, however, professional Clerks also exist. Administrative employees, who are in charge of the entire legal administration, also assist the Court. They may also be asked to manage some Alternative Dispute Resolutions. The Administrative Director of the Courts reports information about his duties directly to the State Governor.

State Courts workload

The State Courts are no slackers compared to the Federal Courts in terms of workload, since they process 93 million cases per year, while the latter handles only a few hundred thousand. One way or another, all Americans are involved in the legal system, even if it's just for paying a fine. Judges have to deal with a wide variety of cases, from the simplest to the most complex. Justices of the Peace fashion American Law day after day, and there are no limits to the types of cases that might be brought before them. Take for example, the Terry Schiavo case, which dealt with the difficult question of ending a life – or the right to life, that went before the Florida State Court, because the Federal Courts refused to become involved. But most of the time, the cases are not so extreme: they most often deal with divorce, child custody, problems with neighbors, or breaches of contract.

A. Say if the following Statements are true or false:

	True	False
1. – In Colonial times, the judges were responsible before Parliament.		
2. – It is to the judge to decide if he prefers to have a Grand or a Petit Jury at a trial.		
3. – R. Pound is famous for succesfully unifyng the U.S. system of Law.		
4. – Two States do not have a higher Court		
5. – Law clerks may replace a judge when he is sick.		

B. What are the three types of crimes a State Court may hear?
....
....

C. What is the role of the Magistrates?
....
....

D. Describe briefly the methods of selecting a judge used in the United States.
....
....

E. What are the differences between State and Federal Courts?
....
....

REFERENCES :

Page 87. "Sheryl Gordon McCloud, Washington State Supreme Court Justice, 2013", by Mike McCloud, Wikimedia. http://commons.wikimedia.org/wiki/File:Sheryl_Gordon_McCloud,_Washington_State_Supreme_Court_Justice,_2013.jpeg
Page 87. "Governor", by Dimitri Champain
Page 90. "Rosco Pound", Wikimedia. http://commons.wikimedia.org/wiki/File:Roscoe_Pound_ca_1916.jpg
"Different places, different laws", Author unknown. Berckman Center for Internet and Society at Harvard University. http://cyber.law.harvard.edu/ilaw/Jurisdiction/Conflict.html
Page 91. "Dissatisfaction with the Administration of Justice", Author unknown. Presented at the annual conventionof the American Bar Association in 1906. Source: Reprinted from 29 A.B.A. Rep.,pt. I, 395-417, 190. http://www.infoplease.com./encyclopedia/society/conflict-laws.html
Page 93. "State Courts", by Dimitri Champain

Page 96. "The judge is off", by Dimitri Champain
Page 99. "NYRA Berkeley voting age protest", by National Youth Rights Association, Wikimedia. http://upload.wikimedia.org/wikipedia/commons/8/80/NYRA_Berkeley_voting_age_protest.jpg
Page 100. "Busy judge", by Dimitri Champain
Page 101. "George Bush". Wikimdia. http://commons.wikimedia.org/wiki/File:GeorgeWBush.jpg
Page 102. "Sheriff of Long View".http://commons.wikimedia.org/wiki/File:DEPUTY_SHERIFF_OF_LONGVIEW_AND_PARTNER._THEY_WERE_CURIOUS_ABOUT_THE_PHOTOGRAPHER%27S_PICTURE-TAKING_AROUND_THE_TOWN_-_NARA_-_547759.jpg
Page 104. "Summary", by Dimitri Champain
Page 105. "Review", by Dimitri Champain
pp. 89, 91, 93, 95, 97, 99, 101, 103 "Review", by Dimitri Champain

Introduction

The structure of the State Court systems varies from one State to the next. Ways of thinking are different as a result of history, geography, and the origins of humankind. Therefore, it is not surprising that we can see all of these variations in Law. States are thus either more "liberal", or more "conservative"; some permit the legal sale of marijuana (Colorado, for example), while others would like to establish a law for refusing to serve homosexual clients in a restaurant (in Arizona, in 2014, for example [eventually vetoed by the Governor]). Whatever the case, each State is free to make its own rules, in its own way, as long as these rules do not contradict the U.S. Constitution. Here are four examples in four States and four very different locations.

6

PART 1 – CALIFORNIA

The foundation for Californian law is its Constitution. It created the State's government, defining its structure and power. California's first Constitution was adopted in 1849, one year before the Republic of California became an American State. The current Constitution was ratified in 1879. It is very long, one of the longest in the world (110 pages). Unbelievably, it was actually shortened by 40,000 words in the 60s and 70s. It should be known, though, that it is a document that continually gets longer, because public referendums are permitted, and frequent; each initiative that is passed, adds itself to the long list of Amendments to the Constitution. Today, there are over 400 Amendments. An amendment may be proposed after a 2/3 vote of the California State Legislature, or signatures that correspond to 8% of the votes cast during the gubernatorial election, which corresponds to one of the lowest thresholds in relation to similar measures in other American States (about 700,000 signatures for a population of around 37 million inhabitants).
The structure of the Constitution is simple: one short

Preamble, 30 Articles and over 400 Amendments. Two strong points of this Constitution are that it protects the rights of cities and counties, and it guarantees extremely broad powers. In this way, cities may pay counties for carrying out certain government functions in their stead, according to Section 8 of Article XI (which gave rise to a strong development of contract cities). Californians' individual rights are also reinforced by a Federal Bill of Rights, notably the rights protected by the 1st Amendment (freedom of expression), or by the 8th Amendment, which forbids "cruel OR unusual punishment", while the Constitution of California specifies "cruel AND unusual punishment".

> One of the strong points of the Constitution is that it protects the rights of cities and counties and guarantees extremely broad powers.

Local ordinances
Locals ordinances are laws usually found in a code of law for a political division smaller than a State or a nation, such as a municipality, a parish, etc.

The Californian legal system is based on Common Law, and the precedents are published in the *California Reports* and the *California Appellate Reports*. The Laws are passed by the California Congress and, like for Texas and New York, are recorded in one of 29 Codes (*California Codes*), which are each specialized in a sector of Law (the 47 other States have a unique Code). Thus, the laws related to civil affairs can be found in the Civil Code; those related to the burden of proof in legal proceedings are in Evidence Code; and those related to crime are in the Penal Code. Cities and counties may also pass rules that are known as local ordinances, which are generally codified in City Codes or County Codes.

Every plot of land is part of a county and California is divided into 58 counties, though some areas are devoid of towns nearby. These areas that are beyond the control of cities and towns are called unincorporated areas and are placed directly under the administration of the County Government. School districts, which are tasked with primary and secondary education, do not report to cities and counties, but to the California State Government. School boards have extended powers, notably to tax, or they have quasi-legal powers, especially in serious cases involving employees or students.

DID YOU KNOW?
The Supreme Court of California, and the various districts of the California Court of Appeal, have generally avoided using law clerks since the late 1980s. Instead, California has primarily switched to using permanent staff attorneys at all levels of the judiciary.

The particular characteristics that distinguish Californian Law from the other States originate in its tradition of popular sovereignty, which is quite powerful. It appears, not only in frequent referendums that are organized in the State, but in each of the legislative, governmental or legal actions, since it must be reminded that they are done in the name of "the People", and not "the State" or "the Commonwealth", as in most of the other American States. The huge concentration of celebrities in California has resulted in the creation of special laws, such as the California Celebrities Rights Act, or a highly specific Family Code, aimed at responding to the numerous matrimonial problems faced by these stars who are rich enough to stay in court forever.

Finally, California has marked the country with some of its laws, sometimes progressive and innovative, and sometimes highly controversial: the Unruh Civil Rights Act and the California Fair Employment and Housing Act are among the most protected civil rights in the United States. But California has also become famous for it tort laws concerning defective products, market-share liability and negligent infliction of emotional distress. There is also the famous Three-Strikes law, which is the source of many a controversy.

ACTIVITY

CELEBRITIES RIGHTS ACT

A. What is the structure of California's Constitution?

....

....

....

....

B. Why are the school districts so powerful? What are their powers?

....

....

C. How would you define California's Constitution in just a few words? What is the main characteristic of this constitution?

....

....

THE GOLDEN STATE

The Three-Strikes law

DOCUMENT 1

In 1992, 18-year-old student Kimber Reynolds returned home to Fresno, Calif., to be a bridesmaid. As she left a restaurant, two men rolled up on a motorcycle and tried to snatch her purse. When she
5 resisted, one of them shot her. She died 26 hours later. As the Reynolds family grieved, they learned that the shooter and his accomplice both had long rap sheets, largely for drugs and petty theft. Outraged that they had been freed, Mike Reynolds, Kimber's father,
10 wrote a proposed "three strikes and you're out" law for repeat offenders.

Two years later, California passed that law, both as a ballot initiative and through the State legislature. Advertised as a way to keep violent repeat offenders
15 off the streets, the Three-Strikes law doubled prison time for a second felony if there was a prior serious or violent felony, as defined by State law. Offenders with two serious or violent priors faced 25 years to life for the third "strike."
20 But to qualify for the life sentence, that third felony did not have to be serious or violent. As a result, California began sentencing people to life for crimes like petty theft and drug possession. The law was challenged for 18 years, including two unsuccessful
25 appeals to the U.S. Supreme Court.

In the meantime, second- and third-strikers made up roughly a quarter of California's large prison population, straining the State budget. Advocates say 3 – 3,500 of California's current third-strikers are ser-
30 ving 25 years to life for nonserious, nonviolent felonies. All of this may explain why 69% of Californians voted last year for Proposition 36, a ballot initiative that radically reformed the Three-Strikes law. Now, defendants may only be sentenced to 25 years to life
35 if their crime was serious or violent, or they have disqualifying crimes – generally very violent crimes or sex offenses – among their priors. All other third felonies will be sentenced to double the time in prison, as if they were second strikes.
40 And more importantly, the law permits inmates who are already serving life sentences for nonviolent, nonserious crimes to petition for resentencing. As with new felonies, their new sentences would still be double the normal penalty for the original crime. But because
45 such inmates have already served up to 19 years, resentencing usually means release from prison.

Los Angeles County, the most populous County in the State and the nation, has by far the most prisoners eligible for resentencing. The Los Angeles
50 Superior Court, the Court of first jurisdiction, had received 1,389 petitions as of late October. To handle this flood, the county has set up a special system that consolidates all petitions under one judge, whose job is to handle nothing but resentencing of Three-Strikes prisoners until at least the end of this
55 year.

The job went to Judge William Ryan, who was already the go-to judge in the county for writs of habeas corpus. He says this is not the first one-judge system for handling special cases. After the 1990s Rampart
60 Scandal, in which corrupt Los Angeles police officers admitted to framing defendants, thousands of petitions for writs of habeas corpus were consolidated in front of one judge. Ryan says the average time from petition to resentencing in Los Angeles County is 148
65 days. It is not clear whether he will be able to finish all of the petitions by the end of December, when his initial appointment is slated to wind down.

"Some inmates are getting impatient," Ryan says. "They didn't use violence when they committed their
70 crime, so they thought the doors of the prison should swing open" the day after voters approved Prop 36. Discussion at those August hearings focused mainly on the defendants' re-entry plans. Ryan emphasizes that success after prison, particularly in the first 90
75 days, depends largely on access to food, housing, jobs and addiction treatment, if applicable. (It often is; Ryan says that 37% of his petitioners' life crimes were tied to drug crimes, and 56 percent more were property crimes that were likely related to drugs.)
80 "Before resentencing, they have to lay that out for me," says Ryan. "When they release them, they give them $200 and a bus ticket and say, 'Good luck.' And that's not necessarily the most humane thing to do."

Thus far, those who have been released have largely
85 stayed out of trouble. The county probation department is supervising only 28 of the 200 people released in the County, but a representative said in mid-August that only two had been arrested again. If that is every new arrest, it is a minuscule repeat offense rate.
90 Statewide, a study by the Stanford Three Strikes Project, a law school initiative advocating three-strikes sentence reductions, found a 2% repeat offense rate in September, when prisoners had been out an average of 4.4 months. That study reported the average
95 repeat offense rate after 90 days – the crucial period during which people are most likely to re-offend – for non-Prop 36 prisoners was 16%.

But Reynolds, the father of the slain bridesmaid and a driving force behind the Three-Strikes law, says it
100 is too soon to determine if that reform has worked. "The full impact of Prop 36, either positive or negative, is really yet to be felt," he says. "Only a handful [of offenders] have really come out in comparison to the full number. Once they are fully released, the real
105 question is: Now what happens?"

The right to delete embarrassing Web posts

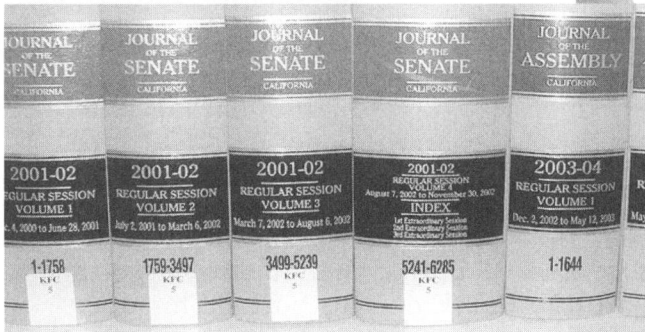

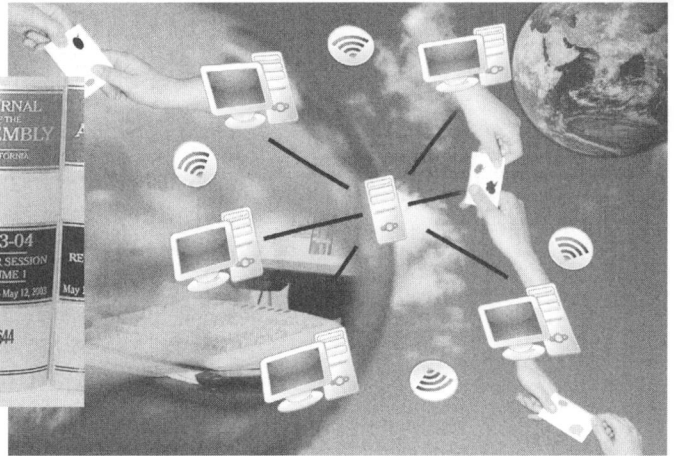

DOCUMENT 2

SACRAMENTO – Gov. Jerry Brown approved a new law Monday giving young people the ability to remove embarrassing information they post on Internet social networking sites.

California is now the first State in the nation to require websites such as Facebook to give minors a way to take down photos and other posts from their sites, according to Common Sense Media, a nonprofit group that promotes children's privacy in digital media and tracks Federal and State legislation on the issue.

The group supported the measure, which also bans website operators from marketing certain goods, such as guns, bullets and dietary products, to Internet users younger than 18.

Senate leader Darrell Steinberg (D-Sacramento) said his measure offered "a groundbreaking protection for our kids who often act impetuously with postings of ill-advised pictures or messages before they think through the consequences."

Minors, he said, "deserve the right to remove this material that could haunt them for years to come."

The bill also prohibits firms from targeting minors with Web advertisements for harmful products that are illegal for them to use, such as alcohol, tobacco and guns.

The measure was opposed by the Center for Democracy & Technology, a nonprofit that promotes Internet freedom and accessibility.

Emma Llanso, policy advisor for the group, said the bill, SB 568, was "motivated by the best of intentions" but could cause confusion among website operators. "If the sites are unclear whether they are covered under the scope of the bill, the response could be to bar minors from the sites entirely," Llanso said.

ACTIVITY

A. *Document 1*: What is the purpose of the Three-Strikes law?

B. What is the main problem with this law if applied strictly?

C. *Document 2*: What is your opinion about the new law adopted in California?

D. Why is such a law voted at the State level and not the Federal one?

E. The U.S. Constitution forbids the various levels of government from having certain powers. What do you think is the reasoning behind this?

PART 2 – NEW YORK

Session laws
All of the laws of New York State are published in Laws of New York. *The Secretary of State publishes them all in a supplement called "session laws". Today, all of these laws can be found on the web at: 72.0.151.116/nycnew/.*

In the State of New York, law is composed of many sources: constitutional, statutory, regulatory and case law. There are also local laws, ordinances, and regulations.

The New York Constitution describes the structure of New York State's government and the citizens' rights. Like most of the American State Constitutions, its text is much more precise and detailed than the Federal Constitution. Many versions preceded the current 8th Constitution, adopted in 1938. A 9th version was rejected in the end by New Yorkers in 1967 and so was never ratified.

The first one dates from 1777 and then had replaced the Colonial Charter under the King's authority. This document profoundly influenced the future U.S. Constitution. It contained its own Declaration of Independence and constitutional principles, anticipating an organization with a bicameral legislative body that had little power but a strong executive power, headed by a Governor. It did not mention judicial power. The subsequent version of New York's Constitution gave rise to very different configuration, but quite close the actual Federal Constitution: three branches with equal powers; the Executive headed by a Governor, a Senate and an Assembly, and a Judicial Branch, containing the State's highest court, the New York Court of Appeals, and the lower courts.

New York is divided into counties, cities, and villages that are all municipal corporations within their government. Only the city of New York (NYC) is unicameral with a unique governing body called the New York City Council. The New York Constitution lists the powers of local governments, such as being able to pass local laws, or electing an assembly. Each local body chooses a journal in which all session laws will be published.

The New York legal system is officially called New York State Unified Court System, with its seat in New York's State Capital, Albany. Common Law is the standard and all precedents are published in law reports: *New York Reports* for Court of Appeals and Appellate Division of the Supreme Court verdicts; and *Miscellaneous Reports* for Trial Court verdicts.

Among specific laws in New York State, one may find laws concerning alcohol, divorce and weapons. The laws about alcohol are some of the most lenient in the USA. However, there are four hours out of each day of the week in which alcohol may not be served: 4:00 a.m. to 8:00 a.m. This was designed to accommodate New York City nightlife, as well as late night workers statewide in general. Despite being generally considered a liberal State, New York has a history of being conservative on issues regarding marriage; but it was the last State in the country to allow no-fault divorce (in 2010) and still maintains a (seldom enforced) law against adultery [*see p.190*]. Until 1966, adultery was the only grounds of divorce; cruelty, one that had long been available in most other States, was not available in New York. New York has among the most restrictive gun laws in the nation. These laws ban handgun possession and provide exemptions, including individuals licensed to carry handguns, or to possess them for some reasons, including sports, repair, or disposal.

ACTIVITY

A. How are the rights of the people secured in the New York Constitution?

....

....

....

B. Briefly explain how the Executive Branch is organized in New York State:

....

....

....

C. How is the 2nd Amendment secured in New York?

....

....

....

A STATE THAT NEVER SLEEPS

DOCUMENT 3

Judiciary of New York

The New York State Court System is divided into 13 Judicial Districts (JDs). There are six upstate JD's, each comprising 5-11 counties. There are five JDs in New York City and two on Long Island.

Court of Appeals

The New York State Court of Appeals is the State's highest court. In civil cases, appeals are taken almost exclusively from decisions of the Appellate Divisions. In criminal cases, depending on the type of case and the part of the State in which it arose, appeals can be heard from decisions of the Appellate Division, the Appellate Term, and the county courts.

Appellate Division of the Supreme Court

The *New York Supreme Court, Appellate Division* is the State's second-highest Court. It hears appeals primarily from State Trial Courts, including the Supreme Court, the County Courts, the Surrogate's Courts, the Family Courts, and the Court of Claims. The Appellate Division also resolves many challenges to actions by administrative agencies. The Court is regionally divided into four judicial departments. The Appellate Division in each department also supervises admission of new lawyers to the State's Bar, as well as disciplinary proceedings against lawyers, duties that most other States are handled by the jurisdiction's highest court.

Trial Court of General Jurisdiction

The court of general jurisdiction in New York is the New York Supreme Court. (Unlike in most other States, the Supreme Court is a Trial Court and is not the highest court in the State). There is a branch of the New York Supreme Court in each of New York State's 62 counties. Counties with small populations share justices. In New York City (NYC), the Supreme Court hears all felony cases; outside NYC, these cases are generally heard in the County Court. The Supreme Court hears civil cases seeking money damages exceeding the monetary limits of the local courts' jurisdiction. The court also has exclusive jurisdiction over matrimonial actions seeking a divorce, legal separation, or annulment of a marriage.

County courts

A county court exists in each county except for the five counties of NYC. Unlike the Supreme Court, each county court is considered distinct. The court has unlimited criminal and civil jurisdiction where the amount in dispute is no more than $25,000. Appeal from a county court is generally to the Appellate Division of the Supreme Court. Where an Appellate Terms of the Supreme Court exists, misdemeanor appeals are heard by that Court and other appeals are directly to the Court of Appeals.

Local courts

• The court system is different at the local court level in NYC. The NYC Courts, mainly composed of the NYC Criminal Court and the NYC Civil Court, are local courts in the 5 boroughs of NYC. City court judges may be elected or appointed, depending upon the city. Full-time city court judges serve 10-year terms. Part-time city court judges serve six-year terms.

• District courts are the local criminal and civil courts in Nassau County and the five western towns of Suffolk County, arraign felonies and try misdemeanors and lesser offenses, as well as civil lawsuits involving claims of up to $15,000, small claims and small commercial claims up to $5,000, and landlord-tenant actions. District Court Judges are elected to 6–year terms.

• Justice Courts (town and village courts) try misdemeanors and lesser offenses in towns and villages. These Courts are the starting point for all criminal cases outside cities, and handle a variety of other matters including small claims, traffic ticket cases and local zoning matters. They also arraign defendants accused of felonies. These Courts may hear civil lawsuits involving claims of up to $3,000 (including small claims cases of up to $3,000). Justices are elected to 4-year terms. The majority of justices are not attorneys. Non-attorney justices must successfully complete a certification course and participate in continuing judicial education. The town and village Justice Courts are locally funded, as opposed to the State-funded city and District Courts.

DOCUMENT 4

New York court structure

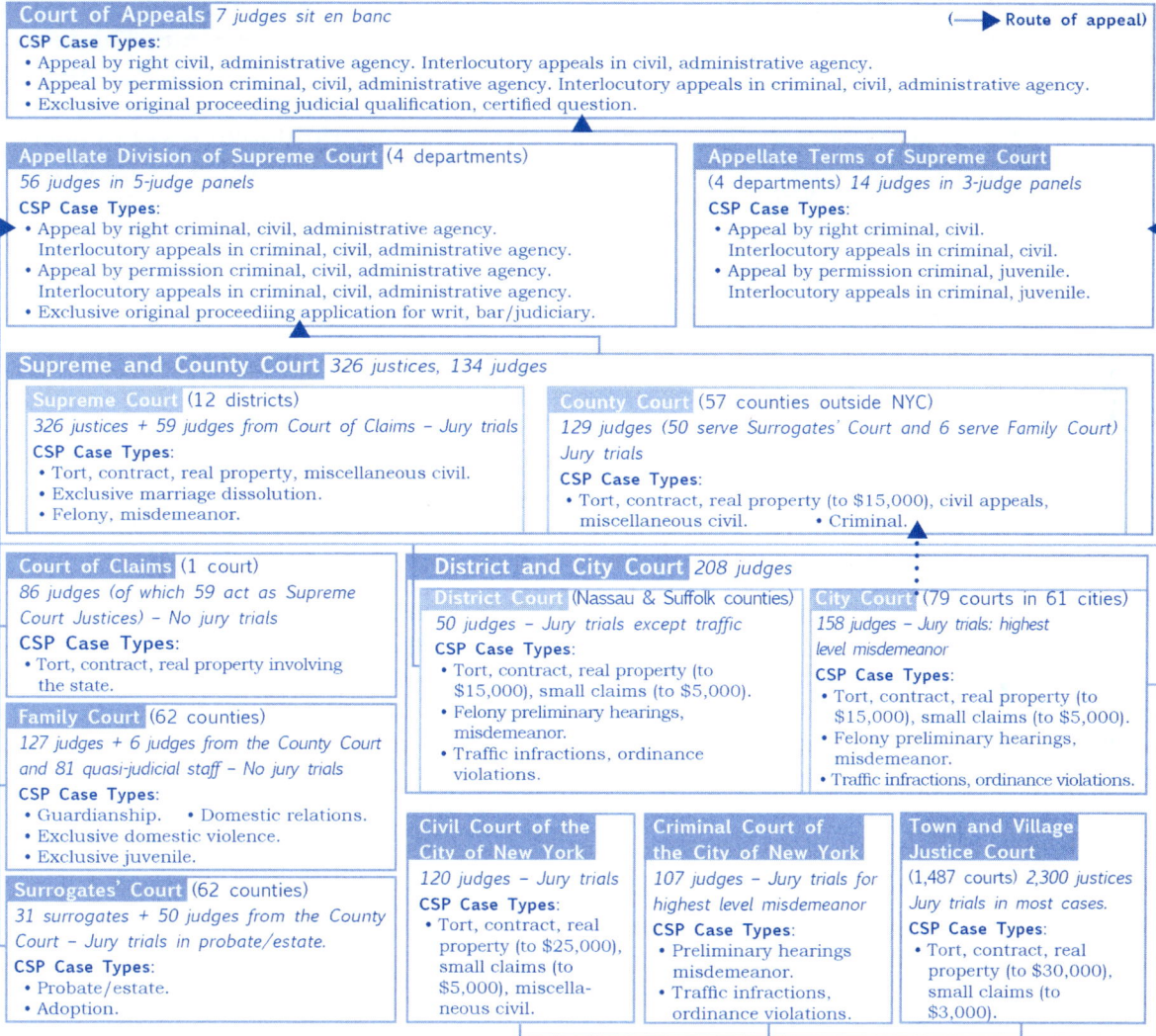

Court of Appeals *7 judges sit en banc*   (——▶ Route of appeal)
CSP Case Types:
- Appeal by right civil, administrative agency. Interlocutory appeals in civil, administrative agency.
- Appeal by permission criminal, civil, administrative agency. Interlocutory appeals in criminal, civil, administrative agency.
- Exclusive original proceeding judicial qualification, certified question.

Appellate Division of Supreme Court (4 departments)
56 judges in 5-judge panels
CSP Case Types:
- Appeal by right criminal, civil, administrative agency.
  Interlocutory appeals in criminal, civil, administrative agency.
- Appeal by permission criminal, civil, administrative agency.
  Interlocutory appeals in criminal, civil, administrative agency.
- Exclusive original proceediing application for writ, bar/judiciary.

Appellate Terms of Supreme Court
(4 departments) *14 judges in 3-judge panels*
CSP Case Types:
- Appeal by right criminal, civil.
  Interlocutory appeals in criminal, civil.
- Appeal by permission criminal, juvenile.
  Interlocutory appeals in criminal, juvenile.

Supreme and County Court *326 justices, 134 judges*

Supreme Court (12 districts)
326 justices + 59 judges from Court of Claims – Jury trials
CSP Case Types:
- Tort, contract, real property, miscellaneous civil.
- Exclusive marriage dissolution.
- Felony, misdemeanor.

County Court (57 counties outside NYC)
129 judges (50 serve Surrogates' Court and 6 serve Family Court)
Jury trials
CSP Case Types:
- Tort, contract, real property (to $15,000), civil appeals,
  miscellaneous civil.   • Criminal.

Court of Claims (1 court)
86 judges (of which 59 act as Supreme
Court Justices) – No jury trials
CSP Case Types:
- Tort, contract, real property involving
  the state.

Family Court (62 counties)
127 judges + 6 judges from the County Court
and 81 quasi-judicial staff – No jury trials
CSP Case Types:
- Guardianship.   • Domestic relations.
- Exclusive domestic violence.
- Exclusive juvenile.

Surrogates' Court (62 counties)
31 surrogates + 50 judges from the County
Court – Jury trials in probate/estate.
CSP Case Types:
- Probate/estate.
- Adoption.

District and City Court *208 judges*

District Court (Nassau & Suffolk counties)
50 judges – Jury trials except traffic
CSP Case Types:
- Tort, contract, real property (to
  $15,000), small claims (to $5,000).
- Felony preliminary hearings,
  misdemeanor.
- Traffic infractions, ordinance
  violations.

City Court (79 courts in 61 cities)
158 judges – Jury trials: highest
level misdemeanor
CSP Case Types:
- Tort, contract, real property (to
  $15,000), small claims (to $5,000).
- Felony preliminary hearings,
  misdemeanor.
- Traffic infractions, ordinance violations.

Civil Court of the City of New York
120 judges – Jury trials
CSP Case Types:
- Tort, contract, real
  property (to $25,000),
  small claims (to
  $5,000), miscella-
  neous civil.

Criminal Court of the City of New York
107 judges – Jury trials for
highest level misdemeanor
CSP Case Types:
- Preliminary hearings
  misdemeanor.
- Traffic infractions,
  ordinance violations.

Town and Village Justice Court
(1,487 courts) *2,300 justices*
Jury trials in most cases.
CSP Case Types:
- Tort, contract, real
  property (to $30,000),
  small claims (to
  $3,000).

ACTIVITY

A. Compare the U.S. Supreme Court and the New York State Court of Appeals in terms of jurisdiction and powers.

B. Which New York courts are not mentioned in *Document 3*? Describe them briefly.

C. Is the New York system of courts more or less complex than the average systems in other U.S. States? Why?

PART 3 – TEXAS

Article I is the Texas Constitution's *Bill of Rights*.
"All political power is inherent in the people, and all free governments are founded on their authority, and instituted for their benefit. The faith of the people of Texas stands pledged to the preservation of a republican form of government, and, subject to this limitation only, they have at all times the inalienable right to alter, reform or abolish their government in such manner as they may think expedient." (Article 1, Section 2)

DID YOU KNOW?
The Governor is supported and surrounded by a Lieutenant Governor, a Comptroller of Public Accounts, a Land Commissioner, an Attorney General, an Agriculture Commissioner, and three members of the Texas Railroad Commission. He or she nominates the members of the State Board of Education and a Secretary of State.

In Texas as well, the Constitution is the main source of Law. The one that currently exists was adopted in 1876 and was the 6th of the State. The first was drafted in 1836. Though it's not as long as California's that was amended over 400 times, or Alabama's (amended over 800 times), Texas' Constitution is still one of the longest in the country: it contains over 100 Amendments. But, in the case of Texas, the Amendments are more remedial than anything else and do not grant broad powers to the government whose creation it authorizes. Incidentally, Texans were so suspicious of too much power that Article I is nothing more than a *Bill of Rights*. The Texas State Legislature is bicameral: a Senate, with 31 Senators, and a House of Representatives, with 150 members who convene in regular session only once every two years. It is located in Austin, the Capital of Texas. Texas applies Dillon's Rule, at the every level of its government (State, County and City), signifying that delegated powers are limited, explicitly stated and cannot be expanded. The Executive Branch is made up of many people who are all elected individually and thus are not answerable to the Governor. Laws are recorded in *General and Special Laws of the State of Texas* in this State. Its legal system is one of the most complex in the United States. Texas has two courts of last resort (only Oklahoma is in the same boat): the Texas Supreme Court, which hears civil cases, and the Texas Court of Criminal Appeals. Except in the case of some municipal benches, partisan elections choose all of the judges at all levels of the judiciary; the Governor fills vacancies by appointment. All members of the Texas Supreme Court (civil) and the Texas Court of Criminal Appeals are elected Statewide. The Republican Party has held all 18 seats (nine in each court) since 1997.
In the 19th century, Texas had the reputation of rendering an arbitrary justice, which was called "Frontier justice". It was said that only two judges administered justice in all of Texas: Judge Winchester and Judge Lynch. It was inhospitable country, which possibly explains why Texas has no laws regarding possession of "long-barreled firearms" or "long guns" (shotguns, rifles and other similar weapons) by people 18 years or older, or handguns by people 18 years or older, without felony convictions.

Texas Courts
One of the most unique features of Texas Trial Courts, including the District Courts, is the tradition of having only one judge per Trial Court. Instead of adding more departments to existing courts in response to population growth, Texas adds more courts.

The lowest court level in Texas is the Justice of the Peace Court (also called Justice Court or JP Court). Each county has a JP Court. JP cases are appealed to the county court level where the case results in a trial *de novo*. The Texas District Courts are the Trial Courts of general jurisdiction. The District Court has exclusive jurisdiction on felony cases, cases involving land titles, and election contest cases. It shares jurisdiction with the County Courts, and Justice of the Peace Courts for civil cases. There are 14 Courts of Appeals, which have intermediate appellate jurisdiction in both civil and criminal cases. Each Court has between three and 13 justices (there are a total of 80). The Texas Court of Criminal Appeals hears appeals on criminal cases, excluding those involving juvenile proceedings. Cases in which the death penalty was ruled are directly and automatically appealed to this Court, bypassing the lower Courts of Appeals. The Texas Supreme Court hears appeals involving civil matters and does not hear any appeals involving criminal matters, except when the defendant is a juvenile. Under Texas law, juvenile proceedings (even those involving criminal activity) are considered civil matters; thus, the Texas Supreme Court hears such appeals, but it defers to the Texas Court of Criminal Appeals in matters where the Texas Penal Code must be interpreted. The Supreme Court also maintains responsibility for attorney licensing and discipline.

ACTIVITY

A. What does Article I of the Texas Constitution tell us about the political views of the people of Texas?

....

....

....

B. Briefly explain how the 2nd Amendment is applied in this State.

....

....

....

THE LONE STAR STATE

D.A. opposed to new handgun law

DOCUMENT 5

Motorists arrested for carrying pistols in their cars without a concealed handgun license will continue to be prosecuted in Houston, despite a new law that purports to give them a legal defense, Harris County
5 District Attorney Chuck Rosenthal said Monday. Although the sponsor said the law should reduce the number of arrests for unlawful handgun possession, Rosenthal said it won't change enforcement practices in Houston after it goes into effect on Thursday.
10 "It is still going to be against the law for (unlicensed) persons to carry handguns in autos," the District Attorney said, adding that the new legal defense can still be challenged by Prosecutors.
The new law, enacted during the regular legislative
15 session last spring, seeks to clarify a longtime law that allowed Texans to carry handguns while traveling, a qualification that was subject to a number of inconsistent court interpretations over the years. The new statute says a person is "presumed to
20 be traveling" if he or she is in a private vehicle, is not engaged in criminal activity (except for a minor traffic offense), is not prohibited by any other law from possessing
25 a firearm and is not a member of a criminal street gang.
It also requires the handgun to be concealed in the car, although weapons can be
30 discovered by officers during routine traffic stops if a driver gives permission for a car to be searched or opens a glove compartment where
35 a gun is secured to retrieve an insurance card or other documentation.
"The intent of the law is to keep innocent people from
40 going to jail," said the sponsor, Rep. Terry Keel, R-Austin, a former Prosecutor and former Travis County Sheriff, who now is a candidate for the Texas Court of Criminal Appeals.
45 The law, House Bill 823, was supported by the National Rifle Association and the American Civil Liberties Union and opposed by various law-enforcement groups.
More than 237,000 Texans have concealed hand-
50 gun licenses. But many other law-abiding adults don't have licenses because they are disqualified by exceptions that have nothing to do with public safety, said Alice Tripp, a lobbyist for the Texas State Rifle Association, an NRA affiliate.
Tripp said people who have defaulted on student 55 loans, who owe the State sales tax or franchise tax payments or are behind in child support payments are ineligible to receive a license.
Keel said he hoped the law will prompt police officers to think twice about arresting motorists who meet 60 the new legal presumption and spare them the expense and "indignity" of arrest and prosecution.
Otherwise, he said, "They basically are going to arrest innocent people and make them prove their innocence."
Rosenthal and Rob Kepple, Executive Director of 65 the Texas District and County Attorneys Association, disagreed.
Rosenthal said the new presumption about "traveling" doesn't define what constitutes traveling and can be challenged in court by Prosecutors, 70 leaving it to juries to decide verdicts "based upon the facts of the case."
A Prosecutor could summon witnesses to successfully argue 75 that a defendant wasn't traveling because he was simply "driving around the corner for a carton of milk," Kepple said. "I really don't think (the law) should affect how 80 police officers respond in arresting somebody," he added.
Houston Police Department spokeswoman Johanna Abad indicated Houston police were 85 going to take their advice from Rosenthal's office.
Unlawful possession of a weapon is a class A misdemeanor punishable by as much as one 90 year in county jail and a $4,000 fine. Rosenthal said most cases are resolved through plea bargains.
The Prosecutor said he asked Gov. Rick Perry to veto the bill because "taking weapons off the street 95 is a pretty good deal." He said his office handled about 5,000 weapons cases of varying degrees of severity last year.
Tripp called Rosenthal's opposition a case of "sour grapes ... and a threat to the general public." 100

DOCUMENT 6

Texas gay marriage ban unconstitutional, Federal judge rules

Lesbian, gay, bisexual, and transgender (LGBT) people in Texas face legal challenges and discrimination not faced by other people. The State denies gays and lesbians the right to marry a same-sex partner, both by statute and in its Constitution.

Until the U. S. Supreme Court declared the applicable law unconstitutional in *Lawrence v. Texas* (2003), certain sexual acts between persons of the same sex were a criminal offense. Despite the U. S. Supreme Court ruling, Texas did not repeal their statutes criminalizing same-sex sexual acts until 2013. In 1997, the Texas legislature prohibited the issuance of marriage licenses to same-sex couples. In 2003, the legislature enacted a statute that made void in Texas any same-sex marriage or civil union. In 2005, Texas voters approved a proposition that amended the State constitution to define marriage as consisting "only of the union of one man and one woman". A lawsuit, *De Leon v. Perry*, challenging the State's ban on same-sex marriage was filed in November 2013. On February 26th, 2014, the Court ruled against Texas' ban on same-sex marriage, but stayed enforcement of its ruling, pending appeal to the Fifth Circuit.

U.S. District Court Judge Orlando Garcia ruled Wednesday that Texas' ban on same-sex marriage is unconstitutional, joining several other Federal judges who have struck down marriage bans, citing the U.S.
5 Supreme Court's June 2013 *U.S. v. Windsor* decision. "Today's Court decision is not made in defiance of the great people of Texas or the Texas Legislature, but in compliance with the United States Constitution and Supreme Court precedent," Garcia wrote. "With-
10 out a rational relation to a legitimate governmental purpose, State-imposed inequality can find no refuge in our United States Constitution."
The ban was approved by the Texas legislature, signed by Gov. Rick Perry, R-Texas, and approved by
15 76% of State voters in November 2005. Residents of 253 out of 254 counties voted for the ban.
Garcia, was appointed to his position by President Bill Clinton in 1994.

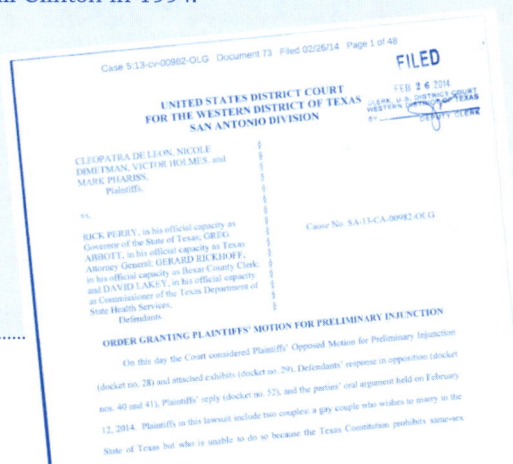

ACTIVITY

A. What is the proposed handgun law about?

B. What is the intent of this law?

C. Briefly explain the opposed points of view regarding marriage law in Texas and at the Federal level.

PART 4 – LOUISIANA

Louisiana's legal system is described in the Constitution by the State Laws: we find a Supreme Court, a Louisiana Court of Appeals, a District Court, the Justice of the Peace Courts, the Mayor's Courts, the City Courts, and the Parish Courts. The Chief Justice of the Louisiana Supreme Court is the chief administrator of the judiciary. Administration of the system is carried out with the support of the Judiciary Commission of Louisiana, the Louisiana Attorney Disciplinary Board, and the Judicial Council of the Supreme Court of Louisiana.

The State of Louisiana is totally unique in the United States: law here is Civil Law, even if one may find some Common Law influence. This special feature is buried in the State's history. Louisiana was originally a French creation and possession. The first code, *Digest of the Civil Laws now in Force in the Territory of Orleans, with Alternations and Amendments Adapted to its Present System of Government*, was adopted on March 31st, 1808. Its structure was modeled after the Napoleonic Code. Its contents are a mixture of Spanish and French Law. Martin O'Callaghan translated it into English. It was very difficult to keep two versions in two different languages, all the while maintaining a necessary coherence and precision. *The Digest* was replaced by the more complete Civil Code in 1825. The Civil Code was modified in 1870, following the abolition of slavery, and, for the first time, the text was published only in English. Other major revisions took place in 1960, and on January 1st, 1992: a fourth book containing the conflicts of law was added. Louisiana kept some Roman law out of this past version, or more so Louisiana's Civil Code, or the Civil Code of 1825. It is the only active civil code in the United States. The Louisiana Code is based on French tradition. Hence, property rights and matrimonial regimes are identical to what exists in France. However, Common Law influenced successive modifications to such a point that the law of the sale of goods today resembles American Law more than French Law.

As for the nature of its Law, there are major differences between Louisiana and the other States, although these differences are slowly disappearing under the influence of Common Law, which is starting to impose itself. The most obvious difference, and which is most often cited, comes from the fact that the judges

A French influence

In 1712, Louisiana was a French colony. Here, the Custom of Paris, along with royal decrees, applied. The Treaty of Fontainebleau gave Louisiana to Spain, and then Spanish Law was in effect. It returned to the bosom of France in October of 1800, before being sold again by Napoleon Bonaparte on December 20th, 1803 to the United States, a Common Law country. The territory of New Orleans became the State of Louisiana.

DID YOU KNOW?

There is no official language in the USA and Louisiana state lawmakers decided in 2014 that road signs in "Louisiana French" were possible. 22 parishes in Acadiana declared themselves interested in putting up bilingual road signs.

in Louisiana, like French judges, are not bound by *stare decisis*, but base their decisions on their interpretations, rather than on the doctrine of precedents.

An other notable difference may be found in the absence of the obligation of having a jury for civil proceedings, or at least, the prerogative is not found in Louisiana's Constitution, but was passed by the Louisiana Revised Statutes. Commercial law was standardized for the other 49 States, who all adopted the *Uniform Commercial Code* (*UCC* or *The Code*), which was published for the first time in 1952. This code is also used in Louisiana, but they prefer to talk about Chapters, rather than Articles, to designate the various subdivisions, because the word Article is used elsewhere to make reference to the Louisiana Code. Besides, Article 2 of the *UCC* (which deals with sales) is not applied because it is tailored for Common Law and incompatible with Civil Law.

Many branches of Law are still influenced by Roman law: Property Law, Contract Law, Commerce, Civil Procedure, and Family Law. Louisiana law and State laws contain words not found in any other State's, such as usufruct, forced heirship, redhibition and lesion beyond moiety. Finally, Law studies and practicing Law are quite different in Louisiana. Moreover, Louisiana does not organize, nor recognize, the MultiState Bar Examination, which allows one to practice in many States.

ACTIVITY

A. What is special about the law in Louisiana? Why is that so?

....

....

....

B. Can you list a few differences between Common Law and Civil Law.

....

....

....

A LITTLE PIECE OF FRANCE

The Louisiana Civil Code.

DOCUMENT 7

INTERSTATE
LOUISIANA
10

CHAPTER 1 – GENERAL PRINCIPLES

Article 1. Sources of law
The sources of law are legislation and custom.
Article 2. Legislation
5 Legislation is a solemn expression of legislative will.
Article 3. Custom
Custom results from practice repeated for a long time and generally accepted as having acquired the force of law. Custom may not
10 abrogate legislation.
Article 4. Absence of legislation or custom
When no rule for a particular situation can be derived
15 from legislation or custom, the court is bound to proceed according to equity. To decide equitably, resort is made to justice, reason,
20 and prevailing usages.
Article 5. Ignorance of law
No one may avail himself of ignorance of the law.
Article 6. Retroactivity of
25 *laws*
In the absence of contrary legislative expression, substantive laws apply prospectively only. Procedural and interpretative laws apply both prospectively and retroactively, unless there is a legislative expression
30 to the contrary.
Article 7. Laws for the preservation of the public interest
Persons may not by their juridical acts derogate from laws enacted for the protection of the public
35 interest. Any act in derogation of such laws is an absolute nullity.
Article 8. Repeal of laws
Laws are repealed, either entirely or partially, by other laws. A repeal may be express or implied. It is express
40 when it is literally declared by a subsequent law. It is implied when the new law contains provisions that are contrary to, or irreconcilable with, those of the former law. The repeal of a repealing law does not revive the first law.

45 CHAPTER 2 – INTERPRETATION OF LAWS

Article 9. Clear and unambiguous law
When a law is clear and unambiguous and its application does not lead to absurd consequences, the law shall be applied as written and no
50 further interpretation may be made in search of the intent of the legislature.
Article 10. Language susceptible to different meanings
When the language of the law is susceptible to different meanings, it must be interpreted as having the meaning that best conforms to the purpose of the law. 55
Article 11. Meaning of words
The words of a law must be given their generally prevailing meaning. Words of art and technical terms 60 must be given their technical meaning when the law involves a technical matter.
Article 12. Ambiguous words 65
When the words of a law are ambiguous, their meaning must be sought by examining the context in which they occur and the 70 text of the law as a whole.
Article 13. Laws on the same subject matter
Laws on the same subject matter must be interpreted in reference to each other. 75

CHAPTER 3 – CONFLICT OF LAWS

Article 14. MultiState cases
Unless otherwise expressly provided by the law of this State, cases having contacts with other States are governed by the law selected in accordance with 80 the provisions of Book IV of this Code.

BOOK I. OF PERSONS
TITLE I. NATURAL AND JURIDICAL PERSONS

Article 24. Kinds of persons
There are two kinds of persons: natural persons and 85 juridical persons.
A natural person is a human being. A juridical person is an entity to which the law attributes personality, such as a corporation or a partnership. The personality of a juridical person is distinct from that of 90 its members.
Article 25. Commencement and end of natural personality
Natural personality commences from the moment of live birth and terminates at death. 95

DOCUMENT 8

Common Law marriages in Louisiana.

Along with Washington D.C., there are only ten
5 States that legally recognize Common Law marriage. However,
10 Common Law marriages in Louisiana are not recognized by judges or the court system. Therefore, if you move from another State in which this
15 arrangement is valid, you may need to consider the possibility of getting formally married.

Louisiana law on common marriage is not recognized for many reasons. States that allow for this arrangement require several conditions from people in this
20 kind of relationship:

• Spouses who are in this kind of relationship must both present themselves to other people on a regular basis as husband and wife. However, doing so will still not lead to the validity of Common Law marriages in
25 Louisiana being recognized.

• Both spouses must be able to legally marry, meaning that they are both of age, in good mental condition and not too closely related. However, meeting all of these requirements still not allow for a Common Law
30 marriage in Louisiana to be recognized.

Spouses who are involved in this kind of benefit are allowed all the same benefits as those who have a formal marriage certificate, such as filing joint tax returns. However, couples who wish to enter into
35 Common Law marriages in Louisiana to take advantage of such rights will not be able to.

It is important to note that if you have entered into this kind of relationship in another State, it may be possible to preserve your status if you move. While Common Law marriage in Louisiana is not an option 40 for those who are already residents, the court system will generally recognize such an agreement if it has already been initiated in another State.

Couples who move to the State and then wish to obtain a divorce may have some difficulty establishing 45 the validity of their relationship. Since Common Law marriages in Louisiana will only be recognized if they were established in another State, a spouse who seeks alimony payments or couples who have minor children will need to establish the prior recognition 50 of their status. This frequently will require calling in witnesses who can testify that both husband and wife presented themselves as such. Arranging transportation for these witnesses to confirm Common Law marriages in Louisiana will add to the expense of 55 divorce proceedings.

Another concern you may have if involved in this kind of relationship involves the handling of your assets after your death. Since Common Law marriage in Louisiana is not recognized, your property will not 60 automatically be inherited by a spouse. To ensure that your wishes regarding inheritances are respected, it is best to draft a will detailing how you wish for your assets to be divided. This way, even though spouses may have difficulty establishing their rights 65 to inherit as members of Common Law marriages in Louisiana, they will still receive their fair share of your estate without having to establish the relationship in probate court.

ACTIVITY

A. Look at *Document 7*. What reminds you of a French document?

B. What is Common Law marriage?

C. What happens if Common Law married people move to Louisiana?

Important Words

**Codes
Initiatives
Session Laws
Lieutenant Governor
Commissioner
*de novo***

California

California Law is based on its Constitution: it gives rise to California's government, giving it structure and defining its powers. It is one of the longest Constitutions in the world, due to the fact that referendums are authorized and frequent, and each initiative passed becomes an Amendment. There is a strong tradition in California of popular sovereignty. The structure of the Constitution is simple: a Preamble, 30 Articles, and over 400 Amendments. California Law is based on Common Law, the precedents being published in case-law reports. The Laws are recorded in the *Codes*, a uniqueness shared by Texas and New York. There are 29 Codes in California. The State is divided into 58 Counties. School districts are under the direct responsibility of the State government. Everyone knows that a large number of celebrities live in California, which led to passing laws specifically for this group of the population, for example, the Celebrity Rights Act, or, a Family Code adapted to people who are rich enough to stay in Court for years.

New York

As in most of the States, the New York Constitution is more detailed than the U.S. Constitution. It has been amended 8 times. The first Constitution of 1777 did not provide for a judicial branch. The one in effect today strongly resembles the Federal Constitution: providing for a Congress with two chambers, an Executive Branch with a Governor in charge, and a Judicial Branch. New York is divided into counties, cities and villages. New York City has a special status, with a unicameral assembly for its governance. The State Constitution defines the power of each local body. The Law conforms to Common Law. Some laws are specific to New York, notably for the right to drink alcohol, which is regulated at night and for marriages, and upholding laws concerning anti-adultery or bearing arms: New York is one of the most repressive States when it comes to possessing a gun.

Texas

There have been six Constitutions in Texas, the first dating to 1876. Just as in California, it is very long, but not quite so long, however. Article I is a Bill of Rights for its citizens. Legislative power is granted to a bicameral house, which sits for two years in Austin. The Executive Branch is composed of many people: a Governor, and all elected officials, all independent of one another. The legal system is also unique, since there are two Supreme Courts (like in Oklahoma): one for civil cases and one for criminal cases. All judges are elected in Texas, during the political elections. The Republican Party has a large majority. In the 19th century, Texas had a reputation of rendering arbitrary justice. It was an inhospitable area, which might explain its very permissive approach to possessing and carrying guns. Crimes committed by children are considered civil cases in Texas and are heard by the civil courts.

Louisiana

Louisiana is totally unique in the United States because it is the only State that applies Roman law; this can be explained by the fact that Louisiana was originally a French territory. Law here is thus based on the Napoleonic Civil Code, the first having been created in 1808. Common Law is however to be found in many areas. Louisianan judges from are not bound by *stare decisis*, but base their decisions on their interpretations. There is no obligation for the Louisiana Courts to hear a civil case with a jury. Family Law, Property Law, Contract Law, Commercial Law, and civil proceedings are still influenced heavily by Roman law. As a result, Louisiana does not recognize the MultiState Bar Examination.

A. Say if the following statements are true or false:

	True	False
1. State laws must follow Federal laws.		
2. All the States must apply the rights guaranteed by the Constitution in the same way (for ex., the right to have a gun).		
3. The laws of the States may be written in Codes.		
4. Louisiana doesn't apply Common Law.		
5. Same-sex marriage is banned in Texas.		

B. Why is the Family Law so important in California compared to other States?

....
....

C. What are the differences in New York City compared to the rest of the State in regard to local courts?

....
....

D. What does the phrase "Judge Winchester and Judge Lynch administered justice in Texas" mean?

....
....

E. How does a marriage become Common Law?

....
....

REFERENCES :

Page107. "Map of the USA with State names", by Eric Pierce, Wikimedia. http://commons.wikimedia.org/wiki/File:Map_of_USA_with_State_names_et.svg
Page109. "Celebrities Rights Act", by Dimitri Champain
Page 110. "The Three-Strikes law", adapted from "After Third Strike, Many Now Walk: California begins to release prisoners after reforming its three-strikes law", by Lorelei Laird, in *Time Magazine*, December 2013, Vol. 99 Issue 12
Page111. "Web posts", created by Jean-Eric Branaa & Keith Sarver "California journals", by CoolCaesar, Wikimedia. image: http://commons.wikimedia.org/wiki/File:California legislaturejournals. jpg?uselang=fr
Page112. "I love New York", by Dimitri Champain
Page 114. "Judiciary of New York", from Wikipedia "Judiciary of New York" (http://en.wikipedia.org/wiki/Judiciary_of_New_York); "New York Supreme Court", by Dimutex, Wikimedia.http://commons.wikimedia.org/wiki/File:New_York_Supreme_Court_at_60_Centre_Street.jpg
Page116. "Texas flag", by Dimitri Champain
Page 118. "DA opposed to new handgun law", adapted from Clay Robinson, *Houston Chronicle*, August 30, 2005
"Natlove", Wikimedia. http://commons.wikimedia.org/wiki/File:Natlove2.jpg

Page119. "Texas Gay Marriage Ban Unconstitutional, Federal Judge Rules", adapted from Steven Nelson, in *US News and World Report*, February 26, 2014
"Sanjaint Warrant", Wikimedia. http://www.usnews.com/news/articles/2014/02/26/texas-gay-marriage-ban-unconstitutional-Federal-judge-rules
Page120. "Louisiana Civil Code", by Dimitri Champain
Page122. "I-10 (LA)". Wikimedia. http://commons.wikimedia.org/wiki/File:I-10_%28LA%29.svg?uselang=fr
"Joseph Riusling Meeker – The land of Evangeline "Wikimedia. http://commons.wikimedia.org/wikiFile:Joseph_Rusling_Meeker_-_The_Land_of_Evangeline.jpg?uselang=fr
Page123. "Regency proposal woodcut". Wikimedia. http://commons.wikimedia.org/wiki/File:1815-regency-proposal-woodcut.gif?uselang=f
"Common law marriages in Louisiana", from Laws.com (http://marriage.laws.com/common-law-marriage-louisiana)
Page124. "Summary", by Dimitri Champain
Page125. "Review", by Dimitri Champain
pp.109, 111, 113, 115, 117, 119, 121, 123 "Activity", by Dimitri Champain

UNIT 7 Review

This Unit will help you to revise the course content seen in Units 1-6. Remember that all the answers contained in this section can be found in these units. So far, we have seen that Americans rebelled against the King and a system in which they were not represented. Their experience in the Colonies allowed them to establish different systems, and they also relied on this experience after the Revolution. But since they were highly suspicious of a centralized power, they created 13 different political and legal systems. However, the need for unity led to a need for a common Constitution, while the Federal system exerted primacy on the system that was developed by the various States. Common Law is the pillar, even if Civil Law still exists in Louisiana. Each State has nonetheless kept its priorities and guards them jealously. You should now be able to discuss and answer questions about Law, its evolution in the United States and the variations that may be found in the States.

7

UNIT 1 **Err... Law**

1. What do we call Laws of Nature?

....

....

....

....

....

....

2. What is *Amicus Curiae*?

....

....

....

....

....

3. Who can write an *Amicus* Brief?

....

....

....

....

....

....

4. What is a lower court?

....

....

....

....

....

5. What is an Appellate Court?

....

....

6. What is Federal Court?

....

....

....

....

....

7. What is the role of State Law in the Federal system?

....

....

....

....

....

8. Can a Court impose an equitable remedy?

....

....

....

....

9. Why would interests groups prefer to go to Court rather than lobby in Congress?

....

....

....

....

....

10. What is known as a test case?

....

....

....

....

....

UNIT 2 — EARLY AMERICAN LAW

1. In what ways is Congress'power of taxation limited?

....

....

....

....

....

2. What are the three limitations on the power of Congress?

....

....

....

....

....

....

3. Which part of the Constitution gives Congress a flexible way of interpreting its powers to act?

....

....

....

....

....

....

4. Is the right to choose one's name protected by the Constitution or not?

....

....

....

....

....

5. Why is this so?

....

....

....

....

....

....

6. Is national Marijuana Smoking Day legal?

....

....

....

....

....

....

7. What is *Habeas Corpus*?

....

....

....

....

....

....

8. What was the Glorious Revolution in England?

....

....

....

9. What do you know about the founding of Harvard?

....

....

....

....

....

....

10. When did the anglicization of American Law start?

....

....

....

....

THE U.S. LEGAL SYSTEM

UNIT 3

1. What does « high crimes and misdemeanors » mean?

....

....

....

....

2. How are the Justices selected?

....

....

....

....

....

....

3. How long can a Justice serve?

....

....

....

....

....

....

4. What do U.S. Supreme Court Justices do?

....

....

....

....

....

....

5. Who are the Justice of the U.S. Supreme Court?

....

6. Who are the current Justices of the U.S. Supreme Court?

....

....

....

....

....

....

....

7. How do U.S. Supreme Court Justices get their jobs?

....

....

....

....

....

....

8. What are the steps the Supreme Court performs in order to decide a case?

....

....

....

....

....

....

9. What is the title given to judges who sit on State Supreme Courts?

....

....

....

....

....

....

10. What is a bill of attainder?

....

....

....

....

....

UNIT 4

THE FEDERAL JUDICIAL SYSTEM

1. How does the Constitution limit the powers of Congress?

....

....

....

....

....

....

2. Do Appellate Courts have original jurisdiction?

....

....

....

....

....

....

3. Can a Court of Appeal overrule itself?

....

....

....

....

....

....

4. Can a Court of Appeal depart from its own decisions?

....

....

....

....

....

5. What can Courts of Appeals do?

....

....

....

....

....

....

6. Can the Court of Appeal increase a sentence?

....

....

....

....

....

....

7. Do Courts of Appeal have juries?

....

....

....

....

....

....

8. What was the constitutional issue decided in *McCulloch v. Maryland*?

....

....

....

....

....

....

9. What Amendment was challenged in *Gibbons v. Ogden*?

....

....

....

....

....

....

10. Did *Gibbons v. Ogden* involve a narrow or broad interpretation of the Constitution?

....

....

....

....

....

UNIT 5

STATE COURTS

1. What are the qualifications for becoming a judge at the Federal level?

....

....

....

....

....

....

2. Who select the State Supreme Court judges?

....

....

....

....

....

....

3. What are the qualifications for becoming a judge?

....

....

....

....

....

4. What qualifications are needed to become a U.S. Supreme Court Justice?

....

....

....

....

5. Are the qualifications of a Supreme Court Justice stated in the Constitution?

....

....

....

....

....

....

6. How do you answer a judge in Court?

....

....

....

....

....

....

7. How many judges or justices are on a State Supreme Court?

....

....

....

....

....

8. How long is the term of office for a judge in higher level of State Courts?

....

....

....

....

....

....

9. Explain the difference between a Petit Jury and a Grand Jury.

....

....

....

....

....

....

....

10. Who is the State Aministrative Director of the Courts?

....

....

....

....

....

UNIT 6   **STATE LAWS**

1. Why is California's Constitution so long?

....

....

....

....

....

....

2. Why is law not made in the name of the Commonwealth in California?

....

....

....

....

....

....

3. What is the Three-Strikes law?

....

....

....

....

....

....

4. What do you know about the administrative organization of New York?

....

....

....

....

....

....

5. Do you know any specific laws only valid in New York State?

....

....

....

....

....

....

6. What is the Peace Court in Texas?

....

....

....

....

....

....

7. How are the judges generally chosen in Texas?

....

....

....

....

....

8. What is the capital of Texas?

....

....

....

....

....

....

9. What does *usufruct* mean, and where can this word be heard in the United States?

....

....

....

....

....

....

10. Is Common Law applied in Louisiana?

....

....

....

....

....

....

REFERENCES :
Page 127. "Time for Review Concept Clocks", by donskarpo,
        Bigstock photo: http://bigstockphoto.com/
        download/bid-2945026.

UNIT 8 Lawyers

Introduction

Each American State has its own legal régime inherited from Common Law, except for Louisiana, which kept private law from the French Civil Code, but integrated public law from Common Law. Federal law takes precedence over State law. None of that complexity is simple for lawyers who work their entire career in only one State; this does not really encourage mobility. The majority of lawyers also specialize either in State, or Federal law.

PART 1 – ATTORNEYS-AT-LAW

The number of lawyers has more than doubled in the USA over the last 40 years, and the numbers are still increasing:
  - 1970: there were 250,000 lawyers in the USA (1.3/1,000 inhabitants)
  - 1980: 350,000
  - 1990: 750,000
  - 2000: 1,000,000
  - 2010: 1,300,000 (3.5/1,000 inhabitants)

Today, it is estimated that the United States has 70% of the world's lawyers. About half of them work for a small firm, or even independently. Many mid-size firms exist, however, which employ between 50 and 200 lawyers. Enormous law firms with over 1,000 lawyers started appearing in the 1970s.

Contrary to most other Common Law countries, there is no distinction in the USA between attorneys that plead (most often called *barristers* in other countries, such as in England) and those who do not plead (often called solicitors). In the US, they are all attorneys at law (or attorneys-at-law). Nevertheless, American lawyers tend to assign themselves specializations as either office lawyers or trial lawyers. The American legal system also does not recognize the title "notary public" from the Roman civil law countries, except for Louisiana. American lawyers deal as much with inheritance and successions, as they do with property transactions, and litigation and representation in court. So, in the United States, the definition is the most general and as liberal as possible: an attorney is a legal professional who is legally qualified to prosecute (*read p.160*) and defend actions in such court on the retainer of clients. Alternative terms include counselor (or counselor-at-law) and lawyer.

> **An attorney is a legal professional who is legally qualified to prosecute and defend actions in court.**

To be admitted into the profession, one need only pass the Bar Exam of the State where one intends to practice, or have a permanent position reserved, and the highest court of the State (usually the Supreme Court), or the State Bar, will issue an authorization to practice. Each State has its own Bar and all lawyers can only practice in the State where they are a member. Lawyers must then register annually with the Bar (which means, pay the annual fees) in return for the license to practice law. The internship as a condition for becoming a lawyer was basically abandoned at the end of the 1960s, in favor of immediately working for a firm as an associate. Lawyers can form teams in a firm, for which any structure is possible: single-member companies, a professional civil law company, or limited liability company. As soon as they are admitted to the Bar, American lawyers can file legal pleadings and argue cases in that state court, provide legal advice to clients and draft important legal instruments such as wills, trusts, deeds and contracts. Arguing cases in the federal courts requires separate admission. Contrary to the glamorous image of lawyers seen in TV shows and films, most of their work is time spent doing library research, or in databases like Westlaw, LexisNexis, or Bloomberg L.P. Along with this research, lawyers must spend a lot of time writing documents, such as legal briefs, contracts, wills and trusts. Few television programs and movies accurately portray the hours required for tasks that form the core of many attorneys' occupational lives.

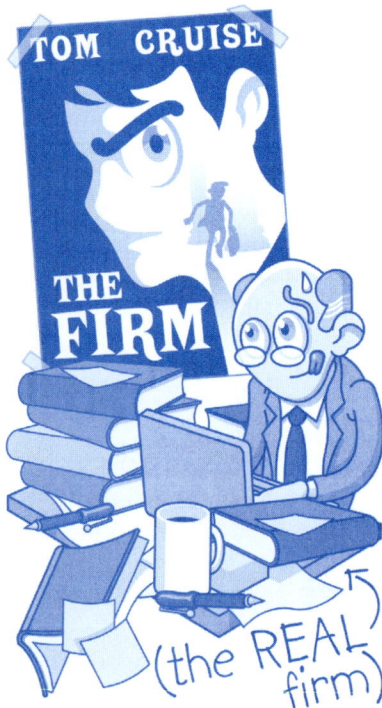

TOM CRUISE

THE FIRM

(the REAL firm)

In litigation, attorneys spend much time discovering the facts of the case to develop a "theory of the case" that integrates facts and law in a way most favorable to their client. Many attorneys believe that the discovery process has reduced the number of civil cases that actually go to trial, since the discovery process often permits a clear evaluation of the merits of each side's position.

Some attorneys are not trial lawyers. Non-trial attorneys are sometimes called transactional lawyers, corporate lawyers, or attorney-advisors in the Federal Government. They specialize in activities that seldom involve them in litigation. Among these activities are writing legal opinion letters, drafting wills or trust documents, advising clients, structuring business transactions, negotiating and drafting contracts, developing tax strategies or preparing and prosecuting filings with government agencies such as the Internal Revenue Service, the Securities and Exchange Commission or the Patent and Trademark Office.

ACTIVITY

A. Compare English and American lawyers. What are the most important differences?

....

....

....

....

....

B. What differs between the image of lawyers on TV shows and the reality of their jobs?

....

....

....

....

....

AN AD FOR A CASE

American Attorney and advertising

DOCUMENT 1

Traditionally, U.S. Bar Associations were opposed to all forms of advertising. The Supreme Court imposed an important change on them in the *Bates et al. v. State Bar of Arizona* judgment (433 U.S. 350 (1977)).
Mssrs. Bates and O'Steen were associate lawyers, and members of the Arizona Bar Association. They had published an ad in the *Arizona Republic* in Phoenix, explaining that their law firm provided legal services for very reasonable fees, giving a list of their prices for some basic services: consensual divorce, undisputed adoption, and excessive individual debt without complications or name changes. The President of the Arizona Bar began a disciplinary procedure against the two attorneys because the Internal Rules of Procedure of the Bar Association forbade any advertising in the press or other media. The disciplinary committee sanctioned them to a temporary one-week ban, which was confirmed by the Supreme Court of Arizona. Mssrs. Bates and O'Steen appealed to the U.S. Supreme Court, claiming that the sanction for the advertizement went against the Sherman Act, which guarantees the freedom of competition, and the 1st Amendment to the U.S. Constitution, which guarantees the freedom of expression.
The first argument was rejected, but the Supreme Court decided that freedom of expression implied the right for lawyers to resort to advertizing, thus the Bar could only sanction false advertizing. The Court observed that the ban on advertizing could result in damage to a lawyer's profession, leaving the public to believe that the former was incapable of making himself known, and the absence of information about his services and fees could dissuade people in need of an attorney. Beyond the respect of fundamental rights, the Supreme Court thus founded the authorization of advertizing for the need of informing the public, which also brings to mind Article 161 of the 1991 decree.
But, that does not mean that we should believe that American lawyers are permitted to advertize with no restrictions. On the contrary, it is regulated. For example, the Alabama Bar demands discretion and objectivity. It forbids its members to give an opinion about the quality of their service or to commit solicitation in their advertisements. The Model Rules of Professional Conduct drafted by the American Bar Association also authorize advertising, while specifying that it must be true (Model Rules of Professional Conduct, Art. 7.1: "A lawyer shall not make a false or misleading communication about the lawyer or the lawyer's services. A communication is false or misleading if it contains a material misrepresentation of fact or law, or omits a fact necessary to make the statement considered as a whole not materially misleading."
They also forbid door-to-door sales and solicitation, except if they are aimed at another lawyer, or someone close to the person soliciting, or if the latter is not offering their services free of charge. Additionally, the mention of a specialization is only possible if the lawyer who is asking holds specialization certificates issued by an organization accredited by any appropriate State or American Bar Association authority.

DOCUMENT 2

The point of view of an insider

Vincent Allard, president at Corpomax, Inc. and at Jurifax, Inc., is a Canadian Lawyer working in the United States, (greater Philadelphia region). He has a blog on which he gives his point of view about his profession, with a great sense of humor (Corpoma).com/blog).

One day I was luxuriating in Florida, to completely empty my depleted lawyer's brain. In a moment of idle curiosity, I was flipping through the Boca Raton Yellow Pages, the area's posh neighborhood. My tired
5 eyes with bags under them fell specifically upon the "Lawyers" section. I was curious: how do my American colleagues inform their neighbors that they exist? I got more than I bargained for.

Printed ad
10 At that time, the Montreal *Yellow Pages* contained only about 20 pages with discreet ads for area lawyers (which would make all the marketing experts cry with rage). On the other hand, those in Boca Raton – a tiny city compared to the Quebec metropolis – reached a
15 whopping 136.
No matter what your problem, a specialized lawyer exists to handle it.
You slipped on a groundhog dying from starvation? No problem: a lawyer specialized in falls caused by
20 groundhogs would be very pleased to represent you. Are you mad at a Police Officer, because he didn't use Tibetan cashmere gloves when he gave you a steep fine? Again, it's child's play: a lawyer with loads of experience on the subject is just waiting to discuss
25 it with you.

Consistent advertising
I am struck by three constants.
First, it says that the first telephone interview is free. So, to set up a meeting and have the directions to the
30 law offices of the Disciple of Themis explained to you, you won't receive a bill.

Then, they promise you, black on yellow, you won't pay a thing if the lawyer isn't paid. You start to earn the trust of a potential client. Except you have to shell out the expenses to follow through with your 35 case. And God knows the expenses can sometimes reach insane levels (expert fees, travel costs, stenography, etc.)
Finally, the local legal advertizers are not stifled by modesty. Grandiose statistics on the number of cases 40 won, showy qualifications, and shocking expressions: anything goes for impressing a future client.

Television ad
Even better: TV commercials. They love to interrupt highly cultural shows, generally blaming young 45 viewers for absolutely unbelievable problems or with smooth-talking hosts convinced they have a Ph.D. in Psychology.
In one typical ad, a man leaps out at you (hardly ever a woman) and looks straight through you with the 50 look of a hungry animal. With one shout, he assures you that you have rights! It's reassuring, even when you don't have a problem.
Then, he informs you that he can obtain the sum of money to which you are due. Hearing that, you 55 instinctively look for a debtor.
Finally, he repeats his telephone number at least 15 times in 30 seconds – a number, of course, chosen with great care so that clients with short-term memory can memorize it easily, something like 555- 60 444-4444, or 1-800-GO-TO-COURT.

ACTIVITY

A. What surprises you about the rights given to U.S. lawyer for advertising?

B. Why was Mr. Allard surprised when looking up the lawyers section in the *Yellow Pages*?

C. What are his criticisms of American attorneys?

PART 2 - EDUCATION

To become a lawyer in the USA, you must first obtain a Bachelor's Degree, in any subject, then, you must pass the LSAT (Law School Admission Test) entrance exam. Once passed, you must study three more years at law school, leading to a Master's Degree (*read more p. 180*). At the end of the first year, students are permitted to work for law firms as "certified student attorneys". Several States even allow students to plead before the Court, under the supervision of a licensed attorney, as a certified legal intern (CLI); but only under the condition that they have finished half of their law school courses. In Kansas and Illinois, in particular, the laws are especially favorable to granting law students free access to the Courts.

The degree awarded to law students in the United States is typically a juris doctor (Latin for "Doctor of Jurisprudence"; abbreviated J.D. or, when conferred in English, D.Jur.). This is not the same as in other Anglophone countries, notably in England, where Law is taught at an undergraduate level and you may obtain a Bachelor of Laws (LL.B.). After that, you may obtain a Master of Laws (LL.M.). In the USA, the LL.B. was replaced by the J.D. in 1902 by University of Chicago Law School. In 1791, every American Bar Association-accredited law school had replaced the LL.B. by the J.D.

Some States recognize foreign degrees. In most jurisdictions, lawyers must also enroll in continuing education (Continuing Legal Education (CLE) requirements). The Bar exams fall under the supervision of agencies set up by the different States. The first Bar Exam was created by the State of Delaware in 1763. In most States, the Bar Exam lasts two days. It includes an essay on the subject of State law (usually subjects such as wills, trusts and community property, which always vary from one state to another). The Multistate Bar Examination (MBE) also exists, which is a standardized test in every State. It was created by the National Conference of Bar Examiners and has been used since 1972. It consists of 200 questions that test your knowledge of six subjects, primarily Common Law issues. The majority of American jurisdictions have also established a more practical exam; the test taker must write a memorandum or closing remarks using a group of documents based on a fictitious case.

Louisiana is still unique, since it uses Civil Law. American lawyers must obtain a degree in Civil Law in this State. It may be noted that Paul M. Hebert Law Center at Louisiana State University now offers a dual degree: J.D./Diploma

Chicago Law School
Lauded as one of the most intellectual law schools in the country with one of the most acclaimed faculties, the University of Chicago Law School has long been rooted as one of the true elites.

Louisiana State University
The Louisiana State University (LSU) Law Center was originally established as the Louisiana State University Law School in 1906. In 1979, the Law Center was renamed the Paul M. Hebert Law Center of Louisiana State University. The Law Center holds membership in the Association of American Law Schools (AALS) and is on the approved list of the American Bar Association (ABA).

of Civil Law (D.C.L.), which takes seven semesters, instead of the usual six required for the J.D.

It is still possible to take the LL.M. in the U.S., but it is usually reserved for highly specialized sectors, such as tax law. The LL.M. is also used for legal practitioners in another country, who choose to study in the United States. Many foreign legal experts try to pass the LL.M. in comparative law, in order to familiarize themselves with American Common Law and to then have the chance to pass the New York or California Bar Exam. After that, they can settle and work in the USA, often for prestigious law firms such as Clifford Chance, or return to their own countries to advise clients at an international level.

Interview with a student going to America

Axelle Vivien is studying at Panthéon-Assas Paris 2 University. She has just been accepted to Duke Law School, in the United States.

Why did you want to go to the United States?
Going to the United States during my studies was always a goal for me. I was first introduced to the American educational system when I was in Junior High School and High School, by attending enrichment camps at Bryn Mawr University in Pennsylvania. I have great memories of those months spent on the Haverford Campus and I still have some very good American friends. After my prep classes, I had already filled out applications to go to NYU. If I'm going to Duke Law School today, it's because that paperwork helped me immensely when I was preparing my application for Duke.

Why Duke?
Duke Law school is, above all, one of the schools that offers exchange programs between my university and the United States. Though Duke is much less well known in France as an Ivy League school, it still ranks as one of the most prestigious universities in the country. Its reputation for having a lively campus life attracted me as well.

Did your teachers support you in this project?
Putting together my application went very quickly, because I had already thought long and hard about it. Because of my previous experience with the NYU application, I was already familiar with the particularities of the American essay. However, I still used some books to help me, such as Essays that worked in Law School, to prepare my personal statement. I was lucky to also have had help in drafting it by an American friend and my English Law professor.

What is the most difficult thing for you, being a young female student coming from France?
It is difficult for me to know in advance today what would be the most problematic for a young French girl going to Law School. Still, I am dreading the first week of adapting to the language and the campus. The same goes for the expectations in terms of the form the work will take, because it's very different from the French dissertation and comments, meaning it will be twice as complicated.

What would you have liked to have learned about American Law at your French university before leaving?
I'm leaving with a very limited body of knowledge about American Law, which is reduced to a few ideas about general culture. I regret that how we learn American Law in the degree is not in accordance with an American Law course which is not a "government course".

ACTIVITY

A. Briefly explain the various steps for becoming a lawyer in the United States.

B. Read Ms. Vivien's interview. What are her expectations and what are her biggest fears? Do you share this point of view? Why or why not?

A STUDENT'S LIFE

DOCUMENT 3

He studied in the U.S.A.

Mr. Alexandre Gelblat is an attorney for Kahn & Associé Law Firm. An alumnus of Panthéon-Assas University (Paris II), he supplemented his degree with some studies in the United States, at Fordham University in New York.

Why did you want to go to the U.S.A.?

Before starting to work, I wanted to have some experience in a foreign country, in order to discover another way of living as well as a different legal system. I was always drawn to the United States so choosing a destination was fairly easy.

Did your teachers support you in this project?

My graduate professors encouraged me to do it and helped me a lot through the tedious process of filling out application forms.

How was your first contact with the students and teachers there?

Contact with the other foreign students happened quickly, because we all had in common the fact that we were far from our families, and that we wanted to discover a new country and a new way of life. Meeting American students took a bit longer, but having an assigned seat in some classes allowed me to get to know those sitting around me. Fordham Law School is in Manhattan, so there was really no campus life, as we imagine it, because the campus is the city. For that reason, the university regularly organized events to help students meet and interact. The professors were always available and easy to talk to.

What was the most difficult thing for you, being a young student coming from France?

The most difficult thing was understanding what was going on in the classes; we didn't have any subtitles! The style of teaching in the U.S. is based on exchanges between the professor and the students, so it's quite easy to feel lost in the first few weeks. Because the classes are most often informal conversations, quite often there were cultural references to a film or an ad made to help us understand a form of reasoning. In those moments, it was fairly easy to see who was a foreign student and who wasn't, because we were the only ones not laughing… Over time and after having bought a TV, things got much better. Another thing that was difficult was the lack of planning and structure in some classes.

What would you have liked to have learned about American Law at your French university before leaving?

I am quite satisfied with what I learned about American Law at Paris II. I think, though, we need to increase the number of hours in learning English in college, so that students can have a sufficient level in English to read and write documents in English. I don't think a Bachelor's level is enough.

You passed the New York Bar Exam. Was that part of your original plans?

Passing the Bar was part of my plans from the beginning.

Did your level of English have an effect on your passing it?

My English level was good, but I don't think that English was the only determining factor. It's obvious that a minimum level is necessary; the TOEFL is useful in knowing if you have the minimum or not.

Did the American way of teaching and practicing law affect your writings?

Having studied in the United States surely improved the way I write in English. As for the contents of my writing, I didn't have enough experience to talk about a transformation in what I wrote. Nevertheless, I think that French law is organic, and those who practice it are naturally interested in what is happening in other countries. The American style of teaching allowed me to sharpen my critical thinking and to ask myself questions.

Do you have any regrets about your year at Fordham, or things that you would suggest to do, if you were giving someone advice?

I don't really have any regrets but the year just flew by too quickly. The only advice I have to give to someone would be to make the most of college life, as much as possible.

DOCUMENT 4

Law rankings by graduates in BigLaw jobs

Rank	Law School	2013 Grads @ NLJ 250	2013 JDs	% of Grads @ NLJ 250	Tuition
1	Columbia	286	437	65.45%	$55,488
2	NYU	295	537	54.93%	$51,150
3	Harvard	309	577	53.55%	$50,880
4	Chicago	114	215	53.02%	$50,727
5	Pennsylvania	136	259	52.51%	$53,138
6	Northwestern	146	286	51.05%	$53,468
7	Duke	117	241	48.55%	$51,662
8	Stanford	89	189	47.09%	$50,802
9	Cornell	87	193	45.08%	$55,301
10	UC-Berkeley	135	301	44.85%	$48,068
11	Virginia	161	364	44.23%	$46,400
12	Michigan	165	400	41.25%	$48,250
13	Yale	80	206	38.83%	$53,600
14	Georgetown	238	638	37.30%	$48,835
15	Texas	120	378	31.75%	$32,376
16	Vanderbilt	65	206	31.55%	$46,804
17	UCLA	101	332	30.42%	$45,221
18	USC	65	220	29.55%	$52,598
19	Fordham	118	481	24.53%	$49,526
20	Notre Dame	45	184	24.46%	$45,980

DOCUMENT 5

Promotion from associates to partners.
Published by *New Law Journal*, February 24 2014
(based on survey responses fro 178 NLJ 250 firms)

Rank	Law School	Associates promoted to Partner in 2013
1	Harvard	41
2	Georgetown	37
3	NYU	31
4	Michigan	27
5	Columbia	26
6	Virginia	23
7	G. Washington	21
8	Debnam	20
9	Boston	17
9	Northwestern	17
9	St Louis	17
12	UCLA	16
12	Iowa	16
14	Stanford	15

ACTIVITY

A. Read Mr. Gelblat's interview. Why wasn't it so difficult for him to adapt to the American educational system?

B. Comment on this interview: what surprised you?

C. Compare the two tables. Why are the university rankings different? What might surprise you in these results?

PART 3 – SPECIALIZATION

All lawyers do not choose to plead in Court. In this case, they are called transactional lawyers, corporate lawyers, or attorney-advisors. The latter mostly work for the Federal government.

Lawyers may become specialized, which results in them not pleading very often. Among the many activities are those that consist in drafting legal opinion letters and wills or trust documents, advising clients, structuring business transactions, negotiating and drafting contracts, developing tax strategies, or preparing and prosecuting filings with government agencies, such as the Internal Revenue Service, the Securities and Exchange Commission, or the Patent and Trademark Office. But, whether they choose to plead or not, most American lawyers specialize in a very specific area of Law.

Legally qualified?

Paradoxically, some jurisdictions will allow a non-attorney to sit as a judge, usually in lower courts or in hearings by governmental agencies, even though a non-attorney may not practice in these same courts. Similarly, in a jurisdiction where a judge is elected by the people, the judge often does not need to be licensed to practice law or trained in any particular way. Likewise, the U.S. Constitution does not provide any such requirement for a U.S. Supreme Court justice or other federal judge, although no non-lawyer has ever been appointed as a federal judge.

The position of one lawyer to the next might be quite different, and they are usually ranked in different categories:

- **Outside counsel** (law firms) **vs. in-house counsel** (corporate legal department)
- **Plaintiff v. Defense Attorneys** (some attorneys do both plaintiff and defense work, others only handle certain types of cases like personal injury, business etc.)
- **Transactional** (or "office practice") **attorneys** (who negotiate and draft documents and advise clients, rarely going to court) **v. litigators** (who advise clients in the context of legal disputes both in and out of court, including lawsuits, arbitrations and negotiated settlements)
- **Trial attorneys** (who argue the facts) **v. appellate attorneys** (who argue the law)

Specialization is a good way for lawyers to find new clients in other States in which they do not practice. However, some States are reticent, or even forbid, lawyers from specializing, except if they are registered with the Bar in the State in question, and/or have been awarded a specific degree in this specialized area, such as California, which created degrees specialized in Family Law, appellate practice, Criminal Law, bankruptcy, estate planning, immigration, taxation and workers' compensation. Other States tolerate suggestive texts, such as *"our practice is limited to . . .",* but lawyers must state so in their advertisements that it is not certified by a state board of legal specialization in the advertised practice area (*read p. 151*).

NYU

Founded in 1831, New York University is the largest private university in the United States. It is composed of 14 schools, colleges, and divisions, and occupies five major centers in Manhattan.

Patent attorneys:
Specializing as a patent attorney is, on the other hand, required for practicing in this area of Law. It is strictly controlled by the Office of Enrollment and Discipline of the U.S. Patent and Trademark Office, and the rules are very strict. Among them, is one that foresees that the lawyer practicing in this sector must have obtained a degree in the hard Sciences or in Engineering.

Plaintiff Attorney   **Defense Attorney**

ACTIVITY

A. Reading about the various specializations available, what would your personal choice be?

....

....

....

B. Why does specialization provide the possibility to find new clients in other states?

....

....

....

PATENT LAWYER

DOCUMENT 6

A Patent Lawyer's job description

A patent lawyer has a fascinating job, learning about new inventions and cutting-edge technology. Applying for a patent can be a difficult and time-consuming process, so inventors rely on patent lawyers to prepare their patent applications and defend them against infringement.

Duties

When preparing a patent application, an attorney must search for any prior work done on the same type of invention and ensure the scientific and legal accuracy behind the inventor's claims. A patent lawyer determines who owns the rights to various parts of an invention. The lawyer drafts the patent application and works with the United States Patent and Trademark Office, USPTO, to resolve any questions the patent examiner may have about the application. The attorney also licenses the patent after it is approved and represents clients whose patents have been infringed upon.

Education and Qualifications

Most patent lawyers have Bachelor's Degrees in a science, such as Physics or Chemistry. They also must have a Juris Doctor, or J.D., degree from an accredited law school. In addition to passing their state's Bar Exam and being a licensed attorney, a patent lawyer must also pass the USPTO's patent bar. The patent bar tests USPTO procedures, ethics and statutes. If an attorney does not have a Bachelor's Degree in a science field, he must take enough science credits, as defined by the USPTO, to qualify to sit for the Patent Bar. Most patent lawyers specialize in a specific area of science or technology, such as chemistry, physics or electrical engineering.

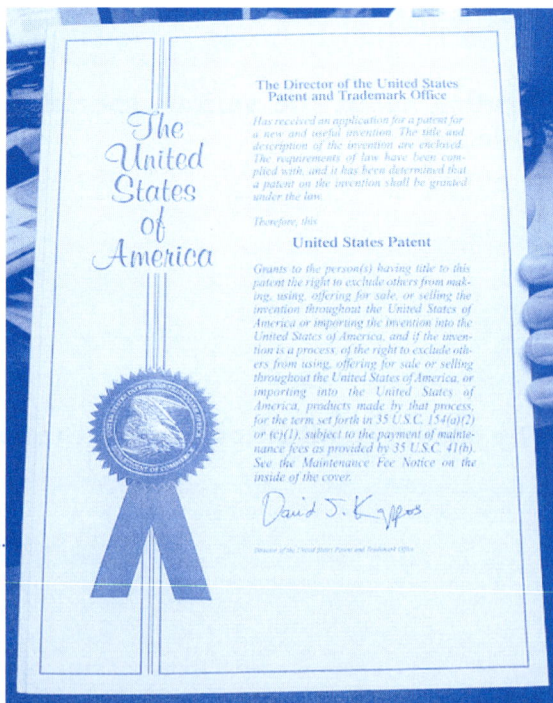

Work Environment

Patent lawyers typically work for intellectual property firms or corporations. Some may also work for universities or organizations that fund inventors and their research. They may also work for the Federal government as patent examiners. The hours that patent attorneys work every week may be very long and intense, since their work requires a high degree of concentration and analysis of very technical information.

Salary and Employment

The USPTO reports that there are approximately 29,000 patent lawyers actively practicing in the United States. The annual average income of a patent lawyer ranges from $110,000 to $121,800. The exact salary depends on an attorney's education, specialization and years of experience. Patent lawyers who are partners at private law firms earn an average of $415,000 a year.

Patent lawyers seen by cartoonists

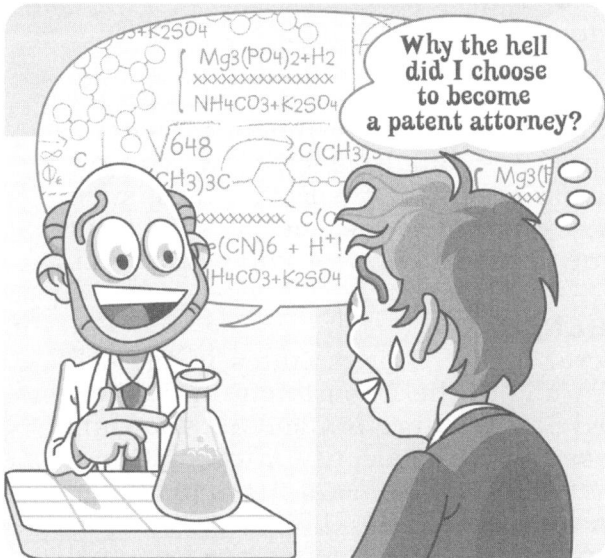

DOCUMENT 7

ACTIVITY

A. What differs in a patent lawyer's education compared to other attorneys?

B. What do the cartoons tell us about a patent lawyer's job and why is that important?

PART 4 – FROM DEFENSE TO PROSECUTION

The Prosecutor is the legal representative of the prosecution in Common Law countries (the adversarial system), or in Civil Law countries (the inquisitorial system). He has the responsibility of presenting the charges brought against the accused during the trial. In the United States, the names given to the prosecutors vary from State to State. It may be City Attorney, as is the most common, but may also be:

- *State's Attorney* (in Connecticut, Maryland, and Vermont),
- *County Attorney* (Arizona),
- *District Attorney* (in Georgia, Massachusetts, New York, Pennsylvania, Oklahoma, and Texas),
- *District Attorney General* (in Tennessee),
- *Prosecuting Attorney* (in Hawaii, Idaho, Indiana, Ohio, Michigan, Washington counties, and West Virginia),
- *Commonwealth's Attorney* (Kentucky and Virginia),
- *State Prosecutor* or *Attorney General* (in Delaware and Rhode Island),
- *County Prosecutor* (in New Jersey),
- *City Prosecutor* (Missouri et Washington),
- *Solicitor* (South Carolina).

Prosecutors are most often elected. United States Attorneys represent the Federal government in Federal Courts, whether civil or criminal. Federal law requires that prosecutors follow certain very specific rules, such as disclosing material evidence to the defense, as a result of the 1963 Supreme Court ruling of *Brady v. Maryland*.

U.S. SOLICITOR GENERAL

The Solicitor General of the United States is the 4th highest in the hierarchy of the Department of Justice, just after the United States Attorney General, who runs the Ministry; his assistant, the Deputy Attorney General; and the Associate Attorney General. He is in charge of leading the representation of the U.S. government in Court, and it is usually he, or his deputy (the Principal Deputy Solicitor General) that pleads for the government in the Supreme Court, either because it is a party to the court proceedings, or because it wished to intervene, or that the Supreme Court had requested his opinion.

His job does not include managing criminal proceedings, in which it is essentially only necessary to show proof of guilt of the accused, since that task is left to the United States attorneys, who are supervised by the Deputy At-

DID YOU KNOW?
Attorneys may be addressed by the post-nominal letters Esq., the abbreviated form of the word Esquire.

How will I dress up?
Unlike their counterparts in other common law jurisdictions, American attorneys are not required to wear wigs, robes or any other items of court dress when they appear in court. They are usually expected to wear contemporary business suits. The one exception is the United States Solicitor General and other U.S. Department of Justice attorneys, who traditionally argue before the U.S. Supreme Court in 19th-century morning dress.

You must be qualified
Some States provide criminal penalties for falsely holding oneself out to the public as an Attorney at law and the unautho-rized practice of law by a non-Attorney.

torney General. But the United States Attorney General intervenes if the case is appealed. He is then the person charged with representing the Federal government before the U.S. Supreme Court. His office, incidentally, is in the same building as the Supreme Court and he is frequently nicknamed the "Tenth Justice". Four Deputy Solicitors General and 17 Assistants to the Solicitor General assist the Solicitor General.

U.S. ATTORNEY GENERAL

The United States Attorney General (AG) is the Minister of the United States Department of Justice. He is part of the President's Cabinet, who, by the way, is the one who nominates someone for the job. The nomination must be confirmed by the Senate, as stipulated in the Consti-tution. He may be replaced at any moment. The official creation of this post was completed with the Judiciary Act of 1789, having the function to "prosecute and conduct all suits in the Supreme Court in which the United States shall be concerned, and to give his advice and opinion upon questions of law when required by the President of the United States, or when requested by the heads of any of the departments." Eric Holder holds the post as of 2014, being the first African-American to do so, and having been nominated by President Obama.

Out-of-State
In most States, the practice of law by an «out-of-state» lawyer is considered unauthorized practice of law within that state, even if the lawyer is licensed in good standing in one or more other states.

Lawyer or Attorney-at-Law?
A person who has a professional law degree, but is not admitted to a State bar is not an Attorney-at-Law but may be considered a lawyer (one learned in the law, according to Black's Law Dictionary) since he or she does not hold a license issued by a state. For example, Presi-dents Obama and Clinton are lawyers, as both men have law degrees and thus are «learned in the law.» Nevertheless, they are no longer Attorneys-at-Law because neither holds a current law license in any State, and thus cannot legally engage in the practice of law.

ACTIVITY

A. How would you translate «U.S. Attorney General»? What is specific to this American position?

B. Why is it untrue to say that, upon being sworn in, American lawyers may choose to become a public prosecutor?

THE CASE OF THE DETECTIVE

The Pinkertons and the Molly Maguires

DOCUMENT 8

Allan Pinkerton, a deputy-sheriff in Chicago, formed the Pinkerton Detective
5 Agency in 1852. The first detective agency in the United States, it solved a series of train
10 robberies. In 1861, the agency was given the task of guarding Abraham Lincoln. While in Baltimore, on the way
15 to the inauguration, Pinkerton foiled a plot to assassinate the President.

Pinkerton became
20 head of the American secret service during the Civil War and in 1875 used an agent, James McParland, to
25 infiltrate the secret organization, the Molly Maguires. McParlan's evidence in court resulted in the execution
30 of twenty of its members.

The Pinkerton Detective Agency was a great success. On the facade of his three-story Chicago head-
35 quarters was the company slogan, «We Never Sleep». Above this was a huge, black and white eye. The Pinkerton logo was the origin of the term private eye. In 1873, Franklin B. Gowen, president of the Philadelphia & Reading Railroad, had a meeting with
40 Allan Pinkerton of the Pinkerton Detective Agency. Gowen had considerable investments in the coalmines of Schuylkill County and feared that the trade union activities of John Siney and the Workingmen's Benevolent Association would result in lower profits.
45 Allan Pinkerton decided to send James McParland to Schuylkill County. Assuming the alias of James McKenna, he found work as a laborer in Shenandoah. Soon afterwards he joined the Workingmen's Benevolent Association and the Shenandoah branch of the
50 Ancient Order of Hibernians (AOH), an organization

$2000 REWARD

DESCRIPTION:

Age—60 years.
Height—5 ft. 8 in.
Weight—125-135 lbs.
Build—Slender.
Complexion—Sallow.
Hair—Jet Black.
Eyes—Dark (bead).
Nose—Prominent.
Teeth, tested toward right side, imitating break.

Remarks:

Walks like an Indian, toes straight forward.
At times uses a disguise.
May wear natural black beard.
He is a lawyer by profession, is well versed in horses and horse racing.
Has conducted a newspaper.
He is a telegrapher.
Owns a large ranch near Chama, New Mexico.

JOHN P. LOONEY

Indicted for Murder in Rock Island County, Rock Island, Ill.

The above reward is offered by the Citizens Committee of Rock Island, Illinois, for the apprehension and return to Rock Island, Illinois of John P. Looney. Any information regarding Looney can be telegraphed at our expense to the nearest of the above listed offices.

Postmasters, Police Officers, Sheriffs, Hotel Proprietors, and all persons receiving this circular will confer a favor by posting it in a conspicuous place.

Under its rules PINKERTON'S NATIONAL DETECTIVE AGENCY does not operate for rewards, therefore will not accept, nor permit any of its employes to accept this reward or any part thereof.

Pinkerton's National Detective Agency

Reward Expires February 1, 1924   117 South Wells St. CHICAGO, ILL.   Telephone Main 282

for Irish immigrants run by the Roman Catholic clergy.

After a few months of investigations McParland 55 reported back to Allan Pinkerton that some members of the Ancient Order of Hibernians were also active in the secret organization, the Molly Maguires. 60 McParland estimated that the group had about 3,000 members. Each county was governed by a body- 65 master who recruited members and gave out orders to commit crimes. These bodymasters were usually ex-miners who 70 now worked as saloon keepers.

Over a two-year period James McParland collected evidence about 75 the criminal activities of the Molly Maguires. This included the murder of around 50 men in Schuyl- kill County. Many of these 80 men were the managers of coal mines in the region.

John Kehoe, one of the leaders of the Molly Maguires, became suspicious of McParland and began to investigate his past. McParland was tipped off that Kehoe 85 was planning to murder him so he fled from the area. In 1876 and 1877, James McParland was the star witness for the prosecution of John Kehoe and the Molly Maguires. Twenty members were found guilty of murder and were executed. This included Kehoe, 90 a former union leader who was convicted of a murder that had taken place 14 years previously.

After Allan Pinkerton died in 1884, the Pinkerton Detective Agency was run by his two sons, Robert Pinkerton and William Pinkerton. The brothers opened 95 their fourth office in Denver. They appointed James McParland and Charlie Siringo to run the Pinkerton's western division.

Private Investigators (P.I.)

DOCUMENT 9

A private investigator (*often abbreviated to P.I. and informally called a private eye*), a private detective or inquiry agent, is a person who can be hired by individuals or groups to undertake investigatory law services. Private detectives/investigators often work for attorneys in civil cases. A handful of very skilled private detectives/investigators work with defense attorneys on capital punishment and criminal defense cases. Many work for insurance companies to investigate suspicious claims. Before the advent of no-fault divorce, many private investigators were hired to search out evidence of adultery or other conduct within marriage to establish grounds for a divorce. Despite the lack of legal necessity for such evidence in many jurisdictions, according to press reports collecting evidence of adultery or other «bad behavior» by spouses and partners is still one of the most profitable activities investigators undertake, as the stakes being fought over now are child custody, alimony, or marital property disputes.

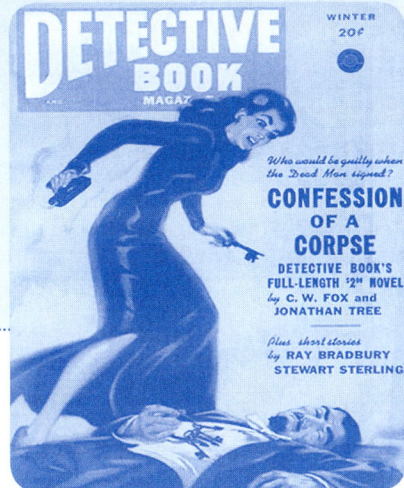

DETECTIVE BOOK MAGAZINE — WINTER 20¢
Who would be guilty when the Dead Man signed?
CONFESSION OF A CORPSE
DETECTIVE BOOK'S FULL-LENGTH $2 NOVEL by C. W. FOX and JONATHAN TREE
Plus short stories by RAY BRADBURY STEWART STERLING

DOCUMENT 10

What a P.I. cannot (legally) get

There are a number of misconceptions about what a professional private investigator can legally obtain. These myths may begin with your matrimonial client's insistence that her husband has secret bank account, or your colleague has boasted about how his investigators found the smoking gun in the opponent's phone records, or it is possible that you picked up some ideas from the latest corporate espionage page-turner... No matter what the reason, you need the information and you need it now! So why cannot your private investigator get it for you? Typically, there are two reasons for this: First, the information may be private and protected by either State or Federal statute. In this case, your investigator may be able to identify where the information is located. Location is extremely useful information for leverage in negotiations, future subpoena requests, or discovery motions. In some cases (*e.g.* employment or insurance fraud investigations), you may have a previously-signed release from the subject that will allow you to access this private information. The second reason is that the information simply does not exist. The information may not be compiled into a single database or a comprehensive format. An investigator may ultimately be able to obtain the information, but the process is not as simple as you might think.

ACTIVITY

A. What was the method used by the Pinkertons for finding evidence to bring to court?

B. What are some of the various names given to private investigators in the United States?

C. Everybody is "Googleing" everybody now. Is it legal to Google someone?

Important words:

**Attorney-at-Law
the Bar
litigation
juris doctor
LL.M.
patent
prosecution**

ATTORNEYS-AT-LAW

Around 70% of lawyers in the world are located in the United States. Most of them work for small firms, or by themselves. Large firms also exist that employ more than a thousand lawyers. There is no difference in the United States between lawyers who plead and the others: they are attorneys-at-law. There are no notaries as in Roman law systems, except in Louisiana. An American lawyer may practice as a Defense or Prosecuting Attorney. To become a lawyer, one must pass the Bar Exam. Once you are admitted to the Bar Association, you can begin to practice, plead, advise clients, and draft or authenticate contracts and official documents. Contrary to the popular image, most of a lawyer's time is spent in case files looking for precedents. In criminal court, they spend a great deal of time creating their strategy. All lawyers do not plead, though; some are specialized in certain editorial or advisory tasks.

EDUCATION

To become a lawyer in the United States, you must pass the LSAT to be accepted into Law School. As soon as they finish their first year in college, students can work for a law firm with the title, Certified Student Attorney. In many States, they are even authorized to plead, under certain conditions. The degree conferred to a law student is the Juris Doctor (J.D.). In all other Anglophone countries, it is typically an LL.B or an LL.M (a Bachelor of Laws or a Master of Laws), but they are reserved to certain specialized sectors, like Tax Litigation, or foreign legal jurists. The Bar Exams are administered by each State, and so are different from one State to the next. You can also take a Multistate Bar Examination since 1972. These exams address Common Law issues, except for Louisiana.

SPECIALIZATION

Not all attorneys choose to plead in Court. Some specialize and work in administration, or for a company. In fact, many types of lawyers exist: those who work for law firms, those who work in companies, those who plead and those who do not, those who work for the Defense, those who are Prosecuting Attorneys, those who plead in trial courts, and those who debate on the interpretation of law in Appeals Courts. Many specialize in a particular area of Law, which may also allow them to find new clients from other States. To become a patent attorney, the legal expert must also hold a degree in Science or Engineering.

FROM DEFENSE TO PROSECUTION

The Prosecutor's job is to present society's point of view during the trial and the charges brought against the Defendant. The title is very different from State to State: States' Attorney, District Attorney, Commonwealth's Attorney, State Prosecutor, etc. Prosecutors are most often elected. U.S. Attorney Generals represent the government at a Federal level. The highest-ranking among them, the U.S. Solicitor General, who is the fourth person in the American legal system, is in charge of representing the United States before the Supreme Court. His office is located inside the Supreme Court building and he is often referred to as the "10th Justice". The Minister of Justice is called the U.S. Attorney General. He is a part of the government, and is nominated by the U.S. President, and confirmed by the Senate.

A. Decide if the following facts about the lawyers are true or false?

	True	False
1. It is estimated that the U.S.A. has 70% of the world's		
2. As soon as they are admitted to the Bar, American layers can file legal pleadings and argue cases.		
3. There are three differents Bars according to lawyers'		
4. Civil Law is recognized by five States: Louisiana, Oklahoma, Vermont, New Jersey and South Dakota.		
5. Some States recognizes foreign degrees.		
6. Becoming a patent attorney is not possible to all lawyers.		

B. What is the waiting period for lawyers to start working after passing the Bar exam?

....
....

C. How was the biggest change in the U.S.A. in regards to advertizing introduced, and what was it?

....
....

D. Why can't you publish a template of a will on your blog, depending on the State in which you live?

....
....

E. When can somebody be called an Attorney-at-Law?

....
....

REFERENCES:

Page 147. "Graduating students", by Sasikiran, Wikimedia. http://commons. wikimedia.org/wiki/File:Graduating_students.JPG
Page 148. "The real firm", by Dimitri Champain
Page 150. "Jeb Williams", by Keith Sarver
"Lawyer's Ad 2", by Keith Sarver
Page 151. "Vincent Allard", rights given by Vincent Allard.
"The point of view of an insider", from Blog de Vincent Allard, http://www. corpomax.com/blog/publicite-des-avocats/ rights given by Vincent Allard.
Page 152. "Education", by Dimitri Champain
Page 153. "Interview with a student going to America", authorization given by Axelle Vivien.
"Axelle Vivien", rights given by Axelle Vivien.
Page 154. "Interview with a student who studied in the U.S.A.", authorization given by Alexandre Gelblat.
"Alexandre Gelblat", rights given by Alexandre Gelblat
Page 155. "Law rankings by graduates in BigLaw jobs", New Law Journal, February 24, 2014 (http://taxprof.typepad.com/taxprof_blog/2014/02/nlj-law-school. html)
"Promotion from associates to partners", New Law Journal, February 24 2014 (http://www.nationallawjournal.com/id=1392735234358?slretu rm=20140204091630)
Page 157. "Plaintiff attorney v. Defense attorney", by Dimitri Champain
Page 158. "A Patent Lawyer's job description", adapted from Stephanie Dube Wilson, in Global Post, January 2014

"Yt Patent". Wikimedia. http://commons.wikimedia.org/wiki/File:Yt_patent. gif?uselang=fr
"D'Amo patent", by Asamouse, Wikimedia. http://commons.wikimedia. org/wiki/File:D%27Amo_Patent.jpg
Page 159. "Patent lawyers seen by cartoonist", by Dimitri Champlain,
Page 160. "Inquisitorial and adversarial", by Dimitri Champain
Page 161. "Inquisitorial and adversarial", by Dimitri Champain
Page 162. "The Pinkertons and the Molly Maguires", in Spartacus. http://www.spartacus.schoolnet.co.uk/USApinkertonD.htm
"Looney reward poster", by Pinkerton detective Agency, Wikimedia. The Pinkertons and the Molly Maguires. http:// commons.wikimedia.org/wiki/File:Looney_reward_poster.jpg
Page 163. "Private investigators". adapted from http://en.wikipedia.org/wiki/Pri vate_investigator
"Detective Book pulp v5n10", Wikimedia. http://commons.wikimedia.org/ wiki/File:DetectiveBook_pulp_v5n10.jpg?uselang=fr
Page 164. "Summary", by Dimitri Champain
Page 165. "Review", by Dimitri Champain

The Judiciary

Introduction

People have the tendency to see judges as the most power-ful players in the judicial system. Their decisions influence the actions of the Police, attorneys and prosecutors. If they show themselves to be more tolerant towards certain crimes, for example, then the Police and prosecutors would be less inclined to sue and to stop those who commit the crimes in question. We always imagine judges in their courtroom; what we do not realize is that the majority of their work takes place outside Court.

9

PART 1 – ADVERSARY v. INQUISITORIAL

More than anything else, a judge is supposed to represent Justice, to insure that the principle of due process is respected and that the accused is treated fairly. The black robe and gavel are symbols of impartiality. We expect a judge to render consistent and wise verdicts, which correspond to the ideals of justice held by every American. Yet, time limitations and a huge number of cases do not always speak in favor of justice that is efficient. All judges are addressed as "Your Honor", and one must stand in deference whenever they enter or leave the courtroom. This does not mean that all judges are highly qualified and fair. Judges often are chosen for reasons that have little to do with either their legal qualifications or their legal conduct. Instead, they may be chosen because of their political ties, friendships with influential officials, or contributions to political parties.

The image of a courtroom is always the same: two opposing attorneys, or a lawyer and a prosecutor. The judge is seated between them, a bit higher, following the debate, and doing what is necessary for the trial to end in a just solution. While lawyers attempt to determine the facts and to inform the jury, the judge endeavors to respect the Law. He interprets the laws at his disposal, whether it has to do with statutes or decisions in prior cases, and he applies his interpretation of circumstances specific to each case. Judges are expected to remain separate from the others who are involved in the trial, and that their decision will be based on their own interpretation of the Law.

> **While lawyers attempt to determine the facts and to inform the jury, the judge endeavors to respect the law.**

Adoption of the Judiciary Act of 1789
The bill continued from where the Constitutional Convention had left off, creating greater compromises between the Federalists and Anti-Federalists. Just as the Federalists wanted, a three-tier federal judiciary came about as a result of the act, while also limiting the jurisdiction of the Federal Courts. It also provided important provisions that the Anti-Federalists wanted: it set a high monetary threshold for diversity cases (cases where the litigants are from different States), and gave the State Courts concurrent jurisdiction over many federal issues. Such compromises meant that each side was sufficiently satisfied.

DID YOU KNOW?
The adversary process is the Court process employed in the United States in which lawyers for each side represent their clients' best interests in presenting evidence and formulating arguments as a means to discover the truth and protect the rights of defendants. In the U.S.A. both state and Federal Courts use the adversary process.

What reinforces the image of American judges is the predominance of the adversary system. Into this system, the Prosecution and the Defense must exhibit a lot of skill to convince the judge and the jury, proving that their client is right, or that he is guilty or innocent, according to which side one is on.

The judge acts as a sort of referee, first working hard to verify that each party respects the applicable rules of court. And this role is even more necessary when both parties are not necessarily subject to the same rules: the Defense Attorney and the Prosecutor do not often have the same experience or knowledge. Moreover, Prosecutors have the advantage of being able to use the work of the Police to find the proof they need. Not all lawyers have considerable resources at their disposal to do the same job, especially those who are appointed to represent poor defendants. That's why many countries choose another system, assigning another role to judges. This is the case in France, which has an inquisitorial system. A judge is specifically nominated to investigate the facts of a criminal trial (the investigating judge). At the end of his investigation, he drafts a report with his conclusions. Then a trial is organized and three judges (a chief judge and two associate judges), along with a jury of nine citizens for the most serious cases, must determine if the accused is guilty and will be sentenced. During the trial, the defendant is questioned in Open Court. In the French system, the Chief-Judge may be active in convincing the jury of the defendant's guilt. In the German system, the Chief-Judge asks questions based on the report prepared by the investigating judge. The Defending Attorney and the Prosecutor are supposed to help the judge discover the truth and must limit their questions to presenting the facts objectively, rather than clearly taking sides and playing the role they have been given. It is difficult to say which system is more just; but American judges think that the adversary system that they use protects the fundamental rights of citizens, while in France, the Police and the investigating judges may very easily pry into people's private lives during their investigations.

The role of the American judge is however more mundane day-to-day: most judges spend their days listening to minor issues and have to cope with hearing after hearing at a fast pace. They make their decisions on their own and sometimes it is routine work, much less exciting compared to major criminal cases.

ACTIVITY

A. How does the public view judges?

....

....

....

....

B. How do the adversary and inquisitorial systems differ?

....

....

....

....

THE SUPREME COURT

DOCUMENT 1

A brief overview of the Supreme Court

Members (as of 2014):

Chief Justice of the USA: JOHN G. ROBERTS, JR.

Associate Justices: ANTONIN SCALIA
ANTHONY M. KENNEDY
CLARENCE THOMAS
RUTH BADER GINSBURG
STEPHEN G. BREYER
SAMUEL A. ALITO, JR.
SONIA SOTOMAYOR
ELENA KAGAN

Retired Justices: SANDRA DAY O'CONNOR
DAVID H. SOUTER
JOHN PAUL STEVENS

"Equal Justice Under Law"
carved on the facade of the Supreme Court

The Supreme Court consists of the Chief Justice of the United States, and such number of Associate Justices as may be fixed by Congress. The number of Associate Justices is currently fixed at eight. Power to nominate the Justices is vested in the President of the United States, and appointments are made with the advice and consent of the Senate. Article III, §1, of the Constitution further provides that "[t]he Judges, both of the supreme and inferior Courts, shall hold their Offices during good Behaviour, and shall, at stated Times, receive for their Services, a Compensation, which shall not be diminished during their Continuance in Office."

Court Officers assist the Court in the performance of its functions. They include the Counselor to the Chief Justice, the Clerk, the Librarian, the Marshal, the Reporter of Decisions, the Court Counsel, the Curator, the Director of Information Technology, and the Public Information Officer. The Counselor is appointed by the Chief Justice. The Clerk, Reporter of Decisions, Librarian, and Marshal are appointed by the Court. All other Court Officers are appointed by the Chief Justice in consultation with the Court.

Jurisdiction. According to the Constitution (Art. III, §2): "In all Cases affecting Ambassadors, other public ministers and Consuls, and those in which a State shall be Party, the supreme Court shall have original Jurisdiction. In all the other Cases before mentioned, the supreme Court shall have appellate jurisdiction, both as to Law and Fact, with such Exceptions, and under such Regulations as the Congress shall make."

Appellate Jurisdiction has been conferred upon the Supreme Court by various statutes, under the authority given Congress by the Constitution. The basic statute effective at this time in conferring and controlling jurisdiction of the Supreme Court may be found in 28 U. S. C. §1251 et seq., and various special statutes.

Rulemaking Power. Congress has from time to time conferred upon the Supreme Court power to prescribe rules of procedure to be followed by the lower courts of the United States.

The Term. The Term of the Court begins, by law, on the first Monday in October and lasts until the first Monday in October of the next year. Approximately 10,000 petitions are filed with the Court in the course of a Term. In addition, some 1,200 applications of various kinds are filed each year that can be acted upon by a single Justice.

Who is the Chief? The Chief Justice of the United States is the head of the U.S. Federal Court system and the highest judicial officer in the country. He also serves as a spokesman for the Judicial Branch. He is directly nominated by the President of the United States to the position of Chief, even if he was not a member of the Supreme Court before (this was the case with John Roberts, who did not have any previous experience in the Supreme Court before his nomination).

«OYEZ! OYEZ!» : The Court and its procedures

DOCUMENT 2

A Term of the Supreme Court begins, by statute, on the first Monday in October. Usually Court sessions continue until late June or early July. The Term is divided between "sittings," when the Justices hear
5 cases and deliver opinions, and intervening "recesses," when they consider the business before the Court and write opinions. Sittings and recesses alternate at approximately two-week intervals.

With rare exceptions, each side is allowed 30 minutes
10 argument, and up to 24 cases may be argued at one sitting. Since the majority of cases involve the review of a decision of some other court, there is no jury and no witnesses are heard. For each case, the Court has before it a record of prior proceedings and printed
15 briefs containing the arguments of each side.

During the intervening recess period, the Justices study the argued and forthcoming cases and work on their opinions. Each week the Justices must also evaluate more than 130 petitions seeking review of
20 judgments of state and federal courts to determine which cases are to be granted full review with oral arguments by attorneys.

When the Court is sitting, public sessions begin promptly at 10 a.m. and continue until 3 p.m., with
25 a one-hour lunch recess starting at noon. No public sessions are held on Thursdays or Fridays. On Fridays, during and preceding argument weeks, the Justices meet to discuss the argued cases and to discuss and vote on petitions for review.
30 When the Court is in session, the 10 a.m. entrance of the Justices into the Courtroom is announced by the Marshal. Those present, at the sound of the gavel, arise and remain standing until the robed Justices are seated following the traditional chant: "The Honorable, the Chief Justice and the Associate Justices of the 35 Supreme Court of the United States. Oyez! Oyez! Oyez! All persons having business before the Honorable, the Supreme Court of the United States, are admonished to draw near and give their attention, for the Court is now sitting. God save the United States and this 40 Honorable Court!"

Prior to hearing oral argument, other business of the Court is transacted. On Monday mornings this includes the release of an Order List, a public report of Court actions including the acceptance and rejection 45 of cases, and the admission of new members to the Court Bar. Opinions are typically released on Tuesday and Wednesday mornings and on the third Monday of each sitting, when the Court takes the Bench but no arguments are heard. 50

The Court maintains this schedule each Term until all cases ready for submission have been heard and decided. In May and June the Court sits only to announce orders and opinions. The Court recesses at the end of June, but the work of the Justices is 55 unending. During the summer, they continue to analyze new petitions for review, consider motions and applications, and must make preparations for cases scheduled for fall argument.

ACTIVITY

A. **What do the words "Equal Justice Under law" mean to you?**

B. **What do you know about the qualifications for federal judges?**

C. **Supreme Court Justices and most of other federal courts judges "hold their offices during good behaviour". What does that mean? What are the advantages and disadvanatages of this system?**

PART 2 – WHO BECOMES A JUDGE?

William Hubbs Rehnquist
(1924-2005) He was an American lawyer, jurist and political figure who served as an Associate Justice of the Supreme Court and later as 16th Chief Justice.

John Glover Roberts, Jr.
(1955-) He is the 17th and current Chief Justice of the U.S.A. (at the time of printing). He has served since 2005, having been nominated by President Bush after the death of Chief Justice William Renhquist.

DID YOU KNOW?
Minority Judges
In 2014, Diane Humetawa was appointed to be the first Native American woman (Hopi tribe) to ever serve as a Judge at the Federal level (District Court of Arizona). The first African American Judge was appointed in 1950 (William Hastie); the first Hispanic in 1961 (Raynaldo Garza); the first Asian in 1971 (Herbert Choy). The first woman, Florence Allen, was appointed in 1950.

In American society, a judge's position is an important one, even judges in the lower courts. Many of those who become a judge could also have a different job and earn much more money. But maybe the prestige, the political power and service to the public are more important motivations in the eyes of some.

Among the factors that might explain why being a judge could be attractive, one may cite the impressive flexibility of work hours. While attorneys must work many more than 40 hours per week, judges are able to create their own schedule and finish at whatever time they wish. So, they can do what they want with their evenings, although the lawyers are preparing a case, preparing a brief or meeting with a client. This benefit is often showcased as being a plus for this job.

Historically, the largest majority of judges were white men with an established political network. Men and women from minority groups had little chance to get a job in the profession. Fittingly, this was a problem for the immense majority of defendants from minority groups. The risk was that these groups would not feel fairly judged because justice was in the hands of small group of privileged individuals who did not resemble them.

The caricature of the white judge, middle-aged, from the middle or upper class of society could have become a problem for the United States. Among the most respected judges, we find those who preside in the Civil Courts and especially those in the Appeals Courts or the Superior Courts of the States. Less attention is drawn to the judges sitting in the Criminal Courts within the judicial hierarchy.

Maybe the status of a judge is directly linked to that of the people he serves. Judges in criminal cases are in contact with the worst members of the society. Even when not involved in the most extreme cases, they spend their days listening to stories where each is just as tragic as the next, surrounded by people confronted by human misery: drugs, poverty, and violence are part of their daily lives and their work takes place in the busiest, noisiest, and least attractive courtrooms.

This is far and above the solemn atmosphere in the higher Civil Courts where wood and marble are often the dominant materials, combined with large, red velvet curtains that give an oppressive and striking impression to the setting. This might explain why many judges spend their careers trying to move from the Civil to the Criminal Courts.

ACTIVITY

A. What are some different motivations for someone to become a judge?

....

....

....

....

....

B. What are some elements in Court that are created to impress people?

....

....

....

....

....

EVERYBODY'S A JUDGE?

DOCUMENT 3

The waves that minority judges make?

Read also «Being a woman or being a judge?», Unit 6, p. 123, Document 9

Justice Thurgood Marshall, the first black member of the Supreme Court, ended his 24 years there bitter and frustrated. He had been unable, he said, to persuade his colleagues in many cases concerning racial
5 equality, the cause to which he had devoted his life. "What do they know about Negroes?" Justice Marshall asked an interviewer. "You can't name one member of this Court who knows anything about Negroes before he came to this Court."
10 But the other justices did get to know Justice Marshall, and even the more conservative ones acknowledged that his very presence exerted a gravitational pull more powerful than his single vote.
"Marshall could be a persuasive force just by sitting
15 there," Justice Antonin Scalia told Juan Williams in an interview for a biography of Justice Marshall, recalling the justices' private conferences about cases. "He wouldn't have to open his mouth to affect the nature of the conference and how seriously the
20 conference would take matters of race."
President Obama's nomination of Judge Sonia Sotomayor to serve on the Supreme Court, where she would be the first Hispanic and the third woman, has raised questions about how her background would
25 affect her decision-making. But there is another question, too: How would she alter the broader dynamic among the justices?
The first woman on the court, Justice Sandra Day O'Connor, often says that wise old women and wise
30 old men reach the same conclusions. Justice Ruth Bader Ginsburg, the second woman to serve on the Supreme Court and currently the only female justice, said that she and Justice O'Connor, who preceded her, brought a distinct perspective to the court.
35 "As often as Justice O'Connor and I have disagreed, because she is truly a Republican from Arizona, we were together in all the gender discrimination cases," Justice Ginsburg recently told Joan Biskupic of *USA Today*.
40 But Justice Ginsburg said her own influence in all sorts of cases at the justices' conferences was uncertain. "I will say something – and I don't think I'm a confused speaker – and it isn't until somebody else says it that everyone will focus on the point," Justice
45 Ginsburg said.
Mark Tushnet, a law professor at Harvard and an authority on the Supreme Court, said Justice O'Connor's arrival at the court "did affect the way other justices responded."

"These are older guys," Mr. Tushnet said. "They 50 haven't dealt with women on a professional basis on the whole." Similarly, he said, "very few of the present justices have interacted as equals with Hispanic professionals." All justices bring their life experiences to the bench in some sense, of course, and Justices 55 Marshall, O'Connor and Ginsburg seemed to devote special attention to cases involving the groups they belonged to.
In a 1992 reminiscence, Justice O'Connor wrote that Justice Marshall was "constantly pushing and prod- 60 ding us to respond not only to the persuasiveness of legal argument but also to the power of moral truth." She recalled the moving stories Justice Marshall would tell to support his view that racism played a pernicious role in the administration of capital 65 punishment.
It is not clear, though, that any of those stories caused Justice O'Connor to change her vote. "Justice O'Connor was not nearly as sympathetic to racial civil rights claims as she was to gender claims," said 70 Lawrence Baum, a political science professor at Ohio State.
Justice Clarence Thomas, the second African-American justice, is by some measures the most conservative justice since 1937, while Justice Marshall was 75 the most liberal. "Thomas is living proof and a daily reminder that not everyone from a particular background has a particular point of view," said David J. Garrow, a historian at Cambridge University, in England. 80
Judge Sotomayor has attracted attention for her musings in a 2001 speech about the impact her background might have on her decision-making, remarks a White House spokesman on Friday said reflected a poor choice of words. 85
"I would hope," she said, "that a wise Latina woman with the richness of her experience would more often than not reach a better conclusion than a white male who hasn't lived that life."
She added, in a less-noted passage, that giants on 90 the Court, including Justice Benjamin Cardozo, the second Jewish justice, had on occasion stumbled. "Let us not forget that wise men like Oliver Wendell Holmes and Justice Cardozo voted on cases which upheld both sex and race discrimination in our 95 society," Judge Sotomayor said.

How judges and Justices are chosen

DOCUMENT 4

Legendary Justice Oliver Wendell Holmes once said that a Supreme Court Justice should be a «combination of Justinian, Jesus Christ, and John Marshall.» The Constitution is silent on judicial qualifications. It
5 meticulously outlines qualifications for the House of Representatives, the Senate, and the presidency, but it does not give any advice for judicial appointments other than stating that justices should exhibit «good behavior.» As a result, selections are governed prima-
10 rily by tradition.

The Nomination Process
The Constitution provides broad parameters for the judicial nomination process. It gives the res-
15 ponsibility for nominating Federal judges and Justices to the President. It also requires nominations to be confirmed by the Senate. More than 600 judges sit on district courts, almost 200 judges sit on courts of appeals, and 9 justices
20 make up the Supreme Court. Because all Federal judges have life terms, no single president will make all of these appointments. But many vacancies do occur during a president's term of office. Appointing judges, then, could be a full-time job. A president
25 relies on many sources to recommend appropriate nominees for judicial posts. Recommendations often come from the Department of Justice, the Federal Bureau of Investigation, members of Congress, sitting judges and justices, and the American Bar
30 Association. Some judicial hopefuls even nominate themselves. A special, very powerful tradition for recommending district judges is called senatorial courtesy. According to this practice, the Senators from the State in which the vacancy occurs actually
35 make the decision. A Senator of the same political party as the President sends a nomination to the President, who almost always follows the recommen-

dation. To ignore it would be a great affront to the Senator, as well as an invitation for conflict between the president and the Senate. 40

Selection Criteria
Presidents must consider many factors in making their choices for Federal judgeships:
- *Experience:* Most nominees have had substantial judicial or governmental experience, either on the State 45 or Federal level. Many have law degrees or some other form of higher education.
- *Political ideology:* Presidents usually appoint judges who seem to have a similar political ideology to their own. In other words, a president with a liberal ideolo- 50 gy will usually appoint liberals to the courts. Likewise, conservative presidents tend to appoint conservatives.
- *Party and personal loyalties:* A remarkably high percentage of a resident's appointees belong to the President's political party. Although politi- 55 cal favoritism is less common today than it was a few decades ago, presidents still appoint friends and loyal supporters to federal judgeships.
- *Ethnicity and gender:* Until relatively recently, almost all federal judges were white males. To- 60 day, however, ethnicity and gender are important criteria for appointing judges. All recent presidents have appointed African Americans, Latinos, members of other ethnic minority groups, and women to district courts and courts of appeal. 65 Because Federal judges and Supreme Court Justices serve for life, a president's nomination decisions are in many ways his or her most important legacy. Many of these appointments will serve long after a president's term of office ends. Whe- 70 ther or not the results are a «combination of Justinian, Jesus Christ, and John Marshall,» these choices can have an impact on generations to come.

ACTIVITY

A. Do you think that personal background may influence decisions made by the judge?

B. Why is political ideology a key question when selecting a judge?

PART 3 – FUNCTIONS OF THE JUDGE

Anthony Kennedy

(1936-) He is an associate Justice of the Supreme Court who was appointed by Ronald Reagan in 1988. He has reliably issued conservative rulings during most of his term, but since the retirement of Sandra Day O'Connor, Kennedy has often been the swing vote on many Court decisions, focusing his interpretation of the Constitution on basic questions of individual liberties.

Everybody knows that the courts are overloaded and that there are too many cases to hear. It is surprising, then, that when visiting a courtroom, you might find some empty rooms and that no one is waiting in the halls. Some studies have revealed that judges spend an average of three hours per day in a courtroom. So, where are they? What are they doing with all of this extra time they seem to have?

In reality, even if everyone imagines the judge presiding over a case in a courtroom, his job encompasses all aspects of the case. The defendants are required to see a judge at each stage of the case and every time a decision must be made about them: for being released with bail, when pre-trial motions are made, when guilty pleas are accepted, when a trial is organized, when a sentence is pronounced, or an appeal is made. However, a judge's work is not only limited to the courtroom.

Judges also have three important administrative functions to fulfill outside of Court:

1. Adjudicator: judges must be absolutely neutral when they render a verdict on litigation or a case with two opposing viewpoints (Prosecution and Defense). They must apply the Law in order to protect the rights of defense in decisions concerning detention, pleading, hearings and sentencing. Judges have some discretion in carrying out these tasks (for example, establishing the amount of bail), but they do it within the context of the Law. They must avoid any biased or prejudiced attitude.

U.S. v. Windsor, 2013

Justice Kennedy described States like New York as embracing «a new perspective, a new insight» that sees the denial of marriage to same-sex couples as «an unjust exclusion.» He also made clear in Windsor that DOMA simultaneously violates the protections of liberty and equality contained within the Fifth Amendment's due process clause. Basically, the Fifth Amendment protects liberty and equality from federal interference to the same extent that the Fourteenth Amendment protects liberty and equality from state interference.

2. Negotiator: most verdicts that determine the defendant's future are taken far from public eyes, in the judge's chambers. They may be a result of negotiation between the Prosecutor and the Defense for a plea bargain, affect the sentence, or deal with the conditions of being released with bail. The judge may act as an arbitrator or mediator, while ensuring that the two parties remain strictly within the context of the Law. Sometimes, the judge takes on a more active role in negotiations, possibly having to suggest the terms of agreement or even insisting that one side accept the bargain.

3. Administrator: one of the roles of the judge that is rarely known is that of being a court administrator. He is actually in charge of the courtroom and all related personnel. In rural areas, a judge's administrative

John Marshall

(1755-1835) He was the 4th Chief Justice of the United States, whose court opinions helped lay the foundation for constitutional law and made the Supreme Court a coequal Branch of government, along with the Legislative and Executive Branches.

tasks may be more broad and he may also be the one who recruits personnel, be in charge of following their careers, the budget for the court and repairs needed for the building. The judge must deal with political players such as county commissioners, legislators and members of the State executive bureaucracy. Chief judges in large courts may also use their administrative powers to push other judges to cooperate in advancing the court's goals. Judges preside over courts at the local, state, and national levels. They are responsible for making sure that disputes between individuals, or individuals and their government, are resolved according to established laws. Courts also are available to protect individual rights from government excess. Judges start out as lawyers, and they typically practice law for a number of years before being appointed or elected as a judge.

ACTIVITY

A. Is a judge's role limited to the courtroom?

....

....

....

....

....

B. What are the three main administrative functions that can be assigned to a judge?

....

....

....

....

....

MARBURY AND OTHER CASES

DOCUMENT 5

***Marbury v. Madison* case (1803) - Brief summary**

Facts

On his last day in office, President John Adams named 42 Justices of the Peace and 16 new Circuit Court Justices for the District of Columbia under the Organic Act. The Organic Act was an attempt by the Federalists to take control of the Federal judiciary before Thomas Jefferson took office. The commissions were signed by President Adams and sealed by acting Secretary of State John Marshall (who later became Chief Justice of the Supreme Court and author of this opinion), but they were not delivered before the expiration of Adams's term as President. Thomas Jefferson refused to honor the commissions, claiming that they were invalid because they had not been delivered by the end of Adams's term. William Marbury was an intended recipient of an appointment as Justice of the Peace. Marbury applied directly to the Supreme Court of the United States for a writ of mandamus to compel Jefferson's Secretary of State, James Madison, to deliver the commissions. The Judiciary Act of 1789 had granted the Supreme Court original jurisdiction to issue writs of mandamus "...to any courts appointed, or persons holding office, under the authority of the United States."

Issues

The issues facing the Court were very clear:
1. Did Marbury have a right to the commission?
2. Did the law grant Marbury a solution?
3. Does the Supreme Court have original jurisdiction to issue writs of mandamus?

Holding and Rule (Marshall)

1. Yes. Marbury had a right to the commission once it was signed by the President and sealed by the Secretary of State. The Court might have held that the commission was not in force until the commission was delivered. However, the Justices stated that the commission went into effect as soon as the President signed it.
2. Yes. The opinion found that a legal solution was required for a legal wrong. Since the government of the United States is one "of laws and not of men," the courts must grant a solution for violation of legal rights. The Supreme Court decided that if an Executive Branch duty is established by the Constitution or Federal law, the judiciary could enforce it.

3. No. Marshall found a conflict between the Judiciary Act of 1789, established by Congress, and the U.S. Constitution. He found that Section 13 of the Act to be unconstitutional because it was in direct opposition to Article III of the Constitution. The opinion acknowledged that Congress has the power to alter jurisdiction of the Court. However, the original jurisdiction for a writ of mandamus as the one in this case, was not permitted by the Constitution. In his opinion, Marshall established that a law in conflict with the Constitution is not valid. It also held that the Supreme Court had the power to invalidate or, at least, disregard such a law. The cornerstone of judicial review today is that the Constitution is the law superior to any enacted by Congress; and the judiciary is required to follow it rather than any inconsistent provisions of federal legislation.

Disposition

Application for writ of mandamus denied. Marbury did not get the commission.

Analysis of the holding

Those in agreement with the decision say that Marshall crafted a solution that was both principled and pragmatic. In fact, the decision required no Court action. Marshall determined that Marbury was justified in his suit. However, the Judiciary Act, on which his claim was based and which allowed the Supreme Court to deal with an original action for mandamus, conflicted with Article III of the Constitution. This Act, changing the wording of the Constitution, was in fact an Amendment and should have been passed through a special required procedure. And it was not the case, this Act being adopted in Congress as a law. The Court then declared the Judiciary Act unconstitutional. In this sense, the decision limited the Supreme Court's power. It meant that the Court could not consider original actions for writs of mandamus. However, critics of the decision say that it was overreaching because the Court, basically, defined its own power for which there was no specific mandate in the Constitution. Nevertheless, the Court then gave itself a new power: that of deciding on the constitutionality of a law. This power is not defined in the Constitution.

Brown v. Board of Education of Topeka (1954)

DOCUMENT 6

Facts: Black children were denied admission to public schools attended by white children under laws requiring or permitting segregation according to race. It was found that the black children's schools and the white children's schools had been or were being equalized with respect to facilities, curricula, qualifications, and salaries of teachers.

Issues: Does segregation of children in public schools, solely on the basis of race, deprive minority children of equal protection under the law, even though the physical facilities are equal?

Holding and Rule (Warren): Yes. The Supreme Court held that the "separate but equal" doctrine, established in *Plessy v. Ferguson*, has no application in the field of education. Segregation of children in public schools, based solely on their race, violates the Equal Protection Clause of the 14th Amendment. First, the Court considered intangible as well as tangible factors. The fact that the facilities and other tangible factors in the schools have been equalized is not the central issue. Segregation of white and black children in public schools has a detrimental effect on black children because it is usually interpreted as denoting their inferiority. A sense of inferiority affects children's motivation to learn. Separate facilities are inherently unequal. Such facilities deprive black children of their right to equal protection under the laws.

Analysis of the holding: *Brown v. Board of Education* is an important example of the Court asserting its power to declare the acts of a state as unconstitutional. In this historic case, the Supreme Court declared that racial segregation in public schools was a violation of the Constitution. Specifically, the Court held that the public schools involved in this case violated the Fourteenth Amendments' rights of minority children, to be treated equally under the law.

Bush v. Gore (2000)

DOCUMENT 7

Facts: In the 2000 Presidential race, Democratic candidates Al Gore and Joe Lieberman filed a complaint contesting the certification (making official) of Florida's results. The Florida Supreme Court ordered a manual recount of ballots entered on machines that did not record votes for the President. Republican candidate George W. Bush filed an emergency application with the U.S. Supreme Court to stop Florida Supreme Court's order for the manual recount. The United States Supreme Court agreed to take the case.

Issues: Does the use of manual recount, for which no standards have been set, violate Equal Protection and Due Process Clauses of the 14th Amendment?

Holding and Rule (Rehnquist): Yes. In a 5-4 decision, the Court decided that there was a violation of the Equal Protection Clause. The Supreme Court held that manual recounts, as ordered by the Florida Supreme Court, did not satisfy a minimum requirement for non-arbitrary treatment of voters. It also held that taking the case to the Florida Supreme Court for it to order a constitutionally proper context was not the appropriate solution. Therefore, it reversed the judgment of the Supreme Court of Florida, and ended the manual recount.

Analysis of the holding: The Supreme Court of the United States ruled that the manual recounts of ballots in Florida should be abandoned because the recounts were unconstitutional and could not be completed by the December 12th, 2000, deadline mandated by Federal law. Without the precedent set in *Marbury v. Madison*, the Court would not have had the power to resolve such a dispute.

ACTIVITY

A. What is common to the three cases?

B. Summarize the concept of separation of powers.

PART 4 – HOW TO BECOME A JUDGE

The first thing to do for those who want to become a judge is to earn a Bachelor's Degree, no matter what the major. Most students get a degree in subjects as diverse as political science, sociology, history, business and economics. Law studies are done at the graduate level, which means that they are undertaken after having earned the Bachelor's. Subjects differ greatly from State to State and there is no federal oversight in the 1,777 accredited Law Schools in the country. They are all however, recognized by the American Bar Association, which is the principle national organization for attorneys in the United States. It is in charge of defining the academic and ethical standards of the profession. The Law Schools vary notably in size: some are very small while others have many thousands of students. To be sure to be accepted into one of these sought-after schools, it is better to have attended one of the best universities, such as the Ivy League schools, Harvard, Yale or Princeton. High school grades are also a determining factor in being accepted into these prestigious universities. Many students obtain apprenticeships with law firms during their undergraduate studies, to show their motivation and to increase their chances of being accepted by these Law Schools. Everyone must take and pass the Law School Admission Test (LSAT) to be admitted.

Most of the schools offer a three-year program, resulting in a Juris Doctor Degree. During the first year of law school, students learn the fundamentals of law, such as civil procedure, contracts, and torts. In the next two years, elective courses in specialized fields of law, such as Family Law and Tax Law are offered. At the end of their studies, students must pass the Bar Exam given by the American Bar Association (each State has its own exam). Judges must work as attorneys prior to attaining a judgeship. Being a prosecutor or government attorney offers a unique chance to become intimately familiar with the way the bench operates. It is not mandatory to be a prosecutor to become a judge, but the majority of people who apply and are appointed to judgeships have plenty of prosecutorial experience. Candidates apply for judgeships through a judicial nominating commission, or can be recommended by Senators or other politicians. Either way, candidates must go through a lengthy application process. At the end of the process, they may be elected or appointed to work as judges, depending on the jurisdiction. Federal, State, and local judges have fixed or renewable terms of office, while some Federal judges are appointed for life. The applicants must be ready to disclose personal information. A judge's past mistakes are always revealed, and sometimes they are rehashed in the press. Most people do not obtain a judgeship on the first try. In fact, failing the first time is almost considered to be a prerequisite for eventually getting a judgeship. Depending on the judgeship pursued, future judges have to be elected, rather than appointed, for the role. They must act as part of a political party and run a campaign to get or keep the seat. Running for an elective judicial office is like running for other political offices; they must have an appealing public persona that makes people want to vote for them. Once the judges have been elected or appointed, they need to complete certain introductory training programs or seminars before they can start practicing as a judge. Trainees may participate in court trials, review legal publications, and complete online exercises. Training may continue throughout their career to ensure they are informed about the latest changes to the law.

ACTIVITY

A. In your opinion, what are the skills needed to be a judge?

....

....

....

....

B. If you were to vote for a judge, what would motivate your choice?

....

....

....

....

I WANT TO BE A JUDGE

So you want to be a judge?

DOCUMENT 8

High status, fascinating issues, great money and perks, no practice-management headaches – what lawyer wouldn't want to be a judge? What lawyer indeed, which is why it isn't an easy gig to get. Supreme Court Justices and others tell how to improve your odds of donning the robe.

Is becoming a judge a lifelong dream of yours? Or are you thinking, now that you've gotten your law degree or have been out in practice for a while, that you might like to throw your hat in the ring, either by applying
5 for appointment to a vacant associate or circuit position or by running in a partisan election for State Circuit, Appellate, or Supreme Court? If your answer is «Yes!» you have plenty of company. That's not hard to understand. As Sheila Murphy, formerly a circuit
10 judge for Cook County, says, «If you're a trial lawyer or litigator, you naturally start thinking at some point, 'I could do that!'»

«By all accounts, being a judge is a great job», says Illinois Supreme Court Justice Anne Burke, «Every
15 day is a challenge and something to love if you're a lawyer. Even more, every day is an honor, because you realize your responsibility to society and, most of all, to the litigants; it is being honest and fair in everything that has to do with them.»

20 The salary's not too shabby, either: Justices of the Illinois Supreme Court make $207,066 annually; Appellate Court Judges, $194,888; Circuit Court Judges, $178,835; and Associate Judges, $169,893, as of July 1, 2010. Add to that great benefits, inclu-
25 ding outstanding retirement pay, reduced or waived bar association dues, and invitations to lavish banquets, judges' nights, and the like, at which you're an honored, nonpaying guest.

The challenges

30 But the judging job has its drawbacks, too. «The most difficult challenge is the public life that you lead» as a judge, says Burke. Your family members may find that challenge even more difficult. Is there something in your background – a nasty lawsuit, perhaps? – that
35 you'd prefer people not to know about? Judicial aspirants should expect that whatever it is will become public, whether to the general community or only to a bar association judicial evaluation committee, during the evaluation of their candidacy, says Burke.
40 If you decide to run for judicial office, you'll have to declare yourself as a member of one or another political party and become involved in that party's activities. You'll almost undoubtedly have to raise money, and lots of it, which, it's safe to say, no can-
45 didate is comfortable doing.

If you succeed and are assigned to a high-profile case – always a possibility for any judge – or if you make rulings you believe are legally correct but end up being heavily scrutinized or controversial, you and your personal life may become the subject of articles 50 and editorials in the press, or you could end up being targeted by one or more special-interest groups for non-retention. Some invitations to those fancy fetes may be more obligatory than optional for you as a sitting judge, though you might prefer spending that 55 time off the bench with your family and personal friends. And, though judicial salaries and benefits are guaranteed by law and are significantly greater than what the vast majority of lawyers earn, a few take a pay cut to go on the bench. 60

Merit vs. political selection

Still, there's no shortage of interested, qualified candidates for judicial vacancies, and competition is intense. No matter how qualified the lawyer, an eventual judgeship is never guaranteed. «Anyone 65 who thinks 'I'll be a judge someday because I'm at the top of my law school class and everyone knows I'm smart,' is very naive,» says Chief Judge Michael McCuskey of the Federal District Court for the Central District of Illinois. Lawyers can, however, take 70 steps to position themselves so as to enhance their chances of being favorably considered for appointment or slating for judicial positions, as McCuskey and other sitting and former State Court Judges told the *IBJ*. As several judges pointed out, Illinois 75 selects its State Court Judges through both «merit» selection and partisan elections. Circuit judges are chosen by popular election, while associate judges are appointed after submitting applications to the circuit judges for their circuit. Additionally, when a circuit 80 judge vacancy occurs mid-term, the Supreme Court justice for that circuit will nominate a candidate for the full court to appoint to serve for the remainder of that position's term. «I don't think you get to either job solely on merit», Mc Cuskey says, «One system is 85 not necessarily better than the other.» Having been elected to State Circuit and Appellate Courts before his presidential appointment to his current position, McCuskey says, «I've seen a lot of great judges elected and a few bad apples. The same goes for those 90

DOCUMENT 9

Resignation of the first woman who was a Supreme Court Justice

Supreme Court of the United States
Washington, D. C. 20543

CHAMBERS OF
SANDRA DAY O'CONNOR

July 1, 2005

Dear President Bush:

     This is to inform you of my decision to retire from my position as an Associate Justice of the Supreme Court of the United States effective upon the nomination and confirmation of my successor. It has been a great privilege, indeed, to have served as a member of the Court for 24 Terms. I will leave it with enormous respect for the integrity of the Court and its role under our Constitutional structure.

     Sincerely,

Sandra Day O'Connor

The President
  The White House
    Washington, D. C.

ACTIVITY

A. Identify the most common method of selecting state judges and give the arguments for and against this method.

B. Find some information about Justice Sandra Day O'Connor and write or make a brief presentation.

C. How can Federal judges be removed from office? What about State judges?

SUMMARY

Important words:

District Court
Circuit Court
Due process
Equal Protection Clause
Standing

ADVERSARY v. INQUISITORIAL

More than anything else, a judge is supposed to represent Justice. It's not always easy, when you think of huge number of cases that fill the newspapers. Moreover, not all American judges are qualified for the job, which they sometimes owe to an election or a political nomination. The role of a judge is to interpret the Law. The stereotype of an American judge is reinforced by the adversarial system that makes him appear like a referee. The Prosecutor has an advantage over the Defense in that he can use all the means at the disposal of the Police to find evidence. That is why some countries, such as France, prefer to use an inquisitorial system, with an investigating judge in charge of an investigation and its completion. In the French system, the Prosecuting and Defending Attorneys are supposed to help the judge discover the truth. In the American system, each one represents his party.

WHO BECOMES A JUDGE?

The judge has an important role in society, even though he might not necessarily make much money. A judge's prestige comes notably from his political power. One advantage of being a judge is organizing your schedule as you wish. In the past, judges were all white, and middle to upper class, which posed a risk to impartial justice. A judge's aura also depends on the kind of justice he dispenses: it is more prestigious to be a judge in civil proceedings, rather than in criminal proceedings, where you deal with drugs, violence and poverty in the poorest courtrooms. In the higher Civil Courts, the formality of the Court, dominated by wood and marble, often with thick, red curtains, creates an impressive atmosphere. This surely explains why many judges spend their entire careers trying to be transferred from the criminal to the civil system.

FUNCTIONS OF THE JUDGE

Everyone knows that the Courts are overloaded, so we might be surprised to find that many courtrooms are often empty. This is because a judge's work typically takes place somewhere other than a courtroom, which he in fact occupies only about two or three hours per day. He works on all the stages of the trial, including those that precede it. The judge has three important administrative roles: he may be adjudicator, negotiator or administrator at the same time. As an adjudicator, he must listen to the Prosecution and the Defense and apply the law that respects the rights of the accused. Many trials are concluded outside the courtroom. The judge intervenes in plea-bargaining between the parties, often very actively. One lesser-known role of judges is that of Court Administrator. He is sometimes in charge of Personnel, as well as Building Management and Maintenance.

HOW TO BECOME A JUDGE

To become a judge, it is preferred that you have studied Law, but it is not obligatory. Law Schools in the States are numerous: 1,777. They vary in size and prestige: the most famous are Ivy League schools, such as Harvard, Princeton or Yale. After having finished Law School, and having earned a Juris Doctor, students take the Bar Exam and become practicing lawyers. Most judges have worked as Prosecutors before becoming a judge, but it is not absolutely necessary. Some become a judge because of their political participation, since some positions are only reserved for nomination by a Senator, a government or a commission. Sometimes citizens directly elect judges. They are not always political elections, but when they are, they give rise to a veritable campaign by the candidates. Once elected, or appointed, the new judges receive training, which they will have for their entire careers.

A. Decide if the following statements are True or False:

	True	False
1. The Federal Courts have limited jurisdiction.		
2. Only one Court is defined in the federal Constitution.		
3. Judicial review came out of *Marbury v. Marshall*.		
4. A case which does not deal with a constitutional question cannot be		

B. Name and define the key concept established in *Marbury v. Madison*.

....
....

C. At the time when Gideon mailed his appeal to the Supreme Court...
1. On what parts of the Constitution did he base his appeal?
2. What was the importance of the writ of *Habeas Corpus*?
3. What was a writ of *certiorari*?
4. What was an *in forma pauperis* petition?

....
....

D. 1. What precedent was set in *Betts v. Brady* 316 U.S. 455 (1942)?
2. What is double jeopardy?
3. Why is it not double jeopardy to try Gideon a second time?

....
....

REFERENCES :

Page 167. "American judge", by Maveric2003, Wikimedia. http://commons. wikimedia.org/wiki/File:American_judge.jpg
"I want to be a judge", by Dimitri Champain

Page 168. "Adversarial trial", by Dimitri Champain

Page 170. "A brief overview of the Supreme Court", adapted from www.supremecourt.gov
"Court Equal Justice", Wikimedia. http://commons.wikimedia.org/wiki/File:CourtEqualJustice.JPG?uselang=fr

Page 171. "OYEZ! OYEZ! : The Court and its procedures", adapted from www.supremecourt.gov.

Page 172. "William Rehnquist", Wikimedia, http://commons.wikimedia.org/wiki/File:William_Rehnquist.jpg?uselang=fr
"Official Roberts", Wikimedia, http://commons.wikimedia.org/wiki/File:Official_roberts_CJ.jpg
"Criminal Court", by Dimitri Champain

Page 174. "The waves minority judges always make?", adapted from Adam Liptak, *The New York Times*, May 31, 2009.
"How judges and Justices are chosen", adapted from USHistory.org

Page 175. "Anthony Kennedy", Wikimedia, http://commons.wikimedia.org/wiki/File:Anthony_Kennedy_%282009,_cropped%29.jpg?uselang=fr

Page 176. "US v. Windsor", by Jean-Eric Branaa

Page 177. "John Marshall by Henry Inman", Wikimedia, http://commons.wikimedia.org/wiki/File:John_Marshall_by_Henry_Inman,_1832.jpg

Page 178. "Marbury v. Madison case - Brief summary", summary of Marbury v. Madison, 5 U.S. 137, 1 Cranch 137, 2 L. Ed. 60 (1803).

Page 180. "From prosecutor to judge", by Dimitri Champain

Page 181. "Nikki Still for Circuit Judge", by Estillbahm, in Wikimedia. http://commons.wikimedia.org/wiki/File:Nikki_Still_for_Circuit_Judge.JPG?uselang=fr
"David Carpenter for Circuit Judge", by Estillbahm, in Wikimedia. http://commons.wikimedia.org/wiki/File:David_Carpenter_for_Circuit_Judge.JPG?uselang=fr
"Denise Pomeroy for Circuit Judge", by Estillbahm, in Wikimedia. http://commons.wikimedia.org/wiki/File:Denise_Pomeroy_for_Circuit_Judge.JPG?uselang=fr

Page 182. "So you want to be a judge?", adapted from Helen W. Gunnarsson, *Illinois Bar Journal*, September 2010, Volume 98, Number 9, page 456.

Page 183. "Oconnor070105 0001", Wikimedia. http://commons.wikimedia.org/wiki/File:Oconnor070105_0001.jpg
"Sandra Day O'Connor", Wikimedia. http://commons.wikimedia.org/wiki/File:Sandra_Day_O%27Connor.jpg?uselang=fr

Page 184. "Summary", by Dimitri Champain

Page 185. "Review", by Dimitri Champain

pp. 169, 171, 173, 175, 177, 179, 181, 183 "Activity", by Dimitri Champain

UNIT 10 It's the Law

Introduction

The goal of Criminal Law is to maintain law and order, and to protect citizens and society. To do that, it forbids a number of behaviors and anticipates that those who do not respect the law will be punished. The criminal procedure begins as soon as the crime is committed. There is no rule of procedure in the United States. The Federal state defines its own rules, and the 50 States do the same. There are no two States that have the exact same legal system and none of them has the same system as the federal one. However, some similarities and shared norms exist.

10

TAOS   N.M.
POLICE   DEPT
G675   7 2 75

PART 1 – IS IT A CRIME?

Hey, I'm not hurting anyone...

LAW

Many crimes are characterized by behavior that wounds someone or affects their property in some way: e.g. rape, assault, theft and causing criminal damage. In each instance, a victim may be determined. For other crimes, however, there is no victim, meaning that no one will suffer directly because of a crime committed. For example, it is a crime to not wear your seatbelt in your car, or your helmet when on a scooter or a motorcycle. When drivers or motorcyclists are fined for these crimes, they experience a feeling of injustice, because they do not realize the severity of their actions and they sometimes say, to justify themselves, that they were not hurting anyone. Actually, in these situations, the law is

trying to protect the "criminal" from himself.

So a crime is not necessarily simply the fact of causing damage or direct harm. An action is defined as a crime if it violates a criminal statute duly enacted by Congress, a state legislature or some other public authority. A crime is a violation of an obligation toward the entire community, and may be punished with a fine, prison time, or even death, in many U.S. States.

> **An action is defined as a crime if it violates a criminal statute duly enacted by Congress, a state legislature or some other public authority.**

California Police Code

187	Homicide
207	Kidnapping
211	Robbery
215	Carjacking
217	Assault
242	Battery
261	Rape
288	Lewd conduct
311	Indecent exposure
417	Person with a gun
419	Dead human body
428	Child molest
459	Burglary
470	Forgery
484	Theft
502	Drunk driving
507	Public nuisance
594	Malicious mischief

In the United States most crimes constitute sins of commissions, such as aggravated assault or embezzlement; a few consist of sins of omission, such as failing to give help after a traffic accident, or failing to file an income tax return. Some crimes are considered as serious by society, such as murder or kidnapping, and this legal classification may be found in the type of punishment incurred, which is most often prison for many years, or the death penalty. Other crimes are only considered as objectionable, such as yelling in the streets at night, screaming or singing too loudly while most others want only to sleep, or double-parking; these crimes will only be punished with a small fine, and more rarely, a night behind bars at the Police Station to give a person time to recover from a too much drinking the night before.

When we take a look at serious or violent crimes, we can still see categories: certain crimes, such as rape or kidnapping, are not acceptable in our society and everyone agrees that they are inhuman. But, for other crimes, even very violent or horrible ones, opinions become divided: what happens when the crime is against a baby about to be born, killed by a desperate mother? Should it be ruled first-degree murder, or should we try to take into account the distress that led to such an act?

There are a large number of crimes and the liability of the criminal is not always just because the crime was committed: let's take the example of international figure skater Tanya Harding in 1998. Would you have condemned her, knowing that she was aware that her husband had hired a man to wound her rival competitor, Nancy Kerrigan, with the only goal of leaving the field open for

CSI: far from the truth

CSI is a popular U.S. TV show which set in Las Vegas, Miami and NYC. But it lacks realism: for instance, the show's characters not only investigate crime scenes, but they also conduct raids, engage in suspect pursuit and arrest, interrogate suspects, and solve cases, which falls under the responsibility of uniformed officers and detectives, not CSI personnel. In the U.S.A., it is considered inappropriate and improbable practice to allow CSI personnel to be involved in detective work, since it would compromise the impartiality of scientific evidence and would be impracticably time-consuming.

her to win the world figure skating title? Law is created by a community, sometimes in response to specific needs at a certain time, and some "crimes" might seem silly to us today: in Wisconsin, it is illegal to sing in a bar; in Nebraska, you can't play Bingo in a church meeting; in Louisiana, it is forbidden to be drunk in a book group meeting. The most serious crimes in the United States are often called felonies. In most States, a felony is a crime punishable with serving time in a penitentiary or with the death penalty, if it is legal in that State. In some other States, a felony is a crime punished with time in prison over one year. Examples of felonies are murder, rape and armed robbery.

Misdemeanors are less serious crimes in all States, punishable by a prison sentence of less than one year, and in a city prison or county prison, e.g. for public drunkenness or vagrancy. Some States have a third category of crimes called infractions, such as parking violations, for which punishment is only a simple fine. Fines my also be assigned for misdemeanors and felonies.

ACTIVITY

A. Can you commit a crime without hurting anybody?

....

....

....

....

....

B. What is a 'misdemeanor'?

....

....

....

....

....

GO TO JAIL AND DO NOT PASS GO

DOCUMENT 1

Rikers Island (New Yok City)

«If you can't do the time, don't do the crime.» So goes the old saying. Yet conditions in some American facilities are so obscene that they amount to a form of extrajudicial punishment. Doing time is not supposed to include being raped by fellow prisoners or staff, beaten by guards for the slightest provocation, driven mad by long-term solitary confinement, or killed off by medical neglect. These, however, are the fates of thousands of prisoners every year—men, women, and children housed in lockups that give Gitmo and Abu Ghraib a run for their money. The United States boasts the world's highest incarceration rate, with close to 2.3 million people locked away in some 1,800 prisons and 3,000 jails. Most are nasty places by design, aimed at punishment and exclusion rather than rehabilitation; while reliable numbers are hard to come by, at last count 81,622 prisoners were being held in some form of isolation in State and Federal prisons. Thousands more are being held in solitary at jails, deportation facilities, and juvenile-detention centers. Nearly 1 in 10 prisoners is sexually victimized, by prison employees about half of the time—more than 200,000 such assaults take place in American penal facilities every year. Suicides, meanwhile, account for almost a third of prisoner deaths, while an unknown number of fatalities result from substandard nutrition and medical care.

Number of inmates: ~10,000

Who's in charge: Evelyn A. Mirabal, chief; Dora Schriro, Commissioner, of the New York City Department of Corrections.

The basics: When it comes to ignominies, New York City's island jail complex has it all: inmate violence, staff brutality, rape, abuse of adolescents and the mentally ill, and one of the nation's highest rates of solitary confinement. Rikers, which contains 10 separate jails, has been the target of dozens of lawsuits and numerous exposés. Yet the East River island remains a dismal and dangerous place for the 12,000 or more men, women, and children held there on any given day—mostly pre-trial defendants who can't make bail and nonviolent offenders with sentences too short to ship them upstate.

The backlash: In 2008, 18-year-old Christopher Robinson, who had violated his probation for a juvenile robbery offense, was beaten and stomped to death in his cell in Rikers youth unit. An investigation revealed that the killers, two fellow prisoners, were part of what was known as "the program," described by the Bronx D.A. as a "secret society run by correctional officers at Rikers Island to extort and beat other inmates," supposedly in the name of maintaining order. Two of the facility's guards pleaded guilty to assault and to charges related to running the extortion program, although the D.A. presented no evidence connecting them to Robinson's death.

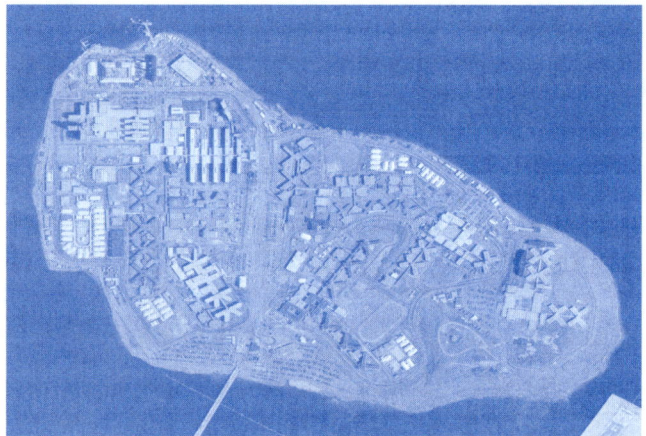

A 2012 lawsuit by the Legal Aid Socicty also documents a "deeply entrenched" pattern of violence by the guards, who "use unlawful, excessive force with impunity" and often send prisoners to the hospital, costing the city millions in legal settlements. Despite the alleged complicity of staff in the rampant violence, the Department of Corrections' response has been to build more solitary cells at Rikers—nearly 1,000 in all, with special isolation units for adolescents and for people with mental illnesses.

Florence, Colorado: Alcatraz of the Rockies

DOCUMENT 2

U.S. Penitentiary Administrative Maximum
(Florence, Colorado)

Number of prisoners: ~440

Who's in charge: David Berkebile, warden; Charles Samuels, director, Federal Bureau of Prisons.

The basics: Known as ADX, and nicknamed the
5 «Alcatraz of the Rockies,» this is among the most secure prisons in the world—and one of the most isolating: Many of its cells, fashioned out of poured concrete with solid steel doors, are equipped with built-in showers and automated chutes that open
10 onto private concrete «exercise yards,» such that occupants need never see a guard or fellow prisoner—much less a visitor. One former warden interviewed by *60 Minutes* called it «pretty close» to hell. Some ADX prisoners have killed guards or prisoners at
15 other facilities, but many others land here by virtue of their notoriety or politics. Unabomber Ted Kaczynski, shoe bomber Richard Reid, and Oklahoma City conspirator Terry Nichols are all notable personages, to be sure, but none of them has been shown to present
20 any special security risks in an ordinary prison environment. Many of those housed at ADX are Muslims serving time for low-level terrorism offenses—such as Syed Fahad Hashmi, convicted of helping to supply al-Qaeda with socks and rain ponchos.

25 **The backlash:** ADX residents have been the plaintiffs in a number of lawsuits claiming cruel and unusual punishment. Consider the following quote from a class-action filed on the prisoners' behalf last June, keeping in mind that the Bureau of Prisons (BOP) has
30 a policy against housing the mentally ill at ADX:
Many prisoners at ADX interminably wail, scream, and bang on the walls of their cells. Some mutilate their bodies with razors, shards of glass, sharpened chicken bones, writing utensils, and whatever other objects they can obtain. A number swallow razor blades, 35 nail clippers, parts of radios and televisions, broken glass, and other dangerous objects. Others carry on delusional conversations with voices they hear in their heads, oblivious to reality and to the danger that such behavior might pose to themselves and anyone who 40 interacts with them. Still others spread feces and other human waste and body fluids throughout their cells, throw it at the correctional staff and otherwise create health hazards at ADX. Suicide attempts are common; many have been successful. 45
This particular lawsuit details the case of Jack Powers, a convicted bank robber who landed at ADX after escaping from another prison. Powers, according to his suit, «had no history or symptoms of serious mental illness» when he arrived at ADX 11 years 50 ago. While there, in addition to repeated suicide attempts, he has removed one of his testicles, bitten off a finger and amputated another one, sliced off his earlobes, and severed his Achilles tendon. ADX officials, the lawsuit alleges, in some instances treated 55 these acts of self-mutilation as disciplinary violations. In June 2012, a Senate Judiciary Subcommittee held the first-ever Congressional hearings on solitary confinement, and grilled BOP director Charles Samuels about conditions at ADX. This past February, 60 the BOP announced that it would be undergoing an «assessment» of its solitary-confinement practices.

ACTIVITY

A. What are some reproaches addressed to the U.S. incarceration system?

B. Compare Rikers Island and Florence. What is your opinion about these prisons?

PART 2 – ELEMENTS OF A CRIME

The illegal act...

...the associated punishment!

Each crime is composed of many elements; the Prosecution must prove the presence of each of these elements in order to find someone guilty.

It is first necessary, however, to clearly and precisely define the illegal act, and specify it as such by a law-enforce-ment agency (such as the Federal Congress, or a State); the associated punishments in cases of non-respect must be clearly defined as well. In this way, citizens know how they should behave and the limits that are established by Law. American Law provides, nevertheless, that it is forbidden to pass laws *ex post facto* (made after the action took place) and that it is also not authorized to pass bills of attainder (laws restricted to a limited group of people or a person, which declare them guilty without the benefit of a trial).

The *Actus Reus* and the *mens rea*

For a person to be declared guilty of a crime, the prosecutor must prove things: the *actus reus* and the *mens rea*. *Actus reus* is Latin for "guilty act", and *mens rea* is Latin for "guilty mind or intention". Imagine a situation where John Doe and Jack Smith have both just been paid a salary of $3,000. They both put the money in their wallets and go for a drink. If John Doe obtains Jack Smith's wallet in a deliberately fraudulent way and spends the money, he has committed theft. The *actus reus* of theft is the voluntary taking of someone else's property and in this case, is the act of taking the wallet. Being dishonest and wanting to 'permanently deprive' Jack Smith of what is legally his, is the *mens rea*.

To be accused of theft, two elements of the crime need be present. Imagine that John Doe leaves with Jack Smith's jacket, which had his wallet in an inner pocket. In this case, John Doe clearly took the wallet and *actus reus* is certainly present. On the other hand, he didn't intend to case harm or be dishonest in this instance; it was actually an error, and *mens rea* is not present. John Doe will not be accused of theft.

It is also possible that *mens rea* be present, but not *actus reus*. In this example, if John Doe voluntarily takes the jacket that he believes to be Jack Smith's and which contains a wallet with $3,000, but he makes a mistake and takes Bob Morane's jacket, which has nothing in it. He irrefutably commits *mens rea* of theft towards Jack Smith, but not *actus reus*, at least for the wallet, because he still must explain himself to Bob Morane about the jacket. *Actus reus* is typically an act, but it may also be an omission. Not stopping at a red light, or not fastening your seatbelt in your car are examples in which *actus reus* is an omission. One might think that most crimes of omission are minor, but it's not necessarily the case, and they may be very serious crimes.

Although *mens rea* means "guilty mind", it does not mean that the defendant necessarily needs to know if his or her action is illegal. That means that the defendant must have the necessary level of intention to commit a specific crime for which he or she is on trial. In the United States, the legal system has always made a distinction between damage caused either voluntarily or not. So, if someone takes another person's life, the State does not automatically label it a murder. If a murder were committed with malice and forethought by a sane individual, it would likely be termed "murder in the first degree". But if it were performed in the heat of passion, it would more likely be termed "second-degree murder", which carries a lesser penalty.

DID YOU KNOW?

In the United States, a sheriff is a county official and is typically the top law enforcement officer of a county. Historically, the sheriff was also commander of the militia in that county. Distinctive to law enforcement in the United States, sheriffs are usually elected. The political election of a person to serve as a police leader is an almost uniquely American tradition.

ACTIVITY

A. What is *Actus Reus?*

....

....

....

....

....

B. What is *Mens Rea?*

....

....

....

....

....

SHOOTING OF TRAYVON MARTIN

DOCUMENT 3

On the night of February 26th, 2012, in Sanford, Florida, George Zimmerman fatally shot Trayvon Martin, a 17-year-old African American high school student. Zimmerman was taken into custody, treated for head injuries, then questioned for five hours. The police chief said that Zimmerman was released because there was no evidence to refute Zimmerman's claim of having acted in self-defense, and that under Florida's «Stand Your Ground» statute, the police were prohibited by law from making an arrest. As news of the case spread, thousands of protestors across the country called for Zimmerman's arrest and a full investigation. Zimmerman's trial began on June 10th, 2013, in Sanford. On July 13th, 2013, a jury acquitted him of second-degree murder and of manslaughter charges.

The dispute at trial turned on, what was in Zimmerman's mind, when he fired the gun. In order to convict Zimmerman, the prosecution had to prove that Zim-
5
merman had criminal intent, or what is called *mens*
10 *rea*. It failed to do that and Zimmerman was acquitted.

What is *Mens Rea*?

Mens rea is a Latin term meaning guilty mind. In the American legal system, every crime has two components which the prosecution must prove to obtain a
15 conviction of the defendant:
  • *actus reus*, or the criminal action, and
  • *mens rea*, or the criminal intent.
If either component is missing, the defendant will be acquitted. For example, a woman who repeatedly tells
20 her friends that she wishes her husband were dead will probably not be convicted of murder if he goes missing. In that situation, the *actus reus* is missing (literally). And, a woman who slips (really) in the kitchen while deboning a chicken and accidentally eviscerates her
25 husband is not guilty of murder, either, because she lacked the *mens rea* for murder (she did not intend to kill him).
But criminal intent does not necessarily mean malicious intent, and a person can be found to have cri-
30 minal intent even when his motives are objectively good. The required intent is the intent to commit the prohibited act. For example, an Earth First activist who breaks into a logging company's yard in order to disable logging machinery may have good intentions
35 (saving endangered old-growth forests) but if the Prosecution proves that he intended to forcibly enter the yard without authorization and destroy the property of others, he will be found guilty. The criminal intent for the trespass was simply the activist's intentional
40 entry onto private property of another.

Levels of *Mens Rea*

Different levels of criminal intent are required to prove different crimes. The levels range from no intent (strict liability, which is rare in criminal cases) to the level of intent required to obtain a death penalty verdict in
45 a first degree murder trial. Generally speaking, lesser crimes carrying lesser penalties may require proof of lower levels of criminal intent. The greater the crime and possible sentence, the higher the level of criminal intent that must be proven.
50

Malice aforethought

The highest degree of criminal intent is malice aforethought, which is usually required to prove first degree murder. A person acts with malice aforethought when he acts with prior intent to do the criminal act.
55 Where a person intends to kill another prior to taking that action and then does kill the other person, the killer has acted with malice aforethought.

Intentional

When a person intends to do the criminal act, but does
60 not form the intent prior to taking the action (which would constitute malice aforethought), the person has acted with intent. So, a person who gets into an argument with another person and pulls a gun and shoots the other person has acted with the intent to
65 kill the victim. But, the killer did not form the intent to kill prior to the killing. Many States' have voluntary manslaughter laws. Voluntary manslaughter is usually defined as the intentional killing of a person but in the heat of passion or some other provocation.
70 A "cold-blooded" intentional killing would generally be charged as murder of some degree.

Knowing

A person who acts without a specific intent to perform a criminal act, but whose intentional actions are such
75 that the person knew or should have known that the wrongful result would occur, has acted knowingly under the law. When a person fires a gun into a crowd, the person may not intend to kill any particular person but

80 would be held to have had the knowledge that adeath of a victim was a likely result of the shooter's action. Some States, including California, require only proof that the defendant had knowledge that death was a likely result of her actions to support a second degree
85 murder conviction.

California woman guilty of 2nd degree murder for killing by her dogs

A California appellate court reinstated a second degree murder conviction of a woman whose two
90 large dogs attacked and killed a neighbor woman in the hallway outside their apartments. Although the dogs were on leash, their owner was unable to control them. The court ruled that the woman knew her dogs had a propensity to attack and
95 that knowledge supported the conviction. Her knowledge established the required criminal intent, or *mens rea.*

Reckless disregard

A person acts with reckless disregard when he
100 consciously ignores a "substantial and unjustifiable risk" that his actions will result in a crime or harm to another. Anyone who engages in reckless conduct may also be found guilty of any crime that results from that conduct. Vehicular homicide laws often require high
105 level of *mens rea,* so a person who drives recklessly and kills a pedestrian may be convicted of vehicular homicide. Involuntary manslaughter typically includes a killing committed by someone acting with reckless disregard for the consequences of their actions.

110 **Strict liability**

Virtually all crimes listed in the criminal codes in the U.S. require some degree of *mens rea.* However, traffic violations, such as speeding, and certain other minor offenses are "strict liability" offenses. This means, as
115 anyone who's ever tried to convince a cop that she didn't realize he was speeding knows that the offender's mental state is completely irrelevant. The "*actus reus*" (speeding) is enough in itself to justify a citation. Note, however, that in many states, «statutory rape,»
120 or sex with an underage person, remains a strict liablity crime.

Effect of *Mens Rea* on charge and sentence

As mentioned, the greater the severity of the crime and the possible penalty for committing it, the greater the level of *mens rea* that the State must prove to convict 125 the person charged.

The Zimmerman Jury considered a lesser charge

Florida prosecutors originally charged George Zimmerman with second degree murder in the killing of Trayvon Martin. After presenting the State's case 130 against Zimmerman, the Prosecution asked the judge to instruct the jury on a "lesser included" charge of manslaughter. The judge granted the request. Under Florida law, prosecutors must convince the jury that Zimmerman had a "depraved mind regardless of 135 human life", to convict him of second degree murder. But, it needed only to prove that he acted with reckless disregard of human life to convict him of manslaughter. This is difference in the *mens rea* requirement makes it easier for the prosecution win a manslaughter convic- 140 tion than a second degree murder conviction. However, Zimmerman's self-defense argument also applied to that lesser charge and the jury accepted that defense for all charges.

Acquittal in spite of proven *mens rea*   145

Some defenses require acquittal even where the state has proven *actus reus* and *mens rea.* These defenses include self-defense and justifiable homicide. George Zimmerman's attorneys argued to the jury that Zimmerman acted in self-defense and offered evidence 150 that they say showed that Trayvon Martin was attacking Zimmerman when Zimmerman shot him. This evidence persuaded the jury that Zimmerman acted in self-defense and the jury acquitted him despite the fact that he intended to, and did, kill Martin.   155

Innocence is a matter of degree

Given the many shades of criminal intent that the U.S. legal system recognizes, the frequent jail-house refrain, "I'm innocent," turns into a loaded phrase. The way intent is viewed under the law is complex and specific 160 to each crime. If you have questions about criminal intent in particular crimes, talk to an experienced defense lawyer in your area.

ACTIVITY

A. What is the «Stand your ground» statute? Search the Internet or try to imagine what it can be.

B. Could it be said that George Zimmermann is a murderer? How did the jury decide the case?

195

PART 3 – PROCEDURE BEFORE

Before a criminal trial is held, Federal and State laws envisage a very strict procedure: certain steps of this procedure are provided for in the U.S. Constitution or in the State Constitutions, in certain Court verdict, or in laws passed by various State Assemblies or the U.S. Congress. This explains how these procedures may differ from State to State.

The arrest

arrest

Everything begins with the arrest. Federal laws provide for two types of arrest: with or without a warrant. For an arrest, a warrant must be issued by a judge who believes there is enough evidence to justify it. But when the crime happens in the presence of a police officer, or when a police officer thinks someone is on the verge of committing a crime, then a warrant is not necessary. In these cases, the police officer files a written or spoken deposition under oath. Approximately 95% of the arrests are made without a warrant in the United States.

Appearance before a judge

appearance before a judge

After an arrest, a suspect is booked at the Police Station. This is when depositions are made and the events that led up to the arrest are written down. The Police may take the suspect's fingerprints and photo, in order to create a document that will serve as a reference in a general file. Then the suspect is brought "without delay" before a judge, a magistrate or a commissioner, depending upon the State. The Supreme Court ruled in 1991 that an individual might not be held over 48 hours by the Police without a warrant, and without going before a judge.

warrant

This presentation is essential to the procedure: the suspect is officially informed of the alleged offenses and is reminded of all of the rights he has as a defendant. Among these rights is the infamous measure that resulted from the *Miranda v. Arizona* (1966), which grants a citizen the right to remain silent, that is, to not testify against himself. This right must be formally announced before all interrogations. The defendant also has a right to a lawyer and, if he cannot afford one, one will be proved by the State. A defendant's basic rights may differ from State to State, and as such we may find the "right to a quick trial" or the "right to confront a hostile witness" in them. After that, a judge decides if the defendant may be released on bail, and if so, the judge sets the amount of bail. The Constitution states that bail may not be

bail

grand jury

excessive, but the issue really depends on how much money the defendant has! Being released on bail is seen as a privilege, not a right, and the judge may refuse bail without any justification. Most often, judges refuse it in the cases of serious crimes, those in which the suspect risks the death penalty, or the risk of flight is too high. At a Federal level, all defendants are guaranteed by the 5th Amendment to be heard by a Grand Jury. It is slightly different, at a State jurisdiction level, because only half of the States enforce it. Others use the preliminary hearing method, or they set up an examining trial.

ACTIVITY

A. What are the pre-trial processes that you can identify? Explain them.

....

....

....

....

....

....

B. Identify the procedural steps that are protected by the Constitution of the United States.

....

....

....

....

....

....

STEP BY STEP

DOCUMENT 4

Dominique Strauss-Kahn denied $1m bail for rape

IMF Chief Strauss-Kahn held in New York jail cell after bail denied over alleged rape and other charges against a hotel maid.

In a badly-fitting black rain-coat, the unshaven 62-year-old was led into the New York criminal court hearing in handcuffs to face charges over a brutal sexual assault which has left the IMF in disarray and sent shockwaves through French politics, almost certainly ending the presidential hopes of the man tipped as the clear winner against Sarkozy in 2012. Strauss-Kahn's defence lawyers denied the charges against him, but failed in a bid for $1m bail. «This battle has just begun,» his defence attorney, Benjamin Brafman, told dozens of reporters gathered outside the court. «Mr Strauss-Kahn is innocent of these charges.» After the hearing, Manhattan district attorney Cyrus Vance set out the case against Strauss-Kahn. He is charged with seven crimes, including attempted rape, sexual abuse, forcible touching and unlawful imprisonment, against a 32-year-old hotel maid who had entered his suite at the Sofitel hotel near Times Square at around midday to clean. Conviction carries a prison sentence of up to 74 years. According to the criminal complaint, Strauss-Kahn shut the door of his hotel room, trapping his alleged victim inside, before grabbing her chest without her consent. John McConnell, an assistant district attorney said: «He sexually assaulted her and attempted to forcibly rape her,» and when that failed, he forced her to perform oral sex. He said the US authorities were now investigating whether Strauss-Kahn «engaged in conduct similar to the conduct alleged in this complaint on at least one other occasion». Asked to clarify by the judge, McConnell said the incident took place «in Europe». Strauss-Kahn did not enter a plea and was remanded to stay in prison until a hearing on Friday after prosecutors argued that the IMF head, who had been detained in the first-class cabin of an Air France jet about to take off for Paris hours after the alleged attack, was a flight risk «like Roman Polanski». District attorney Daniel Alonso compared Strauss-Kahn to the French-Polish film director who fled the US after having had sex with an underage girl and has avoided extradition ever since. Alonso said France had no extradition treaty with the US and Strauss-Kahn was a wealthy man who had been arrested attempting to flee the country. Brafman, who previously successfully defended Michael Jackson against child molestation charges, said it was «quite likely» his client would be «exonerated» and disputed he was trying to flee. Instead, Brafman said his client had a lunch meeting near the hotel and that his lunch partner would be able to testify. He said hotel security found out he was at the airport only after they called him and he told them where he was. He said Strauss-Kahn had been booked on to the Air France flight to Paris for some time.

DOCUMENT 5

Arrest Warrants: What's in them, how Police get them

Police must convince a neutral judge that, more likely than not, a crime has been committed and the subject of the warrant was involved.

An arrest warrant is an official document, signed by a judge (or magistrate), which authorizes a police officer to arrest the person,
5 or people, named in the warrant. Warrants typically identify the crime for which an arrest has been authorized, and may restrict the manner in which an arrest may
10 be made. For example, a warrant may state that a suspect can be arrested "only between the hours of 6 a.m. and 6 p.m." Finally, some warrants also specify the
15 bail that a defendant must post to regain freedom following arrest. If the warrant is for a previous failure of the suspect to appear in court—called a bench warrant—it
20 will probably specify that the arrested person may not be released on bail at all (sometimes termed a "no-bail warrant").

How the Police obtain an arrest warrant

To obtain a warrant, a police officer typically submits
25 a written affidavit to a judge or magistrate. The affidavit, given under oath, must recite sufficient factual information to establish probable cause that a crime was committed and that the person named in the warrant committed it. A description so broad that
30 it could apply to hundreds of people will not suffice. For instance, a judge will not issue a warrant to arrest

"Rich Johnson" based on an affidavit that "a liquor store was held up by a bald, potbellied man of medium height, and Rich Johnson matches 35 that description." That description doesn't establish probable cause to believe that Rich Johnson robbed the liquor store, because the vague description would apply to numerous 40 people. On the other hand, probable cause to arrest Rich Johnson would likely be adequate if the affidavit included the factual information that "the liquor store clerk and three 45 witnesses identified a photo of Rich Johnson as the person who held up the liquor store."

Incorrect Information in Arrest Warrants

Sometimes, arrest warrants contain factual mistakes. 50 For example, the suspect's name may be misspelled, or the wrong crime may be specified. Ideally, the Police should show the warrant to the suspect. And, if the suspect is able to prove that the officer has the wrong person, then the officer should not proceed. 55 As a practical matter, however, the Police sometimes don't show the warrant to the suspect for a variety of reasons real or imagined, and any mistakes as to identity are sorted out later. As for clerical errors, they are not enough to invalidate the warrant. 60

ACTIVITY

A. Why was Dominique Strauss-Kahn initialy refused bail? Was it fair?

B. Do you think the warrant system offers good protection for suspects?

PART 4 - THE ARRAIGNMENT

Civil and criminal cases

A dispute between two or more private individuals and organizations is considered a civil case. This covers disputes ranging from property rights (a conflict between a tenant and landlord), business arrangements, a family dispute, or people seeking damages after a car accident. However, in a criminal case there are not two private individuals. The State is the plaintiff and the individual is the defendant, meaning that charges are brought against a citizen by the State for violating a law. The citizen is thereby in a position to defend him/herself. Criminal cases involve either a felony (a major crime such as murder, rape, assault, arson, or a misdemeanor (a less serious crime, such as littering).

DID YOU KNOW?

9-1-1

Everybody knows this number in the United States: '9-1-1' is the emergency telephone number. It started to evolve to what is called NG9-1-1 (New Generation 9-1-1), to improve public emergency communication services in a growing wireless mobile society. It particularly intends the public to transmit text, image, video and data to the 9-1-1 center.

Arraignment is the stage in the procedure when the accused is presented before the Court and must respond to the Grand Jury's indictment or the Prosecutor's bill of information. It is the formal reading of an accusation in the presence of the accused so that he is aware of the exact reasons for which he is being prosecuted. The accused must enter a plea in answer to an arraignment. The plea may be different in each State or jurisdiction, but generally they must plead "guilty" or "not guilty" in person.

The accused has the option of pleading "not guilty for reasons of insanity", or "double jeopardy" if they were already accused of the same crime(s), or "nolo contendere", which is Latin for saying they do not dispute the charges, but do not understand the charges brought because they committed no crime. In Federal Court, the arraignment happens in two steps: the first must take place within 48 hours of being arrested (72 hours if the accused was arrested on a weekend), so that they may prepare their defense under proper conditions. The judge may also decide to release the accused on bail, and establish the amount of bail. During the second arraignment, a post-indictment arraignment or PIA, the defendant is allowed to enter a plea.

If the accused pleads "not guilty", then the judge sets a date for the trial. If they plead "guilty", they immediately receive a verdict, or the judge sets a future date. He makes sure that the plea is not made against the will of the accused and that he or she understands the consequences of the plea. A guilty plea is the same as a "guilty" verdict.

Plea bargain

Criminal proceedings very seldom go to trial. This is basically due to the possibility given of making a plea bargain between the Defending and Prosecuting Attorneys, between the charges brought and the sentence that the guilty person will receive. In about 90% of cases, negotiation results in an agreement. In reality, a sort of tolerance is usually promised in exchange for a plea of "guilty" and the resulting sentence is less severe. But here again, the role of the judge is very important. He or she must insure that the procedure is respected and that the rights of the accused are not infringed.

There are two types of plea bargains:

- Reduced charges: this is the most common form

of agreement between a prosecutor and a defendant. For the most part, the defendant is able to spend less time in prison but, most importantly, to avoid being accused of a felony, which remains on one's criminal record: by agreeing to plead guilty for numerous misdemeanors, the defendant may convince the Prosecutor to withdraw a more serious charge.

- Reduced sentences: the agreement only depends only on the seriousness of the conviction, which, most of the time, is the time to be spent in prison. The Prosecutor promises to ask for a lower sentence from the judge. Judges are not obliged to accept them, even if they most often do.

ACTIVITY

A. What is an arraignment?

....

....

....

B. How do plea-bargains work? What is your opinion of this system?

....

....

....

ACCUSED OF A CRIME

The Basics of Pennsylvania Law Sentencing

DOCUMENT 6

In Pennsylvania, once you are convicted of a crime or plead guilty to a crime, it is the trial judge's obligation to sentence you in accordance with the law. The trial judge has broad discretion when it comes to senten-
5 cing, and has a wide array of sentencing alternatives available. For instance, the judge may order you to serve probation, electronic home monitoring (house arrest), jail time or pay fines. A judge may order you to perform community service, stay away from the victim,
10 pay restitution to the victim, or enroll in a drug and alcohol treatment program. These are a few examples of the sentencing alternatives at the disposal of the trial judge. However, there are some restraints on the court. If the crime carries a mandatory sentence, by
15 law, the court has to follow the mandatory sentence if the District Attorney's Office enforces it. For example, the mandatory sentence for selling drugs in a school zone is 2 years jail. If the offender is convicted, and the District Attorney's office enforces the mandatory, the
20 judge may not give the offender any less than 2 years jail time. Another restraint on the trial judge is that he may not sentence an offender beyond the maximum penalty provided by law. The following chart outlines the maximum sentences available to Pennsylvania
25 judges. In the right hand column, the number of years indicates the maximum length of the sentence, and the dollar value indicates the maximum fine a judge may impose.

Maximum Sentences

30 18 Pa.C.S.A. §1101 et seq.

Felony 1st Degree	20 yrs	$25,000
Felony 2nd Degree	10 yrs	$25,000
Felony 3rd Degree/Felony	7 yrs	$15,000
Misdemeanor 1st Degree	5 yrs	$10,000
35 Misdemeanor 2nd Degree	2 yrs	$5,000
Misdemeanor 3rd Degree	1 yr	$2500
Summary	90d	$300
Summary		$25

For example, if an offender is convicted of a Felony
40 3rd degree, the judge may not fashion a sentence of probation or incarceration that exceeds 7 years in length or $15,000 in fines.

Pennsylvania Sentencing Guidelines

The Pennsylvania Commission on Sentencing has
45 promulgated sentencing guidelines as a guide for Pennsylvania trial judges to follow. However, the sen-
tencing guidelines are NOT binding on Pennsylvania judges. The common pleas judge that sentences you may deviate from the guidelines. If the court departs 50 from the guidelines, it MUST explain the reasons for the deviation on the record. It is my experience and legal opinion, that 99% of the time, Pennsylvania Court of Common Pleas judges give great weight to the sentencing guidelines and will sentence in accordance 55 with these guidelines. Therefore, if you are facing criminal charge(s) in Pennsylvania it is important to calculate your sentencing guidelines well in advance of your court date.

60

Calculating Your Guideline Sentence

Your sentencing guideline will be based on two things,
1) the seriousness of the offense, known as the "offense gravity score"; and
2) your prior criminal record known as your "prior record score." 65

Offense Gravity Score

Each Pennsylvania crime has an assigned point value. The higher the number value, the higher the offense gravity score. To determine the offense gravity score of the charge you are facing, look up your offense to *204 Pa.Code* §303.15 to determine its offense gravity score. 70 For example, Rape would carry an offense gravity score of 11 while Possession of a Small Amount of Marijuana carries an offense gravity score of 1.

Prior Record Score

Your sentencing guideline will also be based on your 75 prior criminal record. Each defendant is designated what is called a "prior record score." Your score is a point value between 1 and 5. All misdemeanor and felony crimes will be added together in the computa- tion of your prior record score. Out-of-state criminal 80 offenses will be counted toward the prior record score. Out-of-state offenses will be assigned the point value of an equivalent Pennsylvania offense. Juvenile adju- dications that occurred on or after the offender's 14th birthday and the adjudication was for a felony or one 85 of the Misdemeanor 1 offenses listed in §303.7 (a)(4) will be counted toward the prior record score.

DOCUMENT 7

Pennsylvania teacher accused of sexually assaulting a student.

Teacher Emily Nesbit resigns after being accused of sex with student in classroom

An 11th grade English teacher resigned last week after she was accused of having sexual relations with a
5 student at a Pennsylvania high school.

Emily Nesbit, 31, was charged with institutional sex assault, a third-degree felony, on Friday. Police said Nesbit admitted meeting an 18-year-old male student for sex in a classroom after hours at Cumberland Valley
10 High School in Mechanicsburg.

Nesbit is charged based on her position as a teacher, without regard to the age of the student. If convicted she could face up to seven years in prison, prosecutors told *ABC 27 News*. Administrators learned about the
15 alleged inappropriate contact on March 10th after a female student discovered sexual text messages on the alleged victim's phone, according to *Fox 43 News*. These included partially clothed and naked photos of Nesbit and the student.
20 According to the *Patriot News*, Silver Spring Township police interviewed the alleged victim the next day. They learned he and the teacher had been in communication for about two months and met several times in
25 the classroom after school. The student did not deny his relationship with the teacher. Police said the teacher's phone number was listed as «My Lady Friend» in the student's iPhone.

Prosecutors are urging parents to closely monitor their 30 children's phones and social media accounts in the wake of the scandal.

«The message to parents is, you need to 100 percent read your child's text messages, follow them on Instagram, follow them on Twitter,» prosecutor David Freed said, 35 according to *ABC 27 News*.

Nesbit's attorney released a statement Friday, explaining that the teacher «made a series of bad decisions at a low point in her life,» and that she «intends to accept responsibility in court and continue to work on her 40 personal issues that lead to the alleged inappropriate conduct,» *PennLive* reports.

Fox 43 News reports that the recent events caused unease and mistrust among faculty and students alike. Cumberland Valley superintendent Frederick Withum 45 said that teachers felt «betrayed» by the alleged conduct. "It kind of feels dirty a little bit," an unidentified student told the station. "It feels weird knowing what went on in there."

ACTIVITY

A. What is the charge against the young woman?

B. Was she arrested? Why or why not?

C. What is the procedure after the Police were told about the alleged charge?

D. What does the teacher face?

E. What is your opinion about the advice given by the prosecutor to the parents?

Important words

Actus Reus
Mens Rea
Arrest
Appearance
Warrant
Bail

IS IT A CRIME?

To define most crimes, such as rape, assault, or theft, one might think that, at the least, someone must be wounded or hurt, and be recognized as a victim. There are other types of crimes in which there is no victim and no one is hurt or wounded. An action is defined as a crime when a law is not respected. Some crimes are defined as serious by society, such as murder or kidnapping. They are often horrible and punished with a heavy prison sentence, or even the death penalty. Other crimes are much less serious and the punishment is adapted to the gravity of the crime committed. It is sometimes difficult to determine if the crime in question is horrible because circumstances should be taken into account that would change our impression of the alleged act committed. Crimes are defined by society to respond to the needs of a given moment. Laws are long to change, and some acts we call a crime might seem ridiculous to us sometimes.

ELEMENTS OF A CRIME

Laws should be clearly defined and published so that citizens know how to behave. Ex-post facto laws are forbidden in the United States and it also not authorized to make laws that would only apply to a limited number of people. Each crime is composed of two elements: the *acteus reus* and the *mens rea*. The Attorney General must prove the presence of these two elements for the suspect to be convicted. *Actus rea* is Latin for "guilty act", while *mens rea* is Latin for "guilty mind". It is possible to commit a criminal act without meaning to do it. Or, one may have the intention of committing a crime, but never act upon it. It is also possible, that one intends to commit a crime, and one acts upon it, but the circumstances are such that the act does not take place. So, the goal of a trial is to determine the circumstances and the intentions.

PROCEEDINGS BEFORE A TRIAL

A strict procedure must be followed when a crime is committed. Some parts of this process are provided by the U.S. Constitution, or by laws, passed by the U.S. Congress or various States. The arrest is the first step. It may be done with a warrant, or without one, if the crime happens in front of the Police, or if the Police think that someone is on the verge of committing a crime. About 95% arrests take place without warrants in the USA. The second step is going before a judge. The Police may take a deposition, photos, fingerprints, and DNA samples of the suspect, but the suspect must go before a judge within 48 hours. The suspect has the right to be reminded of his rights, some of which are protected by the Constitution, such as the right to remain silent, or the right to an attorney. The Supreme Court confirmed these rights in famous decisions, such as *Miranda v. Arizona*, 1966. A suspect may be released with bail, but the bail must not be excessive. Suspects have the right to be heard by a Grand Jury at a Federal level.

THE ARRAIGNMENT

The third step is the arraignment, which consists in going before a judge, or a Grand Jury if it's a federal trial. During the arraignment, the accused is made formally aware of the charges against him, and he must state his plea: guilty or not guilty. The defendant may also plead not guilty in case of (temporary) insanity, or double jeopardy, or *nolo contendere*, which means that he doesn't understand. A guilty plea leads to a conviction that may be pronounced immediately by the judge. Appearing before the judge must take place within 48 hours of being arrested. The judge may decide to free the defendant on bail. Criminal cases rarely go to trial because it is possible to make a plea bargain, which is quite common. The plea may concern a reduced charge or a reduced sentence.

A. Are the following statements true or false? Check the correct box.

	True	False
1. Misdemeanor is another word to designate aggravated		
2. Rikers Island is the most famous Police Adademy in the		
3. *Mens Rea* is an expression used when a suspect is supposed to have		
4. A warrant is always delivered by a judge.		

B. Why should the State punish a person for not wearing a seat belt when it will only be that person who suffer through not wearing it?

....
....

C. Is it possible to find *mens rea* in a case without an *actus reus*?

....

D. Is it possible to be acquitted in spite of proven *mens rea*?

....
....

E. What happens if somebody pleads guilty?

....
....

REFERENCES :

Page 187. "Dennis Hopper mug shot", Wikimedia. http://commons.wikimedia. org/wiki/File:Dennis_Hopper_mug_shot.jpg?uselang=fr

Page 187. "It is a crime?", by Dimitri Champain.

Page 190. "Rikers Island", adapted from "The 10 worst prisons in America", by James Ridgeway and Jean Casella, May 1, 2013. http://www.theinvestigativefund.org/investigations/rightsliberties/1779/the_10_worst_prisons_in_america?page=entire
"USGC Rikers Island", by U.S. Geological Survey. Wikimedia. http://commons.wikimedia.org/wiki/File:USGS_Rikers_Island.png?uselang=fr

Page 191. "Florence, Colorado: Alcatraz of the Rockies", adapted from "America's 10 worst prisons: ADX", by James Ridgeway and Jean Casella, May 1, 2013.http://www.motherjones.com/politics/2013/05/10-worst-prisons-america-part-1-adx

Page192. "Crimes deserve punishments", by Dimitri Champain.

Page194. "Shooting of Trayvon Martin", from "mens rea its effect criminal cases", by Deborah C. England, in *Criminal defense lawyer*, http://www.criminaldefenselawyer.com/resources/criminal-defense/criminal-defense-case/mens-rea-its-effect-criminal-cases
"George Zimmerman Mugshot." Wikimedia. http://commons. wikimedia.org/wiki/File:George_Zimmerman_Mugshot.jpg?uselang=fr

Page 198. "Dominique Strauss-Kahn denied $1m bail on rape", adapted from *The Guardian*, by Dominic Rushe in New York and Angelique Crisaflis in Paris, May 17,2011
"Dominique Strauss-Kahn media circus", by Patsw. Wikimedia. http://commons.wikimedia.org/wiki/File:Dominique_Strauss-Kahn_media_circus.jpg?uselang=fr

Page 199. "Arrest Warrants: What's in Them, How Police Get Them." in Paul Bergman, J.D., and Sara J. Bergman, J.D., *The Criminal Law Handbook, know your rights, survive the system,* August 2013, 13th edition. 169.
"Samjain-warrant", Wikimedia. http://commons.wikimedia.org/wiki/File:Samjain_warrant.png?uselang=fr

Page201. "Let's plead 'not guilty'", by Dimitri Champain

Page 203. "Pennsylvania teacher accused of sexual assault of student." adapted from the *Huffington Post*, March, 17, 2014, by Andres Jauregui.
"Cumberland Valley high school", by Dimitri Champain

Page 204. "Summary", by Dimitri Champain

Page 205. "Review", by Dimitri Champain

pp.189, 191, 193, 195, 197, 199, 201, 203 "Activity", by Dimitri Champain

UNIT 11 Criminal Trials

Introduction

When there is no agreement for a plea bargain and the defendant continues to claim his innocence, a trial is planned. This is a right protected by the U.S. Constitution: the 6th and 14th Amendments. This right was strengthened by similar guarantees included in various State constitutions; thus, rights that judges must try hard to enforce protect every American. The procedure during a trial is particularly important and its strictness is another way to protect the defendant.

PART 1 – EQUAL JUSTICE FOR ALL

Protecting those accused of a crime is a major challenge in a democracy. Adopting the Bill of Rights should have been an answer to this problem and it gave a number of fundamental rights to those suspected of having committed a crime.

Unreasonable searches and seizures prohibited

It's obvious that you need proof to convict someone. Finding that proof sometimes requires searching people, or inside their vehicle or house. Searches are not forbidden by the Constitution; on the other hand, the 4th Amendment explicitly states that they should not be "unreasonable", without any more details as to what is meant by unreasonable. Because this is a complicated issue, it was established that the Police would have to obtain a search warrant before searching someone or their home. The warrant must specify the location of the search and those involved, as well as the objects for which they are searching. There is no "standard" warrant that would permit searching for anything and everything, since that would go against the principles of the Constitution. However, it is possible for the Police to not have need of a warrant, notably when they witness a crime happening. This situation is far from being the most common in the United States, even though it was largely restricted in 1980, in *Payton v. New York*, in which Police were banned with entering someone's home to arrest a suspect, even if they are convinced that a crime is being committed.

> **It was established that Police would have to obtain a search warrant before searching someone**

Guarantee of the right to counsel

6th Amendment
The 6th Amendment states that a defendant has the right "to have assistance of counsel for his defense." Even lawyers have the right to hire another lawyer to defend them. As the proverb goes, "the lawyer who defends himself has a fool for client."

The Constitution protects the right to a lawyer in Federal proceedings. However, this same right is not guaranteed by all of the State constitutions, so criminal justice has developed quite differently from one State to the next. This right is also unique in having been recognized by the Supreme Court in a 1942 judgment, *Betts v. Brady*. Though, in 1963 the Supreme Court rendered a groundbreaking verdict that saw this problem from the opposite side, in *Gideon v. Wainwright,* providing that the State should furnish an attorney free of charge to those who were too poor to afford one.

Self-incrimination restricted

This right is protected by the 5th Amendment, which states that no one *"shall be compelled in any criminal case to be a witness against himself."* The Courts have interpreted this by meaning that no one is obligated to testify against themselves. In other words, no one is obliged to help the Police find proof against them, and they are under no obligation to testify during their own trial. The goal of this protection is to avoid testimony being obtained by force or under duress. This measure is applied in the States as a result of the 14th Amendment. Two Supreme Court verdicts are the authorities on this issue: *Escobedo v. Illinois* (1964) and *Miranda v. Arizona* (1966)

Double jeopardy prohibited

The 5th Amendment also states that no one will be put "twice in jeopardy of life and limb," which means no one may be judged twice for the same crime. One must not forget, however, that since some crimes may be con-

Jury rights are secured
This right is found in Article III of the Constitution and repeated in the 6th Amendment: "In all criminal prosecutions, the accused shall have the right to a speedy and public trial, by an impartial jury." This right applies to States via the 14th Amendment.

sidered as Federal and State crimes at the same time, it is technically possible to be judged twice (once in Federal Court and once in State Court). Moreover, one deed may fall under several laws and correspond to numerous crimes, again providing the possibility of being judged many times for many reasons; the Supreme Court recognized this in *Blockburger v. United States* (1832). Finally, if a jury cannot decide on a verdict, a second trial will be held (*United States v. Perez*, 1824, confirmed more recently in *Blueford v. Arkansas*, 2012).

Right to trial by jury

Of all of the rights accorded a defendant as part of their proceedings, the most important is surely the right to be judged by 12 citizens chosen at random from within the community. Nevertheless, the Supreme Court has indicated that it is a right that may not necessarily be applied by States to crimes that result in being put in prison for over six months, this leaving it up to the States to decide according to their own policies in less serious offenses. However, the Supreme Court has firmly reiterated this right for all major recent verdicts: *Apprenti v. New Jersey*, 2000 and *Blakely v. Washington*, 2004. Most of the States have decided that there should be a jury for all criminal trials, whether "petty" or not. The selection of the jury start with questioning the prospective jurors, a courtroom process known as *Voir Dire* (which means "to speak the truth").

ACTIVITY

A. What are the Amendments concerned with the protection of the accused?

....

....

....

B. Why is the Fifth Amendment so important?

....

....

....

VOIR DIRE

DOCUMENT 1

A jury selection exercise

Case Overview:

Jonathan Frank, 21, was charged with manslaughter in the death of Jolie Emmanuel, 17, in a fatal alcohol-related car crash last year. On a date with Emmanuel, Frank bought a 4-pack of wine coolers for the young woman and watched her consume 2 bottles over the course of the evening. At the end of the date, Frank took Emmanuel back to her car. It was on the drive home that Emmanuel lost control of the vehicle and slammed it into a cement barrier. She was killed instantly. The police report indicated alcohol levels below the legal maximum and that Emmanuel had been speeding on rain slicked roads at the time of the accident.

JUROR 1 – Carol Brustein
Middle aged woman with two teenage sons. She has served on a jury before, but the trial ended in a hung jury. She lives in the neighborhood where both Frank and Emmanuel grew up, but does not know them personally. She thinks that one of her sons might have heard of Frank, a star basketball player while at the high school.

JUROR 2 – Carl Sweet
Young male college student majoring in Political Science and pre-Law. He works part-time as an intern in the local D.A.'s office and is a member of the debate team at the university. What little free time he has is used for studying and hanging out with the guys from his fraternity house.

JUROR 3 – Elias Kinshak
Middle-aged school librarian who works at the local high school, volunteers for the American Library Association annual book drive, and trains for international marathons in his free time. He recently was ranked third in his age group at the New York Marathon.

JUROR 4 – Steve Davis
Young man who works at an auto repair shop in the valley. Went to the rival high school and completed Vocational Tech program. He knew Emmanuel through his girlfriend but was not close to her. He attends church near where the accident happened and passes the memorial to Emmanuel every weekend.

JUROR 5 – Veronica Rivera
Elderly retired secretary for the police department. She is widowed; her husband was a retired police officer before he passed away two years ago due to complications with adult diabetes. She is a member of the League of Women Voters and tutors adult English as a Second Language students at the community center in Frank's neighborhood.

JUROR 6 – Parker O'Brien
Retired 65-year-old businessman with a strong New York accent who sold his local copy shop to Kinko's three years ago. Has a daughter about Emmanuel's age, but to his knowledge, his daughter does not know Emmanuel personally.

JUROR 7 – Josie Clementine
Doctor in her mid-thirties who is an emergency room physician at the local hospital. Specializes in reconstructive facial surgery. She moved to the area from Washington, D.C., six months ago.

JUROR 8 – Christi Miller
18-year-old college freshman who used to live five streets over from the Frank family. She doesn't know Frank personally. Graduated top of her class at the magnet school in the city and plans to become a broadcast news anchorwoman.

JUROR 9 – Sergio Sowell
Middle aged local banker and town councilman. He is married, has three young children in the local Catholic school system, and enjoys reading true crime stories in his limited free time. He hopes to be elected mayor one day.

JUROR 10 – Alice Klein
Single mother and child care worker in a chain daycare center in the heart of town. Dropped out of high school and received her GED. Has served on a jury once before in a civil trial. Commutes from outside of the city and has no connection to either party involved in the suit.

JUROR 11 – Geneseo Kantakoros
Recent immigrant to the United States who works full time at a local computer software company. Holds two Ph.D.s, one in Physics and the other in Computer Science. He hopes to start his own business one day and work as an adjunct professor at the local university. As a result, he works 60-80 hour weeks. His new house is in the same development as the Emmanuel family's.

JUROR 12 – Claire Tremont
Middle-aged former horse trainer who lives with her husband on a large ranch located in the peaceful countryside. Five years ago, she was involved in an auto accident that left her unable to participate in equestrian competitions. Her truck and trailer were hit head-on by a drunk driver in a red sports car on the two-lane road that leads to her property.

Jury Selection in Criminal Cases

DOCUMENT 2

The right to trial by jury in criminal cases is guaranteed by the 6th Amendment to the U.S. Constitution, as well as the laws of every state. Lawyers and judges select juries by a process known as "*voir dire*," which is Latin for "to speak the truth." In *voir dire*, the judge and attorneys for both sides ask potential jurors questions to determine if they are competent and suitable to serve in the case. Errors during jury selection are common grounds for appeal in criminal cases.

Questioning Jurors

When a case is called for trial, a randomly selected panel of potential jurors (called a *venire*) is seated in the courtroom. The trial judge begins *voir dire* by asking the prospective jurors questions to ensure that they are legally qualified to serve on a jury and that jury service would not them cause undue hardship. For example, most States allow a student who might miss critical exams, a person who has an upcoming surgery scheduled, or someone who serves as sole caretaker of an ill or elderly family member to be excused from jury service for undue hardship. Next, the lawyers for each side question the potential jurors about their biases and backgrounds, as well as any pre-existing knowledge they might have about the case. But the lawyers aren't allowed to ask overly personal questions, and they aren't allowed ask the jurors how they would decide the case in advance.

Challenges to the Venire

After they have completed questioning, the lawyers begin removing potential jurors from the *venire* by making challenges for cause and peremptory challenges.

Challenges for cause. Challenges for cause are made when *voir dire* reveals that a juror is not qualified, able, or fit to serve in a particular case. Lawyers generally have an unlimited number of "for cause" challenges available. In order to serve as a juror, a person must be a U.S. citizen, over the age of 18, live in the court's jurisdiction, and have the right to vote. Also, each person must be able to physically sit through the entire trial, as well as hear and understand the trial testimony. Jurors must also be mentally capable of understanding and applying the judge's legal instructions. Any person who doesn't meet these criteria will be dismissed "for cause."

Actual Bias. Actual bias arises when potential jurors admit that they wouldn't be able to be impartial. For example, a juror who states that she would never vote for a guilty verdict in any case because her religious beliefs prevent her from sitting in judgment of another would be excused for cause.

Implied Bias. Implied bias is present when potential jurors have character traits or personal experiences that make it unlikely for them to be able to be impartial, regardless of what they say during *voir dire*. So, a juror who is a close friend or relative of a key party, a witness, the judge, or an attorney for either side will be dismissed for cause.

Peremptory Challenges. No reason is required for a lawyer to use a peremptory challenge to excuse a potential juror. Such challenges allow each side to dismiss jurors who are otherwise qualified, but appear likely to favor the opposing party. However, peremptory challenges cannot be used to exclude jurors on the basis of race or class.

Striking the Jury

In the process known as "striking a jury," the Prosecution and Defense take turns arguing their challenges for cause. If the judge grants a challenge, the juror will be struck from the jury panel. Once there are no more viable challenges for cause, the sides alternate in striking jurors via peremptory challenges until those are exhausted or each side is satisfied with the jury panel. The States vary in the number of jurors required for a jury, ranging from six to 23. If too many potential jurors have been eliminated after the use of challenges, the judge can either summon additional potential jurors or declare a mistrial.

ACTIVITY

A. Determine whether jurors 1-12 would be permitted to participate in this case.

B. Explain why each one would (or would not) be a "good juror" in the eyes of the Prosecution or the Defense.

C. Now create three of your own jurors – one who'd assist the defense, one who would assist the Prosecution, and a "dream witness" for both sides. Create a short biography as above in jurors 1-9. (JUROR 10 – JUROR 11 – JUROR 12)

PART 2 – OPENING THE TRIAL

The jury is selected according to different judicial philosophies and rules. If a juror's response indicates that he or he will not make fair decisions, the juror may be *challenged for cause.* Then the judge must rule on the challenge and has the final say. There is no limit to the number of jurors the attorneys may challenge for cause. Another method of controlling the jury's composition is through the use of peremptory challenges exercises by the Prosecution and the Defense. The judge has no control here. Usually, the Defense is allowed eight to ten *peremptory challenges*, and the Prosecution six to eight. This permits them to exclude whom they think will be unsympathetic to their arguments. Also, defendants have the right to request to be judged by a judge only, with no jury.

Opening Statement

The opening of a trial takes place with a quick introduction of the case. This is called an *"opening statement"*. The Prosecuting and Defending Attorneys each take turns speaking, but sometimes, for strategic reasons, a lawyer may choose not to speak at this point in the proceeding. When the trial takes place in front of a jury (*a jury trial*), rather than in front of a judge (*a bench trial)*, the opening statement lasts a little longer. The goal of this first phase of the procedure is to familiarize the jury with the laws and procedure, all the while stressing a version or specific proof that will be put forward by one of the other parties, to try to prove the defendant's guilt or innocence. Generally, the Prosecution begins by announcing the accusation for the State, while the Defense speaks next in order to refute the charges.

The case for the Prosecution

After the opening statement, the Prosecutor will deliver the actual accusation in more detail and will begin presenting proof collected by the State against the defendant. This proof may be physical evidence, or witness testimony. There is no limit to the type of physical evidence that can be presented, though we probably think first about bullets, fingerprints and DNA samples that constitute the most common spectrum of evidence collected by the Police. For each piece of evidence, the Defense has the right to object, and if the objection is reasonable and upheld by the judge, then it will be disregarded during the trial. Every piece of evidence is numbered and labeled

Witness testimony
This is one of the most common types of proof. It is presented in the structure of an interview with questions and answers, in which the aim is to focus on a particular point or specific aspect of the case. The Prosecutor must be as clear as possible, and the testimony should reinforce the understanding of what he or she is presenting to the jury or judge. It's not a question of having a series of witnesses who tell a complete version of the events in their own way, since the obvious risk is rendering the discussion confusing and nonsensical. The Prosecutor must also avoid procedural flaws, such as acting as if the defendant has already been condemned for the same crime (though it's not true).

CSI effect

The "CSI effect" is a reference to the phenomenon of CSI raising crime victims' and jury members' real-world expectations of forensic science, especially crime scene investigation and DNA testing. This is said to have changed the way many trials are presented today, in that Prosecutors are pressured to deliver more forensic evidence in court.

by the Court.

The Defense Attorney may then proceed with cross-examination, in which the goal is to show that the witness is possibly not trustworthy. He or she has the right to ask questions that may anger, disturb or perturb the witness. Witness testimony is often uncertain and the attorneys are highly gifted at damaging the credibility of a witness in front of the jury. The Prosecuting Attorney may re-address after cross-examination and question the witness again. The goal here is to clarify a question that may have popped up during the cross-examination led by the Defense.

The case for the Defense

The Defense's statement is identical in form and style to the Prosecution's. The difference is that the Defense is under no obligation to present evidence or witnesses, contrary to the Prosecution. The Defense may "settle for" disproving the evidence presented by the Prosecution or attempting to discredit the testimony.

ACTIVITY

A. What is the difference between a peremptory challenge and a challenge for cause?

LET'S START

Jury pool selection

DOCUMENT 3

	Round One Only people who live in the area and are familiar with the case are allowed to serve (as in Old English Common Law)	Round Two Only people who do not live in the area and are not familiar with the case are allowed to serve.	Round Three Anyone can be eliminated because of potential bias.	Round Four No jury but a judge instead.	Round Five Juror excuses.
1. Ekaterina 2. Jason 3. Charles 4. Veronica 5. Eric 6. Melanie 7. Elias 8. Miroslava 9. Kyle 10. .... 11. .... 12.					

Questioning the jury

DOCUMENT 4

The case is between the plaintiff (Sharon Franks) and the defendant (Express Car Repair). The plaintiff is suing the defendant because she claims she brought her car to Express Car Repair for an oil change and the repair shop damaged her car.

Juror 1: Josie Batch, waitress, age 26.
Describe your work ethic. I work very hard to support myself and help my family.
Have you ever been fired from a job? Yes, I used to work for the plaintiff until she fired me.
So you know the plaintiff? Yes. I really don't like her and don't feel like I can listen to the evidence fairly.

Advantages/disadvantages for the plaintiff:

Advantages/disadvantages for the defendant:

Determination on juror:

Juror 2: Chris Grace, teacher, 55.
Have you ever taken a car to Express Car Repair? I take both of my cars there. A few months ago one of my cars was dented while in the repair shop.
Was it badly damaged? It hasn't affected how my car drives, but it looks bad.
Do you think that experience will keep you from being a fair juror in this case? No, I don't.

Advantages/disadvantages for the plaintiff:

Advantages/disadvantages for the defendant:

Determination on juror:

Juror 3: Janet Casson, owner of Lots to Read Bookstore, age 39.
How long has your business been located next door to Express Car Repair? About two years.
Do you know anyone who works at Express Car Repair? The people who work at the garage are always parking in front of my store, but I don't know any of them by name.
Is there any reason you would not be able to consider evidence fairly? I've taken my car to the repair shop and did not really like their work, but I would try not to let anything influence my judgement.
Adv./dis. for the plaintiff:
Adv./dis. for the defendant:
Determination on juror:

DOCUMENT 5

Opening Statements: What the Prosecution and Defense Can and Can't Say

In a typical criminal trial, after they have selected the jury, the Prosecution and Defense have the opportunity to give an opening statement. The opening statement allows both sides to give the judge and jury an overview
5 of the case, including what they plan to prove and how they plan to prove it (what evidence they will offer in support of their claims).Prosecutors and defense attorneys generally have considerable latitude in what they're allowed to say in opening statement. That said,
10 they're not allowed to "argue" (argument is saved for closing), nor are they allow to refer to inadmissible evidence or facts they don't intend to or can't prove.

Opening Statement Examples

The following are examples of opening-statement com-
15 ments that courts have found improper:
A defense attorney said that the defendant had offered to take a polygraph test in order to prove that he was innocent. [Evidence regarding lie detectors was inadmissible. *Simmons v. State*, 208 Md. App. 677 (2012).]
20 A Prosecutor asserted a fact that could have been proven only if an informant had been available to testify in support of it. The Prosecutor knew the informant would not be testifying. (*State v. Bernier*, 486 A.2d 147 (Me. 1985).)
25 A defense attorney tried to argue legal principles relating to eyewitness identification. (*State v. Elliott*, 69 N.C. App. 89 (1984).)
On the other hand, courts frequently allow lawyers to push the boundaries of acceptable opening-statement remarks. Consider the following comments, which 30 appellate courts validated:
A Prosecutor described the alleged crime as a "mass execution" and its date as "one of the worst and most violent days in the history of Boston." The statements were "enthusiastic rhetoric, strong advocacy, and 50 excusable hyperbole." (*Com. v. Siny Van Tran*, 460 Mass. 535 (2011).)
A Prosecutor said, "You will learn that the defendant is a drug dealer.» The appellate court said this merely amounted to saying the defendant committed the crime 55 in question. (*State v. Smallwood*, 230 S.W.3d 662 (Mo. Ct. App. 2007).)
A Prosecutor commented that the defendant had escaped from a prison camp shortly before abducting the victim. Even though evidence of other crimes by 60 a defendant aren't usually admissible, the Prosecutor had a reasonable expectation that evidence of the escape would be admitted. (*Ex parte Baldwin*, 456 So. 2d 129 (Ala. 1984).)

Intervention
65
If a lawyer goes too far astray in an opening statement, opposing counsel can object—if the objection is proper, the judge will cut off the lawyer and potentially admonish the jury not to consider what he or she just said. The judge will probably let the lawyer resume the ope- 70 ning statement, but intervene if it gets off track again.

ACTIVITY

A. You are the judge in this case and you are trying to to create as fair a jury as possible. Read the description on p.210 carefully. Then go through the selection process for rounds one to four. For each round, mark K for «Keep» or «E» for Eliminate, for each juror.

B. For round five, determine what the excuses could be for each juror (*Read p.211 for explanations*) and decide whether or not to keep them.

C. Decide if the three potential jurors proposed are fair for this case. Write the advantages and disadvantages for the plaintiff, then do the same thing for the defendant, before deciding.

PART 3 – THE JUDGE AND THE JURY

The juror

The jury's role is not an active one during the proceedings. The job of the 12 jury members is, first of all, to listen. In most cases, they are not permitted to ask questions, although it is possible, but always in writing and using the judge as an intermediary. They are also not allowed to record any audio or video, or take notes. There is nothing in the Constitution or the Law to explain this interdiction, but it is the result of tradition and Courts typically apply this rule. Incidentally, it is almost always clearly stated in the Court rules. These considerations are the judge's responsibility; he or she sometimes authorizes different rules: when sitting for the District Court for the Northern District of Illinois, Judge John F. Grady allowed the jury to take notes for over ten years. Many judges who sit in the State Courts permit this practice. Numerous Federal Appellate Courts allow jurists to ask witnesses questions. But, generally, the jury's role is passive.

Judges also have a mostly passive role. They don't participate in questioning the witnesses and play no active role in presenting evidence. During this part of the trial, they restrict themselves to sustaining or overruling a lawyer's motions or the Prosecutor who objects to a question or an answer; or requests the rejection of a piece of evidence, or a witness. Sometimes, the judge asks questions directly to the witness, or will give some comments on the credibility of a piece of evidence, but it is simply forbidden by Law in most States.

The judge's, and the jury's, active role comes into play when the trial is coming to an end. This is the moment when judges take a more active role in delivering instructions to the jury, clarifying the meaning and intention of the Law, and the way in which it should be applied. Instructions to the jury always contain the fundamental elements: the definition of the crime of which a person is accused is part of it. The judge must also provide information about all of the options open to the jury for the type of verdicts it may render. For example, if someone was murdered, judges may explain what first-degree murder is; but they must also explain what second-degree murder is, as well as manslaughter. The latter will be applied if the defendant is found guilty of the crime, but without malice aforethought.

Judges remind the jury that the burden of proof lies with the State and in criminal cases the proof must be solid, with a very high burden of proof at 99%. The jury is reminded that the defendant is innocent until proven

Beware of the girl with high heels!
Anything may be a weapon: In April 2014, Ana Lilia Trujillo was found guilty of murder by a jury in Houston, Texas, in the killing of her boyfriend with the heel of a stiletto shoe. The shoe were a $1,500 present from the victim!

guilty, so long as it has not decided otherwise. This notion should tilt the scales in favor of the defendant if there is too much doubt. On top of that, if doubt persists after the jury's deliberation, it cannot render a guilty verdict. Finally, judges explain a large amount of practical information to the jury, such as how to contact the judge if there is a problem, or if it has questions, in which order to deal with the charges brought against the defendant when there is more than one, and who must sign official documents, etc.

Then, the jury retires for deliberation to decide the defendant's destiny. Jury members deliberate by themselves: no one is allowed to participate in their discussion, not even the judge. Jury members may ask for clarification on a point of Law, re-examine physical evidence, re-read witness testimony, but they are not allowed access to anything else. No law books, no Internet, no telephone. When they have reached a verdict, they return to the courtroom to deliver it. If they have not reached a decision by nightfall, the members return to their homes with orders to not speak to anyone about the case. In high-profile cases, the judge may require that they stay in a hotel in order to assure confidentiality.

ACTIVITY

A. What does the jury do during the trial?

....

....

....

....

B. Who may participate in the deliberation?

....

....

....

....

BE ATTENTIVE

DOCUMENT 6

Summary of trial procedures

1. Attorneys present physical evidence for inspection.
2. Judge states charges against defendant.
3. Prosecution delivers its opening statement. No questioning during opening statements.
4. Defense may choose to deliver its opening statement at this point or may wait to open after the prosecution has completed its case in chief.
5. Prosecution calls its witnesses and conducts direct examination.
6. After each prosecution witness is called to the stand and has been examined by the prosecution, the defense cross-examines the witness.
7. After each cross-examination, prosecution may conduct re-direct examination of its own witnesses if necessary.
8. After prosecution presents all its witnesses, defense delivers its opening statement (if it did not do so earlier).
9. Defense calls its witnesses and conducts direct examination.
10. After each defense witness is called to the stand and has been examined by the Defense, the Prosecution cross-examines the witness.
11. After each cross-examination, defense may conduct re-direct examination of its own witnesses if necessary.
12. Prosecution gives its closing argument, then Defense presents its closing arguments. No questioning during closing arguments.
13. Prosecution and Defense present rebuttal arguments.
14. Judge/jury deliberates, announces verdict in court, and conducts a short debrief of the trial.

DOCUMENT 7

You are the jury

Read about the ins and outs of the pinnacle of a criminal case.

On October 12th, an intruder broke into the town art museum, smashing through an office window sometime between the hours of 2 and 4 A.M. At 4 A.M. the museum security guard noticed that three paintings were missing from the museum. He immediately called the police, who searched the museum and found two other items missing: a pair of replica crowns from 15th-century France. The police found muddy footprints at each crime scene. On December 14th, Robert Smythe attempted to sell a replica 15th-century French crown to a pawnshop. The shop owner contacted the Police, who searched Smythe's home and found a second replica crown and a large collection of swords and armor. They also found a pair of shoes that matched the muddy footprints found at the museum. They did not find any of the stolen paintings. Robert Smythe maintains that he is innocent and that he collects European antiques. He states that he bought the crowns on the Internet and later decided to sell them.

Part I: Juror Notes
(*This part is to be done individually*)
1. What evidence in the case indicates that Smythe is not guilty?
2. What evidence indicates that Smythe is guilty?
3. Based on the evidence, would you find Smythe guilty or not guilty?
4. Is there anything in the case that would change your decision? Why or why not?

Part II: Official Juror Form
1. Did the jury conclude that Robert Smythe was guilty or not guilty?
2. Was the jury verdict the same as, or different from your individual decision?
3. If the jury verdict was different, what made you change your mind about the decision? If it was the same, did anyone with a differing opinion present any evidence that almost convinced you to change your mind?

DOCUMENT 8

Closing Argument in Criminal Trials

Read about the ins and outs of the pinnacle of a criminal case.

In television dramas, closing arguments are the height of the trial: The prosecutor and defense lawyer each deliver an emotional plea for justice. In real life, closing arguments are a way for the attorneys to pull together
5 all the evidence for the jury—they're intended to appeal to jurors' reason, not just their passion.

The Right to Present a Defense
Under the Sixth Amendment, defendants have a right to present a defense. They are also entitled to give a closing
10 argument. Usually, the Prosecution first makes a closing argument, then the defense attorney. The prosecutor, who has the burden of proof, frequently gets the chance to respond to the defense's final argument.
For defense counsel, closing argument is the last chance
15 to remind the jury of the prosecution's high burden of proof and to persuade the jury that there is, at a minimum, reasonable doubt as to the defendant's guilt.

Typical Closing Arguments
An effective closing argument ties together all the pieces
20 of a trial and tells a compelling story. Generally, closing arguments should include:
- a summary of the evidence,
- any reasonable inferences that can be draw from the evidence,
25 - an attack on any weaknesses in the other side's case,
- a summary of the law for the jury and a reminder to follow it, and
- a plea to the jury to take a specific action, such as convict, acquit, or convict only on a lesser charge.
30 For example, in a shoplifting case, the criminal defense attorney's closing argument might go through all the evidence, but focus on the fact that the surveillance video was blurry and the defendant's alibi. Counsel could then remind the jury that it must be convinced of guilt beyond
35 a reasonable doubt, a very high standard. Since there is reasonable doubt about the identity of the shoplifter,

the defense attorney will ask the jury to follow the law and find the defendant not guilty.
In rebuttal, the prosecutor might point out that police found items at the defendant's home that are identical 40 to the stolen goods, and that the alibi came from the defendant's family member—hardly an unbiased source. The prosecutor will then ask the jury to uphold the law and find defendant guilty.

Limits on Argument   45
In practice, judges give attorneys great freedom in closing, as long as the argument has some relation to the evidence presented at trial. Additionally, judges must carefully craft any restrictions on closing so that they don't deny the defendant the opportunity to discuss 50 important considerations for the jury.
Nonetheless, there are limits to properly closing arguments. When attorneys overstep them, usually a judge will simply tell the jury to disregard the improper argument. But when attorneys commit serious misconduct 55 during closing, a judge might declare a mistrial, and if not, a court of appeal might overturn any conviction. Arguments must be based on evidence. Most importantly, the conclusions that an attorney urges a jury to draw must be based on the evidence. Counsel cannot use the 60 closing argument as an opportunity to refer to evidence that wasn't part of the trial. For example, an attorney can't argue that no similar crimes have been committed in the location in question since the defendant's arrest without having presented evidence to that effect. 65
Arguments cannot be irrelevant, confusing, or prejudicial. Judges can also prohibit or exclude arguments that are unrelated to the case, confusing, or inflammatory. For example, name-calling is generally forbidden. And asking the jury to "send a message" to other criminals 70 by finding the defendant guilty may be improper since the focus is only whether the particular defendant on trial committed a crime. (*State v. Woodard*, 2013).

ACTIVITY

A. Write a fictional law story about a trial in which the characters in the story go through the trial procedures.

B. *Document 2*: Read the case, then answer the questions in *Part I*. Do not discuss your answers with your fellow jurors.

C. Work together in groups of 6 to decide whether Robert Smythe is guilty. Everyone in the jury must agree before you can offer a final verdict. When you have reached a decision, answer the questions in *Part II*.

PART 4 – CLOSING A CRIMINAL TRIAL

The power of the jury
A jury may refuse to convict someone even if they think they are guilty as charged. If they find the law to be unjust, they can return a verdict of not guilty. In such cases, the jury is said to have nullified the law.
In the last 40 years, juries have refused to convict marijuana-users accused of non-violent offences or people who have assisted with euthanasia. Men and women on juries have the power to send strong messages to policy-makers with verdicts such as these. But their decision may be controversial, too. Critics asserts that justice requires strict enforcement of the laws. They point to cases like those in the American South were white jurors refused to convict Ku Klux Klan members for murdering African Americans.

DID YOU KNOW?
Death penalty
The debate about the death penalty began anew, on April 29th 2014, when Clayton Lockett died a very agonizing death that lasted 43 minutes after lethal injection. 32 States had the death penalty and eight of them proposed the electric chair or electrocution once more, as an alternative. In Wyoming and Utah, the condemned may also choose execution by firing squad.

In most criminal trials, at the Federal as well as State level, the jury must decide unanimously if the defendant is guilty or innocent. Only Louisiana, Montana, Oklahoma and Texas allow majority verdicts of juries composed of 12 people. In most cases, the jury makes a decision fairly quickly. On average, it takes about an hour and one vote. Though, the decision could be a very difficult one. Sometimes the case has strong media coverage, and the jury members feel some pressure; sometimes one or two of them are totally convinced and refuse to change their minds, even though all the others think the opposite. Whatever the reason, the jury can be deadlocked and not render a verdict. Judges will insist that the jury render its verdict, but if the deadlock can't be broken, they will dismiss the jury and call for a new trial. This is called a jury nullification.

When the jury members have reached an agreement on a verdict, they return to the courtroom and the foreman announces the verdict in open court. At that time, the Prosecutor or Defending Attorney's may ask each member to confirm that the verdict reflects their own opinion, in order to make sure that no one was forced to vote the same as the others, or was not cowed under the pressure of the group.

Two steps of the trial remain: sentencing and a possible appeal.

The formal announcement of the verdict by the Court is what is called sentencing. At a Federal level and in most of the States, the judge alone decides the sentence. Judges possess a great deal of latitude in deciding the sentence and the severity, even in States that have established a Penal Code. Since many judges are actually elected officials, sometimes a fear exists that they will be too severe in order to please voters who expect that type of harsh justice. The Penal Codes adopted by the States grant them significant discretion in what options judges have, but very often, in cases of death penalty, juries of 12 are expected to vote the same way.

In some States, after having voted to determine guilt, the jury must vote again to decide the sentence, like in Missouri, for example. Some States, like Arizona, even foresee setting up a second jury, whose sole function is to determine the sentence. Sometimes months pass by before the sentence is actually carried out. This period of time allows the judge to examine all of the Defense's

Punitive damages

Punitive damages are awarded in addition to actual damages in certain circumstances. Punitive damages are considered punishment and are awarded when the defendant's behavior is found to be especially harmful, but are normally not awarded in the context of a breach of contract claim.

requests and complaints following the trial. It also gives a probation officer the time to make a preliminary investigation of the sentence to be executed and focus on the defendant's profile and his or her chances to repeat the crime or not. The probation officer could recommend a modification of the sentence to the judge, in order to avoid prison time, but the judge is in no way obliged to follow the advice.

At every level of jurisdiction (apart from the higher Courts), everyone has the right to appeal. In reality, very few criminal trials are followed by an appeal. An appeal may be due to a procedural error, or of interpreting the Law, but may not simply be against the verdict.

ACTIVITY

A. Why can the jury system be criticized sometimes?

....

....

....

....

....

B. Should juries know the likely sentence when deciding guilt?

....

....

....

....

....

MOCK TRIAL STRATEGY

BASIC TRIAL PROCEDURES
A. Pre-trial preparation
- information gathering (discovery)
- pre-trial hearing
5 - pre-trial order
- jury selection

B. Courtroom and participants
- judge attorneys
- witnesses jurors
10 - bailiff court reporter

C. Beginning the trial
Bailiff announces: «All rise. The Court of _____ is now in session, the Honorable Judge_____ presiding.»
15 Everyone remains standing until the judge enters and is seated. Next, the judge asks the bailiff to call the day's calendar (the «docket»), at which point the bailiff says, «Your Honor, today's case is _____ v. _____.»
20 The judge then asks the attorneys for each side of the case if they are ready to begin the trial.

D. The trial
Plaintiff/Prosecution rises and introduces him/herself: «May it please the court and ladies and gentlemen of
25 the jury, my name is _____, counsel for _____ in this action.» Attorney for Plaintiff/Prosecution always delivers his/her opening statement first. Defendant/Defense attorney generally gives his/her opening statement immediately after.
30 The actual trial is developed by testimony of witnesses. Plaintiff/Prosecution witnesses are called first. Order of witness presentations is determined by strategy, i.e., chronologically into overall story. Direct examination of Plaintiff/Prosecution witnesses includes Cross-exami-
35 nation by Defense and Redirect examination by Plaintiff and Recross examination by Defense, which occurs in real trials, but in mock trials it is strongly suggested that teachers allow only a very limited redirect, if at all. Defendant/Defense cross-in-chief proceeds when Plaintiff/Prosecution rests its case. Direct examination
40 of witnesses called by Defense and Cross-examination by Plaintiff, etc. After each side has called all of its witnesses, cross-examines its opponent's witnesses, they enter all relevant documents or objects into evidence. The Judge then permits Plaintiff/Prosecution closing
45 argument, then Defense closing arguments. Only the Plaintiff may rebut the Defendant's closing argument. After closing arguments, the judge gives the jury their instructions, a brief explanation of the applicable law and then the jury leaves courtroom to deliberate in
50 private. Most States requires unanimous jury in both civil and criminal cases or «hung jury» requires re-trial before new jury.
When the Jury returns with decision on paper given to judge who announces the decision on open court. If
55 a criminal case, guilty defendant scheduled to return at later date for sentencing.

RULES OF EVIDENCE
In American trials, elaborate rules are used to regulate the admission of proof (i.e., oral or physical evidence). These rules are designed to ensure that both parties 60 receive a fair hearing and to exclude any evidence deemed irrelevant, incompetent, untrustworthy, or unduly prejudicial. If it appears that a rule of evidence is being violated, an attorney may raise an objection to the judge. The judge then decides whether the rule 65 has been violated and whether the evidence must be excluded from the record of the trial. Formal rules of evidence are quite complicated and differ depending on the court where the trial occurs. For purposes of mock trial programs, the rules of evidence have been 70 modified and simplified below.

A. WITNESS EXAMINATION
1. Direct Examination (attorneys call and question their own witnesses)
     a. form of questions: Generally, the attorney 75 who calls them may not ask witnesses leading questions. A leading question is one that suggests to the witness the answer desired by the examiner, and often suggests a «yes» or «no» answer. Direct questions are usually phrased to evoke a narrative answer. 80 However, the witnesses should not be allowed to give long, uncontrolled responses to direct questions. Examples of direct questions:
* Mr. Bryant, when did you first meet Angela?
* Mr. Bryant, how long have you been employed by 85 the factory?
* Directing your attention to Saturday, October 25th, could you please tell the court what you observed?
Examples of leading questions:
* Mr. Hayes, isn't it true that you dislike Daryl Bryant? 90
* You were not in the building that day, were you?
* Mr. Hayes, didn't you see Jack put the money into the briefcase?
     b. evidence about the character of a party to the case: For mock trial purposes, evidence about the 95 character of a party may not be introduced unless that person's character is an issue in the case.
example: In a civil divorce trial, whether one spouse has been unfaithful to another is a relevant issue, but it is not an issue in a criminal trial for theft. Similarly, 100 a person's violent temperament may be relevant in a criminal trial for battery, but it is not an issue in a civil trial for breach of contract.
     c. refreshing a witness's recollection: If, during direct examination, a witness cannot recall a state- 105 ment that he/she made in an earlier affidavit or even pre-trial notes, the attorney may help the witness to remember. The lawyer must first mark and identify the statement as an «exhibit» and show the other side a copy. However, the statement need not actually be 110 admitted into evidence in this situation.

Example: A witness sees a purse snatching, offers to testify and gives a statement of events to the lawyer. At trial, the witness has trouble remembering the events he/she saw. The lawyer may help the witness remember by showing him/her the statement.

2. Cross Examination (questioning the other side's witnesses)

a. form of questions: Attorneys should ask leading questions when cross-examining the opponent's witnesses (i.e., questions should be phrased to evoke a «yes» or «no» answer, rather than a narrative one).

Example of leading questions:
* Mrs. Bryant, you considered marrying George Hayes, didn't you?
* Isn't it true that you are hard of hearing, Mrs. Short?
* Mr. Jones, don't you generally prefer to avoid loud, crowded taverns?

b. what questions may be asked: Attorneys may only ask questions that relate to matters which were brought out by the other side on direct examination or to matters relating to the credibility (believability) of the witness, even if these matters were not gone in to on direct. Note that many judges allow a broad interpretation of this rule.

Examples:
*If the plaintiff in a car accident case never mentions damages to the car when being questioned by his/her own attorney, then the defense may not ask questions on cross examination about the repair costs.
* On direct examination, the witness testifies as to events that took place in a bar in Milwaukee on Friday evening. On cross-examination the attorney may only ask the witness about the events in that bar in Milwaukee on Friday evening. The attorney may not ask the witness what happened at the Toledo Zoo on Thursday afternoon.
However, in order to test the credibility of the witness, the attorney could ask about a situation in which the witness had lied in the past, even if the situation in question had nothing to do with the bar in Milwaukee on Friday evening.

c. Impeachment: On cross-examination, the attorney may want to show that the witness should not be believed. This is called impeaching the witness. It can be done by asking the witness questions about:
* prior bad conduct that makes his/her credibility (truth-telling ability) seem doubtful and shows that the witness should not be believed.
* prior criminal convictions of the witness.
* prior statements made by the witness, which contradict his/her testimony at trial and point out the inconsistencies in his/her story.
* the bias or prejudice of the witness, that is, showing that the witness has reason to favor or disfavor one side of the case.
* the accuracy of his/her sensory perceptions, which is the witness' ability to see, hear or smell.

Examples:
* Prior bad conduct: «Is it true that you have had your credit cards revoked for failure to pay your bills?», or «Isn't it true that you often exaggerate events?»
* Past conviction: «Is it true that you were recently convicted of armed robbery?»
* Prior inconsistent statement: Bill Jones testifies at trial that Joe's car was travelling 90 mph. The opposing attorney asks, «Isn't it a fact that before this trial you gave a statement to the police saying that Joe's car was only travelling 50mph?»
* Bias or prejudice: Mrs. Young is the mother of the defendant. The prosecuting attorney points this out and asks, «Mrs. Young, you don't want to see your son go to jail, do you?»
* Inaccurate sensory perception: Mrs. Block testifies that she saw Sam, who was a block away, take a bag of marijuana from his briefcase and hand it to Joe Smoker.
On cross-examination, the attorney asks Mrs. Block, «Isn't it a fact that you didn't have your glasses on when you claim to have seen Sam and Joe?»

3. Redirect Examination
If the witness' credibility or reputation for truthfulness has been attacked on cross-examination, the attorney whose witness has been damaged may wish to ask a

ACTIVITY

A. Check newspapers or magazines or the Internet for an article that mentions a trial that is currently being conducted in the United States.

B. List the events in a trial in the right order.

C. Make a list of the steps in a trial, first from the plaintiff/Prosecution's point of view (e.g., opening statement, direct examination of plaintiff/Prosecution's witnesses, cross examination of defense witnesses, and closing arguments). Do the same from the defense perspective.

few more questions. These questions should be limited to the damage the attorney thinks was done by the opposing attorney on cross examination, and should be phrased so as to try to save or «rehabilitate» the
200 witness' credibility in the eyes of the jury.

B. HEARSAY EVIDENCE

NOTE: These types of questions may only be asked when the questioning attorney has information that indicates that the conduct actually happened. Any out
205 of court statement that is offered to prove the truth of the contents of the statement is hearsay. These statements are generally inadmissible in a trial.
Examples:
* Joe is being tried for murdering Henry. The witness
210 may not testify, «Ellen was there, and she told me that Joe killed Henry.» The underlined statement is hearsay and would not be permitted at the trial.
* In a civil trial arising from an automobile accident, a witness may not testify, «I heard a by-stander say
215 that Joe ran the red light.»
* Sandy says, «I've heard that Jack has a criminal record.»
Exceptions to the Hearsay Rule:
Though hearsay is not usually allowed at a trial, a
220 judge may sometimes allow it if:
1. The statement (called the ADMISSION) was made by a party in the case and it contains evidence, which goes against his/her side (e.g., in a murder case, the defendant told someone that he/she committed the
225 murder).
2. The statement describes the then-existing state of mind of a person in the case, and that person's state of mind is an important part of the case.
3. The statement is an «excited utterance.»
230 4. The statement is a «dying declaration.»
Examples:
* Joe is being tried for murdering Henry. The witness may testify, «Joe told me that he killed Henry.»
* In the case, the witness may testify, «I once heard
235 Joe say, «I'm going to get even with Henry if it's the last thing I do.»
* Kimberly is shot in the chest and falls into the arms of Mark. Kimberly says, «I never thought she'd really do it, Alison shot me.» Kimberly then dies and Mary
240 may testify that her dying words implicate Alison as the murderer.
* Mark sees Alison with a gun and it's pointed at his friend, Kimberly. Mark yells, «Run, Kim, Alison's got a gun and she's after you.» Kimberly is subsequently
245 shot. Jill, who's back was turned, may testify that she heard Mark warn Kimberly.

C. OPINION TESTIMONY:

As a general rule, witnesses may not give opinions, but «experts» who have special knowledge or qualifi-
250 cations may. An expert must first be «qualified» by the attorney who calls him/her. This means that before an expert may be asked and may give an opinion, the questioning attorney must bring out the expert's qualifications and experience. All witnesses may give
255 opinions about what they saw or heard at a particular

time, if such opinions are relevant to the facts at issue and are helpful in explaining their story. A witness may not, however, testify to any matter of which he or she has no personal knowledge.
Examples: 260
* The witness may say, «Roy was drunk. He had slurred speech; he staggered and smelled of alcohol.»
* A psychiatrist could testify that, «Roy has severe eating problems», but only after the lawyer has qualified the psychiatrist as an expert through a series of 265 questions about his/her background and experience in a particular field.
* The witness works with the defendant but has never been to the defendant's home or seen the defendant with her children. The witness may not testify that 270 the defendant has a bad relationship with her children or that she is a bad mother, because the witness has no personal knowledge of this.

D. RELEVANCE OF EVIDENCE:

Generally, only relevant evidence may be presented. 275
Relevant evidence is any evidence, which helps to prove or disprove the facts in issue in the case. However, if the evidence is relevant but also unfairly prejudicial, potentially confusing to the jury, or a waste of time, it may be excluded by the court. 280
Examples:
* On cross-examination the defense asks Ms. Stone, «How old are you?» This question would be permitted only if Ms. Stone's age is relevant to the case.
* The defendant is charged with running a red light. 285
Evidence that the defendant owns a dog is not relevant and may not be presented.

E. INTRODUCTION OF PHYSICAL EVIDENCE:

There is a special procedure for introducing physical evidence during a trial. Below are the basic steps to use 290 when introducing a physical object or document (such as a pre-trial statement) into evidence in a court: «Your Honor, I ask that this letter be marked for identification as Plaintiff's Exhibit 1.» Show the letter to the judge then hand it to the bailiff or clerk for marking. Show 295 the letter to the opposing attorney, who may make an objection to the piece of evidence at this point. If the opposing attorney does not object, show the letter to the witness whom you are questioning. «Mr. King, do you recognize this document, which is marked Plain- 300 tiff's Exhibit 1 for identification?» The witness then explains what it is (e.g., «Yes, this is the letter I received from the defendant, Marilyn Smith.»)
Ask further questions to establish relevancy and authenticity. «Your Honor, I offer this letter, marked 305 as Plaintiff's Exhibit 1 for identification into evidence.» Give the letter to the judge for his/her inspection. The judge rules on whether or not the letter may be admitted into evidence. If the judge admits it, the attorney may give it to the jury to look at. 310
Example: Suppose this is a personal injury case in which the tenant claims he was injured when he tripped on a loose step in the apartment building. A neighbor who lives in the same building is testifying:
Q. Mrs. Spak, are you familiar with the condition the 315

stairs were in the day before the accident?

A. Yes.

Q. I ask the reporter (or bailiff) to mark this as Defendant's Exhibit 1 for identification.

320 Reporter or Bailiff: This will be Defendant's Exhibit 1 for identification. Counsel now shows the exhibit to opposing counsel.

Q. Thank you. Counsel (showing exhibit to plaintiff's attorney) Now, Mrs. Spak, I show you what has been
325 marked as Defendant's Exhibit 1 for identification. Please examine it and tell us what it is.

A. It's a picture of the back stairs of my apartment building.

Q. Mrs. Spak, turning your attention once again to
330 those stairs as they were the day before the accident, can you tell us whether this picture is an accurate and complete picture of the stairs as they looked at that time?

A. Yes, I would say it is.

335 Q. Thank you, Mrs. Spak. Your Honor (handing exhibit to judge), we offer what has been marked as Defendant's Exhibit 1 into evidence, and we ask permission to show it to the jury so they can see it during Mrs. Spak's testimony.

340 **F. OBJECTIONS:**

Objections can be made whenever an attorney or witness has violated the rules of evidence. The attorney wishing to object should stand up and do so at the time of the violation; that is, the objection should
345 be made as soon as the improper question is asked by the other lawyer and before the witness answers, whenever possible.

When an objection is made, the judge will ask the objecting attorney the reason. Then the judge will
350 turn to the attorney who asked the question and give him/her a chance to explain why the objection should not be accepted (sustained) by the judge. The judge will then rule on the objection, deciding whether an attorney's question or witness' answer must be dis-
355 carded («objection sustained»), or whether to allow the question or answer to remain on the trial record («objection overruled»).

The following are standard mock trial objections:

RELEVANCY - «Objection, Your Honor. This testimony is not relevant to the facts of this case.» 360

LEADING QUESTION ON DIRECT EXAMINATION - «Objection, Your Honor. Counsel is leading the witness.»

IMPROPER CHARACTER TESTIMONY - «Objection, Your Honor. Character is not an issue here.» 365

BEYOND THE SCOPE OF DIRECT EXAMINATION - «Objection, Your Honor. Counsel is asking about matters that did not come up in the direct exam.» (Or, matters that are «beyond the scope of the direct examination»). 370

HEARSAY - «Objection, Your Honor. Counsel's question, the witness' answer, is based on hearsay.» If the witness has already given a hearsay answer, the attorney should also say, «and I ask that the statement be stricken from the record.» 375

OPINION TESTIMONY - «Objection, Your Honor. Counsel is asking the witness to give an opinion.»

NO PERSONAL KNOWLEDGE - «Objection, Your Honor. The witness has no personal knowledge to answer the question.» 380

CREATION OF MATERIAL FACT – «Objection, Your Honor. The witness is creating facts material to the case which are not in the record.» (This objection is not a rule of evidence ordinarily but is used in the mock trial scenario to avoid the creation of evidence 385 by students, which misleads and confuses the issues presented.)

OPENING STATEMENTS

The opening statement should introduce the attorney and his/her client and tell the jury what the case is all 390 about. It is the attorney's first opportunity to present the jury with a clear and concise description of the case from his or her client's perspective. But the opening statement is not an argument. The attorney may not infer from or plead the facts of the case that he/she 395

ACTIVITY

A. What is the purpose of the opening statements?

B. How do they differ from closing arguments?

C. In *Unit 13*, choose one of the cases to use as an exercise in writing opening statements.

D. What are some of the problems with the opening statements?

expects to prove during the trial. The purpose of the opening statement is to tell the jury what the case is about and what you expect your evidence will be.

400 A test of a good opening statement is this: If the jurors heard the opening statement and nothing else, would they understand what the case is all about and would they want to decide in your favor?

An opening statement on behalf of the prosecution should include:

405 * An introduction of yourself and your client: «May it please the court, ladies and gentlemen of the jury, my name is _____, counsel for _____, the plaintiff/prosecution in this action.»

* A cohesive summary or outline of what your evidence 410 will be, presented in chronological order or any other orderly sequence of events. Phrasing includes: «The evidence will indicate that...», «The facts will show...», «Witness X will be brought to testify that...», «Witness Y will be called to tell you that....»

415 * An acknowledgement that the burden of proof rests with you and the degree of that burden.

* A conclusion, which includes a respectful statement to the jury: «Ladies and gentlemen of the jury, it is your responsibility to listed attentively to the statements of 420 the witnesses and to determine the facts in this action.»

The plaintiff/prosecution's opening statement should not include any references to evidence whose admissibility is doubtful or to anticipated defenses or defense evidence.

425 The opening statement on behalf of the defendant should include:

* An introduction of yourself and your client.

* A reminder that opening statements are not evidence.

* A cohesive (but non-argumentative) reference to 430 anticipated deficiencies in your opponent's evidence, plus a summary of what your evidence will be.

* A reminder that the burden of proof rests with your opponent, and a conclusion, which indicates that at the close, you will return and request the jury to find 435 in favor of the defendant.

Again, the defendant's opening statement should not include references to evidence whose admissibility is doubtful.

DIRECT EXAMINATION

440 Direct examination is the heart of most trials. Except for those criminal cases where the defendant calls no witnesses and does not take the stand (where cross-examination, objections and argument are all the defense lawyer does) direct examination is more 450 important than cross-examination, the opening statement or the closing argument. For, unless the outlook is so dismal that the only hope for one side in the trial to win is to create confusion, a coherent statement of the facts by the witnesses is essential to the jury's 455 understanding and acceptance of your position.

The rules governing direct examination are fairly simple. First, leading questions are not permitted.

Uncontrolled narrative questions are also not permissible – the attorney may set his/her witness on 460 «automatic pilot» with a narrative question and let the witness fly alone. Multiple and repetitious questions

are objectionable too.

A well-conducted direct examination must be carefully prepared in advance by the attorney and practiced with the witness. The direct examination is most effective 465 when questions are put to the witnesses in plain language, rather than legal jargon, which may seem unduly long, stilted or unnatural to the jury.

The following is a list of the sorts of questions that might be asked on direct examination: 470

* «What happened then?» or «What did you see?»

* «How long have you worked for Mrs. Smith?»

* «What happened after you saw the yellow car?»

* «How far away was the other car when you first saw it?» 475

* «How long did you stand there?»

* «Did Bill (the defendant) say anything about...»

CROSS-EXAMINATION

The law governing cross-examination is, for the most part, quite simple. First is the right to do it at all. This 480 right is so firmly entrenched in our law that a denial by the court of this right is usually a reversible error, and a witness' refusal to submit to cross-examination usually results in the direct examination of that witness being excluded from evidence. 485

Second, in a majority of jurisdictions, the scope of cross-examination is limited to the scope of direct. However, as long as a line of questioning reasonably relates to what was testified to on direct examination, it is considered within the scope. 490

Also, this limitation does not prevent an attorney from inquiring into the witness' bias or prejudice or using prior convictions or inconsistent statements to impeach him/her.

Third, the cross-examiner has the right to ask leading 495 questions, which is an important advantage in dealing with adverse witnesses.

Just as important to an effective cross-examination as an understanding of the law and rules of evidence, is a firm idea of your objectives at this state of the trial. 500 Generally, they fall into two broad categories: 1) reducing the effect of direct examination, and 2) developing independent evidence on behalf of your side. There are a number of ways to meet these objectives.

CLOSING ARGUMENTS

505

Lawsuits are usually won during the course of the trial, not at the conclusion. They are won by witnesses, exhibits, and the manner in which the lawyer paces, spaces and handles them. Sometimes, however, lawsuits have been lost by fumbling, stumbling and 510 incoherent closing arguments

This is not intended to minimize the importance of closing arguments, but rather to emphasize its proper position as a summation of the evidence and a relation of that evidence to the issues in the case. 515

Closing arguments should include:

* An address to the judge, jury and your opponent.

* An explanation to the jury of your purpose--to summarize the facts and relate them to the issues in the case. 520

* An «argument» telling the jury why it should consider all of the evidence and decide in your favor (i.e., tell them what the verdict should be and why).

525   The attorney should argue but not shout or attack personalities. The testimony of each witness should not necessarily be repeated in chronological order since the jury has already heard all of the witnesses. Instead, the attorney, by referring to the witnesses' testimony, should focus on putting the whole story
530   together for the jury.

AFTER THE TRIAL

In a mock trial, it would be a useful exercise for the student jurors to deliberate «fishbowl style» (in front of the entire class). This enables students to see first
535   hand the process of decision making and to learn what evidence was persuasive to the jury and why. Since the student jury may be representative of the community, their deliberations should provide a good analogy to real jury deliberations.
540   After all mock trials, it is important to discuss the proceedings with the class. This is referred to as «debriefing»; it is designed to put the whole mock trial experience into perspective by relating the mock trial to the actors and process of the American court system. The discussion should focus on a review of the legal   545 issues in the trial and courtroom procedure, as well as broader questions about our trial system.

Questions (and topics for short compositions), which may be pertinent, include:
- Were the procedures used fair to both parties?   550
- Were some parts of the trial more important than others?
- Did either side forget to introduce any importance evidence?
- Could either side have been more effective or   555 successful in their direct or cross-examination of the witnesses?
- Was the verdict a fair one?
- Is the jury system the best possible system for determining the outcome of the case?   560
- What changes could be made to improve the jury system?
- What changes could be made to improve the trial procedures?

ACTIVITY

A. What is the purpose of direct examination? How does it differ from cross-examination?

B. Choose a case in *Unit 13*, or pick one on the Internet. After reading through the facts, determine the information you want to get out of a particular witness (Remember that the witness' answers should be relatively brief and very clear for the jury to understand fully).

C. Then write a series of questions that you could ask this witness.

D. Prepare a closing argument for the same case.

Important words

**Searches and seizures
Double jeopardy
Self-incrimination
Opening statement
Challenged for cause
Peremtory challenges**

EQUAL JUSTICE FOR ALL

The adoption of a Bill of Rights was aimed at protecting those who are accused of committing a crime. Unreasonable searches and seizures are forbidden; this is guaranteed by the 4th Amendment. It is specified that the Police must ask a judge for a warrant to search someone or their property. The warrant must be specific in indicating the location and what is being looked for. The Police do not need a warrant if the crime is committed in front of an officer, or if it thought that a crime will be committed. The right to an attorney is guaranteed by the 6th Amendment. The Supreme Court confirmed this, notably in the decision *Gideon v. Wainwright* in 1963. The 5th Amendment gives suspects the right to not testify against themselves, in order to prevent obtaining a confession through violence or pressure. This was confirmed in *Miranda v. Arizona* in 1966. It is also forbidden to try someone twice for the same crime, as the Supreme Court has recently confirmed in *Blueford v. Arkansas* (2012). Article III the Constitution guaranteed the right to a trial by jury.

OPENING THE TRIAL

Jury selection is made according to different regulations relating to the jurisdiction and the lawyers. A jury may be disqualified for any reason decided by the judge. A peremptory challenge may also be allowed, on which the judge has no control. The trial begins with the opening statement. It is generally somewhat longer if the trial is by jury. It presents the facts, and prepares the jury or the judge to hear a point of view for presenting the facts. Each party speaks in turn during this stage of the trial. The next step consists in the Prosecution presenting all its proof, and questioning the witnesses. The Defense Attorney may cross-examine. The Assistant Public Prosecutor may question the witnesses again, after the cross-examination. When it's the Defense's turn, the procedure is the same, with the presentation of proof, questioning, and cross-examinations.

THE JUDGE AND THE JURY

The jury does not have an active role during the trial. The 12 jury members have only to listen, and to form an opinion. It is possible for them to ask questions, or take notes, but it's fairly uncommon. The judge's role is also passive during the trial. He primarily steps in at the end with instructions to the jury, which is very important. The judge's instruction always contains two essential elements: the definition of the alleged crime and which verdicts the jury may render. The burden of proof is very high in criminal cases: 99%. The judge also provides the jury with useful information about the process of deliberation. The jury retires to deliberate and no one is allowed to interfere, not even the judge. The jury members are not allowed any type of outside contact during deliberation, nor are they allowed any written documentation. When they have agreed upon a verdict, they return to announce it to the Court.

CLOSING A CRIMINAL TRIAL

In most criminal proceedings, the jury must decide unanimously. Some States, such as Louisiana, Montana, Oklahoma and Texas, allow majority verdicts. Juries deliberate for an hour on average, and return with one vote. In cases that are complicated, or if the questioning becomes long and involved, a judge may order the jury members to be sequestered in a hotel. When they are allowed to return home before rendering a verdict, they are obligated to speak to no one about the case. In most States and at a Federal level, only the judge decides the sentence when someone is found guilty. In case of a death penalty, jury confirmation is required in some States, and must be unanimous. Many months go by before a sentence is executed and the probation officer, after an investigation, can ask the judge for a reduced sentence, though he is no way obligated to accept it.

A. Match the term with its definition:
1. Objection
2. Voir Dire
3. Peremtory challenge
4. Opening statement
5. Challenge for cause

a. *The right in jury selection for the attorneys to reject a certain number of potential jurors without stating a reason.*

b. *The removal of any juror who does not appear capable of rendering a fair and impartial verdict.*

c. *A legal phrase that refers to a variety of procedures connected with jury trials. It originally referred to an oath taken by jurors to tell the truth.*

d. *This is the first occasion that the jury or judge has to hear from a lawyer in a trial.*

e. *A formal protest raised in court during a trial to disallow a witness's testimony or other evidence.*

B. What is the first Court appearance after an arrest and what happens?
....
....

C. What happens at a trial?
....
....

D. What about bail?
....
....

E. «No one read me my rights. Does that matter?»
....
....

REFERENCES :

Page 207. "Oil Pastelsdrawing of Superior court Judge Harold M. Mulvey, court reporters and clerks, and jurors probably including foreman Robert L. Gaythier, as well as Frank J. Dilger and Jennie Jesilavich", by Beinecke Library. *Wikimedia*. http://commons.wikimedia.org/wiki/File:Oil_Pastelsdrawing_of_Superior_court_Judge_Harold_M._Mulvey,_court_reporters_and_clerks,_and_jurors_probably_including_foreman_Robert_L._Gaythier,_as_well_as_Frank_J._Dilger_and_Jennie_Jesilavich.jpg

Page 208. "5th Amendment", by Dimitri Champain

Page 210. "Jury", by Mike Faulk, from *Wikimedia*. http://commons.wikimedia.org/wiki/File:Jury_selection_-_Faulk.jpg

Page 211. "Jury selection in criminal cases", adapted from from Sherilyn Streickerreturns, in *Nolo, law for all* at http://www.nolo.com/legal-encyclopedia/jury-selection-criminal-cases.html

Page 213. "Courtroom", by Dimitri Champain

Page 215. "Opening Statements: What the Prosecution and Defense Can and Can't Say", from Micah Schwartzbach, in *Nolo,* *law for all.* http://www.nolo.com/legal-encyclopedia/opening-statements-what-the-prosecution-defense-can-can-t-say.html

Page 216. "The juror", by Dimitri Champain

Page 218. "Summary of trial procedures", from http://www.nolo.com/legal-encyclopedia/closing-argument-criminal-trials.html

Page 219. "Closing argument in criminla trial", adadpted from by Ave Mince-Didier, in *Nolo, Law for all*.http://www.nolo.com/legal-encyclopedia/closing-argument-criminal-trials.html

Page 222. "Mock trial strategy". from http://www.isba.org/sites/default/files/teachers/mocktrial/Mock%20Trial%20Teacher%20Training.pdf

Page 227. "The jury", by Dimitri Champain

Page 228. "Summary", by Dimitri Champain

Page 229. "Review", by Dimitri Champain

pp. 209, 211, 213, 215, 217, 219, 221, 223, 25, 227 "Activity", by Dimitri Champain

UNIT 12 Civil Trials

Introduction

Civil trials follow different rules than criminal trials. Civil Law governs relationships between citizens. The cases heard are not concerned with the protection of the public, but the government may be implicated in certain hearings. In civil cases, the Court tries to rule on cases by examining the legal rights of each party involved. There is no punishment, but a payment of damages, that comes in the form of monetary damages or, when the case is judged in Equity, an injunction to take or not take an action, for example.

PART 1 – GOING TO TRIAL

Though a number of cases are actually resolved by alternative solutions in the end, a large majority of them will end in Court. As in criminal proceedings, we find the method of adversarial process in Civil Law. The rules are simple: one of the parties must have a standing. That means that they must have a vested interest in the case. Another major difference exists: constitutional protection does not necessarily apply in Civil, like, for example, the right to have an attorney provided by the State. On the other hand, the right to a trial by jury, "where the value in controversy shall exceed $20", is strongly retained, and even often reinforced, in laws passed by the States.

Filing a civil suit

The person filing is called the Plaintiff and the person accused is called the Defendant. Civil cases bear the name of the two parties, the Plaintiff being listed first, *e.g.: Doe v. Smith*, Doe being the Plaintiff and "v." signifying against (from the Latin *versus*). The Plaintiff's lawyer lodges a complaint with the Court by sending a complaint or a

Super injunctions
In the U.K., a number a celebrities have stopped details emerging about their private life using «super injunctions». This could not happen in the U.S.A. because it goes against one of the country's founding principle: free speech. The equivalent in the U.S. of a super injunction would be something called prior restraint, but Courts are very reluctant to prohibit somebody from saying something.

petition, along with the payment of a sum required by the Court. The most critical question is to determine which Court has the authority to hear the case. For example, if Suzie Smith from Ohio accidentally wounded John Doe from Texas, and the accident took place in Boise, Idaho, one might think that the Courts of the three States cited would hear the case. If the damages inflicted are higher than $75,000 and since the two parties are from different States, the case could also be brought before a Federal court. According to State laws, the trial will be held in the defendant's State (here, in Ohio). On the other hand, according to Federal law, the trial would most certainly be held in a District Court of Idaho. But laws in Texas and Ohio would provide for other solutions and the lawyers would have to determine if any particular rules would apply in there cases.

> **The right to a trial by jury, «where the value in controversy shall exceed $20», is strongly retained.**

Once the proper Court is determined and the case is brought before the jurisdiction, the Court Clerk attaches a copy of the complaint to a summons, which is then delivered to the Defendant by a representative from the Sheriff's Office, a U.S. Marshall or a private agency. The defendant has 30 days to respond, which is called a pledge. If this is not done, he or she may be judged in absentia.

Pre-trial activities

The Defending Attorney has numerous avenues of attack: he can ask to cancel the filing on the grounds that it was not properly delivered, for example, if it was not delivered to the Defendant in person; he can also file a motion to suppress sections of the claim, if they are prejudicial, improper or irrelevant. A motion asking for clarification upon demand is also possible. The most common motion is a motion to dismiss, for the reason that the Court does not have jurisdiction for handling the request.

Prior restraint

It is very difficult to obtain such a limitation to free speech, even for the government: in 1971, the Nixon Administration successfully stopped the New York Times from publishing the Pentagon Papers, classified documents that included damages about U.S. policy in the Vietnam War. But two weeks later, the U.S. Supreme Court ruled that the government did not have a string enough case to merit prior restraint.

Answer

The following step after the request should be, under normal conditions, the answer. It should contain the admission, denials, defense or counterclaim of the opposing party. The plaintiff should then respond after receiving the document.

Discovery

American procedure anticipates that all of the information a party possesses should be shared with the adverse one, especially the testimonies that are collected during the depositions under oath outside of Court. The lawyers from both sides must be present and are able to interrogate the witnesses. There may also be interrogatories, which are also under oath and intended for both parties during trial. During the period of discovery, all documents required for establishing the truth (letters, drawings, photos, videos, maps, etc.) must be available upon request. The Court may also order expert evaluations, notably about the physical or mental condition of those involved.

Pre-trial Conference

The judge may organize a pre-trial conference that takes place in his chambers and is restricted to the lawyers of both parties. The goal is to try to reach an agreement on all or part of the case. Generally, these meetings are fairly effective and result in a trial that is faster and more focused on one or more legal points, while putting aside that which can be.

ACTIVITY

A. Is a trial by jury guaranteed in the United States?

....

....

....

B. Who can be a member of a jury in a Civil Trial?

....

....

....

THE JURY IN QUESTIONS

Which system is best?

DOCUMENT 1

Jury system		Judge-only system	
Pros	Cons	Pros	Cons

A civil trial

DOCUMENT 2

The case: [*Fake case*]
Katherine Barnes v. John Hoobert (2015)
Katherine Barnes (Plaintiff) claims that John Hoobert (Defendant) installed a roof on her home that is now defective. Just months after the work by John Hobert was completed at the Barnes residence, a series of leaks developed in the new roof, ruining the furniture in the living rom and permanently damaging electronic devices in the kitchen and bedroom.

Jury nowhere to be found

DOCUMENT 3

Charleston (West Virginia) - Bob Engleton couldn't believe his eyes as he stared at the empty seats along the wall. The 12 chairs remained empty as he stood before the judge and heard his name mentioned in a civil lawsuit against his carpeting company. During the entire trial, not a single person showed up to fill those seats; there was no jury to be found.

Ben Engleton, 45, owned a small carpet-cleaning and repair company in Bluefield, West Virginia. In January 2014, he and an employee were cleaning a carpet in the house of Dawn Dabervil of Charleston, West Virginia, when one of their rug cleaners shorted out and caught fire. Soon, the whole house was ablaze. Ms. Dabervil, Mr. Engleton and his employees barely escaped with their lives. A few months later, Ms. Dabervil brought a civil suit against Engleton and his company. The two sides tried to settle out of court but could not come to terms, so the suit was brought to court. In May 2014, Engleton appeared before Judge Lucy Skyrocket, prepared to defend himself in front of a jury of his peers from in and around Bluefield. He and his lawyer were surprised to see, however, that no jury had been called for his case. When Engleton requested trial by jury, he was denied. Judge Skyrocket ruled in favor of the Plaintiff, Ms. Dabervil, and awarded her a settlement of $1.3 million. Bob Engleton had to sell his business and house and declare bankruptcy in order to pay the damages.

Six months of legal battles have led Engleton and his attorney to Washington and the Supreme Court. Engleton hopes to have the ruling overturned bcause of the violation of the Seventh Amendment. He goes before the Court on October 29th to argue his case.

ACTIVITY

A. *Document 1*: **Use the table to compare the jury system to a judge-only system. Do research in the library or on the Internet to help you fill in the table.**

....

....

B. **Write a list of five questions that a lawyer representing John Hoobert should ask a juror, to ensure that he or she will remain fair-minded in this case.**

....

....

C. **Determine what kind of case was brought against Bob Engleton, and who determined the ruling of the case.**

....

....

PART 2 – THE CIVIL TRIAL

Class actions

A class action, class suit, or representative action – popularized by the movie Erin Brokovitch – is a lawsuit where a person sues a group of people, a group of people sues another group of people, or a group of people sues a person. It is wordy to refer to a class action as a «class action suit». Collective lawsuits originated in the United States and are still predominantly a U.S. phenomenon.

SOME COMMON LEGAL OBJECTIONS

«Objection, your Honor,»
Ambiguous
Argumentative
Assumes facts not in evidence
Beyond the scope of direct examination
Calls for a conclusion
Calls for a narrative answer
Calls for an opinion the witness is not qualified to give
Confusing
Cumulative
Hearsay
Immaterial.
Incompetent
Irrelevant
Leading and suggestive of the answer
Misleading
Misstates the evidence
Misstates the witness
Multiple question
No authentication
No probative value
No proper foundation
Not the best evidence
Not responsive to the question
Prejudicial
Privileged communication
Repetitive
Self-serving
Speculative
Vague and ambiguous

The first step in the civil process is jury selection, since the 7th Amendment of the Federal Constitution guarantees everyone the right to a trial by jury and this right is very often reinforced by State Law. The typical number of jury members is 12, but this number could vary, because many States actually authorize smaller juries in Civil law.

Just like for criminal trials, the jury members are chosen at random, and during *Voir Dire* procedures, the lawyers may refuse some of them. The *Voir Dire* procedure refers to the process by which prospective jurors are questioned about their backgrounds and potential biases before being chosen to sit on a jury. *Voir Dire* is then the process by which attorneys select, or perhaps more appropriately reject, certain jurors to hear a case. It should be noted that the 14th Amendment forbids the selection or rejection of a jury member because of his or her race or gender.

Opening statements

The trial begins with the lawyers' delivery of their opening statements, starting with the Plaintiff's Attorney. He briefly explains the reason for the trial to the jury. The Defending Attorney may respond right away, or wait until the end of the introductory arguments.

Presentation of the plaintiff's case

After the opening statements, the Plaintiff's Attorney begins his presentation again, but this time in more detail. This is when all of the proof that the Plaintiff has in its possession is given and all of its witnesses take the stand. They are first questioned by the Plaintiff's Attorney then cross-examined by the defense. In Arizona, the jury members may even ask questions, in writing, through the judge. After the cross-examination, the Plaintiff's Attorney can question the witness again. Witnesses cannot give their own opinions, unless they are experts called to the bench to clarify something complicated for the jury.

Motion for directed verdict

After this presentation by the Plaintiff, the Defendant often introduces a motion for directed verdict. For this, the opposing party argues that the Plaintiff does not have enough evidence to continue the trial and requests to halt the procedure. If the judge believes that the proof is not convincing enough, then the Plaintiff has lost the case.

Presentation of the defendant's case

If the reverse happens, the case continues and the opposing party presents its proof and its witnesses. And here again, the witnesses may be cross-examined.

Plaintiff's rebuttal

After the presentation of the Defendant's case, the Plaintiff may bring forth rebuttal evidence, which is aimed at refuting the Defendant's evidence. The Defending Attorney has the same right.

Closing arguments

Once all of the proof has been presented and the witness eshave come to the bench, the lawyers give their closing remarks, starting with the Plaintiff's Attorney, but this time to close the proceedings. Each attorney's eloquence here is extremely important.

Instruction to jury

The judge then informs the jury that it must base its decision on the proof presented during the trial. He or she also explains the rules and legal principles, which are clarified when necessary.

Verdict

The jury withdraws to a room in which no one else may enter. Deliberations may take a long time.

Judgment

A verdict in favor of the defendant ends the trial. If not, in Civil Court a verdict is rendered and a sum the Defendant must pay the Plaintiff is established, or the remedy, which has been decided to address the wrongs suffered.

ACTIVITY

A. What are the various steps in a civil trial?

....

....

B. How does the jury render a verdict?

....

....

MOCK TRIAL

DOCUMENT 4

The Three Bears family v. Gold E. Lock

SCENE:

The Arapahoe District Court house. The Bailiff comes out and calls the case of Mom A. Bear, Pop A.Bear and Babe E. Bear vs. Golden Locks, also known as Gold E. Locks. The Bears are seated at the Plaintiff's table. Golden Locks is sitting at the defense table.

PARTICIPANTS IN TRIAL

Judge ....*played by:* ....
Mom A. Bear: ....
Pop A. Bear: ....
Babe E. Bear: ....
Gold E. Locks: ....
Mrs Locks: ....
Plaintiff's counsel: ....
Defendant's counsel: ....
Jurors: ....
Bailiff: ....

YOUR TASK (ACTIVITY)

1. Read the script, differentiate between the stages of the trial and fill in the table below.

2. You are a press reporter; write a short article to explain the situation in Court.

3. If you would have been the Defense Attorney who else could have you called as a witness?

4. Give the verdict as delivered by the foreman. What could be the sentence if the Defendant loses her case?

5. Write another mock trial based on the same idea:
    e.g.: - Red Riding Hood v. Big Bad Wolf
    - The three little Pigs v. Big Bad Wolf
    - Ugly Duckling v. Mother Duck
    - Cinderella v. Stepmother

Civil Trial Process

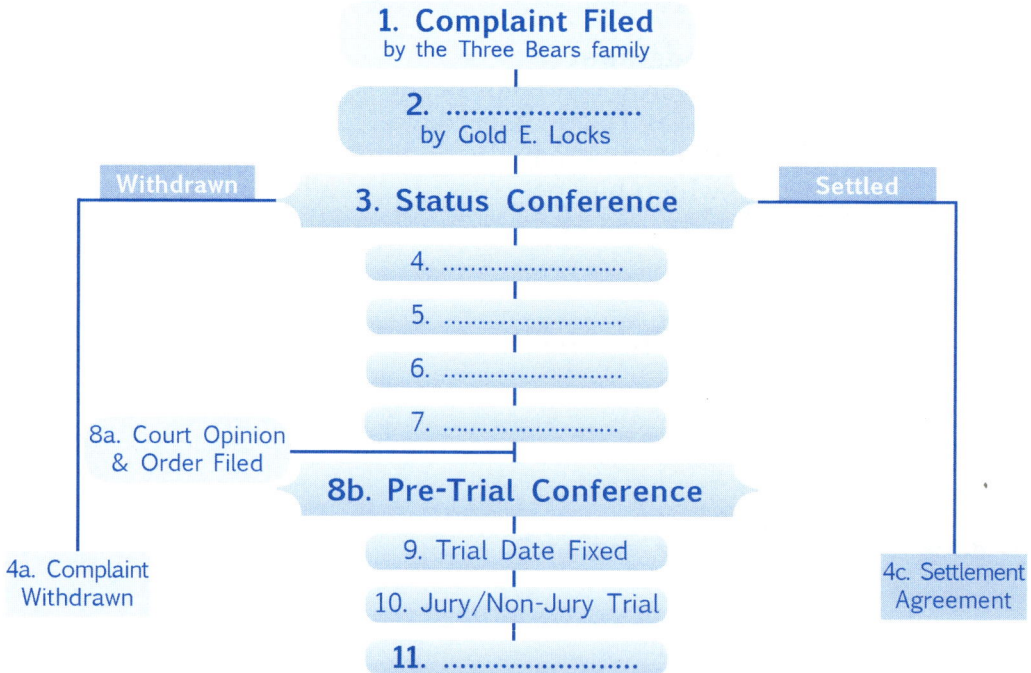

1. Complaint Filed
by the Three Bears family

2. ....
by Gold E. Locks

Withdrawn — **3. Status Conference** — Settled

4. ....

5. ....

6. ....

7. ....

8a. Court Opinion & Order Filed

8b. Pre-Trial Conference

9. Trial Date Fixed

10. Jury/Non-Jury Trial

11. ....

4a. Complaint Withdrawn

4c. Settlement Agreement

JUDGE:

This is the case of Mom A. Bear, Pop A. Bear and Babe E. Bear vs. Golden Locks. As I understand the pleadings, the charge against Golden Locks is that
5 she exhibited bad manners. Are there any opening statements?

ATTORNEY FOR BEARS:

Your Honor, in this case we will show that one crisp fall morning. Mom A. Bear got up early and made a
10 steaming bowl of porridge. She intended to serve the bowl of porridge to Pop A. Bear and Babe E. Bear for breakfast. We will further show that because the porridge was too hot, the Bears decided to take a walk in the forest. While walking in the forest, Gold
15 E. Locks entered the home of the three Bears and ate some porridge out of the bowls of Mom A. Bear and Pop A. Bear. She ate all the porridge from the bowl of Babe E. Bear. After eating Babe E. Bear's porridge, Gold E. Locks sat down in Babe E. Bear's chair and
20 broke it. After breaking Babe E. Bear's chair, Gold E. Locks went upstairs and fell asleep in Babe E. Bear's bed. Through our evidence we will show that Gold E. Locks did was not polite in her actions. Thank you, your Honor.

25 JUDGE: Does the Attorney for Gold E. locks have any opening statement?

ATTY FOR LOCKS: Your Honor, these charges of bad manners against Gold E. Locks are ridiculous. We will show that the Bears invited Gold E. Locks
30 into their homes by leaving the door open. Gold E. Locks was out walking in the forest, minding her own business, and picking flowers, when she smelled the sweet aroma of porridge cooking. She had been in the forest many times before and she knew where the
35 Bears lived. Gold E. Locks merely thought she was invited for breakfast. We will further show that the porridge was so good that Gold E. Locks decided to take a nap so that she could sleep off her breakfast. We will show that Gold E. Locks was a guest – and
40 certainly did not demonstrate any bad manners.

JUDGE: Very well. Call your first witness.

ATTY FOR BEARS: I call Mom A. Bear as my first witness. (*Mom A. Bear gets up, goes forward to be sworn in.*)

45 JUDGE: Please raise your right paw.

(*Mom A. Bear raises her right paw.*)

JUDGE: Do you swear that the evidence you are about to give is the truth, the whole truth, and nothing but the truth?

50 MOM A. BEAR: I do.

JUDGE: Please be seated.

ATTY FOR BEARS: Please state your name.

MOM A. BEAR: My name is Mom A. Bear. That's first name Mom, middle initial A., last name Bear. They
55 also call me Momma Bear.

ATTY FOR BEARS: Where do you live?

MOM A. BEAR: I live in a little bungalow house in the forest. The forest is surrounded by flowers and trees. It is a pretty little house.

ATTY FOR BEARS: Is that forest located in (*insert local city & state*) 60

MOM A. BEAR: Yes, it is.

ATTY FOR BEARS: Who else lives in the house?

MOM A. BEAR: My husband, Pop A. Bear, and our little bear, Babe E. Bear, also live there.

ATTY FOR BEARS: On the Morning of October 26, 65 1977, did you make breakfast for your family?

MOM A. BEAR: Yes, I did. I always make a wholesome nutritious breakfast for my family. Since they are very fond of porridge, I made porridge on that particular day, and as I always do, I sprinkled the 70 porridge with honey, a pinch of cinnamon and two pawfuls of raisins. Pop A. Bear especially likes the two pawfuls of raisins.

ATTY FOR BEARS: Please state your name.

POP A. BEAR: My name is Pop A. Bear. (*growling*) 75

ATTY FOR BEARS: Do you live in the forest with Mom. A. Bear and Babe E. Bear?

POP A. BEAR: Yes, that's our home. It's located out in (*indicate local place*).

ATTY FOR BEARS: Very well. When you got back from 80 your walk in the forest what did you notice?

POP A. BEAR: Well, first I noticed that the door was open. I told Babe E. Bear to close it several times, but I guess she forgot again. I'm going to have to speak to Babe E. Bear about her forgetting to close the door 85 when I tell her to!

ATTY FOR BEARS: Did you smell porridge in the house?

POP A. BEAR: Oh, yes! It smelled delicious. Mom A. Bear is the best porridge-maker in the whole forest. 90 I especially like the two pawfuls of cinnamon and raisins she puts in it.

ATTY FOR LOCKS: Your Honor, we know Mom A. Bear makes good porridge. We will stipulate for the record that Mom A. Bear's porridge is the best porridge in the 95 whole wide world, not to mention the best porridge in (*insert local place*)

ATTY FOR BEARS: When you got back to the house, what did you notice first?

POP A. BEAR: Well, I went over to eat my bowl of por- 100 ridge. When I looked in the bowl there was none there.

ATTY FOR BEARS: Did you say anything?

POP A. BEAR: Yes, I growled, «Somebody's been eating my porridge!»

(*Attorney for Bears takes bowl of porridge labeled «Pop 105 A. Bear» and has it marked as an exhibit.*)

ATTY FOR BEARS: Pop A. Bear, I now hand to you what has been marked as «Bear's Exhibit A.» Is that your bowl?

POP A. BEAR: Yes, can't you see it says «Pop A.» on it? 110

ATTY FOR BEARS: Oh. Is this the bowl of porridge that was sitting on your table?

POP A. BEAR: Yes, it is. I never eat my porridge from any bowl except that bowl.

ATTY FOR BEARS: And when you came back from 115 your walk in the forest, is this the way you found it?

POP A. BEAR: Yes, it was empty, just like it is now! (*Attorney gives bowl to Court.*)
ATTY FOR BEARS: Your Honor, I ask that our exhibit
120 be admitted as evidence.
JUDGE: All right.
ATTY FOR BEARS: Pop A. Bear, after you discovered your porridge bowl empty, what did you do?
POP A. BEAR: I walked into my living room.
125 ATTY FOR BEARS: And what did you see?
POP A. BEAR: My favorite Pop A. Bear chair that Mom A. Bear and Babe E. Bear gave me for Father's Day last year.
ATTY FOR BEARS: Did you say anything upon noti-
130 cing that somebody has been sitting in your chair?
POP A. BEAR: Yes I growled, "Somebody's been sitting in my chair!"
ATTY FOR BEARS: Then what did you do?
POP A. BEAR: Well, I was getting suspicious, so I
135 went upstairs.
ATTY FOR BEARS: What did you notice upstairs?
POP A. BEAR: I noticed that my bed had been messed up.
ATTY FOR LOCKS: Your Honor, I object. We all know
140 that Pop A. Bear never makes his bed, and that the bed just sits there until Mom A. Bear makes it in the morning. How do we know that the bed had not been messed up from Pop A. Bear's sleeping in it?
ATTY FOR BEARS: Pop A. Bear, did you make your
145 bed that morning?
POP A. BEAR: Yes. I made a special effort that morning to make the bed as a birthday present for Mom A. Bear.
ATTY FOR BEARS: And when you got back was the
150 bed messed up?
POP A. BEAR: Yes, it was.
ATTY FOR BEARS: Did you say anything?
POP A. BEAR: Yes, I growled, «Somebody's been sleeping in my bed!»
155 ATTY FOR BEARS: Did you see anybody sleeping in your bed?
POP A. BEAR: No, I didn't. I went back downstairs.
ATTY FOR BEARS: Pop A. Bear, I have no further questions for you.
160 JUDGE: You may step down.
(*Pop A. Bear gets off the witness stand.*)
ATTY FOR BEARS: Next I will call Babe E. Bear to the stand.
(*Babe E. Bear goes forward, raises her right paw and
165 is sworn in.*)
ATTY FOR BEARS: What is your name?
BABE E. BEAR: (*babyish tone*) My name is Babe E. Bear. I live with my Mommy and Daddy Bear in a little cottage in (*write local place*).
170 ATTY FOR BEARS: Do you go to school?
BABE E. BEAR: Yes. I attend the (*insert name of particular school*) in (*insert local city and state*).
ATTY FOR BEARS: I see. And who are your teachers at pre-school?

BABE E. BEAR: My teachers are (*insert name of 175 teacher*)
ATTY FOR BEARS: And do you always respect your teachers at pre-school?
BABE E. BEAR: Well, most of the time I do.
ATTY FOR BEARS: And have your teachers told you 180 to close the door when you leave a room?
BABE E. BEAR: Well, they are trying to teach me to do that, but sometimes I forget. You see, I am still a baby bear.
ATTY FOR BEARS: Did you go for a walk with your 185 Mommy and Daddy in the forest?
BABE E. BEAR: Yes, I did. The porridge was too hot and I could not eat it, so I thought we could go for a walk and see the birdies, the bunny rabbits and the other animals that live in the forest. I like to watch 190 the birdies and the bunny rabbits. One time I even saw a deer in the forest.
ATTY FOR BEARS: When you got back from the forest ,what did you see?
BABE E. BEAR: I went with my Daddy to have my 195 breakfast, and when I sat down, my porridge bowl was empty.
ATTY FOR BEARS: And what did you say?
BABE E. BEAR: (*whines*) I said, «Somebody's been eating my porridge, too, and they ate it all up!» 200
(*Attorney takes bowl labeled Babe E. Bear and hands it to Court Reporter.*)
ATTY FOR BEARS: Please mark this as Bear's Exhibit B.
(*Attorney hands bowl to Babe E. Bear.*) 205
ATTY FOR BEARS: And, is this your porridge bowl?
BABE E. BEAR: Yes, it is. My Grandma gave it to me when I was a tiny baby. I was just a little cub when she gave it to me. She gave it to me because she knew I liked to eat porridge for breakfast. 210
ATTY FOR BEARS: And, is that the bowl that was empty when you came back into your house from your walk in the forest?
BABE E. BEAR: Yes, it is.
(*Attorney hands bowl to Judge as Exhibit B.*) 215
ATTY FOR BEARS: And then what did you do, Babe E. Bear?
BABE E. BEAR: I went into my living room and I saw that my favorite chair was broken! Grandpa gave me the chair for my second birthday so that I could sit 220 with Mom A. Bear and Pop A. Bear. I mainly used it when I watched television. You know, my favorite programs are Yogi Bear and football games between the Chicago Bears and the (*insert name of local team*). Of course, I had to root for the Bears. 225
ATTY FOR BEARS: Yes, I know. And when you saw your chair what did you say?
BABE E. BEAR: I said, «Somebody's been sitting in my chair and they broke it!» I was really sad about my chair being broken, because it was my favorite. 230
(*Attorney picks up broken chair and has it marked as Exhibit C.*)

ATTY FOR BEARS: Babe E. Bear, is that your chair?

BABE E. BEAR: (pouting) Yes, it is. I really feel sad
235 because it was broken. Pop A. Bear was going to fix it,
but he is very slow at doing these things sometimes.
I guess Mom A. Bear will have to talk to him about it.

ATTY FOR BEARS: And then what did you do?

BABE E. BEAR: I went upstairs to my bedroom.

240 ATTY FOR BEARS: And did you make your bed on
that morning?

BABE E. BEAR: Yes, I did on that morning because
it was Mom A. Bear's birthday. Daddy Bear and I
wanted to surprise her because we sometimes, well,
245 most of the time, forget to make our beds. Mom A.
Bear scolds us for it.

ATTY FOR BEARS: I see. But you did make your bed
that morning?

BABE E. BEAR: Well, Daddy Bear helped me, but
250 we made it, yes. I even put my little pillow neatly at
the top of the bed.

ATTY FOR BEARS: And, when you went back upstairs, what did you see?

BABE E. BEAR: (agitated) When I went back upstairs,
255 my little pillow was gone! When I approached the bed
I saw these golden locks. I then peeked under the
covers and I saw a little girl, and I shouted, «Somebody's been sleeping in my bed, and there she is!
It's a little girl!»

260 ATTY FOR BEARS: And, what did the little girl do?

BABE E. BEAR: She got up and ran so fast that I
hardly saw her. I just saw these golden locks as she
ran out the door.

ATTY FOR BEARS: Is the little girl who was sleeping
265 in your bed here today?

BABE E. BEAR: Well, that little girl over there with
the golden hair looks like her, but I really didn't get
a very good look. It could be her.

(Attorney hands pillow, which has been marked as
270 Exhibit C to Babe E. Bear.)

ATTY FOR BEARS: Is this your pillow?

BABE E. BEAR: Yes, it is. My Aunt Cubby made it
for me when I was a baby.

ATTY FOR BEARS: Babe E. Bear, you don't have
275 golden hair, do you?

BABE E. BEAR: No, I don't. My hair is brown and
furry like my Mommy's and Daddy's.

ATTY FOR BEARS: There is golden hair on this pillow.
Could that be Gold E. Locks' hair?

280 BABE E. BEAR: I guess so, it's not mine.

ATTY FOR BEARS: Very well, Babe E. Bear. Do you
have anything further to say?

BABE E. BEAR: Well, I don't blame the little girl for
wanting to eat the porridge and Mommy can always
285 make more porridge, but I wish she hadn't broken
my chair. That really is my favorite chair.

ATTY FOR BEARS: Thank you, Babe E. Bear.

(Babe E. Bear gets down.)

ATTY FOR BEARS: Your Honor, that is all of our
290 evidence. The Bears rest.

JUDGE: Very well. We will now hear Gold E. Locks'
side of the case.

ATTY FOR LOCKS: Your Honor, as my first witness I
will call Gold E. Locks.

(Gold E. Locks gets up, walks forward, raises her right 295
hand to be sworn. Judge administers the oath. Gold
E. Locks then sits down.)

ATTY FOR LOCKS: What is your name?

GOLD E. LOCKS: My name is Golden Locks. I am also
called Gold E. Locks. When I was born, my mother 300
said I had golden locks. And so from that day forward
I have been known as Gold E. Locks.

ATTY FOR LOCKS: I see. You do have very pretty
gold locks.

GOLD E. LOCKS: Thank you. 305

ATTY FOR LOCKS: Where do you live?

GOLD E. LOCKS: I live with my Mother Locks, my
Father Locks, my little baby brother Locks, my kitty
cats Spook Locks and Funny locks at (insert a local
address). Oh yes, I also live with my dog, Melissa 310
Locks. Melissa needs a haircut right now.

ATTY FOR LOCKS: Oh, that's very interesting. And
is your house located anywhere near the house of
Babe E. Bear?

GOLD E. LOCKS: Oh, yes, Babe E. Bear and I see 315
each other quite often while walking in the forest. I
like to walk through the forest and pick flowers. I
also like to watch the bunny rabbits and deer in the
forest. Babe E. Bear and I also attend the same pre-
school, which is (insert the name of a local school). 320
My Mommy takes me every day in the station wagon
to pre-school. Sometimes I take some of the flowers
with me, which I have picked in the forest.

ATTY FOR LOCKS: And, are your teachers also (indicate name of teacher). 325

GOLD E. LOCKS: Yes, they are. We play games and
play in the toy kitchen and sing and have a snack.

ATTY FOR LOCKS: And, I'm sure your teachers, along
with your Mother and Father, have told you never to
go into a strange house. 330

GOLD E. LOCKS: Yes, they have. But sometimes I
forget, especially when the porridge smells so good!

ATTY FOR LOCKS: Now Gold E., on the day in question, were you out walking in the forest?

GOLD E. LOCKS: Yes, I was. I was out picking flowers 335
in the forest early one fall morning. I like to go out
early in the morning because that's when I see the
most bunny rabbits and sometimes I even see a deer.

ATTY FOR LOCKS: And, as you were walking in the
forest what did you smell? 340

GOLD E. LOCKS: I smelled the most yummy porridge coming from a house in the forest. I followed
my nose until I came to a brown house, which had
the name «Bear» on the front. I knocked on the door,
but I did not see anybody at home. The smell was so 345
good and I had not had any breakfast that morning
since Mommy does not fix breakfast until I get back
from my morning walk. In fact, sometimes she even
goes with me.

ATTY FOR LOCKS: I see. And then what did you do? 350

GOLD E. LOCKS: I knocked on the door several times but nobody answered. Since the door was open, I figured that the people who lived in the house must be close by.

355 ATTY FOR LOCKS: Did you enter the house?

GOLD E. LOCKS: Yes, I did, but the door was wide open. I followed my nose right to the kitchen. There I saw three bowls of porridge.

ATTY FOR LOCKS: When you saw the three bowls of
360 porridge, what did you say?

GOLD E. LOCKS: I said, «Oh, my porridge!»

ATTY FOR LOCKS: Then what did you do?

GOLD E. LOCKS: I tasted some porridge from Papa Bear's great big bowl. It was too hot. Then I tasted
365 the porridge in Mom A. Bear's medium-sized bowl, but it was too cold. Then I tasted some porridge in Babe E. Bear's bowl. It was just right, and I was so hungry I ate it all up.

ATTY FOR LOCKS: Were the Bears in the house while
370 you were eating the porridge?

GOLD E. LOCKS: No, but I figured they must be nearby. I guess I got so excited eating the porridge that I forgot about the Bears.

ATTY FOR LOCKS: Then what did you do?

375 GOLD E. LOCKS: Well, my tummy was so full of yummy porridge that I went into the living room to thank the person who had made the porridge and to tell her how good the porridge was. My Mother said I always should say thank you when somebody does
380 something nice for me.

ATTY FOR LOCKS: Did you find anybody?

GOLD E. LOCKS: No, I didn't. So I decided to sit down in a chair to wait for the person to come home so I could tell her how good the porridge was. I wanted
385 her to give me the recipe so I could give it to my Mommy. My Mommy makes good porridge, but it doesn't taste quite as good as the porridge I had at the Bears' house. I think it's the pawfuls of raisins that makes it taste so good.

390 ATTY FOR LOCKS: Did you sit down?

GOLD E. LOCKS: Yes, I did. In fact I sat in this great big chair. But it was too hard and too big. I did not feel comfortable in it. It looked like a Poppa's chair. My Daddy has one like it at home. Then I sat in a
395 smaller chair, but it was too soft. It was kind of like the chair my Mommy sits in at home. Than I sat down in this little chair which seemed to be just right.

ATTY FOR LOCKS: What happened when you sat in the chair?

400 GOLD E. LOCKS: It broke. But I think the chair was already broken when I sat in it and that it was just sitting there as a decoration. As little as I weigh I am sure my weight would not have broken it if it had not already been broken. I was really sad when I saw
405 the broken chair.

ATTY FOR LOCKS: Then what did you do?

GOLD E. LOCKS: I was so sad when I saw the broken chair that I decided to go upstairs and wait for the Bears to come home so I could tell them about it. I
410 went into a room which was decorated a lot like my room at home and sat down on a bed to wait for the Bears to come home. I think I was crying a little bit too, about breaking the chair. Well, the bears did not come home right away and I must have closed my
415 eyes to wait for them. I fell asleep on Babe E. Bear's bed. The next thing I remember before I fell asleep on Babe E. Bear's bed was that I also tried Pop A. Bear's bed and Mom A. Bear's bed. But they were too hard. I guess I messed their beds up a little bit
420 too, although Pop A. Bear's bed had not been made very well. It looked like he did it himself.

ATTY FOR LOCKS: What do you remember next?

GOLD E. LOCKS: The next thing I remember there were three bears standing around me. Pop A. Bear
425 looked very, very mad and he said, «Somebody's been sleeping in my bed!» Then I heard Mom A. Bear say, «Somebody's been sleeping in my bed!» I was so frightened that I got up and ran right out the door to my mother.

430 ATTY FOR LOCKS: Gold E. Locks, as I recall your testimony, you ate the porridge because it smelled so good and you were hungry. You had not knocked the door down, but walked in the open door thinking the people would not care. The chair was broken when
435 you sat down to wait for the maker of the porridge to tell her how good the porridge was, and you accidently fell asleep on the bed.

GOLD E. LOCKS: That's right.

ATTY FOR LOCKS: You didn't mean anybody any
440 harm did you, Gold E. Locks?

GOLD E. LOCKS: Of course not! It looked like such a friendly house and I knew that Babe E. Bear lived there. I see her at pre-school many times. She even told me that sometime I should come over and have
445 some porridge with her because her mother made it so good! I really didn't mean to harm anything and I'm really sorry about the chair, but I still don't think I broke it.

ATTY FOR LOCKS: Thank you, Gold E. That's all the
450 questions. Next I will call Mrs. Locks to the stand. (*Mrs. Locks goes forward and is sworn in.*)

ATTY FOR LOCKS: What is your name?

MRS. LOCKS: My name is Curl E. Locks.

ATTY FOR LOCKS: Where do you live, Mrs. Locks?

455 MRS. LOCKS: We live at (insert localized address).

ATTY FOR LOCKS: And are you the mother of Gold E. Locks?

MRS. LOCKS: Oh, yes, I am. She is my little girl.

ATTY FOR LOCKS: What kind of a little girl is Gold
460 E. Locks?

MRS. LOCKS: Gold E., essentially, is a good little girl. She is mischievous like most little girls, but she tries to always do the right thing. Sometimes she forgets. I do have one trouble with her and that is that she
465 likes to wander through the forest picking flowers. She tells me that she likes to look at the bunny

rabbits and the deer. Most of the time I go with her but on the morning in question I was getting ready for a bridge club meeting.

470 ATTY FOR LOCKS: You say Gold E. is essentially a good girl. Does she say please?

MRS. LOCKS: Most of the time.

ATTY FOR LOCKS: And does she say thank you?

MRS. LOCKS: Oh, I have taught her to say thank

475 you and her teachers at school have taught her to say thank you, and she says thank you most of the time when she remembers. But like most little girls, sometimes she forgets.

ATTY FOR LOCKS: Does she help you with the

480 dishes?

MRS. LOCKS: Well, most of the time. But sometimes; especially when the Muppets are on television, she runs downstairs and watches television and forgets to help me with the dishes. But I understand – espe-

485 cially when the Muppets are on television. That's her favorite show, you know.

ATTY FOR LOCKS: Does she attend pre-school?

MRS. LOCKS: Oh, yes. She goes to (*insert name of school*) every day. She enjoys the music and swin-

490 ging on the swings and the art classes and all the activities. She's really excited about pre-school.

ATTY FOR LOCKS: Well, this trial is about Gold E. Locks having bad manners. Do you think she has bad manners?

495 MRS. LOCKS: Oh, goodness no. She does forget occasionally like most little girls do, but I know she tries to use good manners. I think the only reason she went into the Bear' house was because the porridge smelled so good. And after she ate the porridge

500 she simply wanted to stay there until the Bears returned to tell them how good the porridge was. She certainly didn't intend any harm and I know that she didn't mean to break the chair. But Gold E. has told me that the chair was already broken

505 when she sat in it. You know she's not very big and I don't think she could break the chair.

ATTY FOR LOCKS: Where is Mr. Locks today?

MRS. LOCKS: Oh, he wanted to be here, but he had a very important meeting. He's a lawyer, you know,

510 and lawyers are always going to very important meetings -- at least that's what he tells me. I'm sure he would say the same thing about Gold E. Locks if he were here.

ATTY FOR LOCKS: Is there anything else you would

515 like to say, Mrs. Locks?

MRS. LOCKS: Well, we're sorry that the Bears were inconvenienced, but if they would like to come to our house for breakfast I would be glad to fix them some of my porridge. Maybe Mrs. Bear could even

520 show me how she makes it so yummy.

ATTY FOR LOCKS: Thank you, Mrs. Locks, you may step down

(*Mrs. Locks steps down.*)

JUDGE: Are there any summaries?

ATTY FOR BEARS: Your Honor, we have shown that 525 Gold E. Locks, without being invited, walked into the Bear's home, ate Babe E. Bear's porridge, broke Babe E. Bear's chair, and slept in her bed. She did all of this without being invited and I certainly think that meets the test of bad manners. Even though Gold E. 530 Locks knew better, that is no excuse. I'm sure the jury agrees that one who displays good manners does not do such things.

ATTY FOR LOCKS: Your Honor, we have shown that Gold E. Locks is basically a good little girl. She has 535 said that she meant no harm in going into the house, and the door was open. The porridge was so good that she could not resist it, and after she ate the porridge she merely wanted to wait for the Bears to come home to thank them. She didn't mean to break Babe 540 E. Bear's chair, and in fact there is no real evidence that she broke the chair. I think the chair was broken when she sat in it. She is certainly not big enough to have broken the chair. She is sorry she fell asleep in the bed, but she was merely waiting for the Bears to 545 come home so she could thank them and to ask them how they make the yummy porridge. She certainly did not display any bad manners, in fact she showed good manners by waiting to thank the bears.

JUDGE: Thank you. Does that conclude the evidence? 550

ATTORNEYS: (*both*) Yes, it does.

(*Judge turns to jury*)

JUDGE: You now have heard the evidence. Now it is your job to decide whether Gold E. Locks has bad manners, or not. Will you please go with the Bailiff 555 to the jury room and after you have decided, would you please come back and inform the Court whether Gold E. Locks exhibited bad manners by entering the house of the three bears and eating the porridge, sitting in Babe E. Bear's chair, and sleeping in Babe 560 E. Bear's bed.

(*Bailiff takes the jurors to the jury room. After a while, jurors come back with a verdict.*)

JUDGE: Have you reached a verdict?

JUROR: Yes, we have, your Honor. 565

JUDGE: What is that verdict?

JUROR: The jury has voted and has determined that... [*complete*]

243

PART 3 – CATEGORIES OF LAW

In the American system, it is possible in certain cases to file a complaint in criminal AND civil court for the same events (this is what happened during the famous trial of the American Football star O.J. Simpson in 1980); civil proceedings are obviously considerably more numerous than criminal proceedings. And this is true, whether at the State or Federal level, because almost every action/event in our society could lead to a trial: a client unhappy with a product or a service, an argument, insults, slander, a breach of contract, a separation or a divorce, someone's death... the list goes on and on.

We can nonetheless determine five main categories of civil proceedings:

1. Contract law: this area deals with agreements between at least two people. It might be an agreement related to a purchase or sale, a specific type of work, a type of repair, etc. The problems that arise typically involve a disagreement for a total amount that one should pay the other, or not being paid on the agreed-upon date, or a flaw in a purchased product or the delivery of a service. In the related areas of contractual relationships, we find problems related to bankruptcy or problems with insurance companies, which may affect almost everyone.

2. Tort law: These issues are usually questions of Civil Law. Here, we are speaking about all personal actions that may cause harm to someone, the most serious being when someone is wounded, such as in car accidents. This is the area that has seen the largest increase in the number of cases brought to suit, especially because of injuries due to defects in products: every sector is affected, from food to toys, to medication, cars, and almost anything that can be bought. The incredible explosion of cases in this domain is often explained by the presence of the jury in Civil Court in the U.S.A. Effectively, these may grant two types of damages: compensatory and punitive. Compensatory damages are given to cover the actual expenses a problem may have caused, such as medical bills, or repairs. Punitive damages are awarded to punish the Defendant, so that it will not happen again and/or the possible negligence be righted.

Over the last few years, juries have tended to grant almost unlimited punitive damages, which has whetted a lot of appetites [see p.62-63].

3. Property law: Property rights have always meant a lot in the U.S.A., whether it be a question of real estate, such as land, houses, buildings, but also crops; or personal property, including such things such as money, jewelry, automobiles, furniture and bank accounts. In recent years, the idea of property has expanded to include the right to use the property, which has led to a large number of cases dealing with zoning problems, a practice whereby local laws divide a territory into districts designated for special uses (residential, commercial, industrial).

4. Succession law: American law recognizes the right of each person to dispose of his or her property as he or she wishes, usually through a Last Will and Testament. Without one, major problems may arise, which are then decided in Court within the context of the different State laws.

5. Family law: this area of law deals with all family-related issues: marriage, divorce, child custody, or children's rights. This affects the lives of a large majority of Americans. Problems with child custody and visitation rights are the most numerous in Courts today.

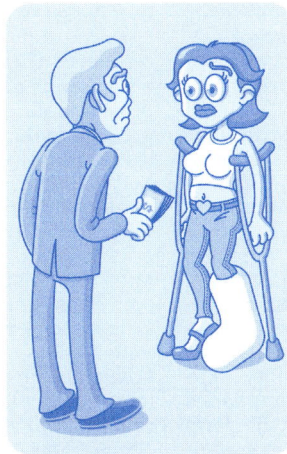

ACTIVITY

Compensatory damages   Punitive damages

A. Can someone file criminal charges while in civil lawsuit?

....

....

B. What are the five main categories of civil proceedings?

....

....

LAW CAREEER ADVISING

DOCUMENT 5

Fields of Law

Knowing which college you want to join is a good thing. But what for? This is the question asked on Brown University website: it's not enough to answer «*to study law*». Because law is a broad topic... Check it out!

Law schools do not expect you to know what kind of law you want to practice before you register. Still, it is a good idea to learn about the various types of law practice well before you decide to submit law school applications. Educating yourself in this area should be part of your career exploration process.

This page summarizes major areas of law practice in alphabetical order, accompanied by links to professional organizations, when relevant. The content is partly based on information from LSAC (lsac.org) and Discoverlaw.org, LSAC's diversity program. The American Bar Association (americanbar.org) is also a good source to explore. *Consult with the Law Careers Advising deans for more information.*

Admiralty (Maritime) Law

Admiralty Law regulates economic transactions and property disputes involving marine trade, sailors, navigation, or land-based activity that is maritime in nature. Admiralty Law is not, however, synonymous with the Law of the Sea, which is in the realm of international public law and deals with rights to navigation, minerals, or coastal waters jurisdiction. *Learn more at: The Maritime Law Association of the United States (mlaus.org).*

Bankruptcy Law

American Bankruptcy Law applies to the insolvency problems of individuals, as well as organizations. This type of law comes directly from the Constitution and is in the domain of Federal law, though State laws have an important effect on bankruptcy procedure. Legal practitioners in this field are experts in the U.S. Bankruptcy Code, which is a subset of the United States Code. *Learn more at: National Association of Consumer Bankruptcy Attorneys (nacba.org).*

Business (Corporate) Law

Corporate Law involves the formation, dissolution, and all other legal aspects of the administration of corporations. Typical duties of corporate lawyers include mergers, acquisitions, internal reorganization, or disputes between corporations and individuals concerning liability, patents, and compliance with State and Federal law, as well as international accords. A legal professional whose sole client is a corporation is generally known as in-house counsel. *Learn more at: Association of Corporate Counsel (acc.com).*

Civil Rights Law

Civil Rights Law aims to balance competing interests between institutions of government on the one hand, and individuals or groups of individuals on the other. Lawyers in such practice may work on cases involving discrimination and unfair practices that infringe on rights and liberties, such as expression, employment, housing, education, or other entitlements. *Learn more at: Civil Rights Trial Lawyers Association (cartl.org).*

Criminal Law

Criminal Law focuses on behaviors that are sanctioned under criminal code and defined as illegal. Prosecutors and District Attorneys sanction illegal behavior, while criminal defense lawyers represent clients accused of criminal activity. Both prosecution and defense professionals deal with issues of individual liberty, basic rights, and responsibilities. In some Common Law countries other than the U.S., and in most Civil Law countries, the roles of a Prosecutor (or Procurator) and Defense Lawyer (or Advocate) are separated more clearly into different professional specialties. *Learn more at: National Association of Criminal Defense Lawyers (nacdl.org).*

Entertainment Law

Entertainment Law predominantly relates to Intellectual Property Law, but is more specifically centered on rights and royalties issues to media in the arts, music, television, cinema, or sports. Sports lawyers ensure compliance with regulations for professional or amateur sports and may represent an athlete for a contractual transaction. With the rapid development of information technology and social media, entertainment lawyers operate in an environment of constant change. *Learn more at: International Association of Entertainment Lawyers (iael.org).*

Environmental Law

Environmental Law concerns a multitude of statutes, treaties, regulations, and conventions based in State, Federal, or trans-national law. Legal professionals practicing in this field may represent government agencies, advocacy organizations, or individuals. Environmental lawyers often focus on cases involving natural resource management, the curbing of pollution, or disputes about land and water-front use. Public health components are increasingly common in the practice of environmental law. *Learn more at: National Association of Environmantal Law Societies (naels.org).*

Family Law

Family Law focuses on legal relations between individuals in the context of the family. Lawyers in this field typically work in smaller firms and specialize in a variety of areas ranging from child welfare, through adoption, to divorce. Child abuse, legitimacy, civil unions, domestic partnerships, and marriages are among the main aspects of family lawyers' practice. *Learn more at: Ame-*

rican Academy of Matrimonial Lawyers (aaml.org).

Health Law
Health Law is a changing field that focuses on legislation related to health care. Health law attorneys may represent patients, clinics, insurance companies, or individual health practitioners. The Federal government employs attorneys in this field to oversee the crafting, implementation, and enforcement of policies. Health Law specialists also work at academic institutions and biotechnology and pharmaceutical companies. *Learn more at: American Health Lawyers Association (healthlawyer.org).*

Immigration Law
Immigration lawyers work with individual clients at all stages of the naturalization process. Other aspects of the profession relate to refugee and asylum seekers, as well as to individuals in the country without legal permission. This field of law varies significantly from country to country. Much of its practice depends on international treaties, bilateral accords, and political conjecture. *Learn more at: American Immigration Lawyers Association (aila.org).*

Intellectual Property Law
Intellectual Property law focuses on protecting the rights of inventors, authors, and businesses to their tangible and intangible creations, inventions and symbols. Legal professionals in this field are often experts in a particular domain, such as Science, the Arts, or an industry. For example, trademark or copyright attorneys manage the legal aspects of contracts, visual identity, brand names, or slogans. Technological advances, notably in digital reproduction and transmission, make this a dynamic field of law. *Learn more at: American Intellectual Property Law Association (aipla.org).*

International Law
International Law is broad in its conception and can be broken down into private and public sectors. In the private sector, specialists in International Law may work in finance and trade divisions of multinational corporations. Familiarity with business essentials, as well as corporate law or intellectual property law would be helpful in this field. In Public International Law, practitioners would work on cases that involve dealings between sovereign nations. Familiarity with Comparative Law or Public International Law would be most helpful for effective practice in this field. Both private and public international Law are Interdisciplinary in nature and would involve an understanding of the differences between Common Law and civil law systems across borders. *Learn more at: http://www.ila-hq.org and http://www.asil.org/mission.cfm.*

Labor (Employment) Law
Labor Law is concerned with the relations between workers and their employers on matters ranging from wages and compensation, through harassment, to discrimination based on gender, disability, or age. Labor law often involves collective bargaining and unions. Attorneys in this field may represent individual clients, a union, a government regulatory agency, or an employer. *Learn more at: National Employment Lawyers Association (nela.org).*

Military Law
Military Law involves codes and procedures that govern legal matters in the Armed Forces. Since 1951, Military Law has been based on the Uniform Code of Military Justice. Legal experts in this field are typically members of the Armed Forces serving in the Judge Advocate General's Corps. *Learn more at: Judge Advocates Association (jaa.org)*

Personal Injury Law
Personal Injury Law deals with intentional or unintentional wrongdoing that affects individuals physically or psychologically. Experts in the field are well-versed in Torts Law and may work on cases involving medical malpractice, accidental collisions, product liability, wrongful death, or workplace injury. Many cases are settled out of Court in this field of legal practice. *Learn more at: National Association of Personal Injury Lawyers (napil.com).*

Real Estate Law
Real Estate law involves land or construction ownership, development, litigation, tenant rights, or landlord disputes. Attorneys in this field may work on residential or commercial transactions, review contracts, or work in planning and other government offices. *Learn more at: Association of Real Estate Licence Law Officials (arello.org)*

Tax Law
Tax Law is a dynamic field that deals with domestic and international transactions. Because of the frequent modifications to local, State, and Federal codes and the complexity of fiscal policy that guides these changes, experts in Tax Law engage in continuous education at greater rates than in many other fields of law. Apart from ensuring the legality of the levies on economic transactions, tax lawyers help clients reduce fiscal liabilities. *Learn more at: National Association of Tax Professionals (naptax.com)*

ACTIVITY

BROWN UNIVERSITY
Located in historic Providence, Rhode Island, and founded in 1764, Brown University is the seventh-oldest college in the United States. Brown is an independent, coeducational, Ivy League institution comprising undergraduate and graduate programs.

A. What topic are you more interested in, and why?

B. Which of these subjects are not commonly taught in France?

PART 4 – TO TRY OR NOT TO TRY?

Though it is common knowledge that the number of lawsuits in the United States is very numerous, many measures exist to settle differences outside of Court. A trial is long in Civil Court and often quite expensive. Hundreds of thousands of trials are avoided using these measures. The cost of a trial sometimes suffices in discouraging some people. Alternative Dispute Resolutions (ADR) are methods permitting a legal and judicial solution to a dispute. Any process aimed at allowing parties with conflicts to search for and accept an amicable solution to stop a conflict will be considered as an alternative, considering that a legal ruling would impose a verdict. Likewise, in a contentious case with an administrative body, using negotiation or intervention techniques via a third party in order to avoid a trial would be considered as an alternative. A number of alternative procedures exist:

1. Mediation: An impartial person tries to help the parties clarify the situation and to reach an agreement that would satisfy both sides. The mediator is not a judge. This solution is a good choice when dealing with complicated family problems (divorce, child custody, etc.), for example, or between neighbors, or employee to employer.

2. Arbitration in contentious cases consists in calling in a third party outside of the judicial system. This party – which could be a group called in by the parties – is in charge of presenting the case, listening to each side, and making a decision. It's a process similar to going to Court, but without having a judge. This procedure is often chosen because it saves a lot of time and money. Arbitration is usually completed in four months, while a trial may last many years.

3. Neutral fact-finding: This is a process by which an organization, a licensed body, or a third party is charged with looking into the problem and drafting a report. This is a method typically used in cases of alleged racial or sexual discrimination. For example, when two parties work for the same company, the directors may prefer to use an outside party so that the final verdict will be accepted by all those involved.

4. Summary jury trial: An alternative dispute resolution technique that is increasingly used in civil disputes in the United States. In essence, a mock trial is held: a jury is selected and, in some cases, presented with the evidence that would be used at an actual trial. The parties are required to attend the proceeding and hear the verdict that the jury delivers. After the verdict, the parties are required to once again attempt a settlement before going to trial for real.

5. Private judging: Lawyers often refer difficult cases to Private Judging. In these cases, an experienced lawyer or retired judge will be hired to serve in some capacity to resolve the issues of a dispute, as a means of keeping a case out of the court system. The private judge may serve in any capacity elected by the parties, from supervising settlement negotiations to making final binding decisions. Government agencies have also been established, with a quasi-legal authority, to deal with some very specific problems. As an example, one may often find a worker's compensation board at the State level, whose mission is to help settle disputes when an employee is hurt on the job.

ACTIVITY

A. What is mediation?

....

....

....

....

B. What are the various alternative procedures?

....

....

....

....

WEIRD LAWS

DOCUMENT 6

Is your sex life against the law?

You can verify the existence of these laws. Go on *Findlaw.com*, where you'll find a listings of sex-related laws for every State in the U.S., along with links to the actual State Codes. HG.org also has some verified listings. For more on bizarre laws, *The Book of Strange and Curious Legal Oddities* by Nathan Belofsky, an attorney, is a goldmine. Finally, DumbLaws.com provides statutory info for some (but not all) of its laws.

Is your sex life against the law? Better make sure. Page 191 has a map of the most bizarre and unnecessary laws regulating what you do, with whom, and where in the U.S. Americans love to lake fools out of their own legal system and you can find dozens of lists of freaky sex laws on the Internet. And guess what? Most of them are urban legends.

When you see laws like "Only sex in the missionary position is legal," or "No sex in an ambulance responding to an emergency call," they're probably just made up or grossly distorted.

But what is true is that several States still have laws against oral and anal sex on their books, despite the Supreme Court shooting down sodomy laws in 2003. Also, a surprising number of States allow necrophilia, along with underage marriage in some circumstances.

Here is a list of surprising regional laws:

Alabama
Incestuous marriages are legal.
Alaska
Moose are banned from having sex on city streets (*in Fairbanks*).
Arizona
You may not have more than two dildos in the same house.
Arkansas
Flirtation and "lascivious banter" between men and women on the streets may result in a 30-day jail term. (*in Little Rock*).
California
It's illegal to sell stuffed items resembling breasts ("boobie pillows") within 1000 feet of a highway.

No man shall dress as a woman without the written permission of the sheriff (*in Walnut, CA*).
Colorado
Male massage parlor workers must wear all white clothing (*in Adams County*). Keeping a house where unmarried persons are allowed to have sex is prohibited.
Florida
Married couples (as well as singles) cannot engage in open "lewdness or lascivious behavior"
Georgia
The term "sadomasochistic abuse" is defined so broadly, that it could possibly be applied to a person handcuffing another in a clown suit. All sex toys are banned.
Illinois
If you sell a reptile, you must give a written warning not to "nuzzle or kiss" them.
It's prohibited by law to "suffer any bitch or slut" (*referring to dogs, in Minooka*).
Indiana
It is illegal for a man to be sexually aroused in public.
Iowa
Kisses may last for no more than five minutes.
Kansas
Illegal "sodomy" includes oral sex, but anal penetration with a finger is allowed under specified circumstances.
Kentucky
Dogs are not allowed to molest property or people.
Until 1975, people wearing bathing suits on any city street were required to have a police escort.
Louisiana
Necrophilia is legal.
It's illegal to reach climax before your partner (*in New Orleans*).
Massachusetts
Making noise in a public

library is a crime against "chastity, morality, decency and good order."
Michigan
A man who seduces or corrupts a married woman faces five years in prison.
Low-riding pants that expose underwear are a Class B offense. But if they expose butt cleavage, they're a Class A offense (*in Flint*).
Mississippi
It's illegal to teach others what polygamy is.
Adultery or premarital sex results in a fine of $500, or 6 months in prison.
Montana
Prostitution is a "crime against the family."
Nebraska
You can't get married if you have gonorrhea.
Nevada
Selling of sex toys is illegal.
New Hamphire
Lingerie must not be hung on a clothesline at the airport, unless there's a screen concealing it (*in Kidderville*).
New Jersey
Flirting is illegal (*in Haddon Township, NJ*).
New Mexico
Nudity is allowed, as long as genitals and female nipples are covered.
New York
Adultery is illegal.
North Carolina
Adultery is illegal. And so is pretending to be married in order to share a hotel room.
North Dakota
It was illegal to swim naked in the Red River between 8 AM and 8 PM (*in Fargo*).
It's against the law to fail to confine a dog or cat in heat (*in Grand Forks*).
Ohio
No person shall solicit sex from another of the same gender if it offends the second person

Oklahoma
It is illegal for the owner of a bar to allow anyone inside to engage in "acts, or simulated acts, of sexual intercourse, masturbation, sodomy, bestiality, oral copulation, flagellation, or any sexual acts which are otherwise prohibited by law." So, no simulated intercourse or animal sex.
Oregon
It's illegal to lie down in a public restroom, or for two people to share a stall meant for one.
Pennsylvania
Oral and anal sex are illegal. You cannot cohabit with an "ancestor or descendant."
South Carolina
If a man promises to marry a woman and she sleeps with him, the marriage must take place.
South Dakota
Public erections are illegal.
Tennessee
Students may not hold hands in school.
Texas
It's illegal to own more than six dildos.
Utah
It's illegal to marry your first cousin before the age of 65 — or 55 if you can prove both parties are infertile.
An adult cannot show sex paraphernalia to a minor, unless they're your own child (*in Salt Lake City*).
Virginia
Adultery is a misdemeanor. Obscenity is a bigger crime if you use a computer.
Washington
If you give a sex worker a ride to work, your car can be confiscated.
West Virginia
An unmarried couple who lived together and were "lewdly associated" could face up to a year in jail (*Recently repealed*).

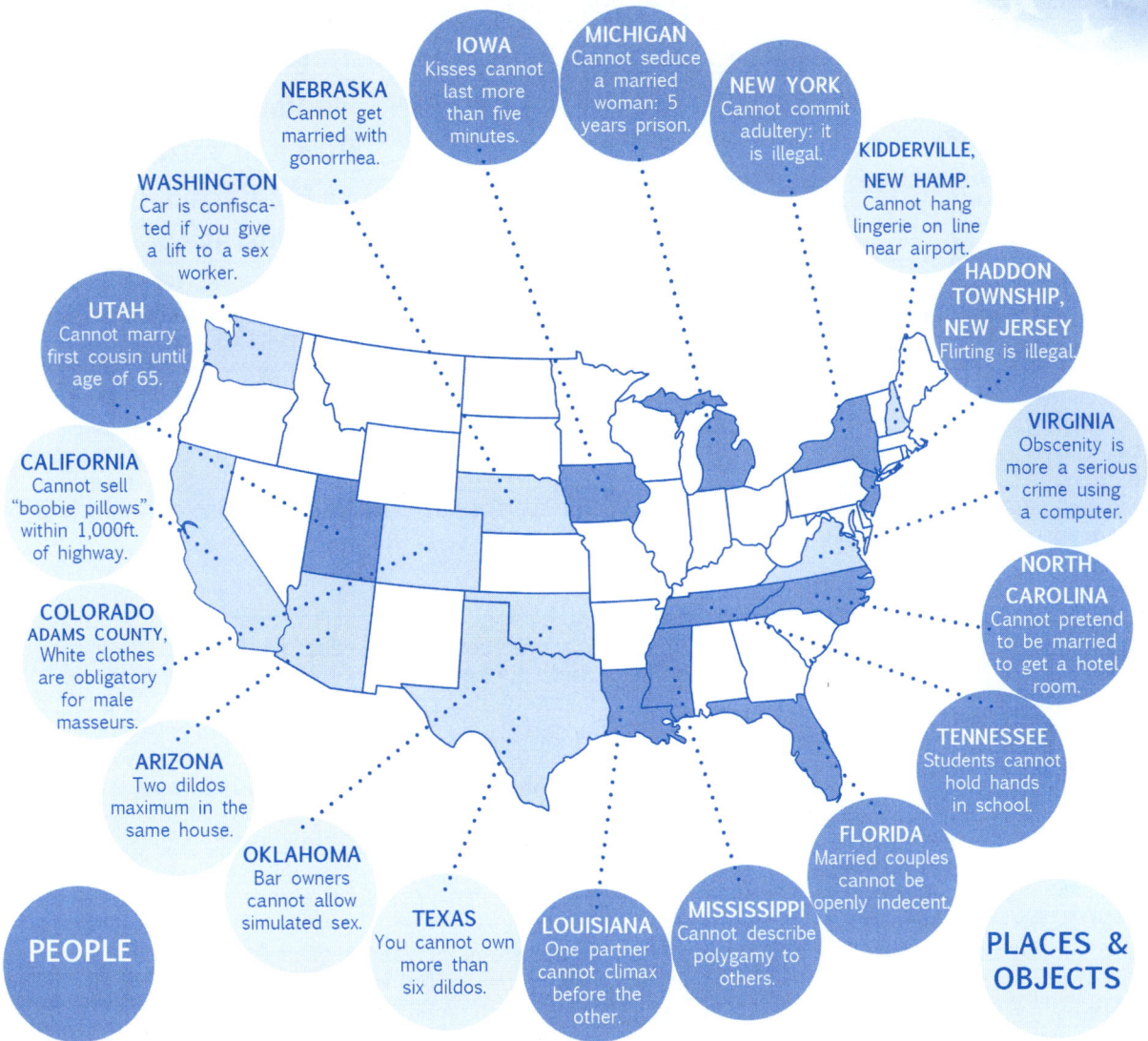

IOWA
Kisses cannot last more than five minutes.

MICHIGAN
Cannot seduce a married woman: 5 years prison.

NEBRASKA
Cannot get married with gonorrhea.

NEW YORK
Cannot commit adultery: it is illegal.

KIDDERVILLE, NEW HAMP.
Cannot hang lingerie on line near airport.

WASHINGTON
Car is confiscated if you give a lift to a sex worker.

HADDON TOWNSHIP, NEW JERSEY
Flirting is illegal.

UTAH
Cannot marry first cousin until age of 65.

VIRGINIA
Obscenity is more a serious crime using a computer.

CALIFORNIA
Cannot sell "boobie pillows" within 1,000ft. of highway.

NORTH CAROLINA
Cannot pretend to be married to get a hotel room.

COLORADO
ADAMS COUNTY, White clothes are obligatory for male masseurs.

ARIZONA
Two dildos maximum in the same house.

TENNESSEE
Students cannot hold hands in school.

OKLAHOMA
Bar owners cannot allow simulated sex.

FLORIDA
Married couples cannot be openly indecent.

PEOPLE

TEXAS
You cannot own more than six dildos.

LOUISIANA
One partner cannot climax before the other.

MISSISSIPPI
Cannot describe polygamy to others.

PLACES & OBJECTS

ACTIVITY

A. What is your opinion after reading this article and looking at the map provided?

B. When you are told about a weird law, how can you check if it is authentic?

C. One law is not an actual law. Go online and figure out which one.

D. Are there any laws on the lists that go against a decision of the Supreme Court or a federal statute?

251

Important terms:

Super injunction
Summons
Voir Dire
Directed verdict
Mediation
Arbitration

GOING TO TRIAL

Numerous court cases between individuals, or against an administrative body, finish in Court: these are civil proceedings. Here, the adversarial system prevails, as in criminal cases. The Prosecution accuses the Defense and has the burden of proof. In civil cases, the burden of proof is less challenging, being reduced to a preponderance of evidence. Constitutional safeguards are weaker in civil cases and there is no obligation to provide an attorney to the Defense. The trial is fairly strict, beginning with the filing of a civil suit, the person filing being the *Plaintiff* and the other party, the *Defendant*. When a case involves two parties from two different States, the case is usually held in the State of the Defense. A summons is first delivered by the Sheriff, or a Marshall, or a private company. Then the parties send each other documents and answer each other with contradictory conclusions. An important part of the procedure is *discovery*: all proof and pieces of evidence must be shared with the opposing party.

THE CIVIL TRIAL

The 7th Amendment guarantees the right to trial by jury, even in civil cases. This right is often supported by legislation passed by the States. In civil hearings, the jury members are selected according to the same rules of procedure, called *voir dire*. The 14th Amendment forbids the selection or rejection of a jury member based on race or gender. Civil cases begin with an opening statement, each attorney speaking in turn, and beginning with the party that filed. After the opening statement, the Prosecution presents its proof and calls its witnesses. The witnesses are questioned then may be cross-examined by the opposing side. They do not have the right to express their personal opinions. The Defense will either ask that the charges be dropped, if they are believed to be too weak, or present its proof and call its own witnesses. After this, the Prosecution may refute the arguments of the Defense. Then, each party addresses the jury, which then retires for deliberation and reaches a verdict for the case and decides on the payment of damages.

CATEGORIES OF LAW

It possible to file a civil and a criminal case in the American system, as was the case in the O.J. Simpson trial in the 80s. There are five major types of civil cases: Contract Law, civil liability, Property Law, inheritance, and Family Law. Problems with contracts are numerous, especially related to commerce. Issues of civil liability are the majority and are also those that result in the highest indemnities. The explosion of the amounts that some have recently been condemned to pay have led to a parallel explosion in the number of trials. Cases involving property have always been high in number in the American Courts. There has been a sharp increase in zoning issues recently. American Law grants each individual the right to dispose of their property after their death, but many cases end up in Court. Family problems have increased the most, notably for divorces and problems with child custody.

TO TRY OR NOT TO TRY

Everyone knows how common trials are in the United States. There are, however, significant measures in place to avoid going to trial, and to encourage resolving conflicts out of Court. Mediation allows an impartial party to help clarify the situation and to find a solution to a problem. Arbitration in cases of dispute consists of asking a third party to listen to each side and then make a decision. It resembles a trial, but there is no judge involved in the verdict. Neutral fact-finding permits an investigation by a specially assigned neutral organization. It draws up a report after its investigation and may then help in resolving a conflict. A summary jury trial is one of the most used in the United States: it is an alternative option that allows setting up a hearing that is not officially a trial. At the end of this process, both parties are asked once more to try to reach an amicable solution. Lawyers try to avoid going to Court with judgments made in private; they ask retired judges or experienced lawyers to offer a solution.

A. Fill in with the words: *case – courts - depositions - law - motions - orders - pleadings - trials*

Civil procedure is the body of (1)........................ that sets out the rules and standards that (2)........................ follow when adjudicating civil lawsuits. These rules govern how a lawsuit or (3)........................ may be commenced, what kind of service of process (if any) is required, the types of (4)........................ or statements of case, (5)........................ or applications, and (6)........................ allowed in civil cases, the timing and manner of (7)........................ and discovery or disclosure, the conduct of (8)........................, the process for judgment, various available remedies, and how the courts and clerks must function.

B. Consider the case on p. 235. Do you think the Supreme Court should have upheld or overturned the previous ruling? Why or why not?

....
....

C. What is the goal of a pre-trial conference?

....
....

D. How many members are there on a typical civil jury?

....
....

E. What is arbitration?

....
....

REFERENCES :

Page 231."Oil Pastel (black) sketch of Superior Court Judge Harold M. Mulvey", by Beinecke Library, Wikimedia. http://commons.wiki-media.org/wiki/File:Oil_Pastel_%28black%29_sketch_of_Superior_Court_Judge_Harold_M._Mulvey._27.jpg?uselang=fr
Page 232. "State justice", by Dimitri Champain
Page 237. "Deliberation room", by Dimitri Champain
Page 245. "Compensatory damages and punitive damages", by Dimitri Champain
Page 246. Fields of Law, from Brown College (Providence) website at http://brown.edu/academics/college/advising/law-school/fields-law.

Page 248. "That is the question", by Dimitri Champain
Page 251. "Is your sex life against the law?", adapted from «The complete list of weird sex laws in the U.S.A.», by Charlie Jane Anders, December 17, 2013.
"U.S. strange laws", by Keith Sarver, adapted from «The complete list of weird sex laws in the U.S.A.», by Charlie Jane Anders, December 17, 2013.
Page 252. "Summary", by Dimitri Champain
Page 253. "Review", by Dimitri Champain
pp. 233, 235, 238, 245, 249, 251 "Activity", by Dimitri Champain

UNIT 13 Landmark Cases and Famous Trials

Introduction

The Founders of the American nation, especially both Thomas Jefferson and John Adams, felt strongly that jury trials were the best defense against government. Thomas Jefferson considered "trial by jury as the only anchor ever yet imagined by man, by which a government can be held to the principles of its constitution." John Adams said it was a jury's "duty . . . to find the verdict according to his own best understanding, judgment, and conscience, though in direct opposition to the direction of the court." Half of these important trials resulted in convictions; the other half resulted in acquittals. Here is a summary of the cases and their influence.

13

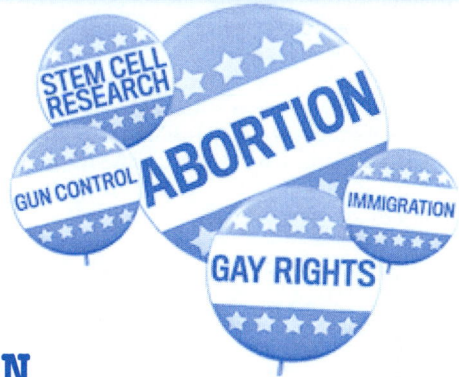

PART 1 – THE BIRTH OF A NATION

1670

This trial took place in England, at a time when the monarchy was aggressively suppressing religious dissent. But, it is closely linked to the history of the Colonies, and, thus, the United States. In 1670, William Penn was 26 years old and the leader of a religious group called the Quakers. But the King didn't care for this religion and forbade it. Penn and another Quaker, William Mead, were arrested during a religious service that they had organized in the street and were accused of "disturbing the King's peace".

During the trial, the jury members listed to witness testimony and the Crown presented no substantial evidence. Penn interrupted the debates numerous times, asking questions or making comments. He was removed from the room and remained confined in a small room, removed from view of the judge and the jury, until the end of the proceeding. The judge finally gave his instructions to the jury before their deliberation, as he should in a trial. They contained the recommendation of declaring Penn guilty. But the jury refused to condemn Penn, and the jury foreman, Edward Bushnell, declared to the Court that the jury believed Penn had simply spoken in public and that there was no violation of any law. So, the judge, who was very angry, sent them back into deliberation to change their verdict.

The judge demanded: "a verdict that the court will accept, and you shall be locked up without meat, drink, fire, and tobacco…We will have a verdict by the help of God or you will starve for it."

They returned with the same verdict as before, and

255

were sent back to deliberate a third time, but they still did not change their verdict.

Finally, the jury members refused to return to deliberations, and the judge had them arrested and imprisoned under the accusation of "misconduct as a juror", which was actually quite common at that time. Of course, Penn was also imprisoned, but under new charges that the judges invented right off the bat, and was made to wear a hat during the trial. He was found guilty of "contempt of court". The jury members were able to make an appeal using a writ of habeas corpus, in which they won and were freed. But not Penn, who had to serve his sentence. Later, he was granted the region Sylvania, located in the American Colonial territory, from Charles II, who wanted to rid himself of the Quakers. The region was later called Pennsylvania, meaning "Penn's Woods".

The impact of the trial was very important for two reasons. First, it established the principle of religious freedom that William Penn defended and brought to America, when he founded Pennsylvania in 1681. Philadelphia became the largest city in the Colonies, on top of being the place where the Declaration of Independence and the U.S. Constitution were drafted. The case also established the principle of "jury nullification", wherein a jury's decision is final, even if it rejects the law. Jury nullification has been used frequently, such as when acquitting Defendants accused of violating the Alien and Sedition Act and the Fugitive Slave Act.

The Witchcraft Trials 1692
Verdict: 29 found guilty.
Sentences: 19 hanged.

Significance: The witch hunts that took place in America resembled the ones that had taken place in England over the centuries; they happened during a time of political instability, but remain uncommon, because they were quite localized to a single area and, in fact, were very brief. They, however, had a visible effect on the collective imagination; each person trying, even today, to try to understand how such an event of mass hysteria could have taken place.

Between June and September 1692, 19 people, all accused of sorcery, were hanged. Hundreds of others were also accused of practicing witchcraft. Dozens of them were held in prison for months without the hope of a trial. Then, as unexpectedly as it started, the hysteria that had overtaken Puritan Massachusetts disappeared into thin air.

So what actually happened? And why there, and at that precise moment in history?

In 1692, a February day of a particularly rude winter, young Betty Paris fell ill: a strange illness resulting in high fever and convulsions. The symptoms were highly similar to those described by an influential Puritan, Cotton Mather, when he was describing the behavior of witches in his book, *Memorable Providences*. Townspeople began to talk more and more about witchcraft, even though many of Betty's playmates exhibited similar symptoms, for example, Ann Putnam, barely 11 years old. The doctor who examined the young girls, William Griggs, concluded that the illness was supernatural in origin. While the number of sick people continued to grow, a neighbor called Tituba, suggested making a rice cake with the urine of the first person to fall ill. At the same time, the girls started pretending to see witches floating in the air around them. Tituba was the first person accused of witchcraft, then, two other women quickly followed. An arrest warrant was issued only four days after the cake incident. Two County Magistrates, Jonathan Corwin and John Hathorne, were placed in charge of the affair. They set up interrogations in a nearby tavern, but hundreds of people wanted to attend, which forced them to move the auditions to a larger venue. The witnesses appeared one after the other and spoke of animals that were born deformed, or about mysteriously disappearing pots of butter, and other things that were naturally attributed to the three "witches". They were interrogated again and again, with the same questions repeated over and over: Were they witches? Had they seen Satan?

Tituba ended up admitting that she was a witch and accused four other women, with whom she supposedly flew; the four other women were arrested. During a religious service, another woman was accused out of the blue of behaving strangely and was also immediately arrested. Then, a little four-year-old girl was next. She was thrown into prison, where she spent eight months. Each arrest was followed by a confession, maybe because confessions avoided a trip to the gallows. Prison filled up quickly, and the Colony fell into chaos. It was at that moment that Governor Phips returned from a trip to England, and decided to take radical measures. Phips created a new court, the "court of oyer and terminer", to hear cases of sorcery. Five judges, including three close friends of Cotton Mather, were appointed to the court. The judges decided to allow the so-called "touching test" (Defendants were asked to touch the afflicted persons to see if their touch, as was generally assumed of a witches' touch, would halt their contortions/deformations), as well as examining he bodies of the accused for evidence of "witches' marks" (moles and similar marks, upon which a witch's familiar might suck). Evidence that would be excluded from modern courtrooms – hearsay, gossip, stories, unsupported assertions, and assumptions – was also generally admitted. Much protection that modern Defendants take for granted was lacking in Salem: accused witches had no legal representation, could not have witnesses testify under oath on their behalf, and had no formal avenues of appeal. However, Defendants could speak for themselves, provide evidence, and cross-examine their accusers. The degree to which defendants in Salem were able to take advantage of their modest protections varied considerably, depending on their own cleverness and their influence in the community. With spectral evidence not being admitted, 28 of the last 33 witchcraft trials ended in acquittals. The three convicted witches were later pardoned. In May of 1693, Phips released all remaining accused or convicted witches from prison. By the time the witch hunt ended, 19 convicted witches had been executed, at least four accused witches had died in prison, and one man, Giles Corey, had been pressed to death. Between 100 and 200 hundred other people were arrested and imprisoned on charges of witchcraft. Two dogs were executed as suspected accomplices.

John Peter Zenger Trial 1735
Verdict: Not guilty

Significance: By accepting truth as a legitimate defense in a libel case brought against a newspaper editor by a public official, the jury laid the foundations of freedom of the Press in America, later codified in the Bill of Rights.

This is the most important case involving the Press. John Peter Zenger was accused of libel for having fiercely criticized the Governor of New York in the columns of the *New York Weekly Journal*. Born in Germany, Zenger immigrated to the Colonies in 1710, and worked as an apprentice for William Bradford, a royal printer. In 1725, together they founded the *New York Gazette*. A majority of people did not appreciate the nomination of the new Governor of New York, William Cosby: he very quickly demanded of the Colonial Assembly to pass a much higher salary in payment for his services. He progressively made more enemies, who ended up making an offer to Zenger to finance a journal that would list their grievances against the Governor. The *Weekly Journal* appeared

for the first time on November 5th, 1733 and rapidly became popular because of its humorous and sarcastic slant. For example, the Sheriff was described as: "a monkey... lately broke his chain and run into the country." On November 2nd, 1734, Cosby ordered four issues of the *Journal* to be burned by the official executioner, but he refused. 15 days later, Zenger was arrested under the charges "of presenting and publishing several seditious libels influencing minds with contempt of his Majesty' government," with a bail of £400, which was two or three times Zenger's annual salary.

It is this excessive bail that later resulted in the adoption of the 8th Amendment against excessive bail.

Cosby assembled the jury, choosing seven New Yorkers of Dutch nationality, who had strong anti-English sentiments and would thus be absolutely opposed to Zenger and his cause. Under Common Law, it had been established that written criticism meant libel, whether the criticism was well founded or not. The jury only had to determine if Zenger was guilty of having printed the articles, which he did not deny. Zenger's defense was that he had the right to print an article that only contained the truth. The judge, in his instructions to the jury, informed the latter that the Law did not recognize truth as an acceptable defense for the crime of which Zenger was accused and thus, they had no authority to acquit him. Nevertheless, they did acquit him, thus establishing the principle of freedom of the Press for the first time.

Marbury v. Madison 1803
Verdict : Plaintiffs could not force Madison to deliver the commissions, because the Judiciary Act was unconstitutional.

IT IS EMPHATICALLY THE PROVINCE AND DUTY OF THE JUDICIAL DEPARTMENT TO SAY WHAT THE LAW IS.

MARBURY v. MADISON
1803

Significance: Marbury v. Madison *may be the most important case in American history, because it established the principle of judicial review (see* **p.178, Unit 9).**

Samuel Chase impeachment
Verdict: Not guilty.
1805

Significance: Congress, for the first and only time, exercised its constitutional prerogative to try a Justice of the U.S. Supreme Court.

Samuel Chase is one of the Founding Fathers. He was active in politics at an early age and was elected to

the Maryland Colonial Assembly. He then represented Maryland the Continental Congress of 1774 in Philadelphia and was one of the signers of the Declaration of Independence in 1776. He was also active in politics after the Revolution within the Federalist Party, and was close friend of George Washington. He was named President of the Baltimore Court and Chief Justice of the Maryland Court of Appeal in 1791. Finally, in 1796, he was nominated to the U.S. Supreme Court, where he overtly worked as a Federalist Justice.

In 1894, the Jeffersonians controlled Congress and attempted to dismiss Samuel Chase from his position as Justice, because he was openly Federalist. The House of Representatives voted for his impeachment and the trial began, with the Senate as jury, as is stated in the Constitution. John Randolph was the Prosecutor. Of 34 Senators in the Senate at that time, 25 were Jeffersonian, and it seemed there was no doubt that the case against Chase would be quickly closed. But, that was not the case. During the trial, Randolph himself criticized Jefferson for something totally unrelated, the Yazoo land fraud in Georgia, which resulted in the dividing the President's camp into two halves. Moreover, what they reproached of Chase were only a few remarks made while he was sitting as a trial judge in a grand jury proceeding. The Senators were not impressed by such little evidence,

and only 19 voted against Chase, far from the required 2/3 needed in such a trial.

The independence of the Judicial Branch was strengthened after this failed attempt to dismiss a Supreme Court Justice from his position. However, this situation inspired future Federal judges to no longer directly engage in politics once in office.

Fletcher v. Peck
Decision: The Court ruled that the State legislature's repeal of the law was void because it was unconstitutional.
1810

Significance: The first case in which the Supreme Court ruled a State law unconstitutional, the decision also helped create a growing precedent for the sanctity of legal contracts, and suggested that Native Americans did not hold titles to their own lands.

McCulloch v. Maryland
Verdict: McCulloch won.
1819

Significance: Congress incorporated a bank of the United States, a branch of which was established in Baltimore. The State of Maryland required all banks not chartered by the State to pay a tax on each issuance of bank notes. It was held that Congress had such a power to incorporate a bank, but Maryland was not recognized to tax a branch of the United States Bank located in Maryland.

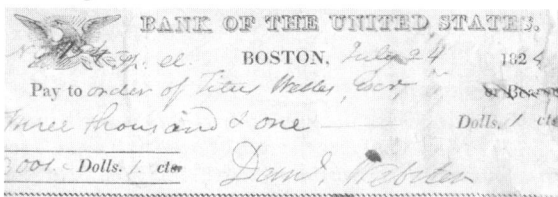

Barron v. Baltimore
Decision: The Supreme Court decided that the Bill of Rights, specifically the 5th Amendment's guarantee that government seizures of private property for public use require just compensation, are restrictions on the Federal government alone.
1833

Significance : The Court established a precedent on whether the United States Bill of Rights could be applied to State governments.

John Barron was a resident of Baltimore, Maryland. He sued his home city because his business, which was located in Baltimore harbor, was damaged. The city of Baltimore passed an adjustment of water flow law which ended up cutting-off water to Mr. Barron's property. Because of the law, Mr. Barron's boats were not able to properly dock in the harbor. The lack of water and the inability to dock resulted in his boats getting damaged. Barron sued Baltimore and was ultimately rewarded money to compensate for his damaged boats. However, the city appealed the ruling and brought the case to the United States Supreme Court. The case of *Barron v. Baltimore* deals with eminent domain. This means that the government can repossess property owned by citizens in the event that the property taken is necessary for public use. The problem was, "public use" was not defined when this case was tried—*Barron v. Baltimore* took place in 1833! John Barron in *Barron v. Baltimore* said that the government's use of eminent domain was a direct violation of the 5th Amendment to the United States Constitution. It states that the government must respect, maintain and uphold the legal rights of all American citizens and that the government must retain a person's liberties and human rights. Mr. Barron thought that is was unfair and illegal for the government to mess with his personal property. He thought that he should be repaid for the damages caused to his boats. The city of Baltimore thought that they were within their rights to restrict water supply. They thought that they were allowed to do this because it ultimately helped out the community.

The United States Supreme Court ruled in favor of Baltimore, stating that the 5th Amendment to the United States Constitution was limited and only should be followed by the Federal government. The 5th Amendment does not state that it must be followed by all State and city governments in the United States. Because of the ruling in *Barron v. Baltimore,* the United States Supreme Court established that a individual citizen's property was not susceptible to the regulation of the 5th Amendment.

President A. Johnson's Impeachment.
Verdict: Not guilty.
1868

He became the enemy of Radical Republicans who controlled Congress after the Civil War. President

Johnson vetoed their legislation and even called their leaders "traitors". Fresh from winning the war, the likes of Republican Senators Thaddeus Stevens (PA) and Charles Sumner (MA) were not about to back down. Sumner, after all, was the guy who once delivered an unconscionably disrespectful speech against elderly South Carolina Senator Andrew Butler, whereupon his outraged nephew Preston Brooks beat Sumner senseless with a cane.

When the House of Representatives impeached President Johnson by an overwhelming vote of 126 to 47, his removal appeared to be a fait accompli. President Johnson had violated the Tenure in Office Act by dismissing his Secretary of War, and he had been excessive in his name-calling of key Senators. Addressing the jury of 54 Senators, the Prosecutor referred to President Johnson as an "accidental Chief" and "the elect of an assassin." Witnesses testified for both the Prosecution and the Defense.

The Prosecutors – called "managers" during impeachment trials – were confident of victory. Manager Thaddeus Stevens described President Johnson as the "wretched man, standing at bay, surrounded by a cordon of living men, each with the axe of an executioner uplifted for his just punishment." Manager John Bingham brought the public galleries to their feet with his oratory: "May God forbid that the future historian shall record of this day's proceedings, that by reason of the failure of the legislative power of the people to triumph over the usurpations of an apostate President, the fabric of American empire fell and perished from the earth."

A 2/3 vote was necessary for conviction, and it all hinged on Senator Edmund Ross of Kansas. Like jury members, he spoke to no one during the proceedings, and no one knew which way he was leaning. But he voted "not guilty," and President Johnson was acquitted by one vote. The Radical Republicans were defeated, and would never again enjoy their unprecedented power.

PART 2 – A BUSY PERIOD

Dred Scott Decision
Decision: That Dred Scott was still a slave, regardless of where his owner took him.

1856

Significance: The Dred Scott decision effectively ended the Missouri Compromise, hardening the political rivalry between North and South, and paving the way for the Civil War.

Tweed's Case
*Verdict: Guilty
Sentence: 12 years in prison.*

1872

Significance: William Marcy Tweed was an American politician and the leader of Tammany Hall. The Tweed Ring, which defrauded New York City of millions, made his name a symbol of civic corruption.

William Marcy "Boss" Tweed began as a volunteer fireman in New York who worked his way to the top of the Democratic New York City political machine by 1863. He developed a corrupt system known as the "Tweed Ring" that faked leases, demanded kickbacks, performed unnecessary repairs and generated other phony expenses that cost New York City from $75 million to $200 million, a huge amount of money at the time. Famed cartoonist Thomas Nast, who created Uncle Sam, and the elephant and donkey for the Republican and Democratic Parties, frequently attacked Tweed in his cartoons.

Eventually, Democratic Federal Prosecutor Samuel Tilden brought an indictment for felony against Tweed, who was defended at the trial by wealthy Republican, Elihu Root, in 1872. But the jury did not reach a verdict. In a second trial, Tilden defeated Root and obtained a conviction, which catapulted Tilden to national prominence and became the Democratic nominee for President in 1876. Tweed was given a 12-year prison sentence, which was, however, was reduced by a higher court, and he only served one year. Arrested once more on other charges, he escaped and fled to Cuba, and then to Spain, but was extradited back to the United States in 1876. He died in prison two years later.

Hans v. Louisiana
Decision: The Supreme Court suggested that the framers of the Constitution had not addressed the possibility of a citizen suing his own State because such a thing would simply be inconceivable to them.

1890

Significance: It determined that the 11th Amendment prohibits the citizen of a U.S. State to sue that State in a Federal Court.

Plessy v. Ferguson
Decision: That laws providing for 'separate but equal' treatment of blacks and whites were constitutional.

1896

Significance: The Supreme Court's decision effectively sanctioned discriminatory state legislation. Plessy v. Ferguson was not fully overruled until the 1950s and 1960s, beginning with Brown v. Board of Education in 1954.

Schenck v. U.S. Appeal — 1919
Decision: Guilty verdict unanimously affirmed.

Significance: This case marked the first time the Supreme Court ruled directly on the extent to which the U.S. government may limit speech.

> Whoever would overthrow the liberty of a nation must begin by subduing the freedom of speech...

Sacco-Vanzetti Trial — 1921
Verdict: Guilty.
Sentence: Death.

Significance: The Sacco-Vanzetti Case started as a simple trial for murder. It ended as an international cause in which the world believed that Massachusetts had executed two innocent men because they held radical views. A study of the trial and its aftermath provides a superb lesson in how myths are made.

Sacco and Vanzetti were two Italian anarchists. They were brought to trial in 1921 for two robberies that had taken place the previous year in Massachusetts: the first, in a shoe-manufacturing factory in Bridgewater, and the second, in South Braintree. The factory's teller, who was carrying $16,000, the amount of the workers' salaries, as well as the bodyguard, were killed. The money was of course stolen. The Police quickly suspected the Italian anarchists of committing the crime, because they supported revolutionary terrorism, and were persuaded that they were trying to finance their attacks and robberies. Sacco and Vanzetti were arrested, a little bit by chance, while they were picking up a friend's car at a garage; their friends were under surveillance because they were suspected of having participated in the robbery. The men were heavily armed, and they were immediately charged with the two robberies. In America, the Liberals protested against the fact that the men were arrested for their ideals, instead of their actions. Questions about how the case was handled existed from the beginning of the situation. No Italians were asked to be on the jury. Witnesses for the Prosecution were weak witnesses, one of them stating, for example, that the murderer spoke English very well (which was not the case of the Defendants), or others who debated about the length of the murderer's moustache. The Prosecution was able to prove that one of the bullets found at the scene of the crime was from Sacco's gun, but was unable to prove where the three other bullets came from. The money was never found.

All of the witnesses for the Defense were questioned about their political opinions. The Defense continuously objected to this line of questioning, but the judge rejected its objections and allowed the questioning. A majority of opinion today is that the judge should not have allowed it to continue.

The jury returned with a verdict of guilty after more than a day's deliberations. The judge's attitude, which was very hostile to anarchists, was highly criticized. He had decided to make anarchism disappear from the United States. The international community protested against the verdict, and in face of such a reaction, the Governor of Massachusetts appointed a

Commission to study the case and the evidence that was presented. Throughout the 20s, this case provoked numerous demonstrations in the United States and around the world. The Commission declared, in the end, that it agreed with the verdict; Sacco and Vanzetti were executed in 1927.

Vanzetti claimed his innocence up until his last day. His last words addressed to the judge, just prior to being executed, were: "I would not wish to [a dog or snake] what I have had to suffer for things that I am not guilty of. But my conviction is that I have suffered for things that I am guilty of. I am suffering because I am a radical and indeed I am a radical; I have suffered because I was an Italian, and indeed I am an Italian; I have suffered more for my family and for my beloved than for myself; but I am so convinced to be right that if you could execute me two times, and if I could be reborn two other times, I would live again to do what I have done already."

The wave of sympathy for Sacco and Vanzetti continued for a very long time afterwards. In 1977, 50 years after their executions, the Democratic Governor and presidential candidate Michael Dukakis signed a resolution demanding their pardon and decided that a day should be established in their memory. But he didn't succeed in exonerating them. This was at the heart of the presidential campaign against George Bush in 1988, which he lost, in part, because of his position against criminals being too lax.

John Thomas Scopes "Monkey" Trial
1925
Verdict: Guilty.
Sentence: $100 fine.

Significance: The John Thomas Scopes Trial examined the influence of Fundamentalism in public education, and stripped William Jennings Bryan of his dignity as a key figure in American political history. It also marked the displacement of religious faith and rural values by scientific skepticism and Cosmopolitanism as the dominant strains in American thought.

In 1859, Charles Darwin published *The Origin of Species* in England. The basis for his theory of evolution, it explains that the diversity of species today is the result of an evolution over time, ruled by natural selection. The theory brings into play another idea, that of Man and apes sharing a common ancestry. This idea contradicts the literal interpretation of the Bible stories recounting that God created Man, who is set apart from animals, and that animals are morally inferior to mankind. American society is torn between progressive and conservative thinkers, so when this theory began to be taught in public schools, many schools in the Bible Belt took action to establish the Butler Act, a law which forbade the teaching of the theory of evolution.

John Scopes was a young teacher in Tennessee who became, in spite of himself, the center of a case leading to the promotion of the theory of evolution being taught in American schools. The ACLU (American Civil Liberties Union) lobby decided to fight the Butler Act in Tennessee. It hired the most famous criminal lawyer at the time, Clarence Darrow, to defend Scope. William Jennings Bryan, a previous U.S. presidential and Secretary of State candidate was persuaded that teaching the theory of evolution would lead to his country's downfall. "The strongest will survive" could only led to war and destruction, in his opinion, providing a justification for the annihilation of other nationalities and races. He led the Prosecution in the trial and defended the Tennessee law.

The judge refused to hear scientific testimony in his court, so Darrow called Bryan, the representative of the opposing side, to testify in the witness box as a biblical expert. Though he was not obliged to, Bryan accepted because of his pride. Darrow asked him question after question for about an hour and a half, on the rationality of the *Bible*: if Adam and Eve were the only humans, how was their son Cain able to meet a woman? Did the fish also drown during the Flood? How did 24-hour days function before the creation of the Sun on the 4th day? Trapped, Bryan was not able to provide believable answers. Scopes was fined $100 by the judge and the trial was over. The Butler Act remained on the books until 1967, and to this day, the theory of evolution is taught very rarely in Tennessee.

Buck v. Bell
1927
Decision: Upheld as constitutional; Virginia's compulsory sterilization of young women considered "unfit to continue their kind".

Significance: Virginia's law served as a model for similar laws in 30 States, under which 50,000 U.S. citizens were sterilized without

their consent. During the Nuremberg trials, Nazi lawyers cited Buck v. Bell *as acceptable precedent for the sterilization of 2 million people in its "Rassenhygiene" (race hygiene) program.*

Al Capone Trial
Decision: 11 years' imprisonment, $50,000 in fines, $30,000 in court costs.

1931

Significance: While the Police were incapable of putting the most famous outlaw behind bars for 10 years, Federal authorities found a way to throw him in prison for tax evasion. This is how the Mob Boss ended up in Alcatraz.

On March 13th, 1931, a Federal grand jury convened secretly to discuss the government's claim that Al Capone owed an amount of taxes reaching $32,488.81 in 1924. Income tax cases such as these, typically took precedence over the violations in Prohibition. The investigation was carried out between the years of 1925 to 1929, with the jury returning an indictment against Capone that was kept secret until the very end.

The judgment later rendered against Capone declared 22 counts of tax evasion, for a total of over $200,000. As a result of this indictment, he and his 68 gang members were charged with 5,000 separate violations of the Volstead Act. His lawyers and the government's Prosecutors secretly made a bargain, for fear of witness tampering, and with doubts that the Supreme Court would actually uphold the six-year statute of limitations. Capone should have pled guilty to a less-serious charge and so expected to receive between a two- and a five-year sentence. The Press was outraged when word got out, and crusaded against what they felt was a blatant cover-up.

The presumptuous Capone, believing he would receive less than five years in prison, suddenly became much less arrogant when he realized that his plea bargain was then null and void. 14 detectives escorted Capone to the Federal Court Building on October 6th, 1931. He wore a conservative blue suit, but not his usual ostentatious jewelry or pinky ring. Authorities were aware of Capone's plot to obtain the list of jury members and bribe them. Capone, of course, had no idea that they knew. So, when Judge Wilkinson entered the courtroom and suddenly demanded to change the jury, he and his lawyer were shocked. The new jury was even sequestered at night, so Capone's mob couldn't communicate with them and try to coerce them. Attorney George Johnson made a mockery of Capone's claim as being a sort of 'Robin Hood' during the proceedings, emphasizing how hypocritical he was in spending thousands of dollars on meals and luxurious items, while donating little or nothing to the poor and unemployed. How could he possess so much property, and so many vehicles

and extravagances, such as diamond-studded belt buckles, when his defense attorneys claimed that their client had no source of income?

On October 17th, 1931, the jury found Capone guilty of several counts of tax evasion after nine hours of

deliberation. Wilkerson denied him bail and sentenced him to 11 years, $50,000 in fines, plus court costs of $30,000. He was transferred from a prison in Atlanta to San Francisco's infamous Alcatraz Federal Penitentiary in 1934. Contact with the outside world was basically eliminated. Privileges he was previously used to were also suspended. He only had minimal contact through few letters and some newspapers. Eventually, his sentence was reduced to 6½ years for good behavior. He became confused and disorientated as his health declined because of a form of syphilis. His condition deteriorated slowly after being released from prison. His wife Mae remained by his side, until he died on January 25th, 1947 of a heart attack, at the age of 48.

Betts v. Brady
Decision : The Court found that Betts did not have the right to be appointed counsel.

1942

Significance: Betts v. Brady *was a landmark United States Supreme Court case that denied counsel to indigent defendants when prosecuted by a state. It was famously overruled by* Gideon v. Wainwright *in 1963.*

In its decision in *Johnson v. Zerbst*, the Supreme Court had held that defendants in Federal courts had a right to counsel guaranteed by the Sixth Amendment. In *Powell v. Alabama*, the Court had held that State Defendants in capital cases were entitled to counsel, even when they could not afford it; however, the right to an attorney in trials in the States was not yet obligatory in all cases as it was in Federal courts under *Johnson v. Zerbst*. In *Betts v. Brady*, Betts was indicted for robbery and upon his request for counsel, the trial judge refused, forcing Betts to represent himself. He was convicted of robbery, a conviction he eventually appealed to the Supreme Court on the basis that he was being held unlawfully because he had been denied counsel.

PART 3 – BECOMING A SUPERPOWER

Alger Hiss Trial
Verdict: Guilty.
Sentence: 5 years'
imprisonment.

1950

Significance: Alger Hiss was the protagonist in a grand, 3-year, human drama that made headlines across America. The case polarized the country from 1948 and 1950, becoming a symbol of American policies at the onset of the Cold War. It accelerated the rise of Richard M. Nixon. The debate about Hiss' guilt remains endless, for either he was a traitor, or he was the victim of being framed for the political advantages of those at the highest levels of justice.

August 3rd, 1948, Whittaker Chambers, an ex-Communist party member, testified before the House Committee on Un-American Activities (HUAC), accusing Alger Hiss of being a Soviet spy. The facts having been decreed at the time of his accusation, the latter was found guilty of perjury. Hiss denied being a spy, and of even knowing Chambers, who claimed, however, that Hiss had been delivering him documents from the State Department for years. Richard Nixon, who was an unknown Representative at the time, was convinced that Hess was lying and questioned him during his examination before the Un-American Activities Committee during the Cold War in 1948. Nixon didn't like Hiss, because of his wealthy background and political connections, which were exactly what Nixon needed to succeed. It was this case, though, that catapulted Nixon to the front of the stage and propelled him into the White House. Hiss and Chambers both testified before the Commission, contradicting each other. One of them was lying. When Chambers supplied the State Department documents and affirmed that Hiss had given them to him, the Federal Prosecutor of Manhattan charged Hiss guilty of perjury.
But Hiss was able to afford the best lawyer and had

assembled a list of very impressive witnesses, including an ex-presidential candidate (John W. Davis) and a future presidential candidate (Adlai Stevenson), two Supreme Court Justices, and an ex-Solicitor General. The jury was unable to reach a verdict, eight of the members being persuaded of his guilt and four believing the contrary. A new trial was organized. This time, the accusation was more aggressive and convincing. Coincidentally, the Defense was less effective and some things were problematic, such as Supreme Court Justice Frankfurter deciding not to testify this time around.

Hiss was found guilty of two charges of perjury and condemned to two 5-year sentences. He maintained his innocence until his death, but the discovery of secret Soviet files after the fall of the Berlin Wall, tended to prove that he was a spy. Be that as it may, this case influenced American politics for 40 years, launching Nixon into the Vice Presidency in 1952, Barry Goldwater into the nomination for President in 1964, Nixon into the White House in 1968, and finally, Ronald Reagan into the Presidency in 1980. The latter awarded Chambers posthumously with the Medal of Freedom.

Brown v. Board of Education of Topeka
Decision: Segregated schools violate the equal protection clause of the 14th Amendment.

1954

Significance: Brown v. Board of Education held that segregated schools were unconstitutional, overturning the "separate but equal" doctrine of Plessy v. Ferguson (1896).

In the 1950's, Topeka's school, like schools in many other cities and towns, were racially segregated. Linda Carol Brown, an eight-year-old black girl, was denied admission to an all-white school near her home and was required to attend a distant all-black school. With the help of lawyers from the National Association for the Advancement of Colored People (NAACP), Linda's family sued the Topeka Board of Education. The NAACP argued that segregated schools were not and could never be equal. Therefore, they were unconstitutional.

In 1954, the Court ruled on this case and similar cases filed in Virginia, Delaware, and South Carolina. In a unanimous decision in *Brown v. Board of Education of Topeka*, the Court overruled the separate but equal doctrine. Chief Justice Earl Warren wrote the Court's opinion. He wrote: "Does segregation of children in public schools solely on the basis of race, even though the physical facilities and other 'tangible' factors may be equal, deprive children of the minority groups of equal educational opportunities? We believe that it does."

The Chief Justice added that such segregation generates in children "a feeling of inferiority as to their status in the community that may affect their hearts and minds in a way unlikely ever to be undone... In the field of education the doctrine of 'separate but equal' has no place. Separate educational facilities are inherently unequal. Therefore, we hold that the plaintiffs... are, by reason of the segregation complained of, deprived of the equal protection of the laws guaranteed by the 14th Amendment." The Court ordered desegregation to begin "with all deliberate speed." The Court's decision did not end segregation in the United States. It did, however, set the basic precedent for a long battle to desegregate the public schools. By early 1970, public schools across the country were no longer public schools reserved strictly for either blacks or whites.

Clarence Earl Gideon Trials (1961 and 1963) — 1961
Verdict: First trial, guilty. Second trial, not guilty. Sentence: First trial, 5 years' imprisonment.

Significance: One man, without benefit of wealth, privilege, or education, went up against entire legal establishment, arguing that his constitutional rights had been violated. In doing so, he brought about an historic change in American trial procedure: all felony defendants are entitled to legal representation, irrespective of the crime charged, and courts are to appoint an attorney if a defendant is

too poor to hire one.

Engel v. Vitale — 1962
Decision: The use of prayer violates the establishment clause of the First Amendment made applicable to the States by the 14th Amendment.

Significance: There is a Constitutional wall of separation between church and State.

The New York State Board of Regents had recommended that the following prayer be said aloud by each class in the presence of the teacher at the beginning of each school day: "Almighty God, we acknowledge our dependence upon Thee, and we beg Thy blessings upon us, our parents, our teachers, and our country."

The parents of ten pupils brought action challenging the use of the prayer.

The Court ruled that using the school system to encourage recitation of the prayer is inconsistent with the establishment clause since this is a religious activity and the prayer was composed by government officials as a part of a governmental program to further religious beliefs.

of six Months, and shall publish the *Journal* of their proceedings monthly, except such parts thereof relating to treaties, alliances, or military operations, as in their judgment require secrecy; and the yeas and nays of the delegates of each State, on any question, shall be entered on the *Journal*, when it is desired by any delegate; and the delegates of a State, or any of them, at his or their request, shall be furnished with a transcript of the said *Journal*, except such parts as are above excepted, to lay before the legislatures of the several states.

Miranda v. Arizona — 1967
Verdict: Guilty. Sentence: 20-30 years.

Significance: Few events have altered he course of American jurisprudence more than the 1963 rape conviction of Ernesto Miranda. The primary evidence against him was a confession he made while in police custody. How that confession was obtained exercised the conscience of a nation and prompted a landmark U.S. Supreme Court decision.

Miranda Rights

- You have the right to remain silent.
- Anything you say may be used against you in court of law.
- You have the right to consult with a lawyer before answering any questions and you may have him or her with your during questioning.
- If you cannot afford a lawyer, one will be provided for you by the State.

Tinker v. Des Moines — 1969
Decision: Reversed the decision of the Court of Appeal (8th Circuit).

Significance: It defined the constitutional rights of students in U.S. public schools and established that school dress codes are not in violation of the First Amendment's guarantee of the freedom of expression.

The Des Moines public school system made a rule stating that any student wearing an armband would be asked to remove it on the grounds that wearing one would cause a disturbance. If the student refused to comply, the consequence was suspension from school. Three public school students wore black armbands to express their opposition to the United States' involvement in the Vietnam War. They refused to remove the armbands and were suspended. The parents of the students argued that the students' actions were not interfering with the rights of the other students. The case was argued in 1968 and the ruling was "handed down" in 1969. The Court ruled that the wearing of armbands was "closely akin to 'pure speech'", and this was protected by the First Amendment to the Constitution. The rule banning armbands lacked the proper justification for enforcement. This ruling eventually had an effect on school dress codes in that the style of clothing one wears indicates an expression of that individual.

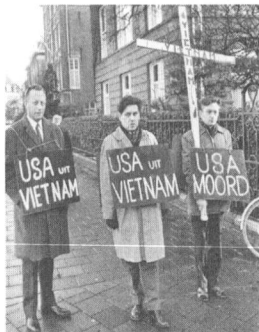

Furman v. Georgia — 1972
Decision: Georgia death penalty statute declared unconstitutional.

Significance: Although **Furman v. Georgia** *did not completely abolish the death penalty, it placed stringent requirements on death penalty statutes.*

Before 1972, many States such as Georgia, granted juries a lot of liberty in deciding to punish criminals with the death penalty. In *Furman v. Georgia*, the case involved a burglary gone wrong: surprised by the home's occupant, Furman attempted to escape. While doing so, he fell and his gun fired, killing the occupant. The Supreme Court found the death penalty was being imposed in apparently arbitrary ways for a wide variety of crimes, and mainly on blacks and the poor. The Court reasoned that capital sentencing based on the unguided discretion of the jury goes against the "cruel and unusual punishment" clause of the Eighth Amendment, because it allows juries to impose the distinctively profound death sentence on some convicted defendants, while other juries would impose the highly different sentence of life imprisonment for large numbers of defendants in similar situations, convicted of exaclty the same crime. The Supreme Court declared that capital punishment as it was then administered was not constitutional.

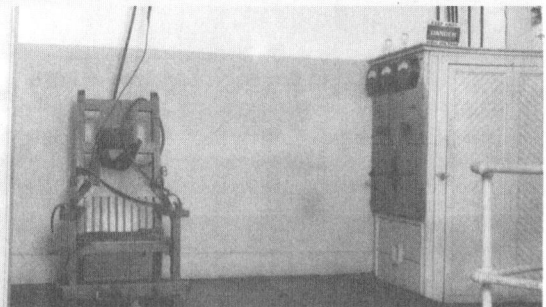

Roe v. Wade — 1973
Decision: Overturned all State laws restricting women's access to abortions during the first trimester of pregnancy and let stand second-trimester restrictions only insofar as they were designated to protect the health of pregnant women.

Significance: This case was first to establish that a woman, rather than her physician, might be the party injured by a State's criminalization of abortion. Moreover, the decision was in large measure based on an implied 'right to privacy' in the U.S. Constitution, which the majority held

Significance: How far should an American citizen be allowed to go in the defense of his life and liberty? That was the question facing a jury in this, one of the most highly charged trials New York had ever seen.

was violated by State laws restricting a woman's right to abort a fetus prior to its viability outside a womb.

Appellant Jane Roe, a pregnant mother who wished to obtain an abortion, sued on behalf of all woman similarly situated in an effort to prevent the enforcement of Texas statutes criminalizing all abortions except those performed to save the life of the mother. Texas statutes made it a crime to procure or attempt an abortion except when medically advised for the purpose of saving the life of the mother. Appellant Jane Roe sought a declaratory judgment that the statutes were unconstitutional on their face and an injunction to prevent defendant Dallas County District Attorney from enforcing the statutes. The appellant alleged that she was unmarried and pregnant, and that she was unable to receive a legal abortion by a licensed physician because her life was not threatened by the continuation of her pregnancy and that she was unable to afford to travel to another jurisdiction to obtain a legal abortion. She sued on behalf of herself and all other women similarly situated, claiming that the statutes were unconstitutionally vague and abridged her right of personal privacy, protected by the First, Fourth, Fifth, Ninth, and Fourteenth Amendments. It was held that statutes that make criminal all abortions except when medically advised for the purpose of saving the life of the mother are an unconstitutional invasion of privacy.

Significance: No matter how unpopular it is to burn an American flag, the First Amendment protects that act and other forms of political expression.

The Supreme Court found in favor of Johnson, the respondent, by a vote of 5-4 and overturned the Texas Venerated Objects Law on the grounds that an individual's right to protected First Amendment political Speech supersedes the State's interest in protecting the flag. Back in 1984, Gregory Johnson participated in a political rally during the Republican National Convention, which was held in Dallas that year. He and other protestors distributed literature and made speeches denoucing President Reagan's 'War Chest' policies. The crowd marched through the streets and staged 'die-ins' on the grounds of several corporations known to support the Reagan administration. The tour concluded in front of Dallas City hall where Johnson unfurled an American flag, doused it with kerosene and set it on fire while the crowd chanted, *'America, the red, white, and blue, we spit on you.'*

Significance: For the first time, the Supreme Court said there could be such a thing as reverse discrimination.

PART 4 – MODERN TIMES

Cruzan v. Missouri Dept. of Health
1990

Significance: While the Constitution protects a person's right to reject life-preserving medical treatment (their "right to die"), States can regulate that interest if the regulation is reasonable.
Nancy Cruzan lay in a permanent vegetative state as a result of injuries suffered in an auto accident. Her parents sought to withdraw life-sustaining treatment and allow her to die, claiming she'd said this would be her wish under such circumstances. The State refused, and the Supreme Court upheld the State's guidelines for the continuation of medical treatment, which allowed withdrawal of treatment only with clear and convincing evidence that this is what the patient would have wanted. The Court said that, given the need to protect against abuses of such situations, the State can continue life support as long as its standards for doing so are reasonable.

Rodney King Beating Trial
1993
Verdict:
Koon and Powell, guilty.
Briseno and Wind, not guilty.
Sentence: 30 months' imprisonment each.

Significance: What was already one o the highest profile cases in American legal history assumed landmark proportions when a second jury had to wrestle not only with questions of guilt or innonence, but how best to assuage outraged civic sensibilities.
A group of white Los Angeles Police Officers were acquitted of State-brought criminal charges for kicking and severely beating African-American Rodney King, whom they had detained after a police chase. The beating was videotaped and shown on national TV. Because the assault carried with it haunting reminders of the vigilantism associated with Scottsboro, the watchful eye of the public monitored the justice system. Riots that erupted after the acquittal

evidenced the perceptions of African Americans and many others that the system can fail to protect all people equally. A Federal trial followed in which the officers were successfully prosecuted for having violated King's civil rights.

O.J. Simpson Trial
Verdict: Guilty (civil).
Not Guilty (criminal).
1995

Accused of brutally slaying his ex-wife and a waiter who happened upon the murder scene, a football legend was tried and acquitted of the crime. More than 100 news agencies, 20 TV companies, and 1,000 correspondents covered the trial, which was held, appropriately enough, in Los Angeles, the nation's entertainment capital. The case's sensationalism is said to have been triggered by the fall of a sports legend, not by the slayings. In civil proceedings that followed, Simpson was found liable for the wrongful deaths of both victims.

The Unabomber Trial
Verdict: Guilty.
Sentence: Life sentence.
1996

Authorities accused Ted Kaczynski of being the domestic terrorist responsible for more than a dozen bomb attacks in multiple States between 1978 and 1995 that killed three people and injured 23 others. The attacker, who called for the «destruction of the worldwide industrial system,» was dubbed the Unabomber because many of his early targets worked at universities and airlines. Investigators zeroed in on Kaczynski after his brother, David Kaczynski, informed the FBI that a manifesto attributed to the Unabomber appearing in *The New York Times* and *The*

Washington Post was similar to papers his brother had written. Ted Kaczynski was ultimately sentenced to life in prison without the possibility of parole.

Oklahoma City Bombing Trial 1997

A homegrown terrorist, Timothy McVeigh detonated a truck bomb in front of the Alfred P. Murrah Federal Building in Oklahoma City on April 19th, 1995. The attack, commonly referred to as the Oklahoma City bombing, claimed the lives of 168 people, including 19 children. A Gulf War veteran, McVeigh was seeking revenge against the Federal government for the 1993 siege of a compound belonging to the religious group Branch Davidians in Waco, Texas. The siege ended in the deaths of sect leader David Koresh and 75 of his followers. The bombing of the Murrah building took place on the two-year anniversary of the Davidians' deaths. McVeigh was convicted of 11 Federal offenses

and was executed on June 11th, 2001.

Impeachment of Bill Clinton 1999
Verdict: Not Guilty.

Significance: The impeachment process is not a substitute for civil or criminal proceedings, but rather exists to address the most serious charges of misconduct that have seriously injured the constitutional system of government, and are linked to an official's public duties. This case showed the common problem of vagueness in the constitutional standard of impeachment.

After having at first denied and later admitting to improper sexual relations with a White House intern, William Jefferson Clinton, in 1998, became the second President of the United States to be impeached. The media circus surrounding the accusations and trial lasted over a year. Finally, however, the Senate

acquitted him, with many of its members concurring with the overwhelming public viewpoint that, even if proven, the allegations against their extremely popular leader did not rise to the level of impeachment. Legal issues surrounding the trial included the legal definition of perjury specific to the case, presidential claims of special exemption, the constitutionality of the Independent Counsel Act and the conduct of the independent counsel in the case, and the implications of the sexual harassment law with respect to the President as employer and Commander in Chief. President Clinton had high ratings in the polls and was just about to choose his successor for the White House at the end of 1998. His leadership enabled the Democratic Party to do surprisingly well in the mid-term elections, and he was looking to leave a lasting legacy.

Michael Jackson Trial
Verdict: Not guilty.

2004

For all of Michael Jackson's talent and hard work, his legacy will forever be tainted by one ugly and recurring storyline. The first allegations of child molestation against the King of Pop arose in 1993, though charges fell apart under scrutiny. Nearly a decade later, footage taken for a documentary by Martin Bashir had enough questionable content that Jackson was arrested in November 2003 and indicted on seven counts of child molestation and other charges. Jackson was acquitted on all charges less than two years later.

Kenneth Lay and Jeffrey Skilling
Verdict: Guilty.
Sentence: 25 years in prison.

2006

One of the most notorious white-collar criminals ever, Kenneth Lay and Jeffrey Skilling engaged in massive securities, wire, and accounting fraud that brought down their $100-billion company, Enron, which at one time employed more than 20,000 people. The aftershocks from Lay's and Skilling's fraud affected many more people (the venerable Arthur Andersen accounting firm went bust) and lost many more dollars than even Bernie Madoff's scam—and led to documentaries and countless hours of media coverage. Lay died of a heart attack before sentencing, while Skilling was sentenced to nearly a quarter century behind bars.

U.S.A. v. Zacarias Moussaoui
Verdict: Guilty.
Sentence: Life in prison.

2006

Zacarias Moussaoui, an admitted member of al-Qaeda, is serving a sentence of life imprisonment after being convicted of six conspiracy offenses pertaining to his role in the September 11th attacks. A native of France, Moussaoui trained in al-Qaeda's camps in Afghanistan and operated a guesthouse in Kandahar, Afghanistan, for jihadists before joining the September 11th plot. While he was in Afghanistan, Usama bin Laden personally selected him to fly a plane into the White House as part of the attacks.

He entered the United States in February of 2001 to obtain flight training as part of his mission. He first obtained flight training on small planes in Oklahoma, but later sought jet training at the Pan Am Flight School in Eagan, Minnesota, even though he did not complete much of his training in Oklahoma. He paid for the flight training with funds wired to him by Ramzi Bin al-Shibh, who served as the coordinator for the September 11th attacks. An attentive flight instructor at the School became alarmed about Moussaoui when the instructor determined that he lacked a foundational knowledge of flying, had paid for the training in cash and had no airline affiliation — all of which were highly unusual. The instructor notified the FBI, who quickly determined that he had ties to other jihadists.

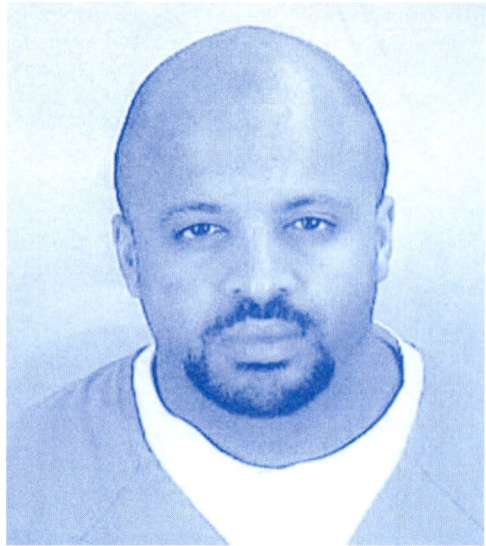

The FBI also learned that Moussaoui was illegally in the United States, because he had overstayed his visa. Agents from the FBI, working with the INS, initially arrested him on immigration offenses on August 16th, 2001, as he left his hotel in Minnesota. A search of his belongings resulted in the recovery of two short-blade knives — one from his pocket and the other from his vehicle. These knives were similar to those used by the hijackers three weeks later to hijack the four planes that were crashed on September 11th, 2001.

The FBI interviewed Moussaoui for two days after his arrest. he denied any affiliation to a terrorist organization, saying instead that he was a tourist who had always dreamed of learning to fly "a big airplane." he further explained that, after his flight training ended, he intended to engage in sightseeing in New York, visiting the Statue of Liberty and the Empire State Building, and then the White House in Washington, D.C. When confronted by the FBI that they believed he was a terrorist, Moussaoui denied the accusation and refused to speak with the agents any further.

After the September 11th attacks, he was charged with six counts of conspiracy related to the attacks. he pled guilty to all of the charges and was ultimately sentenced to life imprisonment by a jury. During his guilty plea, he admitted that he swore "bayat" (loyalty) to Usama Bin Laden and al-Qaeda; was personally selected by Bin Laden to participate in a terrorist operation where commercial airliners would be hijacked and flown into prominent buildings in the United States; came to America to carry out his part in the operation, which was to attack the White House; and admitted to lying to the FBI agents at the time of his arrest so the September 11th plot could move forward.

Conray Murray Trial 2011
Verdict: Guilty.
Sentence: Life in prison.

The Conrad Murray Trial (*People of the State of California v. Conrad Robert Murray*) was the hearing for the private doctor of Pop star Michael Jackson. Murray was accused of involuntary homicide for having caused his death on June 26th, 2009, with an overdose of Propofol. The case began on September 27th, 2011, before the Superior Court of Los Angeles County, presided by Judge Michael Pastor.

In their opening statement, Prosecutors David Walgren and Deborah Brazil address the jury with these words: "misplaced trust in the hands of Murray cost Jackson his life". Murray, in his defense, explained that Jackson, visibly exhausted, had administered the powerful sleeping pill himself, and that he had gone overboard with the dosage. The jury felt that Murray was guilty and condemned him to four years in prison, after 8 hours of deliberation. He was freed from prison on October 28th, 2013.

James Bulger Trial 2013
Verdict: guilty.
Sentence: 2 life sentences in prison + 5 years.

James Bulger, Jr. was working as an informant for the FBI in 1975. His brother Billy Burger was the President of the Massachusetts Senate, and turned a blind eye to his trafficking and organization.

But, in 1997, New England newspapers were investigating organized crime and published a whole series of articles that, in exposing Bulger's role, led to the embarrassment of the FBI.

Bulger then fled to Boston, and went underground. He was on the run for 16 years, until his arrest on June 22nd, 2011, in Santa Monica, California. He was 81 years old.

He was extradited to Massachusetts, and his trial began on August 12th, 2013, with 31 charges against

him, including racketeering and involvement in 11 murders. He was sentenced to two life sentences. He is currently in prison in Tuscon, Arizona.

G. Zimmermann Trial 2013
Verdict: Not guilty.

On the night of February 26th, 2012, in Sanford, Florida, United States, George Zimmerman fatally shot Trayvon Martin, a 17-year-old African American high school student. Zimmerman was taken into custody, treated for head injuries, then questioned for five hours. The police chief said that Zimmerman was released because there was no evidence to refute Zimmerman's claim of having acted in self-defense, and that under Florida's «Stand Your Ground» statute, the police were prohibited by law from making an arrest. As news of the case spread, thousands of protestors across the country called for Zimmerman's arrest and a full investigation. Zimmerman's trial began on June 10th, 2013, in Sanford. On July 13th, 2013, a jury acquitted him of second-degree murder and of manslaughter charges.

Windsor v. USA 2013
Decision: The Supreme Court ruled that a ban on federal benefits for gay couples, enacted under the Defense of Marriage Act (DOMA), is unconstitutional.

Significance: United States v. Windsor is a landmark case in which the United States Supreme Court held that restricting U.S. Federal interpretation of «marriage» and «spouse» to apply only to heterosexual unions, by Section 3 of the Defense of Marriage Act (DOMA), is unconstitutional under the Due Process Clause of the Fifth Amendment.

THE TRIAL OF ....
(Choose a trial in the list)

A. Facts and issues

What are the facts in the case? Who is invloved? What do the participants want to happen? What is the most important issue? (*Begin here and continue on a separate sheet of paper*).

....
....
....
....
....
....
....
....
....
....

B. Arguments

What arguments are made by each side? What interests and values are in conflict? What points of view are represented?

....
....
....
....
....

C. History

What events and circumstances of the time are relevant to the case? How do they affect the case?

....
....
....
....
....

D. Outcome

What is the outcome of the trial? What happens to the participants?

....
....
....
....
....

E. Significance

Why was the trial important in its own time? Why is it important now?

....
....
....
....
....

F. Analysis

Do you agree with the outcome of the trial? Why or why not? How would you judge the case? Why?

....
....
....
....
....

REFERENCES :

Page 255. "Spirit of Justice Rayburn", by Smallbones, in Wikimedia. http://commons.wikimedia.org/wiki/File:Spirit_of_Justice_Rayburn.JPG?uselang=fr
«Buttons», by Keith Sarver
"Lely, William Penn", by Peter Lely, in Wikimedia. http://en.wikipedia.org/wiki/File:Lely,_William_Penn.jpg

Page 256. 'Martha Cory and Persecutors", by James Stark, in Wikimedia. http://commons.wikimedia.org/wiki/File:Martha_Corey_and_Persecutors.JPG?uselang=fr

Page 257. "Appletons' Hamilton Andrew", by Jacques Reich, in Wikimedia. http://commons.wikimedia.org/wiki/File:Appletons%27_Hamilton_Andrew.jpg?uselang=fr
"Marbury v. Madison John Marshall by Smatjester ", by Swatjester, in Wikimedia. http://commons.wikimedia.org/wiki/File:Marbury_v_Madison_John_Marshall_by_Swatjester_crop.jpg?uselang=fr

Page 258. "Samuel Chase", by inconnu, in Wikimedia. http://commons.wikimedia.org/wiki/File:Samuel_Chase.jpg?uselang=fr
"Daniel Webster 1824 Signature"., by CC-BY-SA_3.0, in Wikimedia. http://commons.wikimedia.org/wiki/File:Daniel_Webster_1824_Signature.jpg?uselang=fr

Page 259. "Baltimore Harbor from rest ", in Wikimedia. http://commons.wikimedia.org/wiki/File:Baltimore_Harbor_from_rest.jpg?uselang=fr
"Andrew Johnson impeachment trial", by Theodore R. Davis, in Wikimedia. http://commons.wikimedia.org/wiki/File:Andew_Johnson_impeachment_trial.jpg?uselang=fr

page 260. "Dred Scott ", by Louis Schulze, Missouri Historical Society, in Wikimedia. http://commons.wikimedia.org/wiki/File:DredScott.jpg
"Tweed-Boss-LOC ", from Hoxie Collection, in Wikimedia. http://commons.wikimedia.org/wiki/File:Tweed-Boss-LOC.jpg?uselang=fr
"JimCrowDrinkingFountain", by John Vachon, in Wikimedia. http://commons.wikimedia.org/wiki/File:JimCrowDrinkingFountain.jpg?uselang=fr

Page 261. "Benjamin Franklin freedom of speech quote ", by DonkeyHotey, in Wikimedia. http://commons.wikimedia.org/wiki/File:Benjamin_Franklin_freedom_of_speech_quote.jpg?uselang=fr
"Save Sacco and Vanzetti ", in Wikimedia. http://commons.wikimedia.org/wiki/File:Save_Sacco_and_Vanzetti.jpg?uselang=fr

Page 262. "Rappleyea Byrd Potter", by Smithsonian Institution, in Wikimedia. http://commons.wikimedia.org/wiki/File:Rappleyea_Byrd_Potter..jpg?uselang=fr
"Following the Will-of-the-Wisp", in Wikimedia. http://commons.wikimedia.org/wiki/File:Following_the_Will-of-the-Wisp.jpg?uselang=fr
"Buck v. Bell", by University of Albany, State University of New York. http://www.dnalc.org/view/11254-Carrie-and-Emma-Buck-at-the-Virginia-Colony-for-Epileptics-and-Feebleminded-taken-by-A-H-Estabrook-the-day-before-the-Buck-v-Bell-trial-in-Virginia.html

Page 263. "AlCaponemugshotCPD", by PD-USGOV-DOJ, in Wikimedia. http://commons.wikimedia.org/wiki/File:AlCaponemugshotCPD.jpg?uselang=fr
"Alger Hiss (1950) ", in Wikimedia. http://commons.wikimedia.org/wiki/Alger_Hiss#mediaviewer/File:Alger_Hiss_%281950%29.jpg
"BRVD school ext", by NPS-Photo, in Wikimedia. http://commons.wikimedia.org/wiki/File:BRVB_school_ext.jpg?uselang=fr

Page 265. "Clarence Earl Gideon", in Wikimedia. http://commons.wikimedia.org/wiki/File:Clarence_Earl_Gideon.jpg?uselang=fr
"ElemFlagGathering", by MarketingMan12, in Wikimedia. http://commons.wikimedia.org/wiki/Category:Flagpoles_in_Nevada#mediaviewer/File:ElemFlagGathering.jpg

Page 266. "Spek, Fred van der – Lek, van der – Lankhorst – SFA002019708", by collectie SPAARNESTAD PHOTO/NA/Anefo/jac. De Nijs, in Wikimedia. http://commons.wikimedia.org/wiki/Category:Flagpoles_in_Nevada#mediaviewer/File:ElemFlagGathering.jpg
"Old Sparky ", by Supercowfan, in Wikimedia. http://commons.wikimedia.org/wiki/File:Old_Sparky.jpg?uselang=fr

Page 267. "Knoxville-march-for-life-2013-3", by Brian Stansberry, in Wikimedia. http://commons.wikimedia.org/wiki/File:Knoxville-march-for-life-2013-3.jpg?uselang=fr
"WCWProtest WashingtonD ", by Andrew Selman, in Wikimedia. http://commons.wikimedia.org/wiki/Category:Burning_flags_of_the_United_States#mediaviewer/File:WCWProtest_WashingtonDC.jpg

Page 268. "Cruzan v. Missouri ".
" O.J. Simpson 1990. DN-ST-91-03444", by Gerald Johnson in Wikimedia. http://commons.wikimedia.org/wiki/File:O.J._Simpson_1990_·_DN-ST-91-03444.JPEG?uselang=fr

Page 269. "Theodore Kaszynski", in Wikimedia. http://commons.wikimedia.org/wiki/Theodore_Kaczynski#mediaviewer/File:Theodore_Kaczynski.jpg
"TimothyMcVeighPerryOKApr2195", by Olaf Growald, in Wikimedia. http://commons.wikimedia.org/wiki/File:TimothyMcVeighPerryOKApr2195.jpg?uselang=fr
"Monica Lewinsky", by Helene C. Stickel, Office of the Secretary of Defense, in Wikimedia. http://commons.wikimedia.org/wiki/File:Monica_lewinsky.jpg?uselang=fr

Page 270. "Zacarias Moussaoui", in Wikimedia. http://commons.wikimedia.org/wiki/File:Zacarias_Moussaoui.jpg?uselang=fr

Page 271. "Michael Jackson", by Mjfannnnnn, in Wikimedia. http://commons.wikimedia.org/wiki/File:Michael_-_Jackson.jpg?uselang=fr
"Gay marriage cake – Torta pro matrimonio gay – Foto Giovanni Dall'Orto 26-Jan-2008-2a ", by G. Dallorto, in Wikimedia. http://commons.wikimedia.org/wiki/File:Gay_marriage_cake_-_Torta_pro_matrimonio_gay_-_Foto_Giovanni_Dall%27Orto_26-

UNIT 14 Review

unit 8	Lawyers	unit 11	Criminal trials
unit 9	The judiciary	unit 12	Civil trials
unit 10	It's the law	unit 13	Landmark cases

This Unit will help you to revise the course content seen in Units 7-13. Remember that all the answers contained in this section can be found in these units. You will remember that in the United States, there is only one class of lawyers, called attorney-at-laws. When talking of the law profession, the judiciary is of great importance, since it represents those people who appply the law to the fact of the case before them. In criminal law, it is important to understand that a crime is composed of two elements: actus reus and mens rea. When crime is commit-ted, the accused undergoes a strict procedure, usually starting with their arrest and appearing before a judge. The Constitution, but also State Law, provides important protection for the Defendant, and most Americans are highly sensitive to respecting these rights. The Courts may have to hear criminal cases, but also civil cases, and even here, the trial follows very strict proceedings.

14

UNIT 8   **LAWYERS**

1. What does an attorney do?

....

....

....

....

....

....

2. What is the difference between a lawyer and an attorney?

....

....

....

....

....

....

3. What are the conditions to be registered to a State Bar?

....

....

....

....

....

....

4. What is the Multistate Bar examination?

....

....

....

....

....

5. What is the J.D.?

....

....

....

....

....

....

6. Can a lawyer work in several different States?

....

....

....

....

....

....

7. Who appoints the Attorney General?

....

....

....

....

....

8. Does the Attorney General have to be a lawyer?

....

....

....

....

9. What is the main role of the Attorney general?

....

....

....

....

....

....

10. What is a solicitor in South Carolina?

....

....

....

....

....

UNIT 9 | The judiciary

1. Why might a judge be removed from his position?

....

....

....

....

....

2. Does a person have to be a lawyer to be a judge?

....

....

....

....

....

....

3. In what situation might judicial neutrality be compromised?

....

....

....

....

....

....

4. What is the difference between a judge and a lawyer?

....

....

....

....

....

....

5. What is the adversary system?

....

....

....

....

....

6. What is the inquisitorial system?

....

....

....

....

....

....

7. Who is the chief in the U.S. Supreme Court?

....

....

....

....

....

8. What was wrong with the background of the judges in the United States until recently?

....

....

....

....

9. What are the main criteria in the selection of judges?

....

....

....

....

....

....

10. Who was John Marshall?

....

....

....

....

....

UNIT 10

IT'S THE LAW

1. Which amendments protects the right of an accused person?

....

....

....

....

....

2. Which amendment grants the accused the right to an attorney?

....

....

....

....

....

....

3. What rights does the Fourth Amendment protect?

....

....

....

....

....

....

4. What are the three rights you have if accused according to the Fifth Amendment?

....

....

....

....

....

....

5. What is a criminal frivolous lawsuit?

....

....

....

....

....

....

6. What is the standard of proof for criminal trials?

....

....

....

....

....

....

7. Why is a judge supposed to be a negotiator?

....

....

....

....

....

....

8. What is an activist judge?

....

....

....

....

9. Why was Marbury v. Madison (1803) so critical?

....

....

....

....

....

....

10. Can the judges preside over a trial immediately after they are elected?

....

....

....

....

UNIT 11

CRIMINAL TRIALS

1. What type of jury is a trial jury ?

....

....

....

....

2. Is a trial jury called a petit jury ?

....

....

....

....

....

....

3. Which is better trial by jury of trial by judge ?

....

....

....

....

....

....

4. Does a defendant have to accept a jury trial ?

....

....

....

....

....

5. What is the role of a jury during a trial ?

6. What kind of trial has no jury?

7. How important is the jury selection to a trial?

8. How many people sit in a criminal trial?

....

....

....

....

9. Is it a good idea to let the jury decide on the sentence?

....

....

....

....

....

10. What are some advantages of strong opening statements?

....

....

....

....

....

UNIT 12   CIVIL TRIALS

1. Can someone file criminal charges while in a civil lawsuit?

....

....

....

2. What is a civil lawsuit ?

3. How do you answer a civil summons for a lawsuit?

4. What is the difference between a grand jury and a jury that sits during the trial?

5. What are the names given to the two different parties in a civil suit?

....

....

....

....

....

....

6. Why is the discovery process so important?

....

....

....

....

....

....

7. What is prior restraint?

....

....

....

....

....

....

8. Are you able to cite some common legal objections at Court?

....

....

....

....

....

....

9. What is tort law?

....

....

....

....

....

....

10. What is private judging?

....

....

....

....

....

UNIT 13   LANDMARK CASES

1. Why is William Penn's trial so important?

....

1. What is the point in question in the John Peter Zenger trial?

....

....

....

....

....

....

3. Could you explain *Marbury v. Madison*?

....

....

....

....

....

....

4. Compare *Plessy v. Ferguson* (1896) and *Brown v. Board of Education of Topeka* (1954).

....

....

....

....

....

....

5. What was the conviction against Al Capone?

....

....

....

....

....

6. Has the death penalty always been the capital punishment in the United States?

....

....

....

....

....

7. How can a President be impeached?

....

....

....

....

8. Why was Zacarias Moussaoui's trial so controversial?

....

....

....

....

....

....

9. Is the right to self-defense protected in the U.S.A.? Justify your answer.

....

....

....

....

....

....

10. What do you know about *U.S. v. Windsor*?

....

....

....

....

....

....

Index

INDEX

Cases and statutes

Abbreviations

Correction of the exercises

Answers for the activities contained in this book: these answers are only proposals. It is obvious that many questions can be answered differently, especially according to the opinions, philosophy and ideas of the person answering. The answers given here must be understood as a guide for the thought and the learning process. The reader should focus on the legal elements provided and check his/her answers in order to improve his/her knowledge on the subject.

Introduction - That's the Law

INTRODUCTION - Page 3

STEP 1: America operates on a system of dual sovereignty: the 50 States and the Federal government all retain their own sovereignty. Because each State is sovereign, each State establishes its own laws and has its own Constitution. In addition, the United States Federal government makes laws and has a Constitution. When determining whether a legal issue is governed by Federal or State law, keep in mind that some areas of the law, such as criminal and environmental law, are governed by both State and Federal laws. Generally, the principle of preemption means that a legitimate Federal action supersedes a State law in certain cases

- Although a full discussion of preemption is beyond the scope of this work, you should be aware of some basic principles:

- Federal law preempts State law when the two laws conflict, when Congress expressly or implicitly says so, or when Federal laws are so pervasive that they occupy the entire field of law. There is no preemption issue in your case. So, two sets of laws potentially govern:

- Federal Issues:

Once you are arrested, basic rights ensured by the Fourth, Fifth, and Sixth Amendments of the Constitution come into play. These rights are ultimately governed by Federal law – the U.S. Constitution. Usually, there are State cases adopting the Federal Courts' interpretations of the Constitution. If this is so, you should cite your State case. Be careful, though, to check and see if there are any new Federal decisions governing basic Constitutional rights related to your case.

STEP 2: In your case, the local police arrested you. These police were acting under the authority of Virginia or local statute against pick pocketing. Thus, at this point, you are in a Virginia State Trial Court. Realize, though, that even though you are in a State Court, the Federal Constitutional issues you identified in step 1 can still be heard by that Court. If you lose at trial and need to appeal, that appeal will go to Virginia's mid-level court of appeals, and then to Virginia's highest court. Only if you lose at the State's highest court and believe that the State law violates the U.S. Constitution can you appeal to the U.S. Supreme Court.

If you had been arrested by the FBI or for a Federal offense, then you could be tried in a Federal District cCurt, perhaps in the U.S. District Court of the Eastern District of Virginia. If the case were appealed, it would go to the Fourth Circuit Court of Appeals, then to the U.S. Supreme Court.

UNIT 1. Err... Law?

PART 1 - Page 9

A. We can easily imagine that life was difficult in the American Wild West. There were no police to enforce the law, or provide security, and laws were fairly inconsistent, anyway. This is maybe why citizens were used to taking justice into their own hands, saving the need for a trial, and preferring to hang the accused. Too bad for those who were innocent!

B. Certainly not. It is not possible to live in a world without laws; such a world doesn't exist. If it did exist, it would only be for a short period of time (like in the Old West). People living in communities naturally create a more or less complex system of rules that can become laws. Law occupies an important place in our society. We can't avoid it if we want to live in a peaceful world without problems. Law provides protection for the victims and assigns punishment for those who break the laws.

C. Because of the various levels of the judicial systems: local, State and Federal, and of the mixing between the different sources of law, including Common Law and Case Law, which is not easily understandable for French students, or people in general.

PART 1 - Page 11

A. Reading these documents, we realize that justice is not a unified collection of cases. The story about Judge Roy Bean, who became a judge just because his brother was in a position to nominate him, is a good example of the casual manner in which justice was rendered. In that same story, we realize that he knew nothing about Law, and maybe didn't even know how to read (since he pretended to read the Penal Code). The real problem, as it is stated in the first text, is that men were already forced to fight against nature and the elements. Their first instinct was of survival. Justice wasn't even on the same level of preoccupation. The story of the O.K. Corral shows us armed men who were only looking for threats to eliminate. It was a harsh environment that included numerous dishonest people and outlaws.

B. They didn't appear to receive any legal education, and were appointed by the local authorities (County Commissioners). In the case of Roy Bean, we realize that he most likely knew nothing about Law. This explains why being a judge was most likely not the first thing people dreamed of being when living in the Wild West. We can also imagine that a judge was not very well paid either, since he was certainly paid with money from the community and the community preferred saving money by hanging people, which was faster and cheaper.

PART 2 - Page 13

A. In order to be fully aware of what we can/cannot do while being in a country's territory. Things that someone might be used to doing in their own country might be forbidden in another one. Also, one can cause damage if s/he is ignorant of the law. It can also be useful for businesses; the legal context might be better in a given country for a company.

B. Law may be divided into many categories. In the United States, the most obvious divisions are Federal law and State law; or between public and private laws. The most commonly used division when studying Law is between Civil and Criminal Law.

C. An equitable remedy differs from a Common Law remedy in that it can compel parties to perform some obligations, rather than force them to pay damages. People very often ask for an equitable solution in order to force the Defendant to right their wrong with something other than money (much more creative).

PART 2 - Page 15
A. The problem is that this type of marriage is not recognized by all States. It is very easy to become an ordained minister online, but even some of the States that accept this type of marriage were able to add some special conditions. Thus, in Alabama, Tennessee, and Virginia, it is forbidden to get married without a congregation, meaning a congregation that is numerous and has existed for a while. Of course, everyone does what they want, and in the end, if they decide to say they are married, even if it is not recognized legally everywhere, it's their problem. Problems may arise if they need to divorce, or when someone dies, when the question of what belongs to who needs to be defined, what the rights of each party involved are.

B. This is an individual response that largely depends on each person's imagination. The most obvious answer might be that "420" ends up in prison for drug trafficking, and that the other boy has become a presenter and gives seminars on the dangers of using drugs.

C. *Document 4* is about marriage, so is Civil Law. *Document 5* reveals a problem with drugs, so is Criminal Law. (Please note that in certain States, State law has legalized the use of drugs for those of age, but this is not the case here, since they are both quite clearly minors. Federal law still forbids the use of cannabis.)

PART 3 - Page 17
A. The Legislative Branch has the power to make laws, that is to say, Congress. It is composed of two chambers in the U.S.: The House of Representatives and the Senate.

B. Article IV is also called the Supremacy Clause. It specifically forbids State laws that contradict either the Federal Constitution or national laws, and this is a clear limitation on State legislative rights.

C. This Amendment says that the States are empowered with everything that is not clearly granted to the Federal government by the Constitution. The fact of having a list of delegated powers is then a clear limitation of the power of the Federal government: all remaining powers lie in the State assemblies and in the People.

PART 3 -Page 19
A. Lines 27 and after, Hampden reminds us that the Constitution provides that all rights not expressly granted to the federal government are reserved to the States. Because, in line 75, there is a major risk that Congress might wish to exercise absolute power. And unfortunately, no one could actually stand in opposition to a misuse of power because the Judicial Branch was not granted sufficient power. "It is next to nothing," Montesquieu said in line 45. So, the actual problem is that the Supreme Court has broad powers, but that these powers are highly limited and depend on Congress' decisions and laws.

B. In the case *McCulloch v. Maryland*, the State of Maryland attempted to impose a tax on all banknotes not authorized in Maryland, but this is not clear at all in the text provided.

PART 4 - Page 21
A. There are many different possible motivations: among them are compensation, money, to initiate a change in public policy, for example: a State or Federal criminal statute.

B. Someone is hit by a car and is injured, but cannot afford to pay for the treatment. He would sue the driver in order to obtain compensation.

C. A modern example could be one in which a homosexual couple requests that they get married legally in Oklahoma or in Texas, although they had just been forbidden to do so.

PART 4 - Page 23
A. A test case contains a major Constitutional issue and reaches the Supreme Court. Then, the conclusion of the case will affect a great number of people. The text gives the example of a case (*Wisconsin v. Yoder*), which, in the end, concerned the entire Amish community, and possibly community groups in general in the United States.

B. *Amicus curiæ* is when a third party, someone not involved in the case, brings forth information to bear in the form of witness testimony, or an insight, which could allow resolution of the conflict.

REVIEW - Page 25
A. All the laws are the same in all the 50 States in the USA. FALSE
Litigation is the action of going to court. TRUE
Equity is a system of law tried in a separate court called "Court of Chancery." FALSE
A bill is a proposal for a new law. TRUE

B. We can find two obvious levels of jurisdiction in the United States: the State level and the national level. Then it becomes more complicated, because then we may talk about limited or general jurisdictions, and original or appellate jurisdictions.

C. Everything starts with a proposal made by a member of Congress in one of the two Houses. This proposal is scrutinized, discussed and amended, if necessary. Then there is a vote in each of the two Houses. The final text is sent to the President who signs the bill into Law.

D. Civil cases usually involve private disputes between persons or organizations. Criminal cases involve an action that is considered to be harmful to society as a whole.

E. When a court determines that an individual committed a crime, that person will receive a sentence. The sentence may be a monetary penalty (a fine and/or restitution to the victim), imprisonment, or supervision in the community (by a court employee called a U.S. Probation Officer, if it is a Federal crime), or some combination of these three things.

F. Civil cases typically only result in monetary damages, or orders to do or not do something. We may note that a Criminal case may involve both jail time and a monetary punishment in the form of a fine.

UNIT 2. Early American law
PART 1 - Page 29
A. The Colonies developed very differently. The geography of the Colonies was different. The South had good soil, so it became agricultural, and the North had bad soil, so it became industrial. The social structures were also different, because the New England Colonies didn't believe in slavery, so the social ladders were not the same. Religious tolerance was another major difference among various regions.

B. Native Americans and their governments had a profound effect on many early American laws, and even played an important role in shaping the U.S. Constitution. The Framers were influenced by both "positive" aspects of tribal governance that they were familiar with, and adopted into the Constitution, and by the "negative" aspects of the threat posed by the Indian Nations to the new United States.

PART 1 - Page 31
A. The Laws and Liberties of Massachusetts was written by Nathaniel Ward, a Puritan minister and teacher and reflect the Puritans' concern that members of the community should live a Christian life true to the principles of the group. Laws were meant to guide the righteous and punish the wicked.

B. Of all the constitutional provisions which grant individual rights and liberties, there are two which occupy a very large part of constitutional law today: the Fifth Amendment Due Process Clause, which makes procedural and substantive due process (see p. 16) applicable to the Federal government, and the Fourteenth Amendment Due Process and Equal Protection Clauses, which make procedural and substantive due process and equal protection applicable to the State government. These clauses provide the basis for a substantial portion of individual rights and liberties in the United States today.

C. Harvard College was founded as a Puritan College with its primary purpose to train new ministers. New ministers were needed because with the increasing population of the Puritan Colonies of New England, the parishes were straining under a shortage of ministers.

PART 2 - Page 33
A. The Colonies developed very rapidly and the population increased more and more. As cities and commerce developed, an increasing number of contractual problems and numerous legal proceedings were brought before the Courts. All of that logically led to the emergence of a new profession of lawyers who became involved in public life, especially by being elected into the Assemblies. Once elected, they influenced the passing of laws, rendering them progressively specific and complicated, and consequently creating a stronger need for justice.

B. The term "black codes" was most often used to describe laws passed in the South after the Civil War, which took away the civil rights of newly freed slaves. Both the North and South passed such legislation, however, the term "black codes" is more closely associated with the South. The laws were actually a reaction to abolition of slavery, enacted in the 1860's.

PART 2 - Page 35
A. The Puritans' strong religious beliefs about how God and Satan interacted and their beliefs on Satan's powers, actions and effects on society made their society an easy target for witchcraft hysteria. Gender roles were deeply ingrained in all societies. The ideals of women in early modern Europe traveled across the Atlantic Ocean with the Puritans. Women were seen as inferior beings that needed to be dominated by a male figure, and those who broke the mold were viewed as dangerous. Ultimately, contradictions between the religion and gender roles illustrate the flaws within Puritan society.

B. First, there is no evidence in the novel that shows any attempt by Chillingworth to inflict any physical harm that could be shown as evidence in a court of law. It is clear, from the very start, that his revenge will not be attained in a concrete or physical way; his, is an entirely psychological and subtle attack whose effects simply cannot be proven beyond a reasonable doubt. Second, there is more evidence of Chillingworth doing more good than harm! In Chapter IV, «The Interview», he actually uses his intelligence of herbs and making of medicine to help both, Hester and Pearl! Chillingworth ascertains that he would never hurt Pearl or Hester by making a poison for them, instead of a medicine. In a trial, this could be entered into a debate; if he had wanted to kill both women on that very day when he discovered Hester's shame, he could have easily done it by concocting a drink that would have killed them, either quickly or slowly.

PART 3 - Page 37
A. The King of Great Britain during the American Revolution was George III. He inherited the throne at the age of 12. He ruled Britain throughout the Seven Years' War, the French and Indian War, the American Revolution, the Napoleonic Wars, and the War of 1812. After the conclusion of the French and Indian War, his popularity declined in the American Colonies. In the Declaration of Independence, Thomas Jefferson vilifies George III, and argues that his neglect and misuse of the American Colonies justified their Revolution.

B. They wrote their own Constitutions so they could be independent States; only they could institute the Constitutional Conventions and form the Original United States of America under the Articles of Confederation. For the States to become united, they needed to first become a State. A Constitution was the easiest method of forming a State.

PART 3 - Page 39

A. The Parson's Cause was an important legal and political dispute in the Colony of Virginia often viewed as an important event leading up to the American Revolution. Colonel John Henry, father of Patrick Henry, was the judge who presided over the court case and jury that decided the issue. The relatively unknown Patrick Henry advocated in favor of colonial rights in the case.

B. The first element that recalls English proceedings is certainly the presence of a jury (line 11). We can see that the procedure includes "a writ of inquiry" (line 11), the writs being the basis for Common Law at that time. The vocabulary is also the same: we find "plaintiff" (line 12) and "sheriff" (line 16). Finally, the process for selecting the jury members shows that, as in England, it's a question of choosing people from the surrounding area.

PART 4 - Page 41

A. The Constitutional convention met in Philadelphia in 1787 and drafted the United States Constitution. The Convention was called because the Federal government established by the Articles of Confederation, which was considered to be too weak to effectively deal with State issues. Officially the purpose of the Convention was to revise the Articles of Confederation. Many feel that this was a drastic understatement, and that the real goal of many of its key proponents was to replace the Articles of Confederation and create a strong Federal government. The result of the Convention was the U.S. Constitution, which was signed by 38 delegates on the final day of the Convention, and ratified by most of the States during the following year. The key issues dealt with Congressional representation and slavery. The "Great Compromise' was a bicameral legislature – two houses of Congress where the States would have equal representation in the Senate, but proportional representation in the House of Representatives. Regarding slavery, Congress did not have the power to abolish slavery, but would obtain the power to end the slave trade beginning in 1808. A 3/5 compromise meant that 3 of every 5 States would be counted when apportioning a State's representation in the House of Representatives. George Washington was unanimously elected President of the Convention.

B. Publius was the pseudonym used by Alexander Hamilton (who became the first U.S. Secretary of the Treasury), James Madison (who became the fourth U.S. President), and John Jay (who became the first Chief Justice of the U.S. Supreme Court) to write the 85 papers that make up *The Federalist*. "Publius" was a fairly common *praenomen* (the first or personal name of an ancient Roman.). Some readers of *The Federalist*, therefore, might have understood "Publius" to be the Publius praised in the Acts of the Apostles (28:7), "the chief man of the island" of Melita (probably Malta) who welcomed and housed Paul and his shipwrecked companions for three days. Most readers, however, probably recognized "Publius" as Publius Valerius Publicola, a Roman patriot, general, and statesman, who lived in the sixth century B.C.E. and who, according to *Plutarch's Lives*, saved the early Roman republic several times from tyranny and military subjugation. Publius was one of the founders of the Republic. His republican reputation was regarded by some of the American founders as superior to the republican bona fides of Brutus and Cato, though a problem for the Federalists was that prominent Anti-Federalists had already appropriated the pseudonyms Brutus (Robert Yates) and Cato (George Clinton).

PART 4 - Page 43

A. According to this document, the Supreme Court has absolute power, while in England its powers were limited. It is shown that English judges are under Parliament's control, although this Constitution will, on the contrary, put Congress in the control of the judges in the United States. Their power comes especially from their power of interpretation, while no other power can subsequently oppose their decision.

B. The author is in disagreement with the proposition that is offered because he sees the possibility of having a group of judges that would hold too much power and the People would not be able to hold them in check.

C. If the Anti-Federalist proposition had been approved, it would be impossible for the Supreme Court to exercise the power of Judicial Review and to declare laws as unconstitutional, since legislative power would actually have had this power to change the Constitution. One could also cite Article V of the Constitution, describing how an amendment is to be created would be unnecessary.

D. The two opinions resonate in the idea that judges must be nominated for life, "during good behavior". On the other hand, the Federalists thought that the Judiciary Branch should be granted more powers, and that it should not be the weakest of the three Branches (line 26 and after). They also considered that it should be an independent Branch, not being checked either of the two remaining Branches (line 34). One might think that these two points of view also meet in the idea that, as for the other Branches, care must be taken so that the Judicial Branch does not exceed its powers: thus, it is forbidden to pass ex post facto laws, or bills of attainder.

REVIEW - Page 45

A. Constitution – Philadelphia – government – legislative – judicial – states – Preamble – amendments.

B. The lives of the Colonists in New England versus the South differed dramatically. In New England, society was focused primarily on trade. For example, Boston was huge port city were many imports and exports came and went. As a result, the population farmed for their own subsistence, not to trade their crops. In addition, most New Englander's were Puritans and lived in urban environments, many, in destitution. In the South, however, the economy was focused on cash crops like tobacco and rice. In addition, slavery was very prominent in the South. There, citizens lived in very rural areas. Unlike in New England, social interaction in the South outside of the family was very limited; as a result of this, families became very close. Labor was divided along gender lines as well, which divided family lines – men did the farming and women did indoor tasks such as housekeeping, etc. As a result of the differing economies and daily life, colonial family life in New England was vastly differeent from life in the South.

C. A Virginia planter and militia officer, who eventually became the first President of the United States. Washington participated in the first engagement of the French and Indian War in 1754, and later became Commander-in-Chief of the American forces during the Revolutionary War. In 1789, he became President of the United States. Although Washington actually lost most of the military battles he fought, his leadership skills were unparalleled and were integral to the creation of the United States.

D. The United States Constitutional Convention (also known as the Philadelphia Convention, the Federal Convention at the Grand Convention in Philadelphia) was held from May 14th to September 17th, 1787, in Philadelphia, Pennsylvania, to address problems in governing the United States of America, which had been operating under the Articles of Confederation following independence from Great Britain. Although the Convention purportedly intended to revise the Articles of Confederation, the intention from the outset of many of its proponents, chief among them James Madison and Alexander Hamilton, was to create a new government, rather than repair the existing one. The delegates elected George Washington to preside over the Convention. The Convention produced the United States Constitution, placing it among the most significant events in the history of the United States.

E. Since one can find certain things in common between the first government created by the Colonists, and that of England. Since the Glorious Revolution of 1688, Parliament was to convene regularly and be consulted for every expense. This was also the case in the Colonies, which had granted their Assemblies broad powers. In England, the King and his family were all to be Anglican. Religious problems were not serious in all of the Colonies, but in some cases, like in New England, some Assemblies existed that imposed a theocracy.

F. *The Federalist Papers* are a series of political articles written by James Madison, John Jay, and Alexander Hamilton. The articles, published in 1787 and 1788, were written to gain popular support for the newly proposed United States Constitution. They would establish the tenets of what would become the political philosophy of Federalism in the United States. They would come to be known as the most important political treatise in United States history. The essays, which would become a series of 85 articles, were published over seven months between October 27th, 1787 and May 28th, 1788. They were written by the authors collectively under the pen name "Publius," symbolizing that they were writing for the public. The authors were prominent in the arena of revolutionary American politics. James Madison, the most well known, had been the primary author of the Constitution, and would later become the fourth U.S. President. Alexander Hamilton would later become the first U.S. Secretary of the Treasury. John Jay, who authored five of the *Federalist Papers* essays, was a former president of the Continental Congress and would later serve as the first Chief Justice of the United States.

UNIT 3. The U.S. legal system
PART 1 - Page 49
A. The Constitution limited Congress' power by crea-

ting a Federal system, separating the powers into three different branches, so one would not have more power than another.

B. The Marbury case established judicial review in American courts. This case also established the basis for the Supreme Court as being an active, law-making body, rather than the puppet court it was at its inception. Early on, the Supreme Court was a joke. Justices often left the Court to take other jobs, even judgeships with the States (sitting on a State Court was considered more prestigious at the time). Marbury made Court vital. The Court stood up to the President and flexed its power. Without Marbury, the Supreme Court would be a hollow body with no real authority.

PART 1 - Page 51
A. 1. A member of Congress introduces a new piece of legislation, or a bill.
2. The bill goes to the appropriate committee.
3a. That committee may kill the bill OR 3B. Refer it to a specific subcommittee.
4. A mark-up occurs after the hearing and a bill is voted out of the subcommittee to the full committee.
4a. The committee votes if the bill will be "reported out" OR 4b. Stop there.
5. The bill is debated.
5a. The majority of the House votes in favor of the bill OR 5b. The majority votes against the bill.
6. The bill is sent to the other house.
7. The bill is referred to a Conference Committee to work out the differences in the House and the Senate versions of the bill.
8a. Both houses vote to approve the bill OR 8B. Both houses vote not to approve the bill (the bill is rejected).
9a. The bill goes to the President for signature OR 9b. The President does not agree, vetoes the bill and returns it to Congress.
10a. The required 2/3 majority in both the House of Representatives and the Senate overrides the veto OR 10b. Either or both houses fail to override the veto and the bill becomes a law.

PART 2 - Page 53
A. All American States use Common Law. But Louisiana mostly recognizes Roman law, Common Law being accessory, limited to certain sectors.

B. Common Law is a more flexible system that also leads to more complexity. Thus, a lawyer who must defend a case in Court will have to not only find the appropriate laws that contain the desired response, but also search within a tangled web of verdicts delivered that are related to a similar problem.

PART 2 - Page 55
A. The right to privacy refers to the concept that one's personal information is protected from public scrutiny. U.S. Justice Louis Brandeis called it «the right to be left alone.» While not explicitly stated in the U.S. Constitution, some Amendments provide some protections. The right to privacy is most often is protected by statutory law. For example, the Health Information Portability and Accountability Act (HIPAA) protects a person's health information, and the Federal Trade Commission (FTC) enforces the right to privacy in various privacy policies and privacy statements. The right to privacy often must be balanced against the State's compelling interests, including the promotion of public safety,

and improving the quality of life. Seat-belt laws and motorcycle helmet requirements are examples of such laws. And while many Americans are quite aware that the government collects personal information, most say that government surveillance is acceptable.

The right to privacy often means the right to personal autonomy, or the right to choose whether or not to engage in certain acts, or have certain experiences. Several Amendments to the U.S. Constitution have been used in varying degrees of success in determining a right to personal autonomy: the First Amendment protects the privacy of beliefs; the Third Amendment protects the privacy of the home against using it for housing soldiers; the Fourth Amendment protects privacy against unreasonable searches; the Fifth Amendment protects against self-incrimination, which in turn protects the privacy of personal information; the Ninth Amendment says that the "enumeration in the Constitution of certain rights shall not be construed to deny or disparage other rights retained by the people." This has been interpreted as justification for broadly reading the Bill of Rights to protect privacy in ways not specifically provided in the first eight amendments. The right to privacy is most often cited in the Due Process Clause of the 14th Amendment, which states: No state shall make or enforce any law which shall abridge the privileges or immunities of citizens of the United States; nor shall any state deprive any person of life, liberty, or property, without due process of law; nor deny to any person within its jurisdiction the equal protection of the laws. However, the protections have been narrowly defined and usually only pertain to family, marriage, motherhood, procreation and child rearing. For example, the Supreme Court first recognized that the various guarantees in the Bill of Rights create a «zone of privacy», in *Griswold v. Connecticut,* a 1965 ruling that upheld marital privacy and struck down bans on contraception. The Court ruled in 1969 that the right to privacy protected a person's right to possess and view pornography in his own home. Justice Thurgood Marshall wrote in *Stanley v. Georgia* that, "If the First Amendment means anything, it means that a State has no business telling a man, sitting alone in his own house, what books he may read or what films he may watch." The controversial case *Roe v. Wade* in 1972 firmly established the right to privacy as fundamental, and required that any governmental infringement of that right to be justified by a compelling State interest. In *Roe,* the Court ruled that the State's compelling interest in preventing abortion and protecting the life of the mother outweighs a mother's personal autonomy only after viability. Before viability, the mother's right to privacy limits State interference due to the lack of a compelling State interest. In 2003, the Court, in *Lawrence v. Texas*, overturned an earlier ruling and found that Texas had violated the rights of two gay men when it enforced a law prohibiting sodomy. Justice Anthony Kennedy wrote, "The petitioners are entitled to respect for their private lives. The State cannot demean their existence or control their destiny by making their private sexual conduct a crime. Their right to liberty under the Due Process Clause gives them the full right to engage in their conduct without intervention of the government.»

B. There are some restrictions on what you may choose as your new name. Generally, the limits are as follows:
• You cannot choose a name with fraudulent intent – meaning you intend to do something illegal. For example, you cannot legally change your name to avoid paying debts, keep from getting sued or get away with a crime.
• Your new name cannot interfere with the rights of others, which generally is defined as choosing the name of a famous person with the intent to mislead. For example, most judges will not approve your renaming yourself George Bush or William (Bill) Clinton unless you have a convincing reason not related to the famous politicians.
• You cannot use a name that would be intentionally confusing. This might be a number or punctuation – for example, "10", "III", or "?". (Minnesota's Supreme Court once ruled that a man who wanted to change his name to the number "1069" could not legally do so, but suggested that "Ten Sixty-Nine" might be acceptable.)
• You cannot choose a name that is a racial slur.
• You cannot choose a name that could be considered a "fighting word", which includes threatening or obscene words, or words likely to incite violence.

PART 3 - Page 57
A. It means "the decisions remains". It says that once a decision is made it becomes a precedent, and the Courts have a bias toward respecting and preserving that precedent. It is necessary to ensure that Law be predictable and consistent, and not change every time a different judge or bench looks at an issue. It doesn't mean that the decision will never be overruled or changed, only that the courts have to find a persuasive reason to say that decision was either wrong, or that circumstances have now changed so that it is no longer right. Without it, the American legal system would be wildly unpredictable. People might lose their confidence in it and would be constantly re-litigating old issues.

B. The Courts, including the State Supreme Courts, may interpret the laws very differently. In case of a conflict between these interpretations, it is possible to ask the Supreme Court to give its own opinion. This latter Court is binding to all the Courts in the United States, including the State Courts. So that, one after the other, its decisions tend to create a unified or standardized corpus of judicial precedent that is then followed by all the Courts in the country.

PART 3 - Page 59
A. First, higher courts bind lower courts within their particular State or Circuit. With the exception of the U.S. Supreme Court, Courts of Appeals and State Courts do not bind courts outside the State or Circuit in which they are located. That is, a Federal Supreme Court decision is mandatory on all lower Federal Courts, both Courts of Appeals and District Courts. A Federal circuit decision is mandatory on all Federal Courts within its circuit, but not Federal Courts in other Circuits. For example, a 9th Circuit decision binds the U.S. District Courts within the 9th Circuit, but not Federal Courts in any other Circuit. However, a District Court or Trial Court decision would not bind higher courts. A State Supreme Court decision is mandatory on all Appeals Courts and Trial Courts in that State, but not in State Courts in other States, and a State Court of Appeals' decision binds State Trial Courts in that State.
Second, Federal Courts usually bind only other Federal Courts, not State Courts.
Similarly, State Courts usually bind only other State

Courts. Thus, a decision by the U.S. Ninth Circuit Court of Appeals, a Federal Court, mandatory on Federal Courts within the boundaries of the Ninth Circuit. It is not mandatory on California State Courts, even though California is geographically within the Ninth Circuit. Similarly, a California Supreme Court decision would bind other California State Courts, but not the Ninth Circuit or other State Courts (like Nevada State Courts).

Finally, Federal Courts bind other Federal Courts, only when they interpret and apply Federal Law while State Courts bind other State Courts only when they interpret and apply State Law.

Sometimes a Federal Court must apply a State's law. In that case, the State's interpretation of that law is mandatory on the Federal Court. Even so, the Federal Court can still decide whether the State's interpretation is consistent with Federal Law. Similarly, State Courts must sometimes decide issues of Federal Law, but they are not bound by Federal Courts, except the U.S. Supreme Court. The U.S. Supreme Court, a Federal Court, is mandatory on State Courts when it decides an issue of Federal Law, such as Constitutional interpretation. Other Federal Courts – District and Appellate – are not mandatory on State Courts.

B. Possession of marijuana is a Federal crime. It is therefore against the law in the entire United States. California, Colorado and a few other States have introduced medical marijuana, and have decriminalized possession of small amounts of marijuana, but since Federal Law supersedes State Law, it is still a crime everywhere. However, the Federal government limits the enforcement of drug crimes only to large distributors. It is unlikely that a person possessing less than an ounce of marijuana will be charged federally, so in a State that allows or does not enforce it, people can easily get away with it.

PART 4 - Page 61
A. The twelve equitable maxims are:
1. Equity will not suffer a wrong.
2. Equity follows the law.
3. Where there is equal equity, the law shall prevail.
4. Where the equities are equal, the first in time shall prevail.
5. He who seeks equity must do equity.
6. He who comes into equity must come with clean hands.
7. Delay defeats equities.
8. Equality is equity.
9. Equity looks to the intent rather than the form.
10. Equity looks on that as done which ought to be done.
11. Equity imputes an intention to fulfill an obligation.
12. Equity acts in personam.

B. We can see books, probaly books of law, scales, a desk, a woman wearing a black robe, and another one wearing a white garment. Her eyes are blindfolded. All these objects are symbols of justice. "Lady Justice" is often depicted wearing a blindfold. This is done in order to indicate that justice is (or should be) meted out objectively, without fear or favor, regardless of the identity, power, or weakness of the individuals brought before the Court. Because the blind commonly worn blindfolds, some assume Lady Justice herself is blind. This belief is likely what led to the phrase, "Justice is blind". Justice is most often depicted with a set of scales, typically suspended from her left hand, upon which she measures the strengths of a case's support and opposition. She is also often seen carrying a double-edged sword in her right hand, which divides with the power of Reason and Justice in either direction simultaneously.

—Is it a classical representation of Justice? Is it a good representation of Justice?
When we think of justice today, the imagery that comes to mind is more likely to be of courtrooms and judges than of a woman carrying the scales of justices and armed with a sword (which is the classical representation of Justice)

PART 4 - Page 63
A. Not all injuries will lead to damages for pain and suffering. Simply being annoyed or inconvenienced by a minor injury, for example, usually will not work. In general, damages for pain and suffering can be awarded for past, present, and future physical distress in a personal injury case. A jury typically considers several factors in its deliberations and calculations, such as:
• the age of the injured victim. Younger victims may be rewarded more pain-and-suffering damages, if they will have to live with pain for the rest of their lives.
• the type of injury. Brain injuries, and injuries that cause continuing physical pain, will generally result in larger awards.
• how the injury affects the victim. This includes consideration of past, present, and future pain and suffering – including the certainty of future pain.
Jurors who consider pain-and-suffering claims are generally asked to "reasonably compensate" the victim for non-economic losses. But jurors usually don't get much guidance from the Court, and instead defer to their personal experience and common sense. That's why pain-and-suffering awards can vary greatly, depending on the facts of the case and the jury. A lack of guidance may also be why jury awards for pain and suffering are frequently modified. Aside from these general provisions, States and local jurisdictions may also impose their own limits on pain-and-suffering damages. Florida, for example, limits pain-and-suffering awards to $500,000 per doctor in medical malpractice cases. Other States may require a victim to be conscious for a period of time during the injury, while others may allow a jury to automatically assume pain and suffering is present in certain types of injury cases.

B. This is a very personal answer.

REVIEW - Page 65
A. - It is fair justice = equity
It can be vetoed by the President = statute law
It is forbidden to drink alcohol under 18 = State law
Courts decisions are binding lower Courts: = Common law
Ex-post facto laws are forbidden: Federal law
It can be vetoed by the President = statute law

B. A committee is a group of individuals all working on the same issue. In the case of Congress, these committees are designed to help Members of Congress with their workload.

C. This is a difficult question, because it depends of the judge and the Court. If Santa Claus were to make

the long haul from the North Pole to the Lehigh County Courthouse in Allentown, he'd probably raise his right hand, swear to tell the truth and say he doesn't want anyone else using his name. That's the reasoning a judge used in August 1989, to deny a Catasauqua man's request to legally change his name to Santa A. Claus. Santa wasn't at the hearing where Joseph Patrick Allen asked Judge James N. Diefenderfer to allow him to use the name Santa, on everything from Allen's birth certificate to his driver's license. Diefenderfer said there are limits to which someone can go in using the name and likeness of a famous person. Someone can impersonate Elvis Presley, but he can't use Elvis' name or photograph in advertisements and promotions, as the U.S. District Court of New Jersey ruled in one case Diefenderfer relied on. The Court said that although Elvis died in 1977, his worldwide popularity has survived. The producer was prohibited from using Elvis' photographs and the initials 'TCB' on any ads or promotional materials. Elvis had used the initials 'TCB' and a lightning bolt insignia on promotional materials, a ring he wore, and the tails of his planes. If Elvis is a famous person, there's no doubt Santa is, Diefenderfer said. The New Jersey Court said entertainers can imitate famous people but can't "appropriate another's valuable attributes on a continuing basis as one's own without the consent of the other." That would certainly be the same for Barack Obama, or Hillary Clinton.
But here again, it depends on the State, the Court and the judge. In December 2012, a judge accepted a name-change to... Santa Claus (but in a different State).

D. A Court of Equity is a court that can apply equitable remedies to disputes. These Courts operate within the legal system, but rather than focusing on the application of law, they look at cases and determine outcomes based on fairness. Also known as Chancery Courts, they can be found in many regions of the world. In some areas, they operate entirely separately from courts of law, and in others, a court of law is empowered to handle both legal and equitable remedies. The concept of a Chancery Courts arose in England, when citizens began to express dissatisfaction with legal judgments handed down by the Courts. They argued that the law was sometimes unfair, and that some situations were not covered by the law, making it impossible for the Courts to respond. Courts of Equity arose to handle legal situations in which people might want damages beyond monetary damages, with the judge empowered to act on discretion, rather than following the rule of the Law. A Court of Equity still has some legal responsibilities, but it has more leeway when it comes to judging cases. It can hand down a judgment that includes an equitable remedy such as an injunction, as opposed to simple monetary damages. These Courts can be used for things like specific performance, for example, in which someone is asked to make good on a breach of contract.

E. This is an individual answer, depending on what the students know.

UNIT 4 . *The Federal judicial system*
PART 1 - Page 69
A. When a Federal statute, civil or criminal is violated, or when State cases are appealed to the Federal Courts.

Also, when a civil lawsuit seeks more than $75,000 in damages, AND, when the civil lawsuit is between parties who are citizens of different States.

B. The Supreme Court mainly has appellate jurisdiction, which means 99% of the cases it hears is appeals. However, the Constitution does grant the Supreme Court original jurisdiction, to act as a Trial Court in certain circumstances. But this rarely ever happens.

PART 1 - Page 71
A. Article III, section 1, says Justices of the Supreme Court "shall hold their offices during good behavior." This phrase has been interpreted to mean justices and judges are afforded a lifetime commission that can only be revoked (by impeachment and conviction) if the justice fails to act with integrity, or commits another impeachable offense, as outlined in Article II, Section 4: "Section 4. The President, Vice President and all civil officers of the United States, shall be removed from office or impeachment for, and conviction of, treason, bribery, or other high crimes and misdemeanors."

B. A case starts in a District Court (lower level). The losing party may appeal the decision to the next level of the Court. When an appeal is filed, the Trial Court sends the official case records to the Court of Appeals. When the Court receives the records and attorneys' written arguments (briefs), the case is said to be at issue, and is assigned to a three-judge panel for consideration. All cases filed in the Court of Appeals must be reviewed. The brief of the person filing the appeal (the Appellant) contains legal and factual arguments as to why the decision of the Trial Court should be reversed. The person against whom the appeal is made (the Appellee) has the right to respond to these arguments. Court of Appeals judges have three main choices when making a decision: affirm (agree with) the Trial Court's decision; or reverse the decision (disagree); or remand the case (send the case back to the Trial Court for further action or a new trial). A petition for review is filed with the Supreme Court when a party wants the Supreme Court to hear a case. After a petition for review has been filed, the record is transferred to the Supreme Court. After examining the petition for review and supporting materials, the Court decides whether to grant or deny review of the appeal. In almost all cases, the Supreme Court's review is discretionary. This means the Court may refuse to review the case. In that event, the last decision from a lower court is final. When the Supreme Court agrees to review a decision, the justices study the record and the questions, or points of law, it raises. In most cases, the Court will hear oral arguments from the attorneys involved in the appeal.

C. 1. Jack Silver, a young Bostonian, is accused of theft. S
2. Natalie Anderwood, from Philadelphia, is accused of murder. S
3. Santiago Herrera, a Latin American, accuses his boss of discrimination. F & S
4. The Russian Ambassador is accused of espionnage. F
5. Two men want to get married in Austin, Texas. F & S
6. Edward Snowden makes NSA information classified as Top Secret public. F
7. A woman files for divorce in New York City. S
8. John Rupert aggresses Bill Crosby, his neighbor,

over a private lane, which he says belongs to him. S
9. Walmart accuses Visa of having colluded with banks to charge it fees it should not have had to pay. F
10. Lacoste sues a company that is selling copies of it's polo shirts in Dallas, TX. F
11. Arthur MacCory is fired from his company in Florida. S
12. A plastic surgeon in Las Vegas is accused of negligence. S
13. In Arizona, Wells Fargo Bank, is accused by Keith Ulahoop for having lied about the risks of buying stocks on the Stock Market. F
14. An author of a crime novel in California sues another author in North Carolina for plagiary. F
15. Julie Potter, from Seattle, refuses to pay her Federal income tax, under the pretext that she doesn't want to keep her American citizenship. F
16. Wyoming and Montana have a dispute over a piece of land. F
17. An Afghanistan war veteran, living in Tennessee, contests a denial to pay him disability benefits for being wounded in battle. F
18. A North Korean warship opens fire on an American submarine. F

PART 2 - Page 73
A. Commissioners: When a person is arrested, a District Court Commissioner, a judicial officer, will review the charging documents and set pre-trial release.
Clerks: Clerks provide support for the Courts both within and outside the courtroom.
Judges: A judge hears or presides over cases in District Court.

B. A District Court judge works for the United States District Court system. These individuals are Federal judges, and they must be appointed to their positions. District Court judges, as well as all Federal judges, are appointed by the President of the United States. A District Court judge is responsible for hearing all types of Federal cases. This includes civil and criminal matters that fall under Federal jurisdiction. During the course of a trial, District Court judges are responsible for monitoring witness testimony, ruling on the admissibility of evidence, and settling any disputes that may arise between defense attorneys and prosecutors. When presiding over a trial, a District Court judge may have to establish new rules if standard procedures do not already exist, according to the Law. These judges are also responsible for ensuring that court proceedings protect the rights of everyone involved in the trial. When not presiding over a trial, a District Court judge usually spends his work hours in a private office, referred to as his chambers. His job duties include reviewing motions and legal briefs, holding hearings with lawyers, writing opinions about legal decisions, and researching a variety of different legal issues that may pertain to a current trial. This kind of judge is also usually responsible for overseeing his administrative staff.

PART 2 - Page 75
A. District judges are nominated by the President of the United States and confirmed by the U.S. Senate. But it appears that nominating a judge is very important, politically speaking, because these nominees may judge in a way that may reflect the politics of the President. In the nomination of District judges, there is a tradition – called "Senatorial Courtesy" – according to which the President asks for the opinion of the local Senators. Using the example of Texas, which is a very strong Republican stronghold, and the President being Barack Obama, a Democrat, we might believe that there is clear obstruction from the local Senators, who want to delay the nomination of District judges as long as possible, hoping that it will eventually be done by a Republican President.

B. The case is about a man, Alan Bakke – the Plaintiff – who wanted to attend UC Davis Medical School in 1973, and again in 1974. He was rejected both times. He claimed he had been discriminated against because of race, and went to Court. The case was heard by the Superior Court of Yolo County, California in 1974. The Court declared that the special admissions policy "operated as a racial quota" and violated Federal and State Constitutions. But it did not order Bakke's admission, because he did not prove that he would have been admitted if the special admissions policy did not exist. He appealed to the Supreme Court of California. In 1976, the Court agreed with the Superior Court of Yolo County and declared the special admissions policy as unconstitutional. The Court also ordered that Bakke be admitted to the Medical School.
Davis Medical School appealed of the decision to the Supreme Court of the United States but lost the case, the Court declaring in 1978 that the special admission was unconstitutional. However, it also said that race could be a "plus" in the application process, instituting a precedent for Affirmative Action.

PART 3 - Page 77
A. In the United States Federal court system, a Circuit Court is an appeals court (above the District Court, but below the Supreme Court). District Court is a court where cases are originally brought (started).

B. One requesting a court to review an appeal from a lower court files a document in the form required by that specific Court, asking the Court to review the decision of a lower court. Generally, the petition for a writ of certiorari document must include the parties of the case, a statement of facts, legal questions presented for review, and the arguments for why the Court should review the decision. The superior court is not required to review the decision of the lower court. If the superior court decides to review the decision, it grants a writ of certiorari to the lower court. A petition for a writ of certiorari must be filed in accordance with the rules of the specific court to which the petition is being addressed. The rules vary by jurisdiction. The U.S. Supreme Court, for example, requires that 40 copies of the petition be submitted in booklet format. The petition process is normally regulated by statute in each jurisdiction.

PART 3 - Page 79
A. This case involved the power of Congress to charter a bank, which sparked the even broader issue of the division of powers between State and the Federal Governments. This case presented a major issue that challenged the Constitution: does the Federal Government hold sovereign power over States? The proceedings posed two questions: does the Constitution give Congress power to create a bank? And, could individual States ban or tax the bank? The Court decided that the Federal Government had the right and power to set up a Federal bank, and that states did not have the power

to tax the Federal Government. Marshall ruled in favor of the Federal Government and concluded, "the power to tax involves the power to destroy."

B. The major debate involved the meaning of Article I, Section 8—specifically, the Commerce Clause. What was the meaning of the word commerce in the Constitution? What exactly could the Federal Government regulate under that provision? Was the carrying of passengers a form of commerce? Should the word commerce be read narrowly (that is, boxes and barrels) or broadly (to include all forms of business relations for the purpose of trade)? Were the steamboat licenses of the State of New York in conflict with the National Government's authority to regulate commerce? If so, was the requirement for all steamships in New York's waters to be licensed by that State constitutional?

C. Chief Justice Marshall delivered the opinion of a unanimous (6-0) Court siding with Gibbons. On the definition of commerce, the Court broadly declared, "Commerce, undoubtedly, is traffic, but it is something more: it is intercourse. It describes the commercial intercourse between nations, and parts of nations, in all its branches, and is regulated by prescribing rules for carrying on that intercourse." The decision called Gibbons' federal license a legitimate exercise of the regulation of commerce provided in Article I, Section 8 of the Constitution. The New York State law creating a commercial monopoly was therefore void, since it conflicted with the regulatory power of the Federal Government in the performance of its constitutional responsibilities. The Court ruled that Gibbons must be allowed to operate within the waters of New York State.

PART 4 - Page 81
A. Just because the State doesn't agree, if the U.S. Supreme Court renders a decision, the State must comply! There is no higher Court than the U.S. Supreme Court and the State cannot file an appeal.

B. The judges review the memos and hold a conference to determine which of these cases should go on the Court's docket. The "Rule of Four" controls matters when deciding which issues the high court will hear. If four justices agree that a specific petition for writ of certiorari should be granted, then the case will be placed on the Supreme Court's docket, and an order stating that certiorari has been granted will be issued to the petitioner. Typically, the justices grant certiorari, or "cert" as it is commonly called, to cases that may have far-reaching, interesting issues. The Court may wish to hear a case and issue its opinion so that it can offer guidance to the lower level judges throughout the country who have the same issues come through their courtrooms on a daily basis. Cert is also often granted when there is a conflict among a number of lower-level Trial or Appellate Courts in interpreting a rule of law or a prior judicial decision. In such cases, the Supreme Court will issue an order specifying the correct interpretation of the law to pave the way and set the legal precedent for the lower courts.

PART 4 - Page 83
A. No, the document deals mostly with criminal cases and verdicts. The opinions of the Supreme Court of the United States are published officially in a set of case books called the *United States Reports*. At the beginning of October Term 2013, the *U.S. Reports*

consisted of 554 bound volumes and soft-cover "preliminary prints" of an additional 5 volumes; a final 10 volumes' worth of opinions also existed in individual "slip opinion" form. Volumes are added to the set at the rate of three to five per Term; they are generally between 800 and 1,200 pages long. The *U.S. Reports* is compiled and published for the Court by the Reporter of Decisions.

B. This is a personal viewpoint. We might emphasize that Sandra Day O'Connor, the first woman to serve on the Supreme Court, has often repeated that a wise female judge will come to the same conclusion as a wise male judge. It is indisputable that people bring different experiences to the bench. Doesn't the role of a judge require that the person who holds that position recognize those dispositions resulting from personal experience and try to overcome them?
At their confirmation hearings, both Chief Justice John G. Roberts, Jr. and Justice Clarence Thomas, said that judges should be like impartial baseball umpires. If we consider Justice Ginsburg's point of view as valid, isn't it a claim for filling the Supreme Court with all the existing minorities? And, by the way, what is a minority and who defines what one is?

REVIEW - Page 85
A. 1. FALSE. They are nominated for life.
2. TRUE
3. TRUE
4. FALSE. the District Courts were created by the Judiciary Act of 1789, that is to say by Congress.

B. The Ninth Circuit Court of Appeals is a Federal Court in the United States charged with hearing appellate cases from across the western region of the nation. It is an extremely large and diverse court, and a number of notable cases in U.S. history have worked their way through the Ninth Circuit. As of 2009, 29 judges serve on the Ninth Circuit Court of Appeals at any given time, with courthouses in San Francisco, Portland, Seattle, and Pasadena to provide multiple venues for hearing trials.

C. The Latin phrase "per curiam" means "by the court" and it is used to indicate that a legal opinion is issued in the name of the court, not in the name of a specific judge. The norms about when opinions and judgments are issued per curiam vary, depending on the nation and the court. High courts, for example, tend to more commonly issue signed opinions and judgments, while lower courts may offer per curiam decisions on a more regular basis.

D. Yes, when it involves a federal question preserved in the State Supreme Court's decision. Federal questions like the constitutionality of a State Law are also allowed to be raised and determined in State Courts. If the State action goes to the State Supreme Court, but one party alleges that the State Supreme Court decision is wrong, because it mistakenly interprets the U.S. Constitution or Federal statutes, the U.S. Supreme Court may, if it chooses, take an appeal from the State Supreme Court decision. If the State Supreme Court decision is based entirely on the State constitution or State statute with no issue of a Federal nature, then the U.S. Supreme Court has no jurisdiction and will not hear the case.

Unit 5. State Courts

PART 1 - Page 89
A. During the Colonial period, powers were concentrated in the hands of a governor who was appointed by the King of England. Executive, legislative and judicial powers were combined into his office, rendering the need for an elaborate court system useless.

B. After the Revolution, a wind of defiance blew through the Colonies, taking with it the Governors' power, and also that of the attorneys and even that of English Common Law. Many Governors were stripped of their functions, and many specialized Courts were angrily abolished. The Supreme Court of the United States, a Federal Court, imposed its supremacy by declaring a large number of the Laws passed by the States as unconstitutional. This encouraged the State's distrust of the legal system.

PART 1 - Page 91
A. According to Roscoe Pound, the system of courts is archaic in three respects: (1) in its multiplicity of courts, (2) in preserving concurrent jurisdictions, (3) in the waste of judicial power that it includes.

B. An example of a situation that might involve the different laws from two places is that of a contract signed in one State, and mailed to another. Complications may arise if one of the States provides that a contract so delivered is effective once mailed, while the other State provides that it is not effective until received.

C. There aren't actually any "conflicting laws". The Supremacy Clause states that Federal laws are superior to State laws. So there cannot be conflicting laws, because the Federal laws are enforced in all States.

PART 2 - Page 93
A. Generally, there is a 3-level structure, with a Trial Court, a Court of Appeals and a Supreme Court. The Trial Court may be divided into one or several Courts of limited jurisdiction and one or several Courts of general jurisdiction. There may also be some specialized tribunals.

B. If the size of the State Supreme Courts may differ from one State to the next, these Judges are all the ultimate decision-makers for every issue judged within the State, depending on State law. Most of these Courts follow a procedure that greatly resembles the one adopted by the U.S. Supreme Court: when a case is admitted, the opposing party has to fill out a brief and present its arguments orally. Then, the Judges deliver their verdicts in writing, with their reasons.

PART 2 - Page 95
A. Texas, along with Oklahoma, is the only State to have a bifurcated appellate system at the highest level. The Texas Supreme Court hears appeals involving civil matters, and the Texas Court of Criminal Appeals hears appeals involving criminal matters.

B. Municipal court: terms and qualifications vary across the State.
Justice of the Peace Court: The only qualification required is to be a registered voter! They are elected for a 4-year term.
County Court: They are elected for a 4-year-term.

The only qualification is to be "well-informed about the law".
District Court: They are elected for a 4-year term, and must be at least 25 years old with 4 years' experience as a lawyer or a judge.
Courts of Appeals: They are elected for a 6-year term. They must be 35 years old, a U.S. citizen and a Texas citizen and a lawyer or a judge for 10 years.
Court of Criminal Appeal: same terms and qualifications as the Court of Appeal.
Texas Supreme Court: same terms and qualifications as the Court of Appeal.

PART 3 - Page 97
A. Someone who wants to become a State Judge must be an American citizen and must be at least 18 years old on the day of the term. He must not have been determined mentally incompetent by a final judgment of a court, he must not have been guilty of a felony that has not been pardoned. He must reside in the State where he wants to be a judge for at least one year prior and in the precinct for the preceding six months. He must not have been declared ineligible for office.

B. Law Clerks assist judges in researching legal issues and making informed legal decisions. Contrary to the job title, Law Clerks perform few clerical duties. Clerkships are available in both Federal and State courts, and at both the trial and appellate levels. Serving as a law clerk is a great way to obtain insight into the judicial process and a broad exposure to various areas of the law. Judicial clerkships can serve as an excellent stepping-stone to a wide variety of career opportunities in both the public and private sectors.

PART 3 - Page 99
A. It's method of judge selection that involves the Governor appointing judges from a list that was submitted by a screening committee of legal officials. After being appointed, the judge serves a set term and is then subjected to a retention election (where the judge has no opponent and voters simply vote yes or no as to retain or remove the judge).

B. Who is more likely to be elected according to the different methods of judge selection used?
- In cases of an appointment by the executive, judges are often picked from the Governor's political party. So, it does not ensure that this judge will be competent for the job.
- In cases of an appointment by the legislature, former legislators are preferred.
- In cases of a partisan election, voters tend to favor labels, and vote for a political party, rather than for the skills of the judges.
- In cases of a non-partisan election, voters base their decision on something other than labels, but not necessarily on skills.
- The Missouri system ensures that the person running for election is competent for the job, because he already proved what he is able to do for a few months or a few years.

PART 4 - Page 101
A. Because the State Courts are in charge of 97% of all lawsuits filed in the United States, which equals about 93 billion cases a year (compared to hundreds of thousands at the Federal level).

B. Of course, the case may be of minor or major importance, for a petty or a colossal sum of money. But State Judges, and especially, Justices of the Peace, through the millions of verdicts rendered each year, mold a part of American society. There is no limit to their power, since, for example, they may be led to pronounce judgment on life sentences, to rule in cases concerning human embryos, or on issues of cloning, or euthanasia.

PART 4 - Page 103
A. There are several factors that may explain the high crime rate, but the fact that most crimes are committed in cities, whereas Texas' population is mostly urban, may be the main factor.

B. The fact that Texas leads the nation with the highest incarceration rate and ranks 5th among the 50 states in terms of total crimes committed per 100,000 people, raises questions as to the validity of that philosophy.

C. The death penalty has been used since the beginning in the U.S.A., but in 1972, the Supreme Court outlawed the death penalty in a landmark decision, *Furman v. Georgia*. Since that date, the death penalty was again adopted in 12 States, after they changed their statutes as per the required Supreme Court procedure, which was defined in another decision, *Gregg v. Georgia*, in 1976.

REVIEW - Page 105
A. 1. FALSE.
2. FALSE
3. FALSE.
4. FALSE.
5. FALSE.

B. In criminal matters, for example, the States can hear three types of crimes: minor offenses (the least serious), misdemeanors (more serious), and felonies (the most serious).

C. The State Magistrates, who are sometimes called commissioners or referees, are often those who start civil, as well as criminal, cases. In some States, they may even have to render verdicts in very limited cases. A primary function of the Magistrate is to provide an independent, unbiased review of complaints of criminal conduct brought to the office by law enforcement or the general public. Magistrate duties include issuing various types of documents, such as arrest warrants, summonses, bonds, search warrants, subpoenas, and certain civil warrants. Magistrates also conduct bail hearings in situations where an individual is arrested on a warrant charging him or her with a criminal offense. Magistrates provide services on an around-the-clock basis, conducting hearings in person or through the use of videoconferencing systems. They are the first level of contact with the public.

D. There are five methods of judge selection used around the nation, each with their own advantages and disadvantages. These five methods are partisan elections, nonpartisan elections, appointment by the Governor, selection by the legislature, and the "merit system" or "Missouri system".

E. State Courts enforce only those laws enacted by that particular State's legislature and signed into law by their Governor. Federal Courts enforce only Federal laws – unless a question of law is appealed to the Federal circuit and is deemed by the Federal Courts to address a question of national implication.

Unit 6. State laws
PART 1 - Page 109
A. The structure of the Constitution is simple: one short Preamble, 30 Articles and over 400 Amendments.

B. School districts, which are tasked with primary and secondary education, do not report to cities and counties, but to the California State Government.

C. It is very long, one of the longest in the world (110 pages).

PART 1 – Page 111
A. The main purpose of the Three-Strikes law was to keep violent repeat offenders off the streets.

B. The problem is that the law also concerns non-serious and non-violent crimes. So, one may serve a long period of time, or even a lifetime in jail, for a misdemeanor.

C. This is a personal opinion. It must be noted, however, that this law has sent people who have only stolen something from a store to prison for life, for example.

D. Criminal laws are generally handled by the States and are influenced by public opinion: they reflect a tendency at specific moment in time. At the Federal level, things are seen with much more perspective, and such a law would have little chance of being passed.

E. People are quite different from State to State, and each State has jealously guarded its prerogatives. During Colonial times, the northern States had laws defining people's behaviors because they were borrowed from religious principles. It wasn't acceptable in the southern States, for example, that did not want any laws dealing with their private lives.

PART 2 Page 113
A. The New York Constitution not only describes the structure of New York State's government but also the citizens' rights.

B. The Executive is headed by a Governor.

C. How is the 2nd Amendment secured in New York? New York has among the most restrictive gun laws in the nation. These laws ban handgun possession and provide exemptions, including individuals licensed to carry handguns, or to possess them for some reasons, including sports, repair, or disposal.

PART 3 – Page 115
A. The New York Court of Appeals, like most appellate tribunals, is exclusively for hearing appeals on legal issues. It does not do any fact-finding, and thus holds no trials. Federal Courts may overrule a State Court only when there is a Federal question, which is to say, a specific issue (such as consistency with the Federal Constitution) that gives rise to Federal jurisdiction. Federal appellate review of State Supreme Court

rulings on such matters may be sought by way of a petition for writ of certiorari to the Supreme Court of the United States.

B. Appellate Terms of the Supreme Court: Appellate Terms of the Supreme Court (not to be confused with the Appellate Division) are located in the First and Second Judicial Departments only. In the five boroughs of New York City, the Appellate Term hears cases from the New York City Courts. In the suburban counties, the Appellate Term hears cases from the city, district, town, and village courts, and in misdemeanor cases from the County Courts. Further appeals, when permitted, are taken to the Court of Appeals in criminal cases and the Appellate Division in civil cases.

C. Yes, this system is more complex or, at least, it is more difficult to understand, because the names used are all different from the ones used in the rest of the country. The most striking example is the Supreme Court of New York, which is in fact a first level Trial Court.

PART 2 – Page 117
A. Texans were so suspicious of too much power being given to their government, that Article I is nothing more than a Bill of Rights.

B. Texas has no laws regarding possession of "long-barreled firearms" or "long guns" (shotguns, rifles and other similar weapons) by people 18 years or older, or handguns by people 18 years or older, without felony convictions.

PART 3 - Page 119
A. The new law says a person is "presumed to be traveling" if he or she is in a private vehicle, is not engaged in criminal activity (except for a minor traffic offense), is not prohibited by any other law from possessing a firearm, and is not a member of a criminal street gang. It also requires the handgun to be concealed in the car, although weapons can be found by officers during routine traffic stops, if a driver gives permission for a car to be searched, or opens a glove compartment, where a gun is stored, to retrieve an insurance card or some other documentation.

B. "The intent of the law is to keep innocent people from going to jail," said the sponsor, Rep. Terry Keel. This means that people could carry a gun without fear of being prosecuted.

C. In 1997, the Texas Legislature prohibited the issuance of marriage licenses to same-sex couples. In 2003, the legislature enacted a statute that voided any same-sex marriages or civil unions in Texas. In 2005, Texas voters approved a proposition that amended the State Constitution to define marriage as consisting "only of the union of one man and one woman". A lawsuit, *De Leon v. Perry*, challenging the State's ban on same-sex marriage, was filed in November 2013. On February 26th, 2014, the Court ruled against Texas' ban on same-sex marriage, but stayed enforcement of its ruling, pending appeal to the Fifth Circuit.

PART 4 – Page 121
A. The State of Louisiana is totally unique in the United States: Law there is Civil Law, even if there is some Common Law influence. This special feature is buried in the State's history. Louisiana was originally a French territory and possession.

B. The most obvious difference, and which is most often cited, comes from the fact that the judges in Louisiana, like French judges, are not bound by stare decisis, but base their decisions on their interpretations, rather than on the doctrine of precedents. Another notable difference may be found in the absence of the obligation of having a jury for civil proceedings.

PART 4 – Page 123
It is difficult to qualify the Louisiana Code as "French", only for the fact that it is written in English. But, it may be noted that it follows the traditional organization of older codes. For this reason, the Louisiana Code is constructed like the French Civil Code. One may find a methodical presentation and a division into three parts: people, possessions, and property.
We can see that the Louisiana Code is the same thing: the Law is codified in the form of articles and a classic organization in large divisions seems to even have been respected (cf: Book I: of persons).
Modern codes use a hierarchical structure based on the one which is ruled by the legal system: first, a legislative part whose articles originate in Law, and second, a regulatory part originating in a decree. This is what is found in many State Codes.

B. Common Law marriage is an alternative to traditional marriage. Instead of obtaining a marriage license, a man and woman who live together and "intend to be married" can become Common Law spouses, without a license or a wedding ceremony.

C. All marriages, Common Law or civil, are recognized by every State. If people moving from another State are Common Law married, and move to a State that does not allow such marriages, they are still married in the new State because their marriage was valid in the State where it took place.

REVIEW – Page 125
A. 1. FALSE.
2. FALSE.
3. TRUE.
4. FALSE. Louisiana has civil law, but also applies Common Law.
5. FALSE. The ban has been declared unconstitutional by a Federal Court (as of 2014).
6. TRUE.

B. The huge concentration of celebrities in California resulted in the creation of special laws, such as the California Celebrities Rights Act, or a highly specific Family Code, aimed at responding to the numerous matrimonial problems faced by these stars, who are rich enough to stay in Court forever.

C. The court system is different at the local court level in NYC. The NYC Courts, mainly composed of the NYC Criminal Court and the NYC Civil Court, are local courts in the five boroughs of NYC.
• District Courts, the local criminal and civil courts in Nassau County and the five western towns of Suffolk County, arraign felonies and try misdemeanors and lesser offenses, as well as civil lawsuits involving claims of up to $15,000, small claims and small commercial claims up to $5,000, and landlord-tenant actions.

District Court Judges are elected to 6-year terms.
• Justice Courts (town and village courts) try misdemeanors and lesser offenses in towns and villages. These courts are the starting point for all criminal cases outside cities, and handle a variety of other matters including small claims, traffic violation cases and local zoning matters. They also arraign Defendants accused of felonies. These courts may hear civil lawsuits involving claims of up to $3,000 (including small claims cases of up to $3,000). The town and village justice courts are locally funded, as opposed to the State-funded City and District Courts.

D. It means that justice was rapid in Texas, or that there was no justice at all, since the crowds preferred to judge by lynching, or that Sheriffs killed suspects (Winchester).

E. A man and woman who live together and "intend to be married" can become Common Law spouses. Intent to be married can be proven by a couple simply by acting as if they are married.

Unit 7. Review
All the answers can be found in Units 1 to 6.

Unit 8. Lawyers
PART 1 - Page 149
A. Contrary to most other Common Law countries, there is no distinction in the U.S.A. between attorneys that plead (most often called barristers in other countries, such as in England) and those who do not plead (often called solicitors). In the U.S., they are all attorneys-at-law.

B. Contrary to the glamorous image of lawyers seen on TV shows and films, most of their time is spent working on library search, or in databases like Westlaw, LexisNexis, or Bloomberg L.P.

PART 1 - Page 151
A. This response is an opinion, but one might mention the right American lawyers have to advertize with every possible media outlet, and even going as far as canvassing new clients by telephone, or going door-to-door, while advertizing was only recently authorized in France. The laws concerning lawyers advertizing in France changed in March 2014, now being allowed, including the right to resort to personal canvassing.

B. Because the situation for lawyers in Canada (Montreal) is similar to that in France, he was very surprised to discover more than 136 pages of advertizing for lawyers in the small town of Boca Raton in Florida, while there were only 20 pages in Montreal.

C. First, he says that we find lawyers specialized in any issue that might be of concern to them, even when it is idiotic: "You slipped on a groundhog dying from starvation? No problem: a lawyer specialized in falls caused by groundhogs will be very pleased to represent you." He especially emphasizes that these lawyers are quite expensive, even if they claim, "the first discussion on the telephone is free", since it only serves the purpose of giving someone directions on how to get to the lawyer's office.

PART 2 - Page 153
A. To become a lawyer in the U.S.A, you must first obtain a Bachelor's Degree, in any subject. Then, you must pass the LSAT (Law School Admission Test) entrance exam. Once passed, you must study three more years at a law school, leading to a Master's Degree.

B. She wants to be successful in a very prestigious and challenging university in the U.S. But her biggest fears are not to be able to adapt (to campus life), because of the language barrier and/or the differences she might encounter. She is also concerned about how the work will be presented, because it is very different from the French dissertation and comment style.

PART 2 - Page 155
A. He did not experience any problems adapting to campus life, New York City actually being Fordham's campus. Due to that fact, the university regularly organized events to help students meet and interact. The professors were always available and easy to talk to.

B. This is a personal opinion, but it may pointed out that students had an assigned seat in some classes, which is different from France, or the fact that it seems very easy to take the Bar Exam.

C. The first ranking depends on the number of graduates, whereas the second one depends on the promotion of Associate to Partner. Two things are interesting to note: the first one is that many good universities are State universities (not necessarily Ivy League universities), and second, *Document 5* shows that a career depends on factors other than simply where you got your diploma.

PART 3 - Page 157
A. This is a personal opinion with a wide variety of answers: advising clients, drafting contracts, working for a government agency, external consultation/internal consultation, etc.

B. A specialization gives lawyers the opportunity to know about various laws in different states on similar issues. They may also advise the same client in different states.

PART 3 - Page 159
A. Generally, patent lawyers must obtain a Bachelor's Degree in a field of Science. In addition to passing their state's bar exam, a patent lawyer must also pass the USPTO Patent Bar Exam. If a patent lawyer does not have a Bachelor's Degree in Science, he must earn enough Science credits, as defined by the USPTO, to qualify for the exam.

B. The illustrations show us that the role of the patent lawyer is quite important, maybe just as important as the invention itself.

PART 4 - Page 161
The United States Attorney General is a member of the President's Cabinet. He is the Head of the Justice Department (DoJ). It may be translated as Minister of Justice. It may be noted that he is nominated by the President, with a Senate confirmation.

B. Because prosecutors are elected at a local level in most of the States, so it is not only up to the lawyer to become a prosecutor.

PART 4 - Page 163
A. The most common method was to infiltrate the criminal organization.

B. A private investigator, or private detective, is often abbreviated to P.I., and informally called private eye, or private dick.

C. Yes, it is. There is no law prohibiting someone from searching the web (or Google).

REVIEW - Page 165
A. 1. True - 2. True - 3. False - 4. False - 5. True - 6. False.

B. There is no waiting period. As soon as they are admitted to the Bar, American lawyers can file legal pleadings and argue cases in State Court, provide legal advice to clients, and draft important documents, such as wills, trusts, deeds and contracts.

C. An important change was brought by a landmark decision of the Supreme Court in *Bates et al. v. State Bar of Arizona* in 1977. The Supreme Court decided that "freedom of expression" implied the right for lawyers to resort to advertising.

D. Because being a lawyer is a restricted profession, and in some jurisdictions the practice of law is quite strict. Providing people with the template of a will can be assimilated to practicing law, and if you do not have the required degrees, it is then against the law.

E. A person who has a professional law degree, but is not admitted to a State Bar is not an attorney-at-law, but may be considered a lawyer. So, it is necessary to be admitted to the Bar to be called an Attorney-at-Law.

Unit 9. The Judiciary
PART 1 - Page 169
A judge is supposed to represent justice, to insure that the principle of due process is respected, and that the accused is treated fairly.

B. In the adversary system, the judge acts as a sort of referee, while in the inquisitorial system a judge is specifically nominated to investigate the facts of criminal trial. He writes a report, and only then is a trial is organized.

PART 1 – Page 171
A. "Equal justice under law". It means that under the U.S. system of law every citizen is treated and judged fairly, regardless of who they are.

B. Federal judges: The Constitution sets forth no specific requirements. However, members of Congress, who typically recommend potential nominees, and the Department of Justice, which reviews nominees' qualifications, have developed their own informal criteria.

C. This means that judges have tenure for life as long as their behavior is consequent with their position. They may not, for example be removed from their jobs for political reasons. This guarantees that judges will not let personal employment considerations influence their

judgment. The advantage of this is the autonomy they enjoy. The disadvantage is the possibility of a mediocre or lazy judge sitting on his laurels at the country's expense till the end of their professional days.

PART 2 – Page 173
A. Among the factors that might explain why being a judge could be attractive, one may cite the impressive flexibility of work hours. But, the real reasons may be the power they wield, the professional status that comes from the position, and the prestige that comes with being a judge.

B. There is generally a solemn atmosphere in a court of law, along with a combination of dominating wood and marble, and large, red velvet curtains, which results in a setting that gives an oppressive and striking impression.

PART 2 – Page 175

A. According to what Thurgwood Marshalls aid, we may think that personal background may influence the decision taken by the judge. But the question is should it? (This is a personal opinion).

B. Because, Presidents usually appoint judges who seem to have a similar political ideology to their own. In other words, a president with a liberal ideology will usually appoint liberals to the courts. Likewise, conservative presidents tend to appoint conservatives.

PART 3 - Page 177
A. No, this may be what people think about the role of a judge, but a large part of their mission is performed out of court. They also have a large administrative role.

B. A judge may act as an adjudicator, a negotiator or an administrator.

PART 3 - Page 179
A. All three cases deal with the power of the Supreme Court in the context of judicial review.

B. Separation of powers is a political doctrine originating in the writings of Montesquieu in *The Spirit of the Laws* where he urged for a constitutional government with three separate branches of government. Each of the three branches would have defined powers to check the powers of the other branches. This idea was called separation of powers. This philosophy heavily influenced the writing of the United States Constitution, according to which the Legislative, Executive, and Judicial branches of the United States government are kept distinct in order to prevent abuse of power. This United States form of separation of powers is associated with a system of checks and balances.

PART 4 – Page 181
A. This is a personal opinion, but it can be said that they need to be strong and not take any nonsense. Also they should be able to keep their cool. It's rather hard to say what « skills » a judge needs or has. He/she has been a lawyer before, that much is for certain. Of course, knowing the law or being a lawyer are just the first few basic requirements.

B. This is a personal answer.

PART 4 – Page 183

A. The two basic methods used in the selection of judges in the United States are election and appointment. Elective methods may be either partisan or nonpartisan. In partisan elections the judicial candidate is nominated by a party and runs with a party identification. In nonpartisan elections the judicial candidate is generally nominated in a nonpartisan primary and runs in the general election without a party label. Appointment methods used in other States differ on where the responsibility rests for the important decisions; they are made either by the Governor, the Legislature or a judicial nominating commission. The method which uses the judicial nominating commission is generally referred to as merit selection or the Missouri plan. Some people may see problems in electing judges: Elected judges can be biassed by their constituency votes and become populist like politicians with narrow mindset trying to win elections, instead of deliveringing unbiassed justice to the people.

B. This depends on the research conducted by the students.

C. If we are talking about State Judges: They are elected officials, and therefore must be impeached on applicable grounds. Surprisingly, it starts at the top - in the House of Representatives. The House Judiciary Committee will open up an investigation to see if there are grounds for removal. If they find cause for impeachment, they will vote on it. If the motion to impeach passes, it then goes to the State, where the State Senate will hold a final trial and vote whether or not to impeach. The American Judicature Society defines grounds for impeachment as "malfeasance," "misfeasance," "gross misconduct," "gross immorality," "high crimes," "habitual intemperance," and "maladministration» (among others).
If we are talking about a Federal Judge, like a Supreme Court Justice, the process is essentially the same, except it doesn't go to any State Senate. The U.S. Senate holds the final vote.

REVIEW - Page 185

A. 1. True.
2. True.
3. False (*Marbury v. Madison*).
4. False (*The Supreme Court is also a Court of Appeal*).
5. True.

B. Marshall established that a law in conflict with the Constitution is not valid. He also held that the Supreme Court had the power to invalidate or, at least, disregard such a law. The cornerstone of judicial review today is that the Constitution is the law superior to any enacted by Congress; and the judiciary is required to follow it rather than any inconsistent provisions of federal legislation.

C.1. The appeal was based on the due process clause of the 14th Amendment.
2. Its importance lies in its ability to protect people from illegal incarceration.
3. A writ of certiorari (Latin: «to be informed») is an order from an appellate court to a lower court to send the records for a specified case under review.
4. An in *forma pauperis* petition is a petition filed by a poor person to proceed to court without any extra court fees such as filing fees, etc.

D. 1. *Betts v. Brady*, (1942), was a landmark United States Supreme Court case that denied counsel to indigent defendants when prosecuted by a state. It was later famously overruled by *Gideon v. Wainwright*.
2. Double jeopardy refers to a person being prosecuted again for the same offense (1) after having been being acquitted, (2) a second prosecution for the same offense after conviction; and (3) multiple punishments for the same offense.
3. Gideon's second trial, when he had a lawyer, was a situation when he was not in jeopardy. This is because he was already in jail for theft and the trial was a retrial to see if perchance he might not have been guilty. He had nothing to fear from the trial but only hope that he might be acquitted.

E. Federal Judges are appointed by the President under the advice and consent of the Senate.

Unit 10. It's the law
PART 1 – Page 189
A. Can you commit a crime without hurting anybody? Yes, because, for example, it is a crime to not wear your seatbelt in your car, or your helmet when on a scooter or a motorcycle.

B. What is a 'misdemeanor'?
Misdemeanors are less serious crimes in all States, punishable by a prison sentence of less than one year and in a city prison or county prison, e.g. for public drunkenness or vagrancy.

PART 1 – Page 191
A. What are some reproaches addressed to the U.S. incarceration system?
The United States boasts the world's highest incarceration rate, with close to 2.3 million people locked away in some 1,800 prisons and 3,000 jails. Most are nasty places by design, aimed at punishment and exclusion rather than rehabilitation; while reliable numbers are hard to come by, at last count, 81,622 prisoners were being held in some form of isolation in State and Federal prisons. Thousands more are being held in solitary at jails, deportation facilities, and juvenile-detention centers. Nearly 1 in 10 prisoners is sexually victimized, by prison employees about half of the time—more than 200,000 such assaults take place in American penal facilities every year. Suicides, meanwhile, account for almost a third of prisoner deaths, while an unknown number of fatalities result from substandard nutrition and medical care.

B. Compare Rikers Island and Florence. What is your opinion on these prisons?
Rikers Island Prison in New York has a legacy of prisoner violence. A man named John Reyes, who was a guard at the prison in 1991, mentioned being daily afraid because of the beatings and murders he witnessed there. Because of the prison's history of violence, it is now one of the strictest prisons in the world. Several reform actions at the prison have helped reduce the number of stabbings a year down from 1,000 to 70. ADX-Florence in Colorado is designed to hold the worst prisoners, many in near round-the-clock solitary confinement. A lawsuit was filed in June 2012 by several inmates. The lawsuit charges that the

conditions of the prison create an environment for inmate abuse and torture.

PART 2 – Page 193

A. *Actus Reus* is the fact that a criminal act has been committed .

B. The *Mens Rea* is present when the individual accused was, at the time of the crime, in a mental state to understand that what he/she was doing was wrong / unlawful and thus that there was intent present in the commission of the crime.

PART 2 – Page 195

A. What is the 'Stand-your-ground' statute? Search the Internet or try to imagine what it might be.
'Stand-your-ground' laws are essentially a revocation of the duty to retreat. Stand-your-ground laws generally state that, under certain circumstances, individuals can use force to defend themselves without first attempting to retreat from the danger. The purpose behind these laws is to remove any confusion about when individuals can defend themselves and to eliminate prosecutions of people who legitimately used self-defense even though they had not attempted to retreat from the threat. In many States with stand your ground laws, a claim of self-defense under a stand-your-ground law offers immunity from prosecution rather than an affirmative defense. This means that, rather than presenting a self-defense argument at an assault trial, for example, an individual could claim self-defense under the State's stand-your-ground law and avoid trial altogether.

B. Can it be said that George Zimmermann is a murderer? How did the jury decide of the case?
The essential criteria for deciding the case came from the court itself, which told jurors that Zimmerman was allowed to use deadly force when he shot the teen not only if he actually faced death or bodily harm, but also if he merely thought he did. And jurors heard plenty of conflicting evidence and testimony that could have created reasonable doubt.
Under Florida law, jurors were told to decide whether Zimmerman was justified in using deadly force by the circumstances he was under when he fired his gun. The instructions they were given said they should take into account the physical capabilities of both Zimmerman, 29, and Martin, 17. And if they had any reasonable doubt on whether Zimmerman was justified in using deadly force, they should find him not guilty. «Beyond a reasonable doubt» is the highest standard of proof prosecutors face in American criminal courts. It means the jurors believe there is no other logical explanation for what happened than the defendant is guilty. If faced with two plausible explanations for what happened, jurors are supposed to acquit. The danger facing George Zimmerman need not have been actual; however, to justify the use of deadly force, the appearance must have been so real that a reasonably cautious and prudent person ... would have believed the danger could be avoided only through the use of that force.

PART 3 – Page 197

A. What are the pre-trial processes that you may identify? Explain them.
- The arrest and the appearance before a judge.

Following the arrest of a suspect by the police, a prosecutor decides whether or not to press charges. The prosecutor is the government's lawyer. If the prosecutor decides to proceed, he or she files a charging document with a lower court. A charging document accuses the arrestee of committing a crime. The most common charging documents used are the information and the indictment. Although the information and indictment differ in some respects, each of these contains a statement of the charge. For the first appearance, the defendant is taken from jail and brought before the lower court judge. The judge informs the defendant of the charge in the complaint, explains to the defendant that he or she has certain rights, offers to appoint counsel at the expense of the government if the defendant is indigent (too poor to afford a lawyer), and sets bail.

B. Identify the procedural steps that are protected by the Constitution of the United States.
- Self incrimination is restricted, double jeopardy is prohibited, there is a right to trial by jury and the right to a lawyer
In the landmark case *Gideon v. Wainwright* (1963), the U.S. Supreme Court held that the Sixth Amendment guarantees access to qualified counsel, which is fundamental to a fair trial. Gideon was entitled to a retrial because Florida failed to provide him with an attorney. After this decision, states were required to furnish public defenders for indigent defendants in felony cases. In *Argersinger v. Hamlin* (1972), the Court extended the right to a lawyer to all cases that might result in imprisonment.

PART 3 – Page 199

A. Why was Dominique Strauss-Kahn refused bail on a first time? Was it fair?
The New York judge ordered Dominique Strauss-Kahn to be remanded in custody after prosecutors expressed fears that he might flee to France to escape charges of sexually assaulting a hotel maid. The judge refused a request for bail, agreeing that Strauss-Kahn, who was pulled off a Paris-bound plane and charged with a criminal sexual act, attempted rape and unlawful imprisonment, represented a flight risk. Strauss-Kahn denied the charges but the prosecution compared Strauss-Kahn to Roman Polanski, the film director who fled the U.S. in 1978 after pleading guilty to unlawful sexual intercourse with an underage girl, what was not really fair.

B. Do you think the warrant system offers good protection for suspects?
A warrant is a command from a judge ordering an officer to arrest a person or search a place for evidence or contraband. However, because a general warrant did not specify who was to be arrested or what place was to be searched it conferred discretionary search authority on peace officers. Because discretionary arrest or search authority conflicted with Common Law standards, in the 1760s English courts declared such warrants illegal. Nevertheless, in 1767 Parliament reauthorized customs officers in the American colonies to use a form of general warrant called a "writ of assistance." However, American colonial courts generally refused to issue such writs, and sometimes denounced them as illegal. On independence, several States included bans against general warrants in State

declarations of rights, and the Fourth Amendment was included in the federal Bill of Rights to prohibit Congress from ever authorizing general warrants.

PART 4 – Page 201
A. What is an arraignment?
An arraignment is a reading of a criminal complaint in the presence of the Defendant; it is the formal reading of charges to notify the suspect as to what he or she is being charged with. The Defendant, in response to the arraignment, is expected to enter the plea before the court. At this point, although acceptable pleas will vary among jurisdiction, the suspect will plead either "guilty" or "not guilty."

B. How do plea bargain work? What is your opinion on this system ?
If there weren't be plea bargains as an option in the U.S. justice system, the courts would be so overloaded with cases that nothing would ever get done. Some people believe that plea bargains allow criminals to get off on lighter sentences when they should be serving their full sentences in prison, but in reality, many criminals that would otherwise have been acquitted are at least paying some sort of a price.
A plea bargain is a «deal» made between the Prosecutor of a criminal case and the defendant, usually facilitated by the defendant's lawyer. In exchange for a lesser charge or a reduced sentence, the Defendant enters a plea of «guilty» or «no contest» and does not go to trial.
There are two basic types of plea bargains:
1. Charge Bargain
A charge bargain is a deal made between the Prosecutor and the Defendant, which allows the Defendant to plead guilty to a lesser charge. For example, an alleged murderer might be able to enter into a plea bargain with the Prosecutor by pleading guilty to manslaughter, rather than going to trial for second-degree murder.
2. Sentence Bargain
In a case where the Defendant is charged with a heinous crime, the Prosecutor might offer to charge him or her with the maximum charge, but with the lowest penalty. For example, if the law in their State says that second-degree murder carries a sentence of 12-25 years, then a sentence bargain may assure the Defendant that he or she will receive only 12 years. Sentence bargains are closely monitored by the trial judge, and are usually offered in a case where the Defendant is willing to testify against an accomplice.

PART 4 – Page 203
A. What is the charge against the young woman?
She is charged with institutional sex assault, a third-degree felony.

B. Has she been arrested? Why or why not?
She must have been arrested, because charges were filed against her.

C. What is the procedure after the Police were told about the alleged charge?
The Police interviewed the victim the day after the alleged charges. Ms. Nesbit was then apparently arrested, arraigned and charged, then questioned by the Police. Now, it seems that we're waiting for the trial, because Ms. Nesbit says she intends to accept responsibility in Court.

D. What does the teacher face?
She faces up to seven years in prison, if convicted.

E. What is your opinion about the advice given by the Prosecutor to the parents?
It is obviously good advice, but in reality, very difficult to apply in every situation and with each child. Pragmatically, parents may not have access to contents of their children's phones or social media accounts, if they do not have the passwords.

REVIEW – Page 205
A.1. False - 2. False - 3. False - 4. True

B. Why should the State punish a person for not wearing a seat belt when it will only be that person who suffers through not wearing it?
It can be argued that making such behavior 'criminally' liable to punishment is an infringement on personal freedom. In these 'crimes', it cannot be said that the law is protecting other people. Nevertheless, society also has some other duties, and one of these is to reduce the 'collective' cost for injuries, for example, because this is paid out of the national treasury, that is to say, out of people's taxes. And this cost is sometimes directly impacted by the behavior of a few, who do not respect the laws decided upon collectively to limit the costs.

C. Is it possible to find *mens rea* in a case without an *actus reus*?
Yes, it is possible for *mens rea* to be present, but not *actus reus*. In the example given in the lesson, if John Doe voluntarily takes the jacket that he believes to be Jack Smith's and which contains a wallet with $3,000 inside, but he makes a mistake and takes Bob Morane's jacket, which has nothing in it. He irrefutably commits *mens rea* of theft towards Jack Smith, but not *actus reus*, at least for the wallet, because he still must explain himself to Bob Morane about the jacket.

D. Is it possible to be acquitted in spite of proven *mens rea*?
Some defenses require acquittal even where the State has proven actus reus and mens rea. These defenses include self-defense and justifiable homicide. In George Zimmerman's case, for example, his attorneys argued to the jury that Zimmerman acted in self-defense and offered evidence that they say showed that Trayvon Martin was attacking Zimmerman when Zimmerman shot him. This evidence persuaded the jury that Zimmerman acted in self-defense and the jury acquitted him, despite the fact that he intended to, and did, kill Martin.

E. What happens if somebody pleads guilty?
They are convicted of the crime, but are usually given a lighter punishment than if they had asked for a long, drawn-out trial. 90% of trials in the States end in a guilty plea.

Unit 11. Criminal trials
PART 1 – Page 209
A. What are the Amendments concerned with the protection of the accused?
The Fifth, the Sixth and Eighth Amendments protect the rights of the accused:
Amendment V – "No person shall be held to answer for a capital, or otherwise infamous crime, unless on

a presentment or indictment of a grand jury, except in cases arising in the land or naval forces, or in the militia, when in actual service in time of war or public danger; nor shall any person be subject for the same offense to be put twice in jeopardy of life or limb; nor shall be compelled in any criminal case to be a witness against himself, nor be deprived of life, liberty, or property, without due process of law; nor shall private property be taken for public use, without jut compensation."

Amendment VI – "In all criminal prosecutions, the accused shall enjoy the right to a speedy and public trial, by an impartial jury of the state and district wherein the crime shall have been committed, which district shall have been previously ascertained by law, and to be informed of the nature and cause of the accusation; to be confronted with the witness against him; to have compulsory process for obtaining witnesses in his favor, and to have the assistance of counsel for his defense."

Amendment VIII – "Excessive bail shall not be required, not excessive fines imposed, not cruel and unusual punishments inflicted."

B. Why is the Fifth Amendment so important?
The 5th Amendment states that someone cannot be forced to testify against oneself.
The most reliable convictions are based upon evidence and testimony of witnesses. Anybody can make someone confess to something they didn't do. It guarantees that the people cannot be forced to confess in Court unless they choose to take the stand. It also protects the people against tyranny in judicial proceedings.

PART 1 – Page 211
A. Determine whether jurors 1-12 would be allowed to participate in this case.
This is a personal answer, depending on the student's work.

B. Explain why each one would (or would not) be a "good juror" in the eyes of the Prosecution or the Defense.
This is a personal opinion, depending on the student's work.

C. Now create three of your own jurors – one who would assist the Defense, one who would assist the Prosecution, and a "dream witness" for both sides. Create a short biography as above for jurors 1-9. (JUROR 10 – JUROR 11 – JUROR 12)
This is an individual response, depending on the student's work.

PART 2 – Page 213
What is the difference between a peremptory challenge and a challenge for cause?
There are Peremptory Challenges and Challenges of Cause in both selecting jury members and selecting judges. In the case of the jury, the Peremptory Challenge states the Defense and Prosecution has the right to reject potential jurors if they feel they are biased in any way. They are not required to provide a reason to the juror regarding why they are being let go. In the case of jurors with a Challenge of Cause, it is the juror who is trying to convince the legal parties to release them from being a juror because they may be unable

to come to a fair verdict.

PART 2 – Page 215
A. You are the judge in this case and you are trying to create as fair a jury as possible. Read the description on p. 210 carefully. Then go through the selection process for rounds one through four. For each round, mark «K» for Keep or «E» for Eliminate for each juror. This is a personal answer, depending on the student's work.

B. For round five, determine what the excuses for each juror could be (read p. 211 for explanations) and decide whether or not to keep them.
This is an individual response, depending on the student's work.

C. Decide if the three potential jurors proposed are fair for this case. Write the advantages and disadvantages for the Plaintiff, and do the same thing for the Defendant, before deciding.
The answers to all these questions depend on the group of students and their answers.

PART 3 – Page 217
A. What does the jury do during the trial?
In a jury trial, the jury hears testimony and studies the evidence. After the trial has ended they receive instructions from the judge regarding the law as it relates to the issues, they discuss the evidence and the law and reach a verdict based on whether the Prosecution proved their case in a criminal trial, or whether the Plaintiff proved their case in a civil trial. In a criminal trial, they determine whether the Defendant is guilty or not guilty. In a civil trial, they determine whether or not the Defendant is liable, and if so, for how much.

B. Who may participate in the deliberation?
Nobody but the jury. After receiving the instructions and hearing the final arguments, the jury retires to the jury room to begin deliberating. In most States, the first order of business is to elect one of the jurors as the foreperson or presiding juror. This person's role is to preside over discussions and votes of the jurors, and, often, to deliver the verdict. The Bailiff's job is to ensure that no one communicates with the jury during deliberations.

PART 3 – Page 219
A. Write a fictional law story about a trial in which the characters in the story go through the trial procedures. This is individual work.

B. *Document 2*: Read the case, then answer the questions in Part I. Do not discuss your answers with your fellow jurors.
1. What evidence in the case indicates that Smythe is not guilty?
2. What evidence indicates that Smythe is guilty?
3. Based on the evidence, would you find Smythe guilty or not guilty?
4. Is there anything in the case that would change your decision? Why or why not?
The answers to all these questions depend on the group of students and their answers.

C. Work together in groups of six to decide whether Robert Smythe is guilty. Everyone in the jury must agree before you can offer a final verdict. When you have

CORRECTION OF THE EXERCISES

reached a decision, answer the questions in Part II.
1. Did the jury conclude that Robert Smythe was guilty or not guilty?
2. Was the jury verdict the same as or different from your individual decision?
3. If the jury verdict was different, what made you change your mind about the decision? If it was the same, did anyone with a differing opinion present any evidence that almost convinced you to change your mind?
The answers to all these questions depend on the group of students and their answers.

PART 4 – Page 221
A. Why can the jury system be criticized sometimes?
In recent years, the jury system has come under attack, and the purpose and usefulness of jurors has been questioned and criticized. With the increase in courtroom technology and complex litigation, some argue that the jury system is no longer able to deal with the complexities of modern litigation. Some critics embrace the concept of trial by judge and abandonment of the jury system. They cite cost, inefficiency and unfavorable results as the reason for change.

B. Should juries be aware of the probable sentence when deciding guilt?
Juries shouldn't have this information because it is not relevant to their decision. Knowing the punishment will inevitably change how the jury views the Prosecution's burden of proof. Will a jury be less likely to convict if they know the Defendant will receive a long prison sentence? Will they be more likely if the Defendant will get probation? Juries exist for a limited purpose – to provide a relatively neutral way to resolve a dispute between the government and the Defendant. The jury is not being asked to make a decision in which they need to know "all of the consequences." People who advocate this have a fundamental disrespect for the proper separation of powers and the rule of law.

PART 4 – Page 223
A. Search newspapers or magazines or the Internet for an article that mentions a trial that is currently being held in the United States.
The answer to this question depends on the group of students and their answers.

B. List the events of a trial in the correct order.
• A person is arrested
• Criminal charges are issued or declined
• Initial appearance
• Entering a plea
• Preliminary hearing
• Arraignment
• Pre-trial conference/Court settlement conference
• Plea hearing
• Trial
• Sentencing
• Appeal

C. Make a list of the steps in a trial, first from the Plaintiff/Prosecution's point of view (e.g., opening statement, direct examination of Plaintiff/Prosecution's witnesses, cross examination of defense witnesses, and closing arguments).
Do the same for the Defense.

PART 4 – Page 225
A. The purpose of opening statements by each side is to tell jurors something about the case they will be hearing. The opening statements must be confined to facts that will be proved by the evidence, and cannot be argumentative.

B. The lawyers' closing arguments, or summations, discuss the evidence and properly drawn inferences. Lawyers cannot talk about issues outside the case or about evidence that was not presented.

C. This is an individual answer, depending on the student's work.

D. The length of the opening statement should be proportionate to the trial itself. If testimony is going to last four hours, a five-minute opening statement is too short and a two-hour opening statement is too long. In most criminal cases, the opening should last between 20 and 60 minutes. Some lawyers believe in giving very long opening statements. Unless you are a fabulous storyteller, most jurors tell us they are bored by long openings.

PART 4 – Page 227
A. The purpose of direct examination is to prove all of the necessary factual elements to establish a prima facie case for the client's claim. This is done by presenting the relevant witness testimony and exhibits favorable to the theory of the case.

B. This is an individual answer, depending on the student's work.

C. This is an individual answer, depending on the student's work.

D. This is an individual answer, depending on the student's work.

REVIEW – Page 229
A. 1.e – 2.c – 3.a – 4.d – 5.b

B. The first court appearance is the arraignment. At this hearing, the attorney receives a copy of the charges and usually a copy of the police report for the case. The attorney will enter a plea of not guilty and set a date to return to court for a pre-trial where negotiations can occur to settle the case. If the case cannot be resolved, then the case proceeds to trial. However, most cases do settle without the need to go to trial. If the case is a felony, there is also a preliminary hearing. This hearing requires the District Attorney to present enough evidence to the Court for it to find that probable cause exists for believing that the Defendant committed this crime. The Defendant has a right to a preliminary hearing within 10 court days or 60 calendar days of his arraignment. This protects his right to a speedy trial. There are also numerous motions that can be enforced throughout the course of any criminal case. The most common of these is a motion to suppress the evidence in the case, based on an unlawful search and seizure.

C. First, the attorneys address any legal issues that may need to be dealt with prior to picking a jury. Then the jury is selected. Once a jury is chosen, the attorneys make their opening statements. This is where they tell the jury what evidence they will hear and

323

see. The District Attorney then puts their witnesses on the stand. The Defense Attorney is given the opportunity to cross-examine, or question each witness. Once the District Attorney has presented their case in chief, the Defense presents their witnesses and evidence. The District Attorney also has the opportunity to cross-examine these witnesses, and sometimes presents rebuttal witnesses. Once all of the evidence is presented, the attorneys make their closing arguments. The judge then reads the jury instructions and the jury retires to the jury room to deliberate. This process can take minutes, hours or days. Once the jury has reached a verdict, it is read in open court. If the Defendant is found not guilty, then they are free to go. If they are found guilty, a future date is set for sentencing.

D. Many times people are not taken into custody but are released on their own recognizance. However, if bail has been set, the defendant should contact a reputable bail bond company to post bail for him. It is possible for the attorney to argue that bail should be lowered, or that the Defendant should be released. However, if he chooses to contact a bail company, he must be prepared to pay a fee that is usually 10% of the bail amount. This fee is not refundable. If he pays the entire bail amount directly to the Court and all court appearances are made, then the money is refundable once the case has concluded.

E. The only time that someone must be advised of his Miranda Rights is if the arresting officer intends to question or interrogate him about the offense once he is in custody. Technically, one is in custody once handcuffed and placed inside the Police vehicle. Interrogation also commonly occurs at the Police station. A voluntary meeting with the Police does not require the advisement of rights. Only a custodial interrogation requires that the rights be read. Bear in mind that anything someone says WILL be used against that person, so it is always best to remain silent and hire an attorney as soon as possible!

Unit 12. Civil trials
PART 1 – Page 233
A. Part of the Seventh Amendment to the Constitution is the right to a trial by jury in civil cases. The Seventh Amendment doesn't guarantee a right to a civil jury trial in State Courts but a lot of States do offer this right.

B. Usually in the case of civil trial, a jury is selected from peers. This usually means that the members of the jury are in the same area and should not have a strong bias in the case and be open to hearing all information before making a decision.

PART 1 – Page 235
A. Document 1: Use the table to compare the jury system to a judge-only system. Do research in the library or on the Internet to help you fill the table. Some of the pros and cons of the American Jury System are listed below:Pros:1. In the American jury system, both sides (the Prosecution and the Defense) have the chance to test each other's witnesses and question them. 2. The jury is forced by the constitution to review each case meticulously to eliminate any unfair decisions. Cons:1. Judges might have

some personal biases that could affect their judicial decisions. 2. Lawyers can also manipulate the jury in favor of their decisions.
The pro of the judge-only system is that cases move much more quickly and there is less of a backlog. Cons: no democracy at all. If you get to pick your judge, then it might work out.

B. Write a list of five questions that a lawyer representing John Hoobert should ask a juror, to ensure that he or she will remain fair-minded in this case. For example, it would be important to determine whether or not the potential juror knows Katherine Barnes, or has ever been a client of John Hoobert, as either situation might make the juror biased.

C. Determine what kind of case was brought against Bob Engeton, and who determined the ruling of the case.
It is a civil case and the judge is Lucy Skyrocket.

PART 2 – Page 237
A. Opening statements – presentation of the Plaintiffs 'case – motion for directed verdict – presentation of the Defendant's case – Plaintiff's rebuttal – closing arguments – instruction to jury – verdict – judgment.

B. In lawsuits and civil disputes that are settled at trial, the jurors will either find for Defendant or the Plaintiff. Additionally, the jury will set any financial damage amounts that are to be paid to the either side, pending the verdict. Likewise, the jury, at the same time, will render their decision on the counterclaims that were produced during the trial, made by the Defendants. Following a jury verdict, all aspects of a trial are settled both legally and financially. To ensure the accuracy of the jury verdict, or prevent a rogue juror from throwing a trial, attorneys from either party may request that a jury be polled, or asked to state their agreement or disagreement, regarding the verdict rendered.

PART 2 – Page 238
2. Answer filed - 4b: Arbitration - 5. Discovery - 6. Argument Motions - 7. Brief Filed on Motions - 11. Verdict

PART 2 – Page 245
A. Can a civil lawsuit turn into a criminal lawsuit? A civil suit cannot turn into a criminal case, but it can prompt one. For example, if a party were to file suit against someone for prtoperty damage, the pleadings of evidence presented in the trial may come to the attention of law enforcement, who may opt to begin criminal prosecution. While the Plaintiff in the civil case would probably be a witness in the criminal prosecution, and the evidence in both cases would be similar, they would be two different cases with two different purposes, and the outcome of one is not binding to the other. Likewise, a criminal case may lead to a civil lawsuit. A popular example of this is the O.J. Simpson case. Simpson was tried and found not guilty of criminal murder. Even though he was found not, the victim's family initiated a civil suit for wrongful death, seeking monetary damages. The family won in that case and was awarded substantial damages. Even though one jury did not convict Simpson of the murder, a second jury found him financially responsible for the victim's death.

B. Contract Law – Tort Law – Property Law – Succession Law – Family Law.

PART 3 – Page 247
A. This is an individual answer.

B. Civil Right law is not so commonly taught in France and has the same importance as it has in the United States. Also, Entairtainment Law, Military Law and Real estate Law are not so common.

PART 4 - Page 249
A. Mediation is an effective way of resolving disputes without the need to go to Court. It involves an independent third party - a mediator - who helps both sides come to an agreement. Mediation is a flexible process that can be used to settle disputes in a whole range of situations such as: consumer disputes, contract disputes, family disputes, neighbourhood disputes. The role of the mediator is to help parties reach a solution to their problem and to arrive at an outcome that both parties are happy to accept. Mediators avoid taking sides, making judgements or giving guidance. They are simply responsible for developing effective communications and building consensus between the parties. The focus of a mediation meeting is to reach a common sense settlement agreeable to both parties in a case. Mediation is a voluntary process and will only take place if both parties agree.

B. Mediation – arbitration – neutral fact-finding – summary jury trial – private judging.

PART 4 - Page 251
A. One might think that people's sexual lives are heavily legislated in the United States, and that there is a law for absolutely everything!

B. You can go on the Internet and verify if a law exists at *findlaw.com.*

C. One law is not a real law. Go online and figure out which one.
It's the law from Louisiana: you are allowed to orgasm in front of your partner, even in this State!

D. The laws connected to sodomy are targeting same-sex couples, and that goes against the Supreme Court rulings on this topic.
A few states in the country — Kansas, Texas, Oklahoma and Montana — specifically maintain anti-sodomy laws, according to the Human Rights Campaign. The legislation implies that sodomy (and oral sex in some jurisdictions) is «unnatural.» However, human rights activists note that the law is primary used to target same-sex couples. In Kansas, sodomy between two members of the same sex is considered a criminal offense. This is true despite the Supreme Court's 2003 decision in *Lawrence v. Texas,* which ruled that anti-sodomy laws are essentially unenforceable. In that case, the court ruled that such mandates are an invasion of privacy. Nevertheless, these types of laws still exist throughout the United States, and the anti-sodomy concept remains enshrined in Kansas' Code.

REVIEW – Page 253
A. 1.law – 2.courts – 3.case – 4.pleadings – 5.motions – 6.orders – 7.depositions – 8.trials

B. Anwers may vary slightly, but students should understand that the Supreme Court should have overturned the ruling because the decision was arrived at unconstitutionality: the Seventh Amendment ensures the right to jury trial in civil cases.

C. The judge may organize a pre-trial conference that takes place in his chambers and is restricted to the lawyers of both parties. The goal is to try to reach an agreement on all, or part, of the case.

D. The typical number of jury members is 12, but this number may vary, because many States actually authorize smaller juries in Civil Law.

E. It consists in calling in a third party outside of the judicial system. This party is in charge of presenting the case, listening to each side, and making a decision. It's a process similar to going to Court, but without having a judge. This procedure is often chosen because it saves a lot of time and money. Arbitration is usually completed in four months, while a trial may last many years.

Unit 13. Landmark Cases
REVIEW – pp. 272-273
This is an individual answer, according to the case chosen.

Unit 14. Review
All the answers can be found in the Units 8 to 13.

Table of contents

TABLE OF CONTENTS

TABLE OF CONTENTS

TABLE OF CONTENTS

Imprimé en Italie par «La Tipografica Varese S.p.A.» Varese